FULLY REVISED AND UPDATED

PAUL WELLER

MY EVER CHANGING MOODS

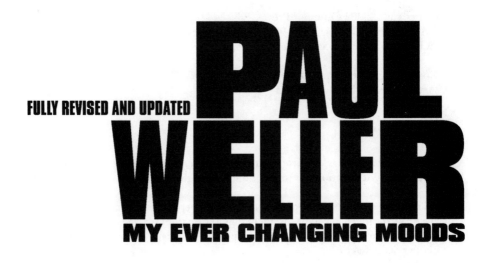

FULLY REVISED AND UPDATED **PAUL WELLER**

MY EVER CHANGING MOODS

BY JOHN REED

OMNIBUS PRESS

Cover designed by Fresh Lemon
Picture research by Nikki Lloyd

ISBN: 0.7119.8866.8
Order No: OP48411

Exclusive Distributors:
Book Sales Limited,
8/9 Frith Street,
London W1V 3JB, UK.

Music Sales Corporation,
257 Park Avenue South,
New York, NY 10010, USA.

Macmillan Distribution Services,
53 Park West Drive,
Derrimut, Vic 3030,
Australia.

To the Music Trade only:
Music Sales Limited,
8/9 Frith Street,
London W1V 3JB, UK.

Every effort has been made to trace the copyright holders of the photographs in this
book but one or two were unreachable. We would be grateful if the photographers
concerned would contact us.

Typeset by Galleon Typesetting, Ipswich.
Printed in Great Britain by Creative Print and Design Wales, Ebbw Vale

A catalogue record for this book is available from the British Library.

www.omnibuspress.com

Contents

Acknowledgements

Writing this book has felt rather like a long and eventful journey – sometimes enlightening, sometimes harrowing, sometimes fascinating. Without the help of very many people, the project would have been considerably more difficult and far less enjoyable.

First, I must first express my undying gratitude to my long-suffering colleagues at *Record Collector* magazine. As a fellow fan, Pat Gilbert has perhaps been the most supportive and the many hours we have spent chatting long into the nights about every conceivable aspect of Weller's life and times and taste in button-down shirts cannot be underestimated. Andy Davis also deserves a medal because, unlike Pat, he has over the years regarded Weller's dress sense as an abomination and found his songs at best passable. As polar opposites in terms of their viewpoints, they helped knock this book into shape with the attention to detail of a micro-surgeon and the patience of a saint. My good editor, Peter Doggett, also cast an eye over the final draft – and left it refreshingly free of red ink, which bolstered my confidence no end. Thanks also to another colleague, Mark Paytress, who got waylaid by a house move but still managed to cast an eye over the early chapters.

A long-time Weller fan, Steve Keegan, read through the early chapters and allowed me access to his unpublished diary of The Jam's live appearances. Hopefully, one day his book may come to fruition. As part of the groundwork for this book, I made several trips to Woking. While Weller's home town may not be the most exciting place on earth, it was where I met some of Paul's oldest friends, whose stories have stuck with me throughout the project. Steve Baker, especially, has the memory of an elephant and offered me the comfort of his living room, as well as a lift to and from Woking station. Steve and Pete Carver were also very helpful and, together with other acquaintances like Tony Pilot, they painted a vivid picture of Paul Weller in the days when he was scarcely out of short trousers.

So too did his elders, such as Arthur Hunte, Status Quo's Rick Parfitt and, most of all, Paul's old music teacher at school, John Avery – thanks especially to John for giving up a couple of hours of his time on a Saturday morning. And I am indebted to the town's historian, Iain Wakeford, committed Weller fan Colin Bird and 10cc fan David Wells for showing me around the sights and sounds of Woking, such as they are.

During the course of my research, I have lost count of the number of people I have spoken to. Of those who consented to be interviewed, Polydor

A&R man Dennis Munday gave up more time than anyone else – Dennis not only shared two afternoons, in and out of the pub, chatting about his recollections of working with Paul since the late Seventies, but he also opened several doors for me and passed on some key phone numbers. Dennis is the prime mover behind Paul's back catalogue and has not only kept me posted on new compilations but drafted me in to write some sleeve-notes – and I was very pleased to oblige. Thanks also to The Jam's original drummer Neil Harris, who was very patient after our first interview was scotched by a technical hitch. His replacement was Rick Buckler, of course, who extended his hospitality to the point that we now have an extra mouth to feed – a cat by the name of Mo'. Rick offered a unique insight into the atmosphere within the band, but sadly, bassist Bruce Foxton wasn't able to help for personal reasons.

Many thanks also to the following people for agreeing to be interviewed: Danny Baker, who I accosted in a pub, Peter Anderson, who also supplied some of the photos, Billy Bragg, who sent me Robin Denselow's book, Ted Carroll, Vic Coppersmith-Heaven, Ady Croasdell, Debsey, Tony Fletcher, John Franklin, Martin Hopewell, Dave Liddle, Glen Matlock, Chris Parry, Mark Perry, Terry Rawlings, Tony Rounce, Dean Rudland, Rudi's Brian Young, Terry Slater, Bill Smith, Jimmy Telford, John Tobler, Pete Wilson and Tracie Young.

During the course of researching articles for *Record Collector*, I also had an opportunity to speak not only to Paul Weller but also to Ben Watt and Tracey Thorn of Everything But The Girl and all of Ocean Colour Scene.

I should also explain the absence of interview material with some of the key players. Because there may be an official biography at some point, many of the musicians who have worked more recently with Paul – for example, Mick Talbot, and the other members of The Style Council, his wife Dee C. Lee and his current drummer Steve White – weren't forthcoming. However, that hasn't stopped the relevant section of the book from representing the most detailed and objective study of that band's six-year life. Neither were his parents available – as his manager, Paul's father has given him a sense of continuity and support which few other performers can claim to have enjoyed in such a volatile industry, and John Weller tells me that he is thinking about writing his own version of events some day. Nor, after some deliberation, would Paul's younger sister Nikki agree to be interviewed. As for Weller himself, he is as reluctant as ever to dwell on the past – and declined to co-operate in the making of this book, although I thank him for the courtesy he has shown to me in the past.

Other small but perfectly formed cogs in the treadmill of this book include Neil Allen (*Start!*), Mark 'Captain Oi!' Brennan, Johnny Chandler, David L. Clark, Dave Clarke, Dave Edwards, Pippa Hall at Go! Discs, Mark Hodkinson, Alan and Deborah Holl, Dizzy Holmes at Detour Records, David Lodge (*Boys About Town*), George Marshall (S.T. Publishing), Andrew

McGibbon, Bob Morris, Iain Munn (*Whole Point*), Lorne Murdoch, Mr Reed (no relation) and Mr Ledger of Bishop David Brown School, Mark Ridlington (*Groovin'*), Liam Sawyer, Mark Smith, Pete Smith (for videos), Simon Smith, Jackie Thurling, Tina at Solid Bond, Adrian T'Vell, Les at Woking Council and Andy Wyness (*Weller Is Back!*). I must also thank Omnibus' editor, Chris Charlesworth, for calling me after a chance meeting at Helter Skelter Books, and picture editor Nicola Russell – they have both been very patient.

Friends and family tended to be neglected while I was knee-deep in news cuttings or catching the train from Waterloo to Woking. Mum and dad smile about it – they still remember when I'd save up to buy the latest Jam single with money earnt in the local supermarket: "Haven't you got enough records, already?" Never. Thanks also to brother Keith, the jazz head. A few friends were especially supportive: Mark Edwards, for early encouragement; Dilys Henry; Piers Butler and Co. for a superb snowboarding break when I really should have been writing; John O'Leary and Tom Kane for the occasional word to the politically wise; Trotski for his atrocious taste; Tom's cousin Jack Kane for being, well, Jack Kane; Calvin and Maxine; and I mustn't forget Andy Moss for those Weller-styled days at college, especially our *A Paris* trip in '85.

But pride of place in this honours list has to go to Angela May, for living through it all. Thank you.

John Reed, June 1996.

Introduction

Paul Weller is the John Lennon of the Grange Hill generation. No other British songwriter since punk has made such an impact – not one. Some might argue a case for Elvis Costello, but he can't match Weller's sustained commercial clout, especially the degree of Weller's renaissance in the Nineties, nor his impact on other artists. Individuals such as Annie Lennox, Chrissie Hynde and Sting, three of the most successful performers to have emerged out of the new wave era, lack Weller's sense of adventure as a musician, not to mention his cult following.

It is this last quality which helps to make Paul Weller, Pop Star, so fascinating. I was part of a generation of kids born around the mid-Sixties who grew up with The Jam as their favourite band. Once The Jam had progressed beyond their punk beginnings, Paul, whether he liked it or not, became both a spokesperson and a figurehead. To paraphrase Lennon, for thousands of young, working class lads, Weller was something to be – a reluctant hero.

During the Nineties, Paul Weller has earned the nickname of the Mod-father, a slightly irritating catch-all term which reflects his near-lifetime passion for the Sixties youth cult which has infused aspects of his image and his music – and those two aspects are inseparable – since the mid-Seventies. A degree of The Jam's omnipotent success – they swept the boards in readers' polls for three years and shared the record for the number of singles to enter the charts at No. 1 – was due to the renaissance of the Mod idea, which pervaded the south of England and the Midlands from 1979 right through until the mid-Eighties.

I saw The Jam half a dozen times in Brighton, a few miles from my home town, a Mod stronghold both then and now, with associations dating back to the Bank Holiday riots of the Sixties. This revival is an overlooked chapter in youth culture, chiefly because it was seen as an embarrassment by the media – who derided the lack of imagination which characterised both the bands and the uniformity of the fashion. But Mod is crucial here, because of Weller's position as the scene's only true icon. Many of the characters with whom Paul has since worked – and many of the movers and shakers in and around the industry, within record labels, or as DJs and musicians – have their roots in the Mod Revival, which goes some way to explain the aura which still surrounds Weller.

Weller's relentless spirit of adventure also redefined and broadened the concept of Mod, and in this respect, his dabblings with psychedelia and soul, and then his fascination with Eighties funk and modern club culture – the ultimate legacy of Mod – felt to like-minded souls like a journey. The Mod net had always embraced a wider catch than other youth cults, which explains its longevity, and allowed Weller to swim around inside it while also reinventing himself on at least two occasions. The Jam were Mod, in the very English sense of mid-Sixties Who or Kinks. The Style Council were Mod in the very cosmopolitan sense of modern jazz, continental stylings and the latest American soul imports. Paul Weller solo is Mod in the sense of a post-Acid Jazz groove and a late Sixties Small Faces-meets-Traffic vibe.

But this is the latter half of the Nineties: while his contemporaries from the late Seventies, The Clash's Joe Strummer and John Lydon, have faded away, Paul Weller has arrived not only at the most lucrative phase of his career, but as a figurehead of the biggest surge in British music since he first signed a record contract back in 1977. Just as Iggy Pop was welcomed by the punk generation, David Bowie was lauded by the New Romantics, Lou Reed by the mid-Eighties indie soundalikes and Neil Young by grunge, Paul Weller was namechecked by those twin peaks of 1995's so-called Britpop sound, Blur and Oasis. Renewed vigour in his own creativity reached its commercial summit with *Stanley Road*. As the hardback edition of this book was being completed, Weller had just played a celebratory outdoor concert in London's Finsbury Park in front of around 35,000 fans, his biggest solo concert to date, which crystallised his renewed popularity. A year later, Paul was on the brink of issuing perhaps the most eagerly awaited LP of his entire career – *Heavy Soul*.

Weller can also boast a songbook to rival any of his peers. While his biggest hits neatly embody their era – from 'Going Underground' in 1980 to 'The Changingman' in 1995 – some of his cleverest lyrics and most enduring tunes have been buried away on albums and B-sides. The sheer scope of his musical adventurism is impressive: over the years, he has fused punk and Sixties R&B, mixed soul and funk, dabbled in jazz and rap and bridged the gap between pop and rock.

He is also one of the smartest icons of our time. As Weller's first idol, The Who's Pete Townshend, remarked, "He is a star. He carefully engineers what kind of star and in what kind of atmosphere he shines: never too grand, never too remote." If his uncanny ability to mix the best ingredients from the past and present and regurgitate them in a modern context has kept his music fresh and alive, then it has also created a chameleon-like picture of the musician.

Weller's twenty-year career presents an unusual scenario. By his own admission, he continues to emulate his musical heroes, a mixture of Sixties (Mod) icons Steve Marriott, Townshend, Lennon/McCartney and Ray Davies, and soul legends Marvin Gaye and Curtis Mayfield. And yet few, if any, of his influences have enjoyed such a durable, consistently popular output. The Who and The Kinks were still stadium-level bands two decades on, but their creative talents had dried up. Weller made his name with The Jam – and like many pop stars, he spent years shaking off the legacy of the band's runaway success, after reinventing himself with The Style Council throughout the Eighties.

But unlike his idols, he finally succeeded in this task during the Nineties. When Weller and McCartney collaborated on the Smokin' Mojo Filters project in late 1995, the latter was still an ex-Beatle – but no one mentioned The Jam. Weller's remarkable renaissance in the Nineties didn't happen by accident, of course. During the late Eighties, he took the idea of The Style Council – an amorphous musical collective which reshaped itself with each album – up a cul-de-sac, alienating his audience before he eventually lost interest himself. His fans returned with *Paul Weller*, his first solo album in 1992, which, by cleverly blending rock and soul influences, bridged the gap between The Jam and The Style Council in one fell swoop. 1993's *Wild Wood* then coincided with the mood swing towards British music which was partly seen as a reaction to the American invasion of grunge.

It dovetailed neatly with Weller's very English sound and he spearheaded a return to a rock orthodoxy which championed traditional instruments, a reverence for established greats like The Beatles and an earnest acceptance that his role in life was to play music – no more, no less. Along the way, he somehow caught the wave of the phenomenon labelled as 'new lad', a reaction to the political correctness of the Eighties. The generation wooed by the *Loaded* mentality could easily relate to Weller's very male rock sound. That's not to denigrate his accomplishments as a musician – but it goes some way towards explaining the platinum-selling popularity of *Stanley Road*, which neither critics nor many fans viewed as his best LP. It might not even be the greatest album of his solo career, but it boasted that indefinable quality of being in the right place at the right time – it encapsulated the mood, the zeitgeist.

Perhaps wishing to avoid the tendency of successful rock stars to settle into a monied, middle-age paunch, Weller reacted to the enormous commercial success of Stanley Road with *Heavy Soul*, a rawer, more rough-and-ready, less compromising album than its predecessor. He even spoke of shunning the music industry treadmill to play Surrey pubs and issue humble mail-order albums, an affirmation that, as far as Paul Weller is concerned, his music is by far the most important factor.

As each year passes, Weller's former musical lives recede into memory, fuelled by his refusal to rest on the laurels of his back catalogue. Few other performers have shunned the temptation to fall back on tried-and-tested hits – and yet, during his at times prolific live schedule, Weller has rarely played a set which comprises simply 'greatest hits'. And yet it is Paul Weller's past which is dealt with in this book. *My Ever Changing Moods* isn't a dispassionate overview of his career, nor an impressionistic survey of the cult of Paul

Weller. This is a factually-detailed fan's eye view – but it's not a hagiography.

Weller isn't the straightforward personality that he seems to convey in the mid-Nineties. One of his friends for many years was Terry Rawlings. "He's three different people – that's how I would see it," says Terry. "There is an incredible, generous side to him. I was having financial difficulties in 1992 after the Black Friday crash happened. My girlfriend was pregnant and Christmas was coming up as well and we were going to lose the house we'd just bought. He said, 'Why didn't you ask me?' Well, I wouldn't have done that. I thought nothing more of it but I was in a bad state. Then I went to watch him rehearse and he gave me an envelope – a cheque which bailed me out. Astonishing, isn't it?"

If Weller has often been accused of being arrogant, then he is also, by all accounts, quite insecure. "He is amazingly unsure of himself and his own fame," suggests Terry. "I remember him telling me about being on a plane, when Eric Clapton recognised him and went over and congratulated him. Paul was absolutely amazed, he was genuinely shocked: 'Clapton knew who I was!' 'You dope!' I said. 'Of course he knew who you were.' I don't think Paul still recognises how big, potentially, he could be. Or what he means to people in this country."

In Rawlings' eyes, though, Weller also has a ruthless side. "There's an unspoken code of conduct that's abided to by the entourage of people who deal with Paul's set-up. If you step out of it, that's your lot. He'll cut you dead. Paul's past is littered with dozens of people who simply don't exist anymore. He can be very cold like that. I got involved with sorting out a couple of secret gigs for him at the 100 Club at the end of 1995. We had an argument and I was deemed as subsequently breaking that code. And that was my lot."

The same multi-faceted aspects pervade his professional life. Much as Weller would despise the link, he has shared Marc Bolan's uncanny ability, as Mark Paytress put it in *20th Century Boy*, to "strike a balance between mainstream acclaim and the decidedly offbeat appeal of a cult artist". Like Bolan, Weller could accommodate a love for poetry and a knack of churning out classic, three-minute slices of urban pop as effortlessly as if they came from a conveyer-belt. Unlike Bolan, and others who have managed the trick for a short burst, Weller has sustained the process – the odd hiccup permitting – for twenty years.

Weller's inner camp hasn't changed over the years and his relationship with his father is unique in the music business. While his public stance on political issues, family life and music itself have fluctuated over the years, the bond which exists between Paul Weller and his dad has proved unshakeable. Other aspects have remained constant: on a more trivial level, during The Jam's three-year reign as Britain's most important pop band, Paul Weller was a pin-up. In 1996, he was voted one of the world's most beautiful men by women's magazine *Elle*, who later ran a cover feature coupling Paul with supermodel Kate Moss, and *Cosmopolitan* listed him as one of the world's "100 Sexiest Men Alive".

More importantly, his life has come full cycle: he now lives on the outskirts of his home town of Woking, next door to his parents. During his days with The Jam, Paul Weller's aim seemed to be to escape his suburban Surrey roots. The band's records and the style of music were starkly urban. During his days with The Style Council, Weller paid scant attention to his past. It is only during his solo career that elements of his background have infiltrated his music. It seems as if, by finally plucking up the courage to go it alone as a solo musician, the real Paul Weller stood up. In doing so, he completed a cycle, and his songs were full of references to his childhood in Woking – which is where this story starts.

Prologue

I KNOW I COME FROM WOKING

"All Weather Shopping And Sparkling Entertainment" – that's the promise which greets visitors to Woking. It's hand-painted on a black-and-white billboard at the mouth of a subway, which leads to nowhere more exciting than the other side of the railway station. The truth is that there's nothing very special about this Surrey town. It has a McDonald's, a Marks & Spencer's, and a Toys 'Я' Us, but there are few distinguishing features.

Since the late Sixties, the town planners have strived to rid Woking of its sleepy atmosphere, ripping down Victorian terraces and erecting uniform, concrete 'leisure' complexes, civic buildings and car parks. In the process, what little individuality Woking may have once possessed has vanished. Today, the town centre shares the faceless functionality that has created a uniformity across the urban landscape of southern England. In the past, Woking's skyline might have been dominated by the outline of its churches; today, it's the Peacock Shopping Centre which looms over the town.

Not that Woking has ever been party to any of history's more exciting events – aside from providing a home for, ironically enough, Europe's largest cemetery and first-ever crematorium. Local guidebooks excitedly point out that the 'sand pits' on Horsell Common, north of the town, inspired H.G. Wells; this is where the Martians are meant to have landed in *War Of The Worlds*. The 19th century science fiction author only lived in the town for a short time – yet over a century later, it's still a local talking point. The suburb of Sheerwater might be familiar to motor racing fans as the home to McLaren's, and the Woking area has been famous for its nursery gardens for nearly 250 years. Musicians as diverse as ex-Eternal singer Louise and Status Quo's Rick Parfitt grew up in the area, but it's no accident that The Jam were given a whole page in the borough's *Welcome To Woking* guide. Paul Weller is arguably the most famous person that the town has ever reared.

Weller fans who've made the pilgrimage over the years and traipsed around the area for a desultory afternoon must have wondered how one of Britain's most consistently successful musicians could ever have risen from such an undistinguished backwater. It hardly feels like a Beatles Liverpool – or even a Manchester still smothered with the landmarks that inspired so many Smiths lyrics.

Woking is located twenty-six miles south-west of London in North-West Surrey. It's the biggest town in the county, with a population which has overtaken that of nearby Guildford – during Weller's lifetime, it has grown from around 60,000 to over 90,000. Five miles outside the M25 motorway which circles the capital and the suburbs, Woking is pure commuter belt: close enough to get to London but distant enough to get away from it. It might only be half-an-hour away from Waterloo on the train but it's easy to see why Weller was so fascinated by the capital from an early age. For a teenager growing up in Woking, the term 'dormitory town' couldn't have been more accurate. Like many towns spread across the Home Counties, Woking was sucked dry by its proximity to the capital. If London buzzed with excitement, then the reverberations didn't ripple out as far as Woking.

What does distinguish the town from its neighbours is the proximity of different social classes – evident in the styles and sizes of housing – huddled together in such a compact area. The railway cleaves the town in two: directly to the north is the town centre, bounded on the east by Stanley Road; and on the north and west by Victoria Way. A third of a mile north of the railway, and running roughly parallel to it, is the Basingstoke canal; these two landmarks not only border the heart of Woking but led to its development in the first place. The area to the south of the line is less congested, stretching down to Old Woking a mile or so away and, to the east, to one of the town's several council estates, Maybury.

Turn right out of the northern exit of the station and it's a five-minute walk to Stanley Road – or what's left of it. Looking north, an anonymous, brown-bricked office block looms on the left; to the right was a nondescript, scruffy area of wasteland cordoned off with rusty chain, which doubled for a car park, but this has now been re-developed into what is described as "affordable housing". All the Victorian terraces, bar a couple, have been knocked down, and it takes some imagination to picture a world that "gleamed in the distance/And it shone like the sun/Like silver and gold – it went on and on", Weller's vivid description of Stanley Road in the song he named after it. The street is scarcely two hundred yards long, starting next to the railway line and ending in a roundabout where it meets the Chertsey Road, which runs from the station north-west out of the town, up past Horsell Common and those 'sand pits', where The Jam later filmed their promotional video for 'Funeral Pyre', and into the surrounding Surrey countryside romanticised in another Jam song from 1981, 'Tales From The Riverbank'.

Not twenty yards from that roundabout, Stanley Road forms the top of a 'T' with Walton Road; it was on the corner, at No. 8, that Paul spent most of the first seventeen years of his life. Until the bulldozers arrived when the road's re-development began in early 1996, all that was left of the house was a patch of weed-infested scrub. Just behind it, at the start of Walton Road, is Woking Working Men's Club, where The Jam – then a duo barely out of

short trousers – played their first, tentative gigs. So close, in fact, was the house to the club that Paul could probably have thrown his guitar over the back garden wall and onto the small, decrepit stage, which still remains today. The club is just as shabby, a faded drinking den for the locals. Opposite, on the north side of the road, is the Youth Club, another of The Jam's earliest testing grounds – together with the Liberal Club around the corner at the end of Stanley Road.

Town planners have been kinder to Walton Road, where most of the houses have stood for a century. This runs east, parallel with the railway, for just over half a mile to the edge of the Sheerwater Estate, and acts as a backbone to a string of small terraced streets that link Maybury Road and Boundary Road, which follows the curve of the canal – alias Boundary Lane, that thoroughfare in Weller's lyrical return to his childhood home, 'Uh Huh Oh Yeh', and its accompanying promotional video. A further ten-minute stroll east along Albert Drive is Bishop David Brown School, previously the Sheerwater Comprehensive. Sheerwater hasn't changed much since Weller's childhood. Apart from the industrial area, which has been rebuilt a number of times, the houses are more or less identical – which can't be said for the town as a whole.

In fact, the Woking town centre of today bears no relation to its earlier, faintly sleepy atmosphere. We can assume that this is the inspiration for The Jam song, 'Bricks And Mortar' ("pulling down houses and building car parks"; there were three multi-storey car parks built in the space of a few years). Today, it may look like any other shopping centre, but it belies a quite unique history lurking beneath the surface.

To understand some of the town's characteristics, we have to go back to the early 19th century. Woking dates back to the Middle Ages and beyond, but two events laid the foundations for the growth of what was then a small village. The first was less significant – the opening of the Basingstoke Canal in 1791 – but it affected the location of the second, the opening of the railway in 1838. It guaranteed that the area between the two would evolve into the new town centre, in place of the old village a mile or so to the south. Nothing much happened, though, until a group of opportunists known as the London Necropolis & National Mausoleum Company acquired over 2,000 acres in the parish in 1852. Their declared aim was to turn Woking and the surrounding area into the world's largest cemetery (and some might argue that they succeeded!) – or rather, to convince the government that that was their plan, so that the land could be obtained cheaply. As Matthew Alexander observed, in his *Tales Of Old Surrey*, Woking was built "if not by fraud, then by some pretty sharp practice".

"It is a very weird story," admits local historian Iain Wakeford, author of several books on the town. "Woking is unique. Early reports described it as a 'Wild West' town, just a couple of streets, a few small shops and very wind-blown. The whole area was then bought to develop as this cemetery

that would serve the whole country. Necropolis means City Of The Dead! Every graveyard, churchyard and cemetery in the country was due to be closed and everybody would be buried at Woking. This company bought the open expanse of heather and gorse that was Woking Common, which included the area around what is now the town centre. They only used 400 acres but Brookwood Cemetery is still the largest in Western Europe. Over the years, they sold the rest of the land off for development, and that's how the town of Woking was built."

The arrangement led to some strange and quite unique landmarks. Wakeford explains: "Many early land sales were for various institutions – an asylum, a prison. One building in the Maybury area started out as what was called the Royal Dramatic College, which was supposed to have been a 'Fame'-type school for teaching the dramatic arts. But unfortunately for those local parents with showbiz aspirations for their offspring, that closed in the 1870s through lack of funds. A Hungarian gentleman bought it, to set up the Oriental Institute, which was a sort of university teaching oriental languages. Because of that, a mosque was built at Woking – the first to be built in this country. And it's because of the mosque that Woking attracted a lot of Asian immigrants. You name any nationality in the world and Woking has probably got them."

By the turn of the century, Woking was fast becoming one of the most cosmopolitan areas outside of Britain's major cities. The local guidebook states: "Today, about 10 per cent of the population were born overseas or have immigrant parents; Italian, Spanish, Chinese, Hindi, Bengali, Punjabi, Portuguese and Greek are some of the languages spoken locally." It's tempting to claim that the town's ethnic diversity affected the young Paul Weller; certainly, its diverse community probably helped him rise above the racist bigotry prevalent among his contemporaries in similar working class areas.

"Woking is still a 'New Town' ", Iain points out. "The Necropolis company sold off all this formally common land for development, which brought about the building of Woking new town centre, starting in the 1870s. They divided the square of land between the railway and the canal, between Stanley Road and Monument Road and, to the north, Boundary Road, into grids of roads. On their plan of 1856, the area where Stanley Road was eventually built was reserved for a church and a school, but these were later located somewhere else." Instead, Stanley Road was built in the 1890s as one of a number of streets of terraced houses to cater for the working classes – the people who served the commuters, both as servants and in the shops. This poorer area stretched east and west of what evolved into the town centre. In contrast, the town's larger houses were built on the higher ground south of the railway. The middle classes also tended to congregate further afield in the small villages which sprang up, scattered among the surrounding countryside: to the east, West Byfleet, Pyrford and Ripley; to the south, Mayford, Kingfield, Westfield and Send; to the west, St. Johns, Horsell,

Brookwood and Knaphill and, further afield, Pirbright and Bisley; and to the north, Chobham. And, to an extent, that pattern remains today. Isolated estates punctuate what is ostensibly a wealthy middle class environment; Woking is widely reported as one of the most expensive places to live in England.

The town's expansion accelerated after the Second World War. During the 1950s, council estates sprang up – Elmbridge, Barnsbury and, largest of all, Maybury – and Woking's growing working class population was naturally reflected in its local politics. "Labour started getting more votes and seats on the council," explains Wakeford. "For quite some years, Woking has had a hung council, whereas every other council in Surrey was Conservative through and through." The first of these estates was built further east along that narrow strip of land bounded by the canal and the railway, once a huge lake that was drained in the 19th century. The area was still waterlogged until London County Council took it over after the war to create the Sheerwater Estate as an overspill to deal with a shortage of housing in the capital, the impact of hundreds of semis and terraces softened by the area's concentration of pine trees. The resulting influx of families from all over London changed the political and social complexion of the town. And one of those families was the Wellers.

1

STANLEY ROAD

"I'm a very, very moody bastard . . ."
(Paul Weller, 1992)

The single most consistent factor in both Paul Weller's life and his musical career has been the unflinching support and devotion of his parents – and, in particular, his father, who has been his manager since the very start. "Paul's dad, John, always reminded me of Spike, the big bulldog in *Tom And Jerry* who says to his little pup, 'That's my boy!' " reckons Steve Baker, one of Paul's first friends at secondary school. "That relationship always struck me. His parents were very young and I think they knew they spoiled him. I mean, I couldn't talk to my mum and dad about music, so I'd go round to Paul's and John would go, 'Did you see *Top Of The Pops* tonight?' He'd be on the ball and very enthusiastic. Without John, there's no way Paul would have got anywhere."

John Weller worshipped his son and the pair were inseparable when Paul was a child – nothing very unusual about that. What is remarkable is that this solid bond appears to have remained unshaken ever since. Theirs seems to be a relationship based on mutual respect that is perhaps unique in a rock world where rebellion against parental values – the older generation – has been a defining characteristic. Perhaps Paul inherited that paternal pragmatism – after all, why change a relationship that got you started and has stood you in ood stead throughout your career? There's a side to Paul Weller that has never broken free of that parental shelter. It's not only fair to say that his dad has been the driving force behind his son for most of his life, it's also highly unlikely that Paul would ever have escaped the clutches of Woking to embark on a musical career without the self-sacrificing dedication, perseverance and unquestioning faith of his father.

This is not to say that there haven't been other notable parent/sibling arrangements in the pop world: with his guidance, Kim Wilde followed her father Marty into the charts of the early Eighties. There have been numerous 'family' operations, of course, behind such neatly packaged collectives as The Jacksons, The Osmonds and Five Star, and Miles Copeland only became involved with The Police because his brother

Stuart was their drummer. But most such relationships disintegrate somewhere along the line, often with tremendous acrimony. Just look, for instance, at the squabbles that have incited the Beach Boys' trials and tribulations, not only between the brothers but collectively against the father who once managed them. In contrast, the bond that was struck between John and Paul Weller at an early age was quite special. "I like his attitude, always have done," Paul admitted in the early Eighties. "He's never been conventional and that's why I like him. He's a lot shrewder than people thought as well. If he jacked it in, I would as well. Definitely. A lot of the times, he's the one that's kept it going."

Born in Brighton on November 28, 1931, John Weller was raised in Lewisham in South East London and cut an imposing figure as a teenager. He was an ambitious, hard-working lad who earned the respect of his peers, with his straight-talking, no-nonsense approach, and his prowess as a boxer. In fact, John shunned school work to become a featherweight champion. "He was an all-round athlete, a trainee journalist after leaving school, a man who boxed for England, who won the ABA," his son later remarked proudly. In addition, people have said of him that he "didn't suffer fools gladly" or "he knew how to handle himself". Traditional, unpretentious and down-to-earth, it's no surprise that John was known for speaking his mind; he may have taken people as he found them but he may also have had an eye for the main chance, and what they could do for him.

John was in his mid-twenties when he met his future wife. Ann Craddock was born in Northamptonshire, on the eve of the Second World War in late summer 1939, and grew up in Chingford, Essex. They married in March 1957 and moved into a terraced house in Walton Road, Woking. Five months later, Ann was pregnant with their first child.

John William Weller was born on May 25, 1958 – or, at least, that was how Ann named him at the hospital for the benefit of the birth certificate. The story goes that having just contracted polio, she was in a shaky state, verging on delirium, and gave the boy the first names that came into her head. The couple soon reconsidered, however, and by the time the family moved around the corner to 8 Stanley Road some two months later, their baby had been renamed Paul. The new parents were besotted with their new arrival; John, in particular, later professed to having always wanted a boy.

Like most young working class families, the Wellers were far from financially secure. They managed the best way they could, John working as a taxi driver and Ann as a part-time cleaner. Their constant if modest income staved off any real hardship and life ticked along without too much difficulty at their spartan Victorian terrace, which Paul later admitted had "an outside khazi, no bathroom and no hot water". The family doted on the toddler, who grew into a shy boy with his mother's features – straight, light-brown hair and blue-green eyes. From an early age, Paul spent much of his time accompanying his dad, either out and about in the cab or going for walks together.

Paul's childhood seems to have been fairly orthodox and passed without incident. When he was four-and-a-half, the family was swelled by the arrival of a baby girl, Nicola, but it doesn't appear to have caused the disruption and the tantrums that occur in some families. Paul neither reacted against the attentions now focused on his baby sister, nor did he grow particularly close to her. Nicky was born in late 1962; within a year, Paul started at Maybury County First School, just off Walton Road and a stone's throw from their house. The school was captured in the video for 1992's 'Uh Huh Oh Yeh'. He was a quiet, solitary boy; Ann later recalled an overriding memory of her son's early love of pop music. "I can remember taking him to see Elvis Presley in the pictures at Woking Odeon and he had a little blue plastic guitar," she told Paolo Hewitt in his Jam biography, *A Beat Concerto*. "He was about five or six and he used to stand in the aisle and play guitar while Presley was on the screen."

With an extra mouth to feed, John Weller found additional work on building sites, while continuing to drive the taxi in the evenings to supplement the family's income. Likewise, Ann once took part-time secretarial work to make ends meet. Both parents were keen music fans, and if it wasn't the latest 45s, then the radio was always on, so Paul was constantly exposed to the hits of the day. It wasn't long before they'd start to buy their son records. His growing interest in The Beatles reached fanatical proportions as the decade wore on, an obsession which has never waned over the years. "I was a Beatles maniac from about '64 onwards," he confessed to *Record Collector*'s Pat Gilbert in 1992, "after 'She Loves You' and 'I Want To Hold Your Hand'. I remember my mum playing them and The Four Tops . . . The Beatles made me think 'this is what I want to do'."

From the mid-Sixties onwards, the youngster bought every Beatles 45 – or had them bought for him – and kept them in a chest-of-drawers. It's not difficult to envisage his excitement when Ann brought home a box of old issues of *Beatles Monthly* that she'd found in a jumble sale one day. Still in short trousers, Paul would while away the hours by sticking the photos into a dozen scrapbooks. "He'd always been into The Beatles from when I first knew him," confides Steve Baker. "And that stayed throughout school. In art lessons, he'd draw a Beatles-type graphic or he'd paint 'We Love The Beatles' and bung it up on the wall."

If today, Paul's childhood memories are vague, then it's his record collection that conjures up the most vivid emotions. "The other day, I was listening to a Beach Boys record and it made me sad, because my father bought me that record and I remembered when we used to go to Heathrow together to see the planes," Paul later reminisced. By the time he was old enough to be aware of it, the youngster was starting to notice there was more to pop than The Beatles.

25

Pop music was slowly mutating into rock – but for a couple of years, he caught the tail-end of a magical era.

"One of my first musical memories was seeing The Small Faces on TV, I think probably *Top Of The Pops*," he wrote in *Cool!* magazine in 1992. "It was them performing 'Tin Soldier' with P.P. Arnold . . . even as a nine-year-old, I was pretty impressed, so much so that even after twenty-five years or so, the image is still with me." Paul later recalled to Andrea Olcese, author of the Style Council biography, *Internationalists*, "me and my friend singing 'Fire Brigade' by The Move with me on a plastic 'Beatle' guitar and him playing drums on a biscuit tin!" Another favourite was The Kinks' 'Waterloo Sunset'. "That's my favourite record of all time, my Desert Island Disc," Weller told Ian Cranna. "It's the most complete song I've ever heard. It's got everything – it's an emotional record, the lyrics are brilliant and it's got a great melody . . . Ray Davies' songwriting – I think he's *the* greatest songwriter."

By 1968, pop had flowered into something rather beautiful, the culmination of the most innovative, fastest-moving half decade in the history of British popular music. The transition from bland imitations of American artists to the emergence of some of the world's most talented and successful musicians was remarkably fast. In 1963, The Beatles (and the accompanying Merseybeat craze) consolidated the guitar/bass/drums set-up of instrumental acts like The Shadows and The Ventures but with several crucial differences: they were a vocal group and, in addition to writing their own material, covered the very best in American soul and rhythm and blues. During 1964, British pop lost some of Merseybeat's shrill, saccharine qualities, toughened up and got dirtier. Steeped in American blues, bands like The Animals, The Yardbirds, The Rolling Stones and The Kinks were rougher and cruder than, say, Gerry & The Pacemakers and Billy J. Kramer.

The sound grew harder still in 1965, as groups like The Who and The Small Faces fused teenage aggression (helped by the louder amps which were being developed) with soul music, which seemed to encapsulate the lifestyle of the prevailing youth cult of the time, Mod. By the end of the following year, though, The Beatles had regained the lead in creating a more sophisticated, studio-based music that married rapidly developing recording technology with the first murmurings of what was labelled psychedelia – music that sought to re-create in sound the heightened consciousness that a growing number of young people, notably musicians, were experiencing through drugs. In 1967, this backdrop of marijuana and LSD blossomed into a style of pop which, at its best, boasted both melodic subtleties and obscure lyrics which progressed beyond the traditional boy-meets-girl message. This is the music which filled the ears of a very impressionable young boy whose love affair with pop was just beginning.

★　★　★

When he was eleven, Paul switched from Maybury First School to Sheerwater County Secondary. It was a long walk, nearly two miles from his house, towards the other end of Albert Drive, the main road which runs through the estate. A model school with a reputation for solid academic and sporting achievements, Sheerwater was built in the mid-1950s to cater for the suburb's overspill. It merged with nearby Monument Hill school in the early Sixties and around half-a-million pounds' worth of improvements were made at the start of the 1970s. Despite the stigma attached to the estate as a consequence of local snobbery, the school was far from the notorious, rough and ready dumping ground that has since been implied.

During the Sixties, the school housed around a thousand pupils – a large number for the time – but this figure had dropped to around 700 by the early Seventies. "There were eight groups for every year," explains Steve Baker. "We had six houses: if you were in the first three, you were in group A or B. It was like, 1A was the really brainy or posh kids, the swots, and then group B seemed to be the intelligent working class kids. Group C was the less intelligent ones and group D was the ones who did the gardening! We were all in group B. We were all fairly bright but didn't work. 'Doesn't try – needs to apply himself'!"

The school brought Paul into contact with the first generation offspring of Sheerwater's London-born population – which is one reason you won't hear any hint of a Surrey accent in his voice, the other being his father's gruff South London bark. "It drew in quite a wide area," Baker points out. "You went there from your primary school and probably only knew two people in your class. We'd all come from little areas dotted around there – it was probably made up from five local schools. Most of the kids' parents came from London and all the rest who didn't live on Sheerwater had lived in Woking all their lives. So it was a funny atmosphere: Sheerwater was a pretty cliquey place. We were the outsiders – so we all went round together. There were lots of different races, Asians and orphans from the children's home."

Paul's taste for records was soon augmented by a growing obsession with clothes, and he took on two paper rounds – one in the morning, one in the evening – to supplement his pocket money. By the end of the Sixties, fashion had kept pace with the rapidly changing face of music, and had splintered into many different styles. While flares and long hair were becoming the order of the day, not just among middle class hippies but the wider community too, a largely working class fashion cult evolved which was cut from a sharper cloth than the one commonly available in the high street. Just as East End Mods' younger brothers adapted the look by cropping their hair and evolving into skinheads, so the boots and braces image gave way to what was labelled the suedehead look – taken from the smarter end of the skinhead's wardrobe but with longer hair. "The name suedehead came from the grown-out crop which takes on a suede appearance," explained George Marshall in *Spirit Of '69*. "It wasn't until the end of 1969 that suedeheads began to take on a cult identity of their own, particularly in London and the south."

Like the Mods, the skinheads and suedeheads adopted classic designs, but by mixing traditionally formal garments (smart suits, the Crombie-style overcoat, Ben Sherman button-down shirts, brogues and loafers) with working men's attire (Dr. Marten's boots, straight-legged jeans, Sta-prest trousers) and general leisure/sportswear (Fred Perry T-shirts and Harrington or Air Force jackets), they'd created a whole new uniform. This was the look which Weller was keen to adopt, but since most of these clothes weren't available in Woking – at least, not in Paul's size – he would save up for trips to Petticoat Lane, London's famous East End market, held every Sunday.

Every group of youngsters has a fashion leader. And Sheerwater's was Paul Weller. "He had all the trendy gear and a different outfit on every week," admits Steve Baker. "Paul had style. When I first met him, he was already fashion conscious and then got us all into clothes. Paul had grown miles ahead of us. The first pair of good shoes I had were Frank Wright loafers, on his recommendation. By that time, he also had brogues and Doc Martens. There was a shop in Woking called Dazzles – it was actually a house – and an old fella used to sell wholesale stuff. Paul would be down there all the time – he had an account!" The teenage Weller even made his school uniform something to be proud of, as Baker explains. "He didn't dress out of uniform, he used to adapt it. It was, like, dark grey trousers but he'd come in with pale grey Sta-prest, and his tie might have a red line through it or he'd wear a lemon-coloured shirt instead of white. He was a bit rebellious; he never wanted to conform. The blokes a couple of years above used to consult him about fashion and clothes."

But Paul wasn't the gregarious individual that his flashy threads might have suggested. In fact, he was shy and guarded at school. As his mother told Paolo Hewitt, "Paul is a very reserved sort of person. When he was young, he wouldn't speak unless he was spoken to, really, not because he was being stand-offish but I think basically because he's a very shy person." This view was confirmed by Paul himself in *Flexipop* magazine: "I think I was a quiet adolescent – 'a bit deep' as my mum put it. Music completely enveloped me."

Of course, music and fashion have always lived hand-in-hand, and the soundtrack for the skinhead/suedehead movement, of which Weller was an initiate, was reggae. Previously an underground phenomenon in Britain among West Indian immigrant communities in cities like London and Birmingham, Jamaican music evolved during the Sixties from the frantic ska sound, the object of a brief craze in 1964, via a slowed-down version known as rocksteady, to reggae itself, which had crossed over to the mainstream by

1969. The next couple of years witnessed a golden era for Jamaican music and several records even topped the British charts, as reggae replaced soul as the predominant form of popular dance music. The highly structured sound was seen as a reaction against the excesses of the prevalent progressive rock movement and its long-haired proponents, who championed lengthy musical improvisation.

Most lads on the brink of their teens are keen on football, but Paul wasn't that fussed about it – or sport, generally, for that matter. "John wanted his son to be somebody," reckons Steve. "He organised this soccer team when we were about twelve. Paul couldn't play to save his life and all these lads who were really good footballers were on the subs bench. And there's John up there, shouting, 'Get the ball, Paul, score a goal'. That didn't last long." Instead, Paul was preoccupied with music and fashion, pursuits in which his father was equally supportive. John Weller bought his son a guitar for Christmas – a proper electric one that he would learn to play, unlike his gimmicky old Beatles souvenir with its mock-signatures. At twelve, Paul was still too young to take the gift too seriously, though, and the instrument gathered dust under his bed for several months.

Instead, he ventured out on his own in the evenings to discover a life beyond the playground or the bedroom. The fact that John and Ann were relatively young contributed to his liberal upbringing. Few restrictions were placed on him, as he was allowed to roam free from parental constraints – but Paul soon discovered that there wasn't much on offer for pre-teens. Iain Wakeford agrees: "Woking was pretty dead in those days. People had to entertain themselves."

The town's premier night spot had been the Atalanta Ballroom in Commercial Road in the heart of Woking, described in *Surrey In The Sixties* as "the place to be . . . many top rhythm and blues bands played there, including The Rolling Stones. The venue boasted the best-sprung dancefloor in Surrey." However, the club was restricted to over-18s – and, in any case, it closed down long before Paul was eligible to attend. Aside from the Guildford Civic Hall over five miles away, the only other local venue was the Bisley Pavilion, which played host to jobbing progressive rock acts like The Pink Fairies and Brewers Droop.

The eleven-year-old suedehead had to look elsewhere for entertainment, and discovered local discos at the Football Club south of the station down in Old Woking, the twice-weekly 'Sounds Around' event at the nearby Old Woking Community Centre, and another disco over at Knaphill. Steve Baker: "We were about twelve. Some girls had a party and it was the first time we'd been out anywhere. I'll always remember the girls were dancing. Then we put on T. Rex and I thought, all we've got to do is dance like they do on *Top Of The Pops*. Paul scoffed and said, 'That's how greasers dance. This is how *we* dance'. And he knew all these synchronised skinhead dances – in the end, there were about eight of us in a line. He was well ahead of us. When I asked where he'd learnt all that, he said, Woking Football Club, an under-16s disco on a Tuesday night. Reggae and Motown – that's all they played. Paul knew all the artists – Max Romeo and Desmond Dekker. He bought this record into school one day, Dave & Ansell Collins' 'Double Barrel'. Two weeks later, it was No. 1. We went to a party once. It was, like, bring your records along and we all had two singles each. Paul had a whole boxful. I think his mum and dad would buy them."

Paul's fashion sense didn't go unnoticed by the opposite sex, either. "All the girls used to fancy him, I think mainly because he was so stylish," admits Baker. "He was quite shy but very arrogant at the same time. He said to me one day, 'I think they all fancy me. It's really who I wanna go out with, isn't it?' When he did pluck up the courage, he did seem to have the pickings. Sometimes, he was very upfront. He'd go up to a girl and shout, 'alright! darling' and grab hold of her." But maybe all the attention went to his head. "We did a school play once," adds Baker. "Somebody had to be king and Paul piped up, 'Yeah, I'll do that. King Weller – I like the sound of that!' I thought, you arrogant bastard. And then, on the day of the play, he was off sick – his bottle went!"

It wasn't long before the teenager's interest in girls went beyond furtive comments and awkward lunges, though. "Sharon Boxall was his first love," remembers Baker. "She was really trendy – the suedehead hair and all that – and a bit tough. All the girls were scared of her. Sharon was in the year above us. Usually, boys go out with girls in the year below, but with Paul, it was vice versa. Janice Furnow was another." Paul told his own version of events in *Flexipop*: "I think I had my first girlfriend when I was around thirteen. All lovey-dovey and cuddling. Then, when I was fourteen, I went 'steady' with a girl for eight months (she's my cousin now!). My mum and dad thought I was ill because I spent all my time with her and didn't go out playing football with the lads. My parents were dead against it. I didn't get on with them for ages around that time."

Paul Weller had reached puberty and like thousands of other lads before and since, it dawned on him that being in a band, playing on a stage, wouldn't do his chances with the girls any harm. Dusting off his guitar, he set about learning the rudiments of how to play, and for the rest of 1971, he managed to master the basics without the threat of disturbing the neighbours. John Weller hadn't realised that an electric guitar needed something to power it. "We didn't know about amplifiers until a lot later," Paul admitted to Paolo Hewitt in *Days Lose Their Names And Time Slips Away*. "I got right into [the guitar]. I loved it and cherished it. I even slept with it on top of my bed."

No-one else at school seemed to share Paul's new passion – until he bumped into a new arrival. Steve Brookes had been born only one day later than Paul at St. Mary's Hospital in Paddington, but family troubles had disrupted his upbringing, and Sheerwater was the latest in a string of schools when his family arrived in Woking around Christmas 1971. Paul and Steve met via a tall, colourful, ginger-haired wild card named Roger Pilling, as Steve told Barry Nield in a filmed interview for the *Highlights And Hang-Ups* documentary, later published in full in *Boys About Town* fanzine. "Pilling dragged me across the playground to meet Paul [who] sort of looked me up and down and wandered off. It improved from there, really!"

In fact, the pair hit it off immediately, kindred spirits with a shared love of Sixties beat music. As Steve Baker sees it, Brookes offered Weller the escape route he was looking for: "He had this notion that he didn't want to work and thought about what he could do to avoid it. Paul said, I can play guitar, I'll teach you to play as well and we'll do that for a living." Brookes probably laughed at the idea. But Paul was serious – deadly serious.

★   ★   ★

Although they were in different classes (Steve had previously been to a Grammar school, so he joined a higher stream), Paul and Steve became inseparable. Brookes quickly got up to speed on the guitar when the pair had lessons with a chap known affectionately as Smithy (Ricky Smith), who ran Woking's main musical shop, Maxwell's. "Steve picked up the actual guitar playing more naturally than Paul – he was really good," adds Baker. Other sources have suggested that the pair were taught by a lad in the sixth form at school; whatever the case, the pair rehearsed together after school in Paul's bedroom with a well-thumbed copy of *The Beatles Songbook*. They weren't content just to bash out cover versions, though. "We wrote from day one, really," reckoned Brookes. "When we first started, the quality of his songs were always better than mine but we did collaborate."

Weller had fond memories of these early endeavours, commenting in *Internationalists* that "they were fairly good songs, considering, and quite advanced for our age and a bit Beatle-ish in style." Brookes more or less moved into Stanley Road for weeks on end. "Steve's parents split up," explains Baker. "Sometimes, he'd live with his mum and sometimes his dad and then Ann Weller said, why don't you come and live with us? So he used to kip on the floor in Paul's room in a sleeping bag." Brookes had fond memories of the time, when he spoke to Barry Nield: "We used to get up at five o'clock in the morning during the summer, and walk around the streets with no shoes on – just for inspiration."

After six months or so, the duo were ready to play their first proper show, having had a lunchtime trial run in the school music room playing shaky original compositions like 'Crossroads', 'Wicked Woman Blues', 'Together' and 'Buster'. During that summer, John Weller secured them another lunchtime slot – this time, at the Albion pub opposite Woking

31

station. Paul and Steve had just discovered the hippie sounds of the late Sixties and, nervous in front of the bemused locals, they chose to perform Donovan's 'Colours'. John Weller was also a regular at the Woking Working Men's Club in Walton Road, right next to the Wellers' house, and on a winter's Thursday night in late 1972, the two fourteen-year-olds hurried through their set with tiny amps in front of an indifferent audience of local drinkers. The set included Sixties covers of Chuck Berry, Donovan and Tom Jones, as Steve recounted to Nield: "We did about eight songs, mostly Beatle songs. We had this idea of wearing the same gear . . . We both had a black-and-white Elvis Presley shirt along with the orange loon pants with training shoes!"

Paul was already convinced that playing music was his true vocation in life and, ever the open-minded parents, John and Ann indulged what at this point must have seemed like a fantasy. With such a tolerant attitude at home, Paul was hardly likely to enjoy the discipline of school life, and his school report for the summer of 1972 stressed his under-achievement and lack of concentration.

"I used to worry about going to Sheerwater Secondary School," Paul admitted in *Flexipop* magazine in 1981. "For the first two years, I really tried to work hard. But by the time I was fourteen, I started discovering sex, music and drinking and there was no way I was gonna stay in and do some poxy maths homework . . . I hated all my teachers passionately . . . School is where I decided I would show bastards like that that I didn't need their rules or their education to get anywhere in life. I suppose I do have some happy memories of school life – bunking off and going down the canal for a smoke. But most of my school recollections are very painful. I didn't like other people having authority over me and that's why I hated the teachers . . . I was very good at English and TD but that was all. I read *1984* for my English CSE and they let me write a poem for it rather than an essay. It was called *Room 101*. Oh, and they put one of my paintings in the school hall."

Paul had grown equally disillusioned with the pop music of the time. "I never turned onto all that glam-rock stuff. I thought it was really boring, all that music in the Seventies," he later commented. But he was also sure that the future didn't lie with Simon & Garfunkel-style duos. No, the pair needed to recruit some other members.

"The idea was to get a band together with people that we actually liked," revealed Brookes to Barry Nield. "It didn't really matter whether they could play an instrument or not." That was certainly the case with another refugee whose family had moved down from London. "Dave Waller became quite a good mate of ours," explained Steve, "and we wanted him in the band . . . We encouraged him to play the guitar but he never really caught on."

Paul may have been the fashionable one, but Dave Waller had the streetwise Fulham background. Born on January 24, 1958, Waller had already expressed his love of poetry and the written word by the time he and his sister enrolled at Sheerwater, but his unstable nature made him a disruptive influence at school. "He was rebel leader, really," smiles Steve Baker. "He spent a whole term doing a project on the history of flight. Then he ripped the whole lot up, hurled it in the air. 'This is what I think of history', he screamed, and walked out. He burnt his blazer once and had a scrap with a teacher. Dave was the one who'd stand up and shout about it." These characteristics earned him a reputation as a bit of a beatnik, which enthralled Paul from the start. Dave brought something else with him from London: the fact that he smoked dope lent him a certain glamour, especially in the eyes of two impressionable teenagers with dreams of making it big as a rock band.

"I was drawn in by the whole sex, drugs and rock'n'roll ethic," Paul later confessed. "Even when I was playing at a youth club, you'd notice a girl looking at you more because you're standing on a stage. When you're 14 or 15, these are the things which impress you." Like most teenagers, the lads dabbled with drugs – dropping acid, smoking spliffs, swallowing pills and even sniffing shoe polish! Sold on the myth of the apocryphal rock'n'roll lifestyle, they wrote psychedelic poems, grew their hair long and travelled to free festivals. Paul had reached that inevitable stage in puberty when he rebelled against family life – and he apparently argued with his mum, in particular.

Persuaded to buy an £18 guitar, Dave Waller took on the role of rhythm guitarist in the band. Paul switched to bass after his parents pawned a couple of his guitars for a Hofner they'd spotted in a music shop in Kingston – the very model that Paul McCartney had immortalised in the Sixties. Now all they needed was a drummer.

★　★　★

Born on January 28, 1958 as a second child and only son, Neil Harris was given the nickname 'Bomber' (after the World War Two Air Marshal, Sir Arthur 'Bomber' Harris) while at Monument Primary. By the time he joined junior school, he was already a proficient musician. "I had my first drum kit when I was six and had lessons from about seven-and-a-half, taught by a professional big band drummer, Bill Wayne," he remembers. "That's when I learnt to read music." When he reached senior school, Harris involved himself in the school band, which played everything from big production musical numbers to mainstream classical tunes.

This project was run by the school's head of music, John Avery, who was struck by Harris's enthusiasm: "Bomber was great. We used to do concerts at school where the brass and percussion sections from the BBC Concert Orchestra came down and played. He got really excited by all this and actually then joined a brass band."

Another pupil enlisted by Avery was Bruce Foxton, who was two years above Harris. "There was a school concert coming up – a cantata, with piano, bass and drums," says Avery. "I said to Bruce, could he play a bass guitar? He said yes, having never taken part in any formal public music before and knowing he'd only got two weeks. Bruce was terrific. He really sweated his socks off learning it, note by note, and then turned up and played it in a very formal concert situation."

Foxton was also forming his own band, as Harris recalls: "Bruce and a guy called Chris Giles were in the same year as my sister Susan. They were looking for a drummer and my sister suggested I was available." Harris jumped at the chance of playing in a band with these lads who were two years his senior, although it was a primitive set-up: they had no bass player or vocalist and the trio didn't even have a name. "I was getting on for 13 then. Bruce was on lead guitar, Chris was on rhythm. We rehearsed at dinner times and performed at school concerts, like at the end-of-term. We covered stuff like The Shadows' 'Apache', simple instrumental stuff. I should imagine that ran for about a year-and-a-half, on-and-off. It wasn't a permanent thing." The band fizzled out altogether when Bruce left school and started a printing apprenticeship in summer '72, but early in 1973, Neil was approached again.

"I first met Weller when I was eleven or twelve, and just started senior school, and we became mates. He must have seen me play at one of the concerts. He said he was starting a band up, and would I fancy playing with them? We had a meeting round Richard Burfield's house – in fact, it might have been Richard who put me onto Paul. The first practice was in Paul's bedroom. I remember it was about 12 feet by 10, and he had lots of pictures on the walls. His parents were very nice, his mum especially. She couldn't do enough for you, really. Dave Waller turned up once and Paul said he'd joined the band. Dave was a good laugh but he wasn't much of a musician. I suppose, all in all, I had half-a-dozen rehearsals with them over a couple of months, mainly down the Working Men's Club on Sunday afternoons when it was closed. Both Paul and Steve sang. We covered stuff like The Rolling Stones. We did a couple of Beatles ballads, 'Yesterday' and 'If I Fell', and a couple of Chuck Berry's, 'Johnny B. Goode' and 'Roll Over Beethoven'. And then Paul started scribbling notes of his own songs down."

The neighbours were good-natured about the lads' ham-fisted, enthusiastic rehearsals – and they weren't the only people who noticed. "I'd go round Paul's house after school and sit and watch them rehearse," remembers Steve Baker, "and there'd be musical instruments all over the place – a piano in the hall, amps up and down the stairs. One Saturday afternoon, they were playing a lot of rock'n'roll stuff like 'Blue Suede Shoes' and 'Jailhouse Rock' – they did a lot of Elvis – and there were a load of greasers outside dancing on the pavement. I don't know whether they were digging it or taking the piss!"

The origin of the band's name has been a source of conjecture over the years. It may have evolved from their numerous jamming sessions, a theory supported by Foxton and drummer Buckler in their book, *Our Story*. Steve Baker agrees: "It was Dave Waller's mum's idea, because he was the one who'd say, we're having a jam this afternoon, talking hip to his mum." Paul and Steve Brookes' version of events, on the other hand, suggested that Paul's sister concocted the name one morning over the breakfast table, the scenario running something like this, as she took a bite out of a piece of toast: "Hey Paul, there's already been a band called Bread and another called Marmalade . . .". Whatever the inspiration, the name stuck – The Jam.

2

REMEMBER HOW WE STARTED

As luck would have it, the lads had stumbled across a rehearsal facility at school, which meant they didn't have to rely on Paul's cramped bedroom and the few occasions they gained access to the Working Men's Club. John Avery was one of the few teachers who managed to strike up a rapport with Weller, and he let the band use his music room to practise at lunch times and after school.

"Paul came to me because I'd got facilities that he wanted: a semi-soundproofed room," explains Avery. "That was my contribution. It was purely a personal thing rather than a school ethos, because they were thought of as oiks, as untouchables. I crossed that boundary as being the acceptable face of authority. I was only recently out of college and wanted to give everyone a crack of the whip, a chance to express themselves. And I wasn't interested, ultimately, in whether kids were going to be disciplined but just in letting them have their say – God, I sound like a social worker!"

Avery's liberal attitude gave the teenagers a breathing space within the confines of school life. He is honest about his contribution to Weller's musical development, though: "If you asked me, did I teach Paul?, the answer is no. But if you were asking whether I encouraged and sympathised, then the answer is yes – against the tide of current thinking about the behaviour and expectations of pupils at that time. I used to leave them to their own devices. I wouldn't even say he showed a great interest in music. I wish I could say he was a star pupil but I can't. He did opt for a CSE in music. The public exam clearly had a fairly academic approach to the subject – and that's not what Paul wanted out of music, quite rightly. There was nothing he could relate to. If you're just doing cover versions, you don't need to know about keys or modulations or the structure of music."

Something in Paul's single-mindedness struck a chord with Avery's own rebellious streak. "I always dealt with Paul as an individual, a one-to-one relationship. I definitely had a soft spot for him. There was a certain chemistry between us which might just have been toleration. I didn't crave his attention any more than he craved mine. But we were kindred spirits. Paul was quite a loner – that's how I observed him from a distance. He had his own ideas. I mean this in the nicest way: he was an angry young man. I always found him intense, keyed up, full of energy and a lot of aggression as well, but I never saw that displayed in a violent way, apart from in the culture. I think that's how he gave vent to his feelings – through his poetry, through playing loud music, rather than duffing people up. I found him a gentle person in many ways. He was always polite to me."

On the one hand, Weller has always displayed a moody edginess, a pent-up energy which is often interpreted as nervousness, and on the other, he is reported as having a pleasant demeanour and a good sense of humour. It is no surprise that these two conflicting sides to Weller's personality manifested themselves in his music. The Jam made their name with a sound that was forceful, exciting, hostile even, but there was also a softer side to many of their songs. For every self-assertive, vitriolic anthem there was a melodic, introverted ballad, and this contrast has continued throughout Paul's life.

There was nothing extraordinary about the school's music room itself: "There were instruments, but the most basic classroom type: the odd triangle or pair of bongos. There was a school drum kit, but they would have brought their own guitars. The place was not a hub of musical or academic excellence! I guess it was the only room in the school which didn't have the word 'Jam' engraved into the desks and tables, because Paul knew that the facility would be removed. School was not really for him. He wasn't very popular with the staff, mainly because he was uncooperative and wanted to do his own thing."

Avery wasn't the only teacher to show some interest, however. "Paul had a real command of language and wrote quite good poetry," he adds, "and there was an English teacher, Roly Brown, who admired the work that he did." Another English teacher was Penny Allen, who encouraged her student as best she could. Paul also started to immerse himself in books. "If we studied something which interested him, like politics or romantic poets, he'd get into it," agrees Steve Baker. "He seemed to be into George Orwell years before anyone else took an interest in the social aspect." But it eventually became obvious that Paul Weller had already dismissed school life as a necessary inconvenience until such time as he could leave – or before.

Tucked away from the school's main thoroughfare, the music room acted as a haven not only for the band but as a meeting place for a gang of friends including Pete Carver, Charlie Barrow and Philip Self, plus the inimitable Roger Pilling. "Roger was the clown," laughs Steve Baker. "Paul was the instigator. He'd wind him up and make everybody laugh. That was our main aim at school. 'Go on, Roger. Get yourself in trouble and we'll all have a good laugh.' Dave Waller was always getting stick for things. Paul was quite sneaky and a bit sly. He'd land someone else in the shit but get himself off the hook at the same time."

"There would be times when he'd come in at lunchtimes, disappear in the afternoon and come back after school," remembers Avery. "Paul was not overtly rebellious," he adds. "I think that's what he admired about Dave Waller." The teacher also met John Weller: "His father was very protective of Paul. He was quite a hard man – I wouldn't want to get on the wrong side of him! Paul was a definite leader and very much his own man, but he was aided and abetted by John."

It was Paul's dad, in fact, who hustled gigs. In *Boys About Town*, Brookes described John as the "making of the band . . . the concrete in between the bricks". Far from resenting the fact that Paul's father was so strongly involved, Steve was positive about his crucial role: "He had total dedication from day one. John had come up the hard way . . . and knew how hard it was to go out and earn a buck. He always had this idea that if his boy could go and do something that didn't involve getting his hands dirty, then that would be the best way to go in life. When he saw that Paul had a talent, he encouraged him . . . It got down to a very tight little unit and there was a golden period of about a year when everything was going really well. The band were sounding good and getting plenty of gigs and it was all down to the fact that John was the driving force."

The story that the Wellers had their phone cut off, in order to buy an amplifier for Paul, is an example of the sacrifice Paul's parents endured, and the occasional tension between Ann and John over the house-keeping was overcome by a 100% commitment to their son's future. "He used to be a hod carrier. There's not a lot of show business in that," Paul said of his father in *The Independent* in 1987. "But he was the one who used to try and get us crummy gigs in pubs, beg, steal or borrow to buy equipment or get hold of a Transit."

Around Easter 1973, John entered the band in the Sheerwater Community Association talent contest. Each district of Woking Borough had its own heat, and The Jam won theirs at the Sheerwater Community Centre on April 22. The final was to be held at Old Woking Community Centre, actually located between Old Woking and Kingfield, on May 12, prompting the local paper to announce the details with the words, "Will a Woking audience be applauding any future stars of tomorrow during the final heat?"

The safe money might have been on Fairlands' Rock Island Line, a rock'n'roll act who'd already appeared in the hit David Essex film, *That'll Be The Day*. As it transpired, the Teddy boys came third and the prize for the best 'Group Of Instrumentalists', one of nine categories in the contest, went to 'Paul Weller & The Jam', who climaxed their brief set with a rendition of Chuck Berry's 'Reelin' And Rockin' '. The band walked away with a "small cash sum" and an engraved silver trophy.

"For the big do, Paul's mum had been down the market and bought us some shirts," adds Harris. "They were mauve/blue, like the old Brutus design with the round collar. We had this attitude that we didn't care. We went on stage and Paul and Steve arranged that when the curtain opened, they had their backs to the audience, facing me. And then, when the music started up, they jumped round suddenly. It sounds a bit weird but it did have some kind of stage effect."

The band had a helping hand from one of the biggest rock acts of the day, as Harris explains: "I borrowed a cymbal off John Coghlan, who was then the drummer for Status Quo; Rick Parfitt's mum and dad lived on Sheerwater and John Weller knew them well. We went to see Quo at the Guildford Civic Hall, in between the heat and the final, which gave us a high." Paul Weller had never been to a rock concert before, but the event doesn't seem to have made a big impact on the teenager. Although early Jam gigs featured a shambolic cover of 'Paper Plane', Status Quo's most useful contribution to The Jam's development came via the Quo guitarist's acquaintance with John Weller.

In fact, Parfitt had grown up about three doors along from Sheerwater Comprehensive. "Paul's dad and my dad were drinking partners at the Woking Working Men's Club," explains Rick. "John Weller would say, 'Paul would like to get into the business. Can Rick give him some encouragement?' I was in no position, really, because I didn't know what the fuck was going on myself! But I went round and saw Paul, who was then a fresh, young lad. He was withdrawn in those days, and didn't say a lot. I found it hard to get through to him, but I understand that he was thrilled that I'd given him some words of advice."

Over the next couple of years, the Quo frontman occasionally lent them equipment and helped out whenever he could – which lends Weller's relationship with Oasis, a band who've attracted the odd Quo comparison, a certain circular appeal. "I got a call one day," Rick recalls. "Did I have a spare amplifier? I happened to have a quite expensive amp in my garage and said they could borrow it as long as they needed it. It wasn't a common model – it had lots of dials and effects built into it. And I never got it back!"

No sooner had they won the talent contest than The Jam lost their drummer. "I went off to Canada for about a month around June/July to play in a football tournament," reveals Neil Harris. "A gig came up so Paul Buckler stood in – or Rick, as he became known. When I came back, Weller's dad came round and said, how do you feel? I said, well, it was understandable if I'm away. He said, well, we're thinking about signing him on now. I said fine. I should kick myself!" In any case, Harris's musical tastes were drifting away from those of the rest of the band: "When I was in Canada, I saw Chicago and The Eagles. My music tastes turned and I was getting into all this West Coast music and The Beach Boys," he adds. To the fifteen-year-old Weller, there was probably no greater crime than liking The Eagles: they epitomised a brand of slick, highly produced American country rock prevalent during the mid-Seventies, a style which Paul has despised to this day.

★   ★   ★

Paul Richard Buckler was born on December 6, 1955, roughly five minutes before his twin brother Peter. His family then lived in Church Street, off the Goldsworth Road just to the west of the town centre. His father Joe (or Bill, as most people knew him) was a postman and, later, a GPO telephone engineer, while his mother Primrose looked after two older brothers, Andy and John. The Wellers may have accepted that their son's talents lay with music, but the Bucklers had a more traditional idea of how to raise their Paul, pushing him to work hard at Goldsworth Primary School and then at Sheerwater, and encouraging him to join the Boys Brigade and the local Baptist Sunday School. Both he and his brother Pete took piano lessons, but Paul wasn't interested and took to the drums instead.

When they were fifteen, the twins formed a rough approximation of a power trio called Impulse. A friend, Howard Davies, played guitar, with Pete on bass. "Vocals? No, we didn't bother with that," laughs Rick. "We were rubbish, really! We were music fans and just wanted to have a go ourselves." This was 1970/71, so Impulse gravitated to those heavy rock bands who were taking the charts and the rock festivals by storm – Led Zeppelin, Black Sabbath and Deep Purple. They were an influence which the drummer retained – albeit quietly – for many years. Unlike Weller, Paul Buckler enjoyed school and even became a prefect in his last year. He did well in his CSEs and 'O'-Levels – he was especially good at woodwork, which is his trade today – and stayed on to study for 'A'-Levels in the Sixth Form.

However, the drummer dropped out halfway through the first year, leaving school at 17 to work for a motorcycle spare parts warehouse. It didn't last long, and after spells in a fishmongers at weekends and as a draftsman in a drawing office, Buckler ended up in electronics quality control. There'd been a lull of perhaps a year since Impulse had folded when he'd got the nod from Paul's dad, who asked him along to a rehearsal. Since he shared the same Christian name as Weller, the drummer became known by his middle name, Rick – later, he attracted the rather less attractive nickname of 'Pube', which was passed on from Steve Brookes. Rick was a natural choice, since he was already acquainted with Paul and his friends. "He used to come and chat with us in the music room," says Baker. "We'd mess around with guitars and he'd always beat hell out of the drum kit."

Buckler was another refugee from the school's brass band. Teacher John Avery had drafted him in to replace the troupe's regular drummer for assembly. "Rick was in my tutor group," adds John. "He was just a pleasant, quiet lad, not one that would stand out." In *Boys About Town*, Steve Brookes described Buckler as "a bit of a hippie. He was dreadful to start off with." Paul also lent the newcomer a couple of Chuck Berry records, and since the school kit was tiny, he borrowed one from the Guildford YMCA (still only one cymbal, a snare and a bass drum), in time for a night at Sheerwater Youth Club – "the first proper gig with a full set," as Baker remembers it.

The Jam inaugurated their new line-up in front of forty school mates, but the event didn't bode well: their equipment packed up and the band retired to the pub, partly to quell their nerves and partly because they thought the whole evening had fallen through. They returned in no fit state to perform, but after a barrage of verbal abuse from an incensed John Weller, the band stumbled onstage to slur their way through a shambolic set.

Aside from the group's drunken antics, the Sheerwater Youth Club gig was memorable for two other reasons. Steve Baker laughs: "Halfway through, Dave Waller's guitar lead broke and they couldn't fix it. So, what are they gonna do? They didn't have a spare, so Paul took the lead out of his bass and grabbed the piano at the side of the stage. He dragged the instrument to the front and played it instead of bass. I didn't even know he could play the piano."

Secondly, that night's set included one of those love songs Paul had been writing with Brookes: 'Takin' My Love' was performed in a country rock style, but its chord structure mirrored the rest of their repertoire. "I think every song was a twelve-bar," reckons Steve Baker. 'Takin' My Love' and 'Blueberry Rock', another new composition written solely by Paul, were chosen for The Jam's first studio session, and a handful of acetates were cut with one song on each side. "It was recorded at Eden Studios in Kingston – some little demo place," Paul told me in 1992. "It was the very first thing we ever recorded as a four-piece."

'Takin' My Love' was later reworked as the B-side of the first Jam single, but 'Blueberry Rock' has since passed into the annals of The Jam's mythology; it would seem that no-one other than the band and close acquaintances has ever heard it. However, once they'd tired of the song, Weller donated it to Steve Baker, who was in the process of forming his own band, Squire – so called because they rehearsed above "an old hippie shop" of that name. "Paul would teach us and show us a few tricks," he adds. Sitting in his living room in Woking over twenty years later, Baker still remembered the song, strumming the twelve-bar riff and recalling the first verse, a mish-mash of easy rhymes and rock'n'roll clichés.

Demo cassettes were run off to help John Weller secure The Jam some more gigs. By now, Paul's dad was actively hustling for the band, driving them to and from events, such as the recent talent contest, in his taxi. His son was equally dedicated on stage, as Baker remembers: "It was always struck me the way Paul put himself across. He really threw himself into it, shouting ad-libs. I think it was the McCartney influence; he was more into him than Lennon, with that Hofner bass. My mum and dad saw them play at a wedding and said, 'That Paul Weller thinks he's Paul McCartney!' "

The Beatles influence could also be detected on a second Jam acetate featuring two Weller-Brookes compositions. It's patently obvious that the pair's infatuation with Lennon/McCartney affected their style of song-writing. Light years away from the prevailing music of the day, the tracks also seemed to hark back to a golden age of American rock'n'roll in a style reminiscent of, say, Dave Edmunds' 'I Hear You Knocking'.

Paul's occasionally wayward lead vocals were clearly evident on both songs. The plaintive melodies of 'Some Kinda Loving' also featured crooned backing vocals. Together with Rick's gentle drumming, it created the effect of a shaky barber's shop tune. Weller's intricate bassline was surprisingly nimble and the four-note rock'n'roll guitar riff and two-chord strumming was joined by a short guitar solo in the middle, supported by more "oooh"s. It sounded like a group with plenty of influences but no experience. Nevertheless, the results were very promising, bearing in mind the primitive recording facilities and the band's age – Weller was still only fifteen, which may explain the song's somewhat gauche, adolescent lyrics.

'Makin' My Way Back Home' had a stronger twelve-bar R&B flavour and galloped along at a more frantic pace – but this was youth club boogie rather than pub rock. As the middle-eight kicked in, Weller boasted in a cod-US accent that "baby, baby, don't you know that I'm right, so come on baby, baby, let's make it tonight – well, alright!" There followed a clean, echo-laden guitar solo that was part Hank Marvin, part early Beatles, before the song ambled to a close.

The handful of acetates bore the imprint Fanfare Records, which was based in London. "One Saturday in October or November of 1973," wrote Steve Brookes in his account of The Jam's early days, *Keeping The Flame*, "we were booked into a studio just off Finchley Road, near Swiss Cottage. We were told not to worry about bringing amplifiers . . . we fantasised about this studio full of Vox AC30s and Fender Twin Reverbs. Wrong again. When we arrived, we realised why – there wasn't enough room!"

"Rick borrowed our drummer's hi-hat," adds Baker, "because he said his sounded like two baked bean tin lids banging together! We used to borrow gear off each other a lot."

Baker also remembers other early Jam compositions like 'Pucker Up, Buttercup'. "I think 'Old Jam Pie' was their first. It was a two-chord thing – it might not even have had words. I don't think they got further than Paul playing them, sitting on a chair." Another Weller-Brookes song was 'Forever And Always', followed later by titles like 'Lovin' By Letters', 'More And More', 'One Hundred Ways' and 'Nothing You Can Say' (a ballad which, according to Baker, sounded like The Doobie Brothers). "There are dozens more," revealed Brookes to Barry Nield. "And even at the Working Men's Club, we were doing fifty per cent of our own material. In fairness, we were always prone to pinching a chord sequence when we were stuck for inspiration. We used to drag out the *Beatles Complete* songbook."

Dave Waller left The Jam towards the end of 1973. His frustration with his inability to master the guitar was shared by the others. "Dave said that he got pissed off with it; Paul said they kicked him out because he was no good," recalls Baker. "I think it was six of one and half-a-dozen of the other." Waller's real interests definitely lay elsewhere. His sombre, intense personality was animated by heated, lengthy rants about politics and, perhaps intimidated by his serious nature, the rest of the band tended to make him the butt of their pranks. Dave was left to concentrate on his poetry, but his passionate socialist convictions and command of the written word had a profound influence on not only Paul Weller's beliefs but also his lyrics. "Dave was very angry," admits Baker, who reckons Waller had no time for love songs. "He said, there's that Elton John song, 'Saturday Night's Alright For Fighting' – why don't we write songs like that? Real songs about taking drugs, getting drunk. It got Paul's mind ticking over. I think he did borrow ideas from Dave right through The Jam era."

Soon afterwards, John Weller organised the trio's first photo shoot with James R. Holl of Woking's Bermuda Studios. Weller, Buckler and Brookes posed, surly and pouting, with shoulder-length hair, but looked relatively smart in broad 'kipper' white ties, black teardrop-collar shirts and hip-hugging bell-bottoms – the idea of a stage uniform was later retained with The Jam's distinctive black-and-white stage attire. The shots were presumably designed to reassure local tenants, bingo hall owners and soon-to-be-married couples that The Jam were respectable young lads, who wouldn't sully an evening with heavy rock music or attract an unsavoury audience.

Like most small towns, Woking had a tightly knit community, and Holl's older brother later married Deborah Bird, who was in Paul's class for the first two years at secondary school. "Paul went out with a friend of mine, Christine Ferguson," she mentions. "He was a nice enough guy. A little crowd of us sat at one end of the classroom, larking around. We used to have a giggle and muck about. I remember quite vividly one particular religious education lesson. Paul decided to throw the tomatoes out of his lunchbox at the blackboard. I remember him showing us the guitar his dad had just bought him."

The bookings continued. "I got them a gig at Chobham village youth club," Baker remembers. "They had a disco once a month, so I said, why don't we have my mate's band instead, on a Friday night? They're really good. I negotiated a fee, twenty or thirty quid. And that was the best night the club ever had – they wouldn't let them off the stage. They played one song for half-an-hour, jamming it through." The group also played regular slots at the Woking Working Men's Club, bashing out inane requests as best they could. It was good practice, but the novelty soon wore off, especially because the band's friends were too young to be admitted. "John would say, I can't get you in. They were really fussy down there," bemoans Baker.

The Jam visited Old Woking Community Centre again towards the end of 1973. "I'll always remember they started with Status Quo's 'Caroline'," says Baker. "They had the curtains draped halfway across and then, singing, they crept out from behind the curtains with their guitars – what a load of prats!" Around Christmas that year, The Jam entered another competition at Woking cinema, together with Baker's band Squire. "There was a week of auditions for local talent," Steve reminisces. "We went down in our flares and played a Status Quo song. We were on different nights but neither of us won our heat."

Not that Paul Weller would have been disheartened. Those who knew Paul – and John, for that matter – in the mid-Seventies share the consensus that he always believed in himself and had a vision that grew clearer, at least publicly, as the embryo of The Jam progressed from broken guitar strings and fumbled plectrums through to their first gigs and beyond. From the day he'd dragged that guitar back out from under his bed, it seems Paul Weller had one goal in life – not only to play music but to become successful at it.

Neil Harris: "Paul always said to me that he was going to make it and be a star." Steve Baker: "We used to drink in the Red Lion in Horsell. I think we were fifteen and still at school but we'd pretend we were older – 'What's it like at work, then?!' Paul was drunk one night and said to me, 'When I make it, 'cos I know I'm going to, I'll make sure I look after you, I'll see you alright. I won't forget you.' He was definitely sure he was going to make it. There was no question in his mind." Steve Brookes: "I don't think it was fame and I don't think he was obsessed. [But] he was confident of success – totally confident."

Paul was resolute that his dream would become a reality, and he made it clear not only to friends (who'd respond with a raised eyebrow), but also to teachers at Sheerwater like Tony Ledger: "I recall on one occasion, Paul was in the music room in a playtime. 'What do you feel like doing when you leave school,' I asked? And he said, 'If I tell you, you'll only laugh – the other teachers laugh when I tell them'. I promised I wouldn't laugh. So, after some hesitation, he said he wanted to play pop music, and awaited my reaction. I didn't laugh but said, 'You've got to realise there are hundreds of kids who've got their eye on this. Give it a go but you mustn't be disappointed if it doesn't work out.' I pointed out that one of the things that was important was to get a good manager."

Paul Weller already had one. And John Weller also knew that, one day, his son would be a star.

★　★　★

On January 22, 1974, John Weller used his connections to secure The Jam an audition at Michael's, an insalubrious nightclub on the Goldsworth Road, heading west out of the town centre. The venue, which had opened in 1964, was owned by, and named after, two Greek Cypriot brothers, Hermes and

Homer Michaelides. They were always in the market for any attraction which lured in more than the usual post-pub clientele – and that usually meant strippers. John's boys turned in a good set, and The Jam were offered a long-standing Friday night residency upstairs. Hermes and his assistant Pepe even let the band rehearse there when Michael's was shut on Wednesday nights. And so began The Jam's own Hamburg years – only their Star Club was but a few hundred yards from Paul's doorstep – and they seem to have enjoyed Michael's, despite the aggravation that inevitably ensued with drunken punters in the early hours.

"The violence was a bit overstated, though," reckons Arthur Hunte, a friend of the Weller family who frequented Michael's. "It wasn't a smooth, sophisticated club, but if you were into funk music, you couldn't want a better place. People from London used to come down, because the DJs were very good. That was downstairs. For an extra drink, which went onto two in the morning, you went upstairs. There were a few people who liked the band but by the time people got to the club after a few drinks, they'd listen to anything."

The boys had created their own little world of rehearsals and drunken gigs, skiving the last few months off school. "For a bunch of fifteen-year-olds, we were quite a showy sort of band," Brookes boasted to Barry Nield, "leaping around the stage doing a lot of Chuck Berry songs and playing the guitar behind my head! Because we were so young, we got away with a lot of things that were basically naff." The band's mates would turn up to cheer them on, although the regulars were sometimes less impressed with their young following. "They wouldn't let us in because we were only sixteen," says Baker, "so John would leave the back door open and we used to sneak up the back stairs. Michael's was a drinking hole, the only place you could get a drink after 11 o'clock. There was a disco downstairs and they had the band upstairs, which was the more relaxed part, where you needed a membership. And it would always be, 'Turn it down lads, we're trying to play cards over here'."

Rick Parfitt remembers seeing The Jam at Michael's: "Johnny would say to me, 'Do you think they've got a chance?' And yeah, I found them different. The music didn't really appeal to me because I was set in my ways with the Quo, but they were refreshing. I didn't really know what to make of them, but being honest, I didn't think they'd get anywhere – which just shows how much I knew! I seem to recall that Johnny asked me to come in on the management side of The Jam. I had so much to do because Quo were flying, so I said no, partly because I knew bugger all about managing!"

Dave Waller might not have been the most proficient guitarist but his absence was certainly felt now that the band were playing regular gigs. In May 1974, they held auditions above a Woking pub for a second guitar player. One of the hopefuls was Bruce Foxton, who'd been recommended by The Jam's old drummer, Neil Harris. Bruce's name cropped up when Paul's dad had approached Harris to sit in for Rick Buckler one evening. "John Weller turned up on my doorstep in Maybury one Saturday afternoon," remembers Neil. "He said, can I borrow a pair of sticks? I'm thinking to myself, aye aye, what's wrong? I said, yeah, no problem. Then he said, how do you fancy playing tonight? We've got a gig on. I think it was Michael's. I said, sorry but I'm working with another band tonight. I couldn't let the guys down. Then he asked me, did I know a guitarist?"

Harris had kept himself busy after returning from Canada, reuniting with his old partner from their school trio. "I got a phone call from Bruce," he recalls. "He asked me to join this band, Rita, with these guys from Godalming on bass and lead guitar. It was a bit heavy, like Deep Purple – Seventies rock. My dad had a factory and used to hire Tellings Farm, over at Weybridge. They had these old barns and we'd go over there in the evenings. I had a garage at Byfleet so we rehearsed down there as well. We didn't play any gigs. In fact, it only lasted a couple of months. Rita were just splitting up, I think, when I spoke to John Weller."

So it was that Bruce Douglas Foxton joined The Jam. Born September 1, 1955, Bruce grew up on Albert Drive, Sheerwater, the youngest of three boys. Like most local residents, his parents originally came from London: his dad Henry worked first as a painter and decorator for the council and later as a sales collector for "Charringtons the coal people". His mum Helen drifted through various local part-time jobs, including a spell in a baker's shop and another at a sports shop where one of her workmates was Mrs Buckler. Educated at Sheerwater Junior and Secondary, Bruce had excelled at football and technical drawing. He became interested in music in his early teens, courtesy of guitar lessons with a fifth year lad, remembered only as Tony. Later, he absorbed his older brother's Motown collection while sharing Rick's love of contemporary hard rock bands like Bad Company.

Having left school in 1972, Foxton joined his older brother Derek, becoming apprentice compositor for a printing firm, Unwin Brothers. He'd formed Rita with two mates from work, but their reluctance to progress beyond light-hearted rehearsals frustrated Bruce, and although he wasn't sure about The Jam's reliance on covers of oldies like 'Blue Moon', he jumped at the chance of playing a couple of gigs a week.

Paul Weller officially left school in the summer of 1974, although his attendance during the last term was what might be described as sporadic, aided by lengthy periods of suspension courtesy of the headmaster, Mr Osbourne. Paul had all but given up on academia, although a booklet for Sheerwater's 22nd anniversary prize distribution, held that November, showed that he passed two CSEs – English and Music. Needless to say, his name was absent from the lists of 'Special Prizes' and 'House Year Group Awards'. It's interesting that the hymn on the back of the pamphlet was 'Jerusalem'. Twelve years later, the William Blake poem would inspire, and lend its title to, the musician's first venture into cinema with The Style Council. Perhaps Paul did learn something of value from his school education – then again, maybe it was just a coincidence.

During the summer of 1974, The Jam were earning an average of £15 each per week gigging, a reasonable income considering that two members were school leavers. Bruce and Rick still had their day jobs, however, and John Weller coerced Steve and Paul into finding gainful employment. The pair made a vain stab at window cleaning for a spell, and also helped Paul's dad out on the building site. Brookes eventually settled for working part-time with a removal firm, "humping furniture about", but Paul never adapted to manual labour. Maybe he was work-shy, or just plain incompetent, or perhaps he didn't fancy the idea. Brookes' anecdote from the *Highlights And Hang-Ups* documentary is worth repeating: "Paul and I were always short of money and we got a job with his dad, working on an extension he was building. One day, John was on top of the scaffolding and I went up with some bricks. While Paul was fiddling around trying to pack some bricks, John said, 'Look at the wanker. If he couldn't play the guitar, what fucking hope would there be for him?'"

His parents supported him when he preferred to stay at home, practising the guitar and writing songs. "Paul would be there during the day," says Arthur Hunte, "because he didn't actually go out to work. Sometimes, I'd pop round there and he'd say, could you listen to this number I've written, and he obviously believed in his music. But because Stanley Road was quite near Boomerang Taxis, the radio transmission would come over on the amplification when he was trying to play a tune!"

For his first few months with the band, Bruce only played on stage intermittently, sometimes joining them, say, for the last four songs. Sources conflict as to whether he struggled with the guitar or whether Paul was unhappy with playing bass. Whatever the case, he and Paul soon switched instruments, and Bruce sold his guitar to Enzo Esposito, Steve's partner in Squire (Enzo later introduced Paul to another local lad of Italian origin, Paolo Hewitt). "Because Paul was such a strong rhythm guitarist, we decided they'd have to swap, at which point Foxton got the hump," says Brookes. "Bruce had never really played bass before and he just did one-note stuff, but with Paul back on rhythm and Bruce doing very basic bass, it sounded a lot better."

The gigs diversified as the band played further afield, accepting offers to perform anywhere from weddings and birthday parties to bingo halls. John Weller had cards printed advertising The Jam as a "rock & roll group". On June 20, they even reached the pages of *Woking News And Mail*. "Fun At Club's First Fair", ran the headline: "There was more fun about than money at Sheerwater Youth Club's first summer fair last Saturday. The Woking girls' weight-training team gave demonstrations throughout the afternoon, and there was also trampolining. Music was provided by 'Jam'. Members dressed as clowns to keep the children amused . . ." Alas, no photos of the event appear to have survived. Now that Paul had left school, the band also found a new rehearsal facility at Horsell Village Hall, storing their equipment in a waterlogged lock-up garage nearby.

In the autumn, The Jam were booked to support Rock Island Line, their old sparring partners from the talent contest, at a "horrid discotheque" called Bunters in Guildford. "I had arranged to meet my friends at the nearby Horse & Groom, further up the street," Bruce told Alex Ogg in *Our Story*. It was October 5, 1974, the night the IRA chose the pub as one of their targets. "I was forced to go home with the rest of the band, who were later telephoned and told the gig was off." The band had soundchecked across the road, just a few hours before a bomb blast ripped the whole street apart.

Closer to home, The Jam were booked for a show at the Hindhead British Legion Club, about fifteen miles south-west of Woking, on the border of Surrey and Hampshire. By chance, they got chatting with a woman after-wards, who happened to be married to the head of EMI Publishing, Terry Slater. "My wife Sheila went to a local Parent Association dance," Terry explains. "There was a little band there, she said, who were pretty good and wanted to get into the music business. There was a guy with them who was one of their dads. She had his card: John Weller. I'm always one for checking things out, so I called him up. He said, 'My boys are in this band, can you come and see us? What I can do, Terry, is give 'em a few quid on a Sunday morning and rent the room above this club where the boys can play for you.'"

The date was March 2, 1975. "I drove up the A3 to Woking," says Terry. "It was something like 10 o'clock, a really cold hour for them to play. And there was John with the boys, sat on these spindly stools, with their little amplifiers. We chatted and got on well and then they auditioned for me. They played some blues songs, mainly covers and a bunch of Beatles things – not much original material. I really liked them. I thought they had a lot of energy. We had a Coca Cola and I drove home." Slater then attempted to secure The Jam a record contract. "Later, John sent me some demos but I couldn't get them a deal," he continues. "Just because EMI Publishing is run by the same company as the label, that doesn't mean you automatically have an open door. I still see John occasionally: funnily enough, I was in the showroom of a classic car company a year ago on a Sunday afternoon. John and Paul came in and we chatted. Paul was looking for an old Aston Martin."

Slater's failure to interest EMI Records isn't surprising, since The Jam relied heavily on Sixties cover versions – they were a club band, after all. But the stagnant pop scene of the mid-Seventies wasn't any more exciting. Whatever glam had represented, whether it was the grand, ground-breaking art rock of David Bowie and Roxy Music, the rock'n'roll flavours

of T. Rex and Gary Glitter, or the bubblegum pop of The Sweet, Mud and
Alvin Stardust, the glitter was rapidly fading. Weller may not have cared
for most of these bands but, to rewrite John Lennon, it *could* get much
worse. This was the age of kids' TV stars The Wombles, easy listening
crooners like Terry Jacks and the Fifties-meets-glam of The Rubettes.
Three days before The Jam's audition at Michael's, bland vocal harmony
group The New Seekers had made No. 1 . . . again. These were artists that
Paul Weller abhorred.

As far as Paul was concerned, the first glimmer of hope arrived with Dr.
Feelgood, hailing from the butt end of the south-east of England, Canvey
Island. As with Woking, most music journalists had never even heard of
the place. A phenomenon known as pub rock was already very popular
around London – a straightforward, good-time brand of music which
ditched the excesses of the prevailing form of serious popular music,
progressive rock, for traditional, more tuneful influences like rock'n'roll
and R&B. Dr. Feelgood were different. Sure, they played John Lee
Hooker, but there was a meaner, tougher streak to them. On stage, they
had a threatening manner – ugly, scruffy and surly. Had The Rolling
Stones never broken out of playing West London pubs they might have
evolved into the Feelgoods.

The band's singer, Lee Brilleaux, spat out his lyrics rather than sang them,
his gravelly voice the product of a chain-smoking habit that would eventually contribute to his early death. But it was Wilko Johnson's guitar technique which captivated Paul Weller. His staccato style was a frenetic collision
of rhythm and lead playing. Prior to hearing Dr. Feelgood, The Jam had
ambled along at a relatively gentle pace – with about as much energy as The
Everly Brothers. Now, Paul stepped up the urgency of their live set. The
Feelgoods made far more sense to him than glam rock: he could identify with
their R&B covers, for a start. Steve Baker takes the credit: "I said I'd seen this
really good band, Dr. Feelgood, but he'd never heard of them. They were on
telly the next week – amazing! Paul said, 'That's the band for me', and we
went to see them live. Two months later, The Jam had completely changed
their style – it was all Dr. Feelgood-type stuff. The first thing they did was
change 'Takin' My Love' by speeding it up double-time and putting a Wilko
riff into it."

The Jam beefed up their sound after hearing the Feelgoods' highly
acclaimed début album, *Down By The Jetty*, in the weeks which followed its
release in January 1975 – and Terry Slater would have caught them during
this transition. Around the same time, Weller came across a record which
would have a far more lasting effect. Again, Steve Baker remembers the
occasion. "We stumbled on it in the same way. We both had younger sisters
who went to see that David Essex film, *Stardust*, and they both bought the
soundtrack album. It had a lot of interesting stuff, including 'My Generation'
by The Who. I never knew it was that good, and when I spoke to Paul a few

weeks later, he said, 'Nicky's got that – I've been getting into that'. Then he just went mad, getting into the *My Generation* album. I had the later Who LPs like *Quadrophenia*. He said, I don't like the music. Can I just keep the cover? Because it had a booklet inside with all those Mod pictures."

Later a highly accomplished film, *Quadrophenia* was a concept album based around a Shepherds Bush Mod named Jimmy growing up in the mid-Sixties. The front cover depicted the Parka-clad teenager astride a chromed and lavishly decorated Vespa scooter, a potent image of rebellious British youth culture. Paul Weller had just become a Mod.

3

THIS IS THE MODERN WORLD

"They were a Mod group. Well, Mods liked them . . . The guitar player was a skinny geezer with a big nose who twirled his arm like a windmill. He wrote some good songs about Mods . . . They played Tamla stuff and R&B."

(Sleeve-note to *Quadrophenia* LP, The Who, 1973)

"Mods were magpies. They took the best from wherever . . ."

(Kevin Pearce, *Something Beginning With O*)

"I fully realised that there existed a complete Mod way of life."

(Richard Barnes, *Mods!*, 1979)

"It's like a code, in a way. It gives something to my life . . . I'm still a Mod. I'll always be a Mod. You can bury me a Mod."

(Paul Weller, 1991)

It's tempting to think of Paul Weller's discovery of the Sixties' Mod lifestyle as a kind of religious conversion. Certainly, he seems to have worshipped at the shrine of the one band who crystallised the essence of Mod – The Small Faces – ever since. Yet this process wasn't so much a sea-change in his tastes, as a focusing. All the ingredients were already in place: The Jam dressed smartly and played Sixties covers with a healthy dose of R&B (the bedrock of the Mods' musical tastes). And the suedehead look of his pre-teen days had been a logical development, via the more brutal skinhead uniform, of the Mod image. By late 1974, Weller already lived for music, first and foremost, and then fashion. But what he hadn't known is that a whole lifestyle had been built on these same foundations a decade earlier.

The Mod cult wrapped up Weller's interests into a convenient package. It was more than a hobby for him, though, or merely a fashion statement. At last, he felt a sense of identity. Paul's obsession with Mod ever since has, for the most part, been a private rather than an evangelical one because, as an all-embracing concept, it has remained so closely married to what has mattered most in his life. In 1974, existing within an artificial world of little else

51

than band practices, he had drawn away first from the throng of school life and then later, the reality of finding employment. The idea of Mod affirmed his fantasies, because he saw in those Sixties bands exactly what he wanted to achieve for himself.

Over the years, he has quietly read around the subject, continuing to learn about the roots of Mod culture, and its different strands. The results are present in his music, in his fashion sense – in his whole outlook on life. It's no coincidence that The Jam's second and third albums were entitled *This Is The Modern World* and *All Mod Cons*, but these are obvious, transparent examples. Most of the time, Weller has translated this private fascination into something modern by giving it a new twist, or a new meaning.

Few have captured the essence of Mod in words as perfectly as journalist Kevin Pearce in what he described as an "intensely subjective description of obsessives, outsiders, risk takers, explorers", *Something Beginning With O.* "The real mod spirit," he wrote, "has nothing to do with scooter-riding, beach-fighting, lumpen mod lore. The best mods had the best record collections, the best wardrobes, the best bookshelves, the best minds. What else? The real roots of the mod uprising lie in the late Fifties modern jazz world. An extension of the beats, but sharper." It was a world of competitive one-upmanship, of being one step ahead of the game. The Mod movement – or Modernists, as they were first labelled – had originated more as a concept or an attitude than as a movement. The idea was rooted in a late Fifties obsession with 'cool', a nebulous term which embodied cosmopolitan sophistication, cleanliness against the grime of urban life, sharp, continental styling and living in 'the now'. To attain 'cool' was to be in control. It was something to strive for. "The Mod way of life consisted of a total devotion to looking and being 'cool'," wrote Richard Barnes, an old friend of The Who's Pete Townshend, in his definitive account of the cult, *Mods!* "Spending practically all your money on clothes and all your after-work hours in clubs and dance halls. To be part-time was really to miss the point." The title of the Small Faces' 'All Or Nothing', then, had a message that was just as Mod as The Who's 'My Generation'.

Of the various factors at work, the initial impetus that sparked the Mod lifestyle was the affluence of post-mid-Fifties Britain and the abolition of National Service, which had given school leavers greater disposable income and time to spend it, particularly so with the introduction of hire purchase in the Fifties. "The two essentials that a full-time Soho Mod needed . . . to keep him on the go," wrote Barnes, "were money and energy." This environment contributed to the evolution of the teenager, as distinct from a 'young adult', in the mid-Fifties. Suddenly, there was a generation who could deliberately set themselves apart from their elders. *The* youth cult of the Fifties was the Teddy Boy, a working class image that was unequivocally English. Their most distinctive garment, the drape jacket, was inspired by early 20th century Edwardian dress; indeed, this was the origin of the word 'Ted'.

In its most clearly defined sense, Mod couldn't have been more different. "The Teds' uniform was exactly that – a uniform," wrote Mark Paytress in *The Marc Bolan Story*, in a chapter discussing the teenager's involvement in Mod. "It consisted of little more than buying the correct outfit and adorning it with the appropriate accessories. The Modernists, meanwhile, were nothing if not eclectic. Instead of sticking to one readily recognisable style, they sought continually to adapt and evolve their dress, combining functional garments designed for the country gentleman with sportswear, ladies' fashions with suits aimed at the city gent. What lay behind this obsessive one-upmanship was the new spirit of competitive individualism that had supplanted the austerity years and, in this respect, Modernist culture in its pure form marked a sharp break with the insular, herd-like outlook of the Teds' world."

Modernists applied the same élitism to their music as they directed towards their immaculate dress sense. Modernist culture centred on authenticity – to use that familiar quote from US soul singer Dobie Gray's Mod anthem, 'The "In" Crowd', "the originals are still the greatest". It was natural, therefore, for those pioneers to dig deep into the urban music of American blacks, where they found a whole new world, modern jazz – hence the term Modernists. Colin MacInnes immortalised the world of the Modernist jazz fan in his book *Absolute Beginners*. Its vivid images captivated Paul Weller, who wrote a song that borrowed the book's title before eventually contributing to the soundtrack of a musical film based around the novel.

To these trendy young aesthetes, rock'n'roll was deemed sweaty and raucous and the antithesis of sophistication. Modern jazz, in contrast, was refined, musically intoxicating and thoroughly new – it had nothing to do with preconceptions of jazz at the time, whether it was the big band swing of Benny Goodman or the torch singer balladry of, say, Ella Fitzgerald. Modern jazz was the underground. Buried away from the pop mainstream, modern jazz music was hard to locate in Britain, even in the capital, a fact which appealed to the Modernists' delight in élitism. None of the artists could perform in Britain due to archaic Musicians' Union laws and few of the records were issued here, which created a mystical aura around characters like Miles Davis, Charlie Parker, John Coltrane and Dizzy Gillespie. They became the epitome of cool – and as such, they were the quintessential Modernist icons.

The third factor in shaping the Mod idea was fashion. Fifties' Britain was a conservative environment for teenagers, who looked abroad for cultural inspiration in the shape of a new, exciting range of products: America was seen as the future, as teenagers took to Levi's, and the Italian look popularised by Italian-American actors like Tony Curtis influenced formal dress. Snug-fitting three-button suits with narrow trousers were *de rigeur*, and the Modernists developed a taste for fancy trimmings and garish colours.

The last piece of the Mod puzzle was transport. Just as Britain embraced Italian styling in the world of fashion, thousands of youngsters took to the motor scooter. It was the product of its time – clean, contemporary, convenient, reliable and graced with smooth continental lines. Italy ruled supreme – they produced the two major scooter manufacturers, Vespa and Lambretta – and during the late Fifties, the scooter's popularity had soared. Scooter clubs opened up all over the country, although its members weren't necessarily Mods. But the scooter proved irresistible to this new breed of individual, as the coolest means of self-expression for those who couldn't afford a flash sports car – and a more practical vehicle for swanning around London. Within a few months of hearing 'My Generation', Paul Weller had invested in an old Lambretta.

During the early Sixties, the Modernist idea spread beyond isolated pockets of individuals. The term was shortened to Mod, with a look and a lifestyle which spread first through London and then the south of England. One of the keys to its success was the shift in emphasis in the Mods' musical tastes. Modern jazz was elbowed aside as American R&B and its more sophisticated cousin, soul, entered a golden era – music that Mods could dance to. Detroit's Tamla Motown empire forged a brand of catchy, upbeat and highly danceable music which managed to cross both geographical and racial boundaries – and hot on its heels was the Stax/Atlantic camp, with a more earthy, down-home style of soul, as well as the bluesy world of Chess and the ultra-hip Sue. A nightclub scene was born, where audiences danced to the latest US imports. With it, the Mods developed a taste for drugs – 'uppers' that kept them keen, wide-eyed and sharp. Pills were an essence of Mod, and if Weller continued to dabble in drugs, he now chose a stimulant like speed over sedatives or hallucinogens.

Soul and R&B prompted a revolution in British pop: The Beatles' early repertoire was heavily reliant on Motown covers, for instance, while The Rolling Stones plagiarised Chuck Berry, Bo Diddley and the whole R&B songbook. Between 1962 and 1966, black music provided the backbone both to the Mods and to the harder end of British pop, but it took a while for any bands to express the Mod experience directly. In any case, Mods weren't interested in the charts, by virtue of their élitist nature and because their new icons – immaculately dressed soul artists like Marvin Gaye, The Impressions or Otis Redding – weren't yet popular in Britain.

In 1965, however, two London bands aligned themselves both to the sound and the style of Mod: The Who and The Small Faces. Ignoring the familiar boy-meets-girl tales peddled by The Beatles *et al*, The Who's Pete Townshend created songs which embodied teenage rebellion. Their first three 45s were among British rock's first anthems: 'I Can't Explain' spoke of that teenage collision of frustration and confusion; 'Anyway Anyhow Anywhere', the other side of that coin, was arrogant youthful bravado on full throttle, dissolving into feedback-ridden, nihilistic chaos; and 'My

Generation' read like an 'us and them' manifesto, set to two chords and loads of attitude: "People try to put us down/just because we get around/The things they do look awful cold/I hope I die before I get old."

By the time 'My Generation' was issued in October 1965, the Mod look was a nationwide phenomenon – making it precisely the opposite of how it started out, creating the paradox of an accepted uniform versus the desire for individuality. Hair was now shorter than the moppy style that had swept the country after The Beatles' arrival. Sculpted, neat and sharp, often spiky with a high fringe but low and pointed over the ears, it was a reflection of the angular styles favoured by the top London hairdresser of the day, Vidal Sassoon, and also in line with the continental look. Expensive mohair suits, silk shirts and fancy leather shoes gave way to more casual sports wear: Fred Perry T-shirts, Harrington sports jackets, suede desert boots, colourful striped jumpers, checked button-down shirts, fancy 'hipster' trousers and tight roll-neck sweaters. Mod was now the cutting edge of high street fashion. It mutated into the living embodiment of what was labelled 'Swinging London', as the capital led the way not only in fashion but also popular culture.

The 'look' of most youth cults tends to be assimilated into the mainstream, fragmenting into new sounds and styles in the process. To over-simplify matters, Mod split in two. A largely working class contingent dropped the frills and evolved into skinheads, swapping soul for Jamaican ska, rock-steady and reggae. The other style grew fancier, as it evolved into the dandy parodied by Ray Davies in The Kinks' 'Dedicated Follower Of Fashion', "eagerly pursuing all the latest fads and trends", and the hippie chick embodied by Fresh Windows' cult psychedelic single from 1967, 'Fashion Conscious': "She follows trends/Where will it all end?/Trousers that flare, people that stare/Military store, jackets galore/'Cos she's a short-skirted, fashion-conscious, long-haired girl". Popularised by the West End fashion set and pop stars alike, this flamboyancy culminated in the brightly coloured psychedelic images of 1967.

Fashion took its natural course, and by the mid-Seventies, the flares and the long hair weren't just for the style conscious, they had become the norm. Men who might previously have sworn by short-back-and-sides were wearing their hair over their ears with pride. By 1974, Mod had dissipated into little more than a footnote in the history books. When Paul Weller started dressing as a Mod, he was making a retrograde statement. He looked unusual. Heads turned.

Paul couldn't relate to the grandiose, ambitious adult rock of The Who's *Quadrophenia* but when its Mod imagery led him back to the band's mid-Sixties origins, it gave him a template for The Jam. He didn't come from Soho – or even London – but that didn't matter. "The ticket living in some dreary suburb, sitting in the Wimpy trying to make his cheeseburger last all night, staring out at the rain, was still part of the Mod myth," wrote Barnes. "He was *going* to get a chromed scooter and five suits in Tonik or ice-blue

Mohair, *and* have some basket-weave shoes hand-made, *and* get his hair styled in Wardour Street *and* go dancing in the West End clubs every night. He *was* a Mod. He had his stake in the Myth." Paul Weller was from the suburbs, and he could dream, too, especially if that myth was cloaked in the allure of some ten years past. "True is the dream, mixed with nostalgia," Weller would later confirm in the lyric to The Jam's 'Tales From The Riverbank' in 1981.

"I first became interested in the early Sixties Mods in late 1974," wrote Weller in *Cool Cats* in 1981. "It interested me deeply and I tried to find out more about it. The most important aspect was the music of the Seventies: I hated it all, until the glorious, liberating Sex Pistols in 1976. Before then, it was all clutching at straws, glam bollocks; all the soft nonsense, Philly 'soul' and the terrible MOR stuff. Bowie and Bolan were okay but I even lost interest in them after their third or fourth LPs. I saw that through being a Mod, it would give me a base and an angle to write from, and thus the group would take on an individual identity. We went out and bought black suits and started playing Motown, Stax and Atlantic covers. I bought a Ricken-backer guitar, a Lambretta GP 150 and tried to style my hair like Steve Marriott circa '66."

By the end of 1974, The Jam's repertoire might already have passed for an early live set by The Who, or even the Stones. Chuck Berry favourites ('Little Queenie', 'Johnny B. Goode', 'Roll Over Beethoven'), and other vintage R&B classics ('Hi-Heeled Sneakers', 'Dimples', 'A Shot Of Rhythm'n'Blues') rubbed shoulders with early Motown ('Hitchhike', 'Do You Love Me', 'Mickey's Monkey'), Stax-styled soul ('Shake', 'Walking The Dog'), and a handful of R&B tracks that had been covered by The Beatles ('Twist & Shout', 'Some Other Guy', 'Slow Down', 'Kansas City'). Now Weller was taking the lead, as Steve Baker reveals. "Otis Redding was a great influence on Paul. I'd never heard of this bloke. I think he came into Paul's life at the right moment." There were only two original compositions: 'Save Your Loving' and 'Takin' My Love'. Weller summarised these developments in *Internationalists*: "Around 74/75, I became musically changed by three sources: Dr. Feelgood and Wilko Johnson, Motown, Early Who."

Soon after hearing the song 'My Generation', Paul borrowed the first Who album of the same name from Paul Neill, an acquaintance who lived in Byfleet. Later, Neill used to hitch a ride up to London with the band on the pretext that he'd take some snaps. "He always bummed a lift on the bus," laughs another friend of Paul, Steve Carver. "We went through it every time: 'Are you going to London? I'll take some photos of you.' He'd wait by this roundabout and Paul would say, 'pull over, dad'. On he'd come. He always forgot his camera. Every day, it was the same story: 'Can I have my LP back?' Paul was always, 'He ain't fuckin' getting that back!' Paul never even lent it to me, however many times he said I ought to listen to it!"

According to Weller, the LP "blew him away", and duly affected his

56

writing, his playing and his image. "It sounded different from anything I'd heard before," he told Ian Birch in 1978. "I liked the Morse code stuff and feedback, which was totally new to me." A decade-and-a-half later, its impact was just as strong, with Weller choosing the album among his Top Ten in *Record Collector* magazine. "This was another record that changed my life," he admitted to Pat Gilbert. "It was a massive influence obviously on The Jam . . . I've plagiarised the whole album, I think – I just changed the titles!"

It wasn't long before The Jam were decked out in black, three-button suits – their trademark stage image – courtesy of local gentleman's outfitters Hepworth's. Over the next few months, the four-piece moulded itself into the image of the young Who, scraping together the money to buy Rickenbacker guitars (popular with both Townshend and The Beatles) and matching Vox AC30 amps – a must for any aspiring beat combo in the mid-Sixties. Rick Buckler hid behind the kind of rectangular shades worn by The Byrds' Roger McGuinn, and Bruce Foxton's basslines grew more clipped and distinct. The Dr. Feelgood factor was still strong, too, as Bruce later admitted to *Negative Reaction* fanzine: "When we first started as a three-piece, that was all we could knock out. So we dropped numbers like 'Goin' Back Home'. We try not to get associated with them."

Baker also recalls working on Paul's newly acquired Lambretta: "I used to work at a little engineering shop down Walton Road and he used to come in on his scooter. He'd have a parka on with 'Mod Class A' in a big circle on his back and all the blokes there, who were eight years older than me, were Mods. They'd go, 'Who's that wanker?' 'I want some mirrors for my scooter,' Paul would say. 'Can you drill some holes so we can screw them on?' So I'd spend my lunch break working on his scooter so he could have fifteen mirrors all over it." Legend has it that Weller rode up to Shepherds Bush one afternoon to see if he could find Pete Townshend. Needless to say, he didn't. "We used to make trips to the coast on our scooters," Paul later told *NME*.

Weller wasn't the only Mod of his age in the neighbourhood. Baker remembers a chap called Mick Walker. Paul and Mick discovered that the Bisley Pavilion, about three miles west out of town, played host to regular Northern Soul events – the so-called Thursday [sic] Club organised by the Inter-City Soul Show – playing the brand of soul music favoured by the original Mods. So-named because of its popularity in the north of England, the Northern Soul movement had begun in the late Sixties. By the end of the decade, soul had evolved into the syncopated funk rhythms pioneered by James Brown, or smoothed out to create a slicker sound epitomised by Philadelphia acts like The O'Jays. Dissatisfied with this progression, DJs at isolated clubs scattered across northern England returned to the classic Tamla Motown sound of the mid-Sixties, and so was born a whole underground cult, based around rare, deleted 45s, a new, expressive style of dancing and a fanaticism which extended to travelling hundreds of miles, if necessary, to these 'all-nighters' which started around ten and didn't finish until dawn.

By 1975, Northern Soul had spread south into a national phenomenon, and the charts were full of reissues of old classics and new cash-in groups like Wigan's Ovation. And it reached Woking and the teenage Paul Weller, who'd ride up to the Bisley Pavilion on his scooter. It made such an impact that he even wrote a song about the experience – 'Non-Stop Dancing', which appeared on The Jam's first album. "Paul thought, this is it – it's a Mod revival," says Baker. "Him and Mick used to wear loud clothes and bright yellow jumpers, and we were still wearing 100% jeans. Paul started to drift away from everybody. It was like, 'Your mate's a bit weird, isn't he? He wears some funny clothes.' He was into this Sixties image."

This image was enough to catch the eye of Terry Rawlings, who later befriended Paul. He remembers Weller from annual summer holiday trips in the mid-Seventies to the south coast – the Selsey Bill of The Jam's 'Saturday's Kids', where Weller later wrote both that song and 'The Eton Rifles'. "I remember seeing this kid down there," says Terry. "Paul had a caravan at West Sands. There were three caravan sites and three clubs. The one at West Sands was called the Wagon Room. All the families would be down there with the kids. He had this home-made target T-shirt and I got to recognise him. You'd just nod to people down there. Kids often looked like Mods because your mum bought your clothes at C&A's or Marks & Spencer's, and cheap clothes were Mod style with straight trousers. You couldn't help but grow up with that. The site was owned by John Bunn and, irony of ironies, John and Ann Weller later bought his house."

Paul's obsession with the Sixties Mod scene brought with it a growing fascination with its birthplace, as Steve Carver told Paolo Hewitt. "He used to love London. I remember he used to say, 'I'm going up to London with a tape recorder.' I'd say, 'What for?' And he'd say, 'I want to tape London.' I think he idolised it, you know. He always thought of it as magical."

Weller wasn't the only one drawn to the big city. There was a growing realisation, shared by the band and John Weller, that they weren't getting anywhere by playing around the Woking area. In fact, The Jam never had a following in Woking to speak of, outside their circle of friends. "Everyone was into disco and we were playing rock'n'roll and Sixties stuff," Brookes admitted to Barry Nield. "All the kids who were our age didn't really take any notice . . . I think we were the subject of a certain amount of ridicule around the town because we were so different." This fact is evidenced by their lack of coverage in the local papers of the time.

Realising that London gigs were essential if the band was ever to get noticed, John contacted an old friend from his boxing days, Duncan Ferguson, who owned the Greyhound pub in the Fulham Palace Road. The result was a support slot with Thin Lizzy in November 1974, the first of many journeys to West London. "The Greyhound was an old hippies' pub then," says Steve

Baker. "It had a stage in one corner and there were little balconies before they knocked it into one big room." Another of John's contacts was a trainer at Chelsea FC, who booked them for a date at Stamford Bridge football ground on April 21, 1975. A pattern was quickly set: if The Jam were offered a gig, they took it, whether it was close to home at a local police ball or a venue like HM Prison Coldingly in Bisley, three miles west of Woking. Sometimes they went as far afield as Folkestone, but the dates out of town were few and far between. With as many as 400 bands on their books, The Fulham Greyhound could only offer The Jam occasional slots and most of the band's bookings remained local. An extract from Paul's diary for that month, reproduced in *Beat Concerto*, revealed that their continuing Friday night slot at Michael's was occasionally supplemented by a Sunday night, or with other dates at the Peabody Club and the Tumble Down over at Farnborough, about ten miles away.

The band were fed up with pandering to indifferent audiences and their inane requests, though. On March 23, 1975, they had played at the Woking Liberal Club opposite the Working Men's Club in Walton Road. The evening rapidly descended into a brawl when Brookes' boredom led him to clamber on top of the club's piano. Paul explained his frustration to *Melody Maker*'s Brian Harrigan in 1977: "We just had to play other people's music in these little working men's clubs . . . people coming up to you and asking if you could do *The Last Waltz* or mainly just people telling you to turn it down!"

And that wasn't their only problem. Despite the camaraderie which binds any band together, the tensions started to grow. Rick was sometimes moody and violent, and he and Paul used to bicker. Similarly, Brookes never saw eye-to-eye with Bruce, while relations once got so bad that Paul didn't speak to either Bruce or Rick for a short period. But the single biggest rift within the band was caused by the fact that Steve never related to Paul's obsession with Mod. By the spring of 1975, Steve had been forced to find a job to support his mother and was now committed to a serious relationship with his girlfriend. If Weller was jealous that his friend's attention was elsewhere, then Brookes was uncomfortable with the musical direction of the band. Inevitably, it drove them apart.

"That was when the rot started to set in as I think he felt I wasn't really giving the time to the band," Steve admitted to Barry Nield. "As far as he was concerned, it was 100% dedication . . . plus we were growing apart musically . . . He was going for this hard Mod edge and I wanted to keep it more pop-based because we had always said that the idea was to get into the mainstream, get a name and then experiment with the music after that – much like The Beatles had done. The important thing was the record deal." Eventually, Steve left the band soon after another Fulham Greyhound slot supporting West Country rockers Stackridge on July 6. "It wasn't like one big day. It just fizzled out, gradually deteriorated . . . we just grew apart. It's like anything at that age – you're charging off in different directions." There was an epilogue to his departure, though. "Paul phoned me one day and said, 'Look, EMI are interested but they want us as a four-piece rather than a three-piece. Do you fancy giving it another crack?' By that time, I was already solo and I said no."

If EMI had resumed negotiations, then Head Of Publishing Terry Slater has no recollection of it. Perhaps it was a ruse on Weller's part to lure Brookes back into the band. After all, as Beatles fans, the idea had always been to have a four-man line-up. But Steve must have known it was always going to be Paul's band, even though it was he who originally formed The Jam with Weller. (Back at that talent contest in 1973, the band had been credited to 'Paul Weller and The Jam', remember.)

There might not have been any head-to-head power struggles but "he did get a bit fraught and have temper tantrums," Brookes admitted to Nield. "It was a strain because he was a very blunt, temperamental and tactless person . . . He was always quite spoilt, although he would never admit it. His parents doted on him and when things didn't go his way, he would stamp and shout and break things." Brookes's departure was sudden, as Rick Buckler recalls. "When a friendship breaks down with Paul, he cuts it off one hundred per cent and that's exactly what happened with Steve," he says knowingly. "One minute they were thick as thieves and the next minute there was nothing between them. They didn't see each other."

At first, the band looked for a replacement for Brookes, with a terse advert in the music press on July 9 stating that "The Jam require lead guitarist". According to *Our Story*, Pete Jessop was the most suitable applicant but he failed to materialise for the band's next clutch of gigs. Frustrated by such indifference, Weller and the band settled as a trio, and much of the friction which had plagued them over the previous year evaporated. It wasn't all sweetness and light, though: Bruce and Rick quit over money after a gig at Michael's on September 26, 1975, and John Weller went so far as to draft in professional backing musicians to back Paul. The affair was purportedly a disaster and The Jam's rhythm section quickly returned, but the incident showed beyond any doubt where John's allegiances lay: if the other two weren't up for it, he'd find some other musicians who were. After all, his son was the singer, guitarist and songwriter in the band – even though, from then on, he was careful not to show Paul favouritism. John's level-headed nature kept the trio on an even keel, and without his pivotal role, The Jam would probably still be playing pubs around Woking.

Steve Baker confirms the extent to which Paul's father took the helm: "The Jam wouldn't have made it without John," he states adamantly. "He could sell ice to Eskimos or bacon sandwiches at a Jewish wedding. He'd give them, 'That was the best, absolutely brilliant' – all the old crap – and people would buy it, partly because he's such a big, forceful bloke that they'd feel intimidated. And he wouldn't have a Tuesday night gig! Oh no. It was top billing on a Saturday night."

John didn't instigate their audition for *Opportunity Knocks*, though. It had been Ann's idea to enter the band, so they drove up to that fertile breeding ground for blossoming young talent – Surbiton Town Hall – on August 12, 1975. "We went up there in an old Thames trailer van," laughs Arthur Hunte, "a smoking old thing that we never thought would make it – but it did. They were taking turns with tap dancers and that kind of thing, and after The Jam played, they basically said, don't call us, we'll call you!"

Brookes was right about the band's keenness to secure a record contract. Some time in 1975, The Jam taped a faithful if primitive version of Stevie Wonder's mid-Sixties Motown classic, 'Uptight (Everything's Alright)', one of several demos the band circulated around the major record companies. They sound tougher on this tape than on the 1973 recordings. Gone are the gentle shamblings and pleasant melodies, to be replaced by a tension and urgency, with a snatch of Wilko Johnson-esque soloing towards the end. The recording survives on a bootleg EP, and is a fascinating glimpse into the pre-punk Jam sound. Buckler thinks this may have been one of several songs taped by a local enthusiast while the band rehearsed at Michael's.

Recordings of around twenty other tracks are known to exist, which are now in Paul Weller's possession. These are mostly cover versions: The Supremes' 'Back In My Arms Again' (a live performance of which was later captured on a Jam B-side), Martha & The Vandellas' 'Dancing In The Street', The Who's 'So Sad About Us', Dr. Feelgood's 'Cheque Book' (a Mickey Jupp song), and Rufus Thomas's 'Walking The Dog'. There were also prototypes of songs like 'I Got By In Time', 'In The City', 'Sounds From The Street' and 'Time For Truth' which The Jam later chose for their début album; plus compositions like 'Again', 'Soul Dance', 'I Will Be There', 'When I Needed You', 'Please Don't Treat Me Bad' and 'Left, Right And Centre', which have yet to be released.

Handwritten notes from Rick Buckler's old scrapbooks reveal recording dates for some of these songs: March 1, 1975 ('Walking The Dog' and 'I Will Be There'; the session also included 'Hundred Ways' and 'Forever And Always'); December 10, 1975 ('Again' and 'Takin' My Love'); and May 28, 1976 ('Left, Right And Centre', plus another tune retained for the first Jam LP, 'Non-Stop Dancing').

These last two self-funded sessions, together with some of the other demos listed above, were recorded at a studio owned by local impresario Bob Potter (once the owner of Woking's Atalanta venue), in Mytchett, a village near Frimley, several miles west of Woking. The engineer for the last of these sessions was John Franklin, who ran a fairly basic set-up. "It was a four-track studio," he explains. "Bob used to manage groups – the I.E.A. or International Entertainment Agency – and the studio was affiliated to that. Interestingly, the equipment had belonged to [legendary sixties producer] Joe Meek, which Bob had bought in an auction soon after Meek's untimely demise – with valve mics, an Ampex four-track made out of angle iron, and a Fairchild reverb.

"We got on famously but it was a fragmented affair," Franklin continues. "Multi-track recording was starting in a big way and most groups of that ilk wanted to record everything separately – i.e. the rhythm track and then the overdubs and then the lead vocals – but Paul and the guys wanted it down in one hit, which was a nightmare for me, the engineer. Because of the quick tempo, it was a bit of a cacophony, so it was hard to record them. We had a little vocal booth and I persuaded Paul to go in there to do his vocals.

"As far as I know, it was all new stuff, and they did two or three Beatles-type songs which Paul had written. From a melody point of view, the songs were quite attractive but were going down in a very raw state, very disjointed, which was what the band wanted – certainly what Paul wanted. I wouldn't say they were the tightest band in the world. They weren't a Dr. Feelgood by any stretch of the imagination, although that was the stuff they were trying to do. They were going through a learning process. I think they were using that tape as a demo to do a presentation."

The next year-and-a-half was a blur of pubs, clubs and late nights, as The Jam tried to break out of Surrey, torn between solid earnings from Woking gigs and the chance to reach a wider audience in the capital. "My fondest memory of The Jam and the most important for the group and me was the hours we spent travelling up and down the motorway in a Ford Transit," Weller later commented with affection. And if they weren't actually playing a gig, then they'd moonlight to London to flypost the area with handmade leaflets designed and produced by Bruce at the printers where he worked – although it wasn't always easy.

On March 8, 1976, journeying home one night from a poster-sticking spree in London, Rick was involved in a road accident and fractured his ankle. "He was still playing drums, though," remembers Baker, "so me and Enzo carried in the guitars, and Paul and Bruce carried Rick on with this plaster. Everyone thought it was a gimmick." Buckler's ensuing six weeks off work only exerbated the strain on their day jobs caused by his and Foxton's increasing number of sick days and afternoons off. "Bruce would stumble in looking white as a sheet," laughs an old colleague of Foxton, Neil Wakeford. "He was like death warmed up. We'd let him have a kip in the backroom and cover for him."

The Jam continued to exist in this limbo until the summer of '76. Intermittent dates at The Greyhound weren't enough to build a following. Paul and Bruce topped up their income with a local country and western band. "I would go out and earn an extra ten pound a night playing bass in a friend of ours' band," Weller later recalled. Meanwhile, John scraped together fixtures for The Jam at such well-known London pub venues as the Hope & Anchor in Islington (May 8) and the Windsor Castle on the

Harrow Road (June 6), but the band were essentially treading water. Something had to give.

That something happened at London's Lyceum on July 9, after Paul read about a young, disruptive new group who were already attracting a degree of notoriety after only a handful of London club dates. "In the summer of '76, I read a review in the *NME*", Weller told the self-same paper in 1994, "and it sounded like just what I was looking for, really: a young band who had loads of attitude. So we decided to go and see them at an all-nighter."

By now, The Sex Pistols were an amazing spectacle, as *Sounds* journalist Jonh Ingham related to Jon Savage in the definitive history of the Pistols and punk, *England's Dreaming*: "That was the night that John [Lydon] stubbed out cigarettes on the back of his hand when he was singing: that frightened me. He was the most maniacal thing alive: it was back to Iggy, that unpredictability." It wasn't just about visual theatrics but they certainly looked the part. Remember, this was still an age of flares and shoulder-length hair. Within this prevailing post-hippie climate, the Pistols' image was like an extremely brutal bastardisation of Mod – all narrow trousers, scruffy tops, cropped spiky hair and facial sneers. The Pistols weren't Mods, of course, but there were enough reference points for Weller to be hooked. For a start, their set included the mid-Sixties Who and Small Faces classics, 'Whatcha Gonna Do About It' and 'Substitute'. And then there was the Pistols' sound – raw, cacophonous rock stripped to its bare bones – led by the nasal whine of Lydon's voice. "At the Lyceum, there was suddenly this major step up in musical ability," reckoned Ingham. "Glen was phenomenal, Paul was right on the beat. It was in one night: they were all just there. Suddenly you knew this was a great band."

On July 15, just a few days after the Pistols' all-nighter, an advert appeared in various music papers, saying that "The Jam are looking for keyboard/ vocals, age 18–20, into early Tamla Motown, R&B. Good prospects of recording contract, clean image". It didn't stipulate that applicants should still own all their own teeth, but the cosy, conservative wording seemed a world away from the maelstrom created by Rotten and Co. a week earlier. It made sense, though: singing and playing guitar without the support of a second guitarist wasn't the easiest task for a front-man, and the attraction of adding an organ to flesh out the sound was obvious – but the ad wasn't successful. Foxton commented in *Negative Reaction* fanzine in February 1977 that one of the band's biggest influences was "the Small Faces, which is why we were going to bring in a keyboard player".

The punk scene may not have had much to do with the true Mod spirit: punk buzzwords were nihilism and chaos, while the Mod ideal was of a constructive individual in control of his surroundings. Punk dictated a certain disregard for physical appearance, while The Who's early manager Peter Meaden once famously described "Mod-ism" as "an aphorism for clean living under difficult circumstances". Alternatively, the punk scene may have had everything to do with the true mod spirit. It was obsessive, competitive, forever changing, narcissistic, asexual, speed-driven and defined by sharp lines. If punk was self-destructive, then maybe this was because it had taken a leaf out of The Who's equipment-smashing stage antics.

The Pistols shared the bill that night with rock band Supercharge and Sixties survivors The Pretty Things. "They were the last band on – six in the morning or something – and we were all speeding out of our heads. French blues," Weller remembered. Or maybe he was just elated by the rush of the music. Tony Pilot, a friend of Paul, says that "all of us scored some speed that was no good that night. We got pretty pissed in the end." What they all agreed on was the impact of The Sex Pistols – none of the teenagers had ever seen a band that was so powerful or striking – and, according to Pilot, the lads could talk of nothing else as they waited around on Waterloo Station for the 'milk train' back to Woking.

"By now everyone was being very serious about making this happen," Ingham told Jon Savage. "It was quite clear that this was the only thing that was going to break through and create a new generation of music." The journalist wasn't the only one who was impressed. "It was brilliant," Paul later commented. "The whole experience swung it for me. There was a scene going on and I wanted to be part of it." It didn't take Weller long. As Paolo Hewitt observed on the sleeve for The Jam's *Extras* compilation, "witnessing punk's birth was just the shot he needed and from that day onwards he has always viewed the role of the artist as that of a tightly sprung alarm clock, designed and destined to wake up the rest of the world."

4

HERE'S A NEW THING

"Everyone's bored with all that shitty technical stuff . . . Led Zeppelin is for middle-aged students to sit and listen to in their bedrooms. What relevance have the old groups got today? I think the whole scene now is just a progression that goes, Mods . . . Skinheads . . . Punks."

(Paul Weller, *48 Thrills*, 1977)

" 'Sod them,' I thought, 'they're going to do Who rip-offs, I don't care. I'll write the songs I want to write.' "

(John Lydon on early Sex Pistols' rehearsals, *England's Dreaming*, 1991)

"The most sudden, violent, high-fly, low-fi, hopelessly brilliant, helplessly gormless, long-sighted, short-lived outpouring of all was punk. Punk Rock."

(Danny Kelly, Q, 1996)

If his discovery of old Who records focused Weller's musical vision, then Punk moulded his wider views. "The Sex Pistols completely changed my attitude towards music," he later wrote in *Internationalists*. "This led me to see The Clash in '76 as well and it was the first time I was exposed to political music and the importance of lyrics." Despite Jon Savage's summary in *England's Dreaming* of the Mod movement as "that era of smart, violent pop that was the Sex Pistols' first influence", the band's main musical inspiration lay elsewhere. The foundation of the Pistols lay in the gritty, unfriendly American rock of The Stooges and The New York Dolls – misfits whose flamboyant attire, and indulgence in a self-destructive rock'n'roll lifestyle, meant nothing to Weller. Neither did the Pistols' cries of 'Anarchy In The UK', for that matter. The Clash, on the other hand, were a tight ball of energy with both an image and rhetoric reminiscent of a young Pete Townshend – speed obsession, pop-art clothing, art school ambition. Behind the mask, they were Gene Vincent-obsessed rockers, but that wasn't how they came across at the start.

"The Clash began as a classic Mod group," wrote Savage, "angry, smart, mediated, pop. They speeded up the heavily chorded, stuttering sound of

The Who and The Kinks." The back sleeve of their début single, 'White Riot', even went so far as to reproduce a clipping about the '64 bank holiday riots from *Generation X*, the mid-Sixties psychological study which centred on the Mod lifestyle. The Clash were fronted by a man whose lyrical invective and confrontational interview stance didn't go unnoticed by Paul Weller. "Around '76, Joe Strummer told me that people have gotta start writing about more important issues," he told American magazine *Trouser Press* in 1979. "That made an impression." Weller reacted by whittling down the number of cover versions in The Jam's set, and dropping some of his flabbier originals as he busied himself writing new, more contemporary material. Collectively, these bands shared one common denominator: "It wasn't that I saw the Pistols," Paul told the *NME*. "It was that for the first time in years, I realised there was a younger audience there, young bands playing to young people which was something we'd been looking for in a long time."

The blazing heat of the summer of '76 witnessed the emergence of several new punk bands – Manchester's Buzzcocks, The Adverts, The Damned, closely followed by The Subway Sect and Siouxsie & The Banshees – while others, like The Stranglers and The Vibrators, disguised their pub rock roots with a hastily assembled punk image. The Jam never tried to be part of the punk vanguard but neither were they within the pop mainstream. "They weren't seen as part of what was happening, but nothing was really happening at that stage," observes the Pistols' bassist Glen Matlock. "They were part of what *wasn't* happening. They were different enough – they were young and played three-minute songs."

Meanwhile, their Stanley Road terrace having fallen into disrepair, the Weller family were given council accommodation at a more modern and spacious terrace – 44 Balmoral Drive on the Maybury Estate – where Paul became reacquainted with two old school friends, Steve Carver and his younger brother Pete. "We really got to know him when his mum and dad moved, and our back garden backed onto theirs," remembers Pete. "He had a parka, and his scooter in the garage," adds Steve. "Chatting to Paul and friends like Tony Pilot and Dave Waller in our local, The Princess Of Wales, the name Sex Pistols cropped up. 'We're going to see them Tuesday,' said Paul. 'Come up with us, we've got a lift.' John Weller had a Transit van and we all drove up to the 100 Club. We saw the Sex Pistols and the earth moved! I didn't know Paul was in a band at this time. Of course, John was there to put out flyers because The Jam were playing The Greyhound on the Monday. 'Come up and see us,' Paul said. And that was it: we were inseparable."

Posters were plastered across the capital, proclaiming The Jam as "most rock'n'roll, maximum rhythm'n'blues" in the style of The Who's famous black-and-white 'Maximum R&B' adverts from their Marquee days. "We kept seeing these little cards everywhere," adds Glen Matlock. "It was like their first publicity device. This was when all the punk bands were forming. I went to see them at the Greyhound with Steve and Paul [from the Sex Pistols] and Bernie Rhodes and Mick Jones from The Clash. We didn't think they were punk – which, obviously, they weren't – but they *were* interesting. They were always a bit of an oddment, to our way of thinking. They seemed very suburban as well. They had the suits. The thing that got me most, though, was Bruce's haircut, which never changed or moved. It was that real 'Dmitri' style – like those drawings of haircuts in barbers' windows."

Foxton's 'bog-brush' style seemed to emphasise his and Rick Buckler's apparent caution about punk. In contrast, Weller held an unshakeable conviction about this new movement. To him, it seemed inextricably linked with his growing fascination with London itself – which had flowered from the seed of his discovery of Mod. There was that story of Paul taking a cassette player up on the train to tape the hubbub of the capital. And one of his new compositions, 'In The City There's A Thousand Things I Wanna Say To You', was written as a tribute to the excitement of Punk London. "I still get that feeling now," Paul told me in 1992. "Maybe it's because I don't come from London, but just driving down the Embankment at night-time, with St. Paul's lit up on the South Bank, feels like being in a film set – like, a big red bus goes by. That's when I know why I live in London, because there's nowhere in the world like it. For all its faults, there's something magical, an energy about it."

On September 8, The Jam played Upstairs at Ronnie's, above Ronnie Scott's famous Soho jazz club, before returning to the Greyhound on the 17th. But they struggled to make an impact on London. One night, at that pub rock haven, the Hope & Anchor in Islington, there were apparently just eight people in the audience. By early October, punk was the talking point of the weekly music press, after Sex Pistols' manager Malcolm McLaren organised a two-night Punk Festival at the 100 Club in late September. Suddenly, record companies were swarming around acts like the Pistols and The Clash. If The Jam didn't hurry up, they would be left behind, so they devised a publicity stunt to get themselves noticed.

It was staged on October 16, on a sunny Saturday lunchtime in Soho Market in the heart of London's West End. Around 12.30pm, The Jam set up their equipment on the pavement in Newport Court, just off the Charing Cross Road. Paul was already a regular customer of a second-hand record stall in the market, Rock On, who agreed to supply the power, and the band played to a mixed crowd of fans, distracted shoppers, locals from neighbouring China Town and firemen on the station roof in Shaftesbury Avenue. As Miles put it in *The Jam By Miles*, the event was "deliberately engineered to give them maximum exposure" – and it succeeded. The music press were invited along and the fact that The Clash just happened to be having breakfast in a café opposite helped secure The Jam's first coverage. The event was reported in both *Melody Maker* and *Sounds*, the latter's Jonh

Ingham commenting that "with bands far exceeding the number of London clubs, sometimes you *really* have to take it to the streets . . . they ripped it up for almost an hour. A small appreciative crowd developed, complete with beggar."

The stunt may have had, as Jon Savage put it, "the required result: immediate attention", but opinion was divided among punk's cognoscenti: "Although they were genuinely teenage (unlike some of the other punk groups), The Jam unfashionably paid explicit homage to the 1960s in general – wearing smart Mod suits and ties – and to The Who in particular. The Jam were young, fast and working class but the reaction to them was equivocal."

The Jam were approached with caution, since the most immediate impact of punk was a vociferous rejection of everything that had gone before. Weller may have injected a new vigour into the group's live performances but many of his new songs were still structured around mid-Sixties Who riffs. Punk bands treated old music with disdain – at least, publicly – with the odd exception of US cult figures like Iggy Pop, The New York Dolls and The Velvet Underground. The music press hired hawkish young journalists to document its rapid explosion; record companies dropped whole rosters of bands to sign up punk acts who'd barely played a gig. Those enterprising punk observers who didn't fancy forming a band soon absorbed the scene's anyone-can-do-it atmosphere and bypassed the establishment, setting up their own DIY magazines – fanzines – and creating independent record labels.

Mark Perry, alias Mark P., did all three: he produced the most widely acknowledged punk fanzine, *Sniffin' Glue,* in the summer of '76, before forming Alternative TV and running a punk label, Step Forward. Naturally, such a forward-thinking individual was cautious about The Jam. "I went down with *Melody Maker*'s Caroline Coon, who heard about the Soho gig on the grapevine," he explains. "There was only a few people there who we knew. Mostly, it was just people walking past, checking it out. I wasn't that impressed, it was just a little PA in the open air. But suddenly, they had a bit of a name." Mark P.'s write-up at the time encapsulated some of the reservations held by punk's inner circle. "They're a restricted band 'cos they play '60s R&B but within that structure they're great," he reasoned in *Sniffin' Glue.* "This Sixties revival thing's alright for a start but what we need now is more serious bands who have got something to sing about. The Jam are good but they've got a lot to think about (and change) before they break into the London scene with any credibility."

Perry is equally nonchalant about the band today. "I always thought they were a bit of a joke," he says. "I just thought it was ridiculous that these guys, dressing in suits and having all the Mod-ish moves, tried to latch onto punk. When you compared them to the Pistols, they seemed opposite to what punk was supposed to be about. During punk, we put aside what we'd liked before. I was into Zappa and Little Feat, but the idea was to forget what you'd known before: it was like, Year Zero with punk rock. Within that context, The Jam's Sixties connotation was a revival. I didn't like that idea of wearing a uniform."

The group's stark Mod image definitely raised a few eyebrows: black suits with three buttons and narrow lapels, neat white shirts with narrow black ties. They were so closely associated with their outfits that their pointed two-tone spats became known as 'Jam Shoes'. "They looked as though they were just released from school, though this could be to invoke mid-Sixties Beat Boom correctness," suggested Ingham in his review of the Soho Market event.

Whatever reservations insiders may have had, the lunchtime gig was a watershed for the band. "Prior to that, The Jam was still on bread-and-butter money," admits Steve Carver, "playing Woking Working Men's Club, 'Tie A Yellow Ribbon'-type crap. They knew they couldn't drop it because they needed the money to subsidise the proper London gigs, but they started having to say no because of the credibility – 'Shit, we're in the paper now'!" In the autumn, The Jam abandoned the drudgery of those hometown gigs once and for all, after a disastrous night out near Camberley.

In the audience was Tony Pilot: "Paul finally had enough after they played at someone's wedding reception. They had two different sets – one for the locals and one for the London crowd – and that night, Paul was pretty pissed off, so they played the London set with songs like 'In The City'. Everyone was saying, 'Aye aye, what's he up to?' He sounded bloody terrible on stage, because he was pissed, and he'd just bought a twelve-string Rickenbacker but hadn't learnt to play it properly. They were booed off stage in the end. From then on, that was it – no more community centres." In any case, Michael's club closed down in September 1976 after undercover police disguised as "sailors in civvies" visited the venue and found it in breach of its licence, which brought to an end the era when The Jam could rely on local gigs to supplement their income.

★   ★   ★

After failing to find a suitable candidate as keyboardist, the band accidently stumbled across a lad from Sheerwater, Bob Gray, who played piano. He joined them at a 100 Club date and supporting The Sex Pistols on October 26, at the Queensway Hall, Dunstable, near Luton. "It was a massive oval room," remembers Glen Matlock. "The Jam had this bloke with a waistcoat on, who looked like a pub pianist with an upright piano." Earlier that month, the Pistols had signed to EMI Records (and, courtesy of The Jam's old friend Terry Slater, EMI Publishing), prompting extensive features in the music press. But the punk movement had still to spread beyond the confines of the capital. "There was hardly any fucker there," says Matlock of the Dunstable gig, "and Weller goes, 'Here, I thought you pulled?' There was about six people."

Sniffin' Glue's Steve Mick wrote, with some insight, "The Jam are a band of moods. One night, they can be so laid-back that you fidget almost to sleep, and another night they're so edgy they almost knock you off your feet . . . It's about time they stopped spoiling their set with all that tuning up." The suggestion wasn't warmly received, as Mark Perry explains: "It was very easy to wind them up (and we did!), because Paul Weller was always so serious about his work and his lyrics – a bit too serious. Weller got all excited and at a Marquee gig, I believe he burnt a copy of *Sniffin' Glue* onstage, which is a nice gesture for him – like, he's got bollocks. But also, obviously, he must have felt prickly. He probably thought, *Sniffin' Glue*, who fuckin' cares, but deep down, he probably would have preferred a good review."

That wasn't Paul's only public reaction to press criticism. After accusations of "revivalism" from *Melody Maker*'s Caroline Coon, he wore a placard around his neck on stage, stating, "How can I be a revivalist when I'm only fucking eighteen?" Weller later defended himself by claiming that, "It's not jumping on bandwagons or anything like that. I don't even remember the Mod thing. I was too young to take much notice then." The Jam's technical proficiency also swam against the tide of popular thinking. "I thought Paul was a bit élitist, because he was very much a musician," explains Perry. "He could play the thing that was hanging off his neck whereas a lot of us couldn't. You see, the three-piece idea was quite interesting as well. I knew he was a good guitarist because he played in that style which is rhythm and lead at the same time – it sounded like two guitarists. The band were always very tight – and that's one reason why they got the piss taken out of them!

"Saying that, you couldn't deny the amount of energy they had, once you'd seen them live. They were very exciting, even though they dressed in stupid clothes! Everybody went to their gigs, because they seemed worth supporting. There were the half-a-dozen bands that played the 100 Punk Festival and not many others. We were looking out for other stuff and when The Jam came along, they were acceptable. The Adverts, Chelsea and Gen X in late '76 had a ready-made audience. It wasn't obscure by then. People were looking around for punk bands. It was very easy to get noticed, which is why bands jumped on the bandwagon – Kilburn & The High Roads became 999, and The Vibrators, an R&B band, were suddenly punk. The Stranglers were making the change. It was very much the climate."

Two other fanzine writers were more openly supportive of The Jam: Adrian Thrills featured them on the cover of the first three issues of *48 Thrills* while Shane McGowan, widely regarded as their most colourful, outspoken fan, enthused about them in *Terminal Bondage*. "Bruce Foxton had problems with his bass and got annoyed," wrote an enthusiastic McGowan of an Upstairs At Ronnie's gig. "Later on, Paul Weller smashed a guitar to bits . . .

climaxing in [him] going mad and throwing his amp to the people at the front." Weller's anger and frustration clearly echoed Pete Townshend's famous Sixties stage act of destroying his guitar as the finale to The Who's shows.

★   ★   ★

The Jam progressed quickly from playing half-empty pubs to sell-out events. "It took off very quickly. After *Sniffin' Glue* got hold of them, it spread like wildfire," recalls Pete Carver. "Sweaty frantic Red Cow residency," wrote Weller on the back of The Jam's live swansong album, *Dig The New Breed.* "1st week 50 people, 2nd week 100, by the 4th week a queue round the block!" Over the next few months, the band played occasional gigs and residencies at popular London pub venues like the Red Cow in Hammersmith, the Nashville Rooms in West Kensington, the Rochester Castle in Stoke Newington or more prestigious locations like the 100 Club – and another date above Ronnie Scott's jazz club.

Upstairs At Ronnie's must have been packed that night; Weller's parents had organised coachloads of the band's friends and family to travel up from Woking, eager both to lend support and to discover what the fuss was all about. Back in their hometown, news about punk had slowly filtered through – in early December, 'Anarchy In The UK' made the Top 40, fuelled by the scandal which followed the Sex Pistols' infamous appearance on Bill Grundy's early evening TV chat show, *Today*. "We were the first punk rockers in Woking!" boasts a proud Steve Carver. "We were like a gang by that time. There was seven or eight of us who we regarded as punks and no-one else wanted to know us because we dressed strange. "

Steve's brother Pete agrees: "We used to take 'Anarchy In The UK' and 'New Rose' by The Damned with us up to the local nightclub and ask the DJ to play them." Bored by disco hits by the likes of the Bee Gees and Tavares, Paul and his mates would sit on the sidelines until their moment came. "Instead of just putting it on, the DJ would say, 'Ladies and gentlemen, can you all please stop dancing? I've just been handed a copy of the Sex Pistols' single.' He'd put it on and being young and foolish, we'd pogo about. Halfway through, he'd say, 'No wonder they failed their audition, on with the real music.' We were fighting a losing battle!"

As a result, punk's serious-minded Woking contingent spent as much time as possible within the more sympathetic environment of London's punk fraternity. "We lived by the *NME* and *Sounds*," explains Steve Carver, "to find out whether it was the Roxy on a Friday, or the Vortex on a Saturday, to see X-Ray Spex or Adam & The Ants. People say now that punk was just a laugh. It wasn't to us – it was a way of life." According to Pete, their London peers were regarded with a certain amount of awe: "They were the punks as such and we were country lads who just looked up to them. None of us had the clichéd punk purple hair. It was more subtle:

71

the token safety pin. I remember Paul used to wear a plastic bag with a photo of himself when he was a baby." "And this nylon white boiler suit," laughs Steve. "He'd sit in the pub and draw on it but, by the next day, his mum had washed it clean."

To friends like Steve Baker, who hadn't yet taken to the punk look, the conversion seemed strange. "Paul came down the pub with painted stripes all down his trousers," he mentions with a smile. "I said 'What's that on your trousers?!' and he replied, 'It's the new look! That's what people wear now. It's like a revolution going on.' He'd have safety pins all down his shirt and all his hair sticking up."

Despite Weller's off-stage interest in punk fashion – by this time, he'd sold the scooter and the parka was gathering dust in his wardrobe – The Jam stuck steadfastly to their black-and-white suits. Steve Carver: "We told him, 'Paul, you're out-of-date, mate! You've done it wrong. Get rid of the suits.' But no, he stuck to his guns. He wouldn't change their stage appearance." Weller was shrewd enough to perceive punk's in-built transience. The Jam had kitted themselves out in Sixties suits because of Paul's Mod obsession but, in doing so, their image stood them apart from the 'ripped and torn' brigade – perhaps more than their sound, described by Steve Carver as "punk with a twist". As their fan-base grew, so too did their 'look'. Steve Carver: "Shane and Adrian Thrills started turning up in school blazers and ties. We looked up to them for being London punks and then they gave us a backward compliment – a mutual admiration society. Then it mixed into a new nucleus with people like Suzy Catwoman."

By the end of 1976, punk was exerting a stranglehold on the music industry that bore no relation to its modest record sales. After three months spent courting outrage, The Sex Pistols had caused the biggest commotion in the media if not since the dawn of rock'n'roll, then certainly since the drug-related scandals that threatened to topple The Rolling Stones *et al* in the late Sixties. Behind them were a growing number of bands, but The Jam had one significant advantage. "They were so quickly on the ball, because they could play," observes Steve Carver. "They hadn't picked up a guitar last Saturday. The Sex Pistols were always going to get signed. The second choice was The Clash, wherever you went. After that, The Jam were on the hit list."

Mark Perry agrees: "After all, we weren't a bunch of dunderheads. We did know. Despite the punk rhetoric, you could tell a mile off that Paul Weller's were decent songs, just like The Clash stood out. Anyone could play loud and fast but it was obvious The Jam had good songs: the lyrics had some sort of meaning, he had a commitment to them and they were bloody good tunes – instantly recognisable poppy punk. Bands like Slaughter & The Dogs and The Vibrators were OK live, but they didn't have any songs, which you need if you want to progress and make records. At the end of the day, they did sign on the back of the punk movement.

Let's face it, a band that looked like they did, coming out of Woking, would never have got a deal otherwise."

★ ★ ★

Ron Watts, the main gig promoter at the famous Oxford Street venue, the 100 Club, was an early admirer of The Jam and gave them regular support slots. On November 9, they played there with The Vibrators; a week later, they preceded The Count Bishops, an R&B act who'd launched the first of a new breed of independent labels, Chiswick Records, run by the owners of the Rock On record stall, Ted Carroll and Roger Armstrong. Together with the recently formed Stiff label, they were sniffing around the punk scene – Stiff issued the first British 'punk' single, The Damned's 'New Rose', in October – and Chiswick courted The Jam towards the end of the year.

Carroll, in particular, was impressed. "Most punk bands were moving in hip, art college circles," he says. "The Jam, on the other hand, reminded me of the Feelgoods – these totally unhip guys from the suburbs, who were so great that they wiped out preconceived notions. When The Jam came on the scene, right at the beginning, punk wasn't defined. All the bands were, to a certain extent, using Sixties groups as role models, buying old records to do covers. They basically imitated The Pistols, whereas The Jam weren't punk, except that they played very fast. They were highly visual, with their suits and Rickenbacker guitars – a strong Sixties commitment – and Foxton and Weller jumped around a lot. It's much harder as a three-piece to break through, but they had their act together. They were professional, tight and highly rehearsed; there was none of the casual approach of The Pistols' chaos between numbers. And they came as a complete unit with Paul Weller's dad, who drove them to gigs and managed them."

In Carroll's view, this arrangement was The Jam's greatest weakness. "The word around town was, well, John Weller's gonna fuck things up," Ted claims, "because he doesn't know about the business. If you put it in perspective, The Pistols, The Clash, The Jam and perhaps The Damned were the four main bands that emerged. Now, The Pistols had Malcolm McLaren, The Clash had Bernie Rhodes, Andy Czezowski was looking after The Damned – sussed people in the centre of the whole thing." John Weller may not have had the experience but he certainly had the tenacity, since he has remained Paul's manager ever since – without any major public blunders along the way.

Specialising in pub rock, R&B and rockabilly with around half-a-dozen singles under their belt, Chiswick had yet to lure any of the punk bands – or those on the fringes of punk who, like The Jam, were now being labelled 'New Wave'. "They were building up a following and I could see they were going to be successful," Carroll admits. "We talked to John Weller and the band a number of times. I knew we weren't in a position to sign them up long-term, so we offered them a deal: let's do a single and we'll pay studio costs. It would act as a stepping stone for them to a major label."

Both parties courted each other into the early weeks of 1977 and there was talk of a £500 advance with free use of a PA – not so much an offer as a gesture of good faith. "John Weller came up one evening to my flat, which was over Rock On in Camden Town," recalls Carroll. "Paul was quiet, as I remember. That night, they had suddenly been offered a deal by Polydor's Chris Parry. I later learnt that Chris thought he was about to sign The Clash and saw them go to CBS, so he was after The Jam. I was surprised they were still interested in talking to us but I think they wanted to be sure; they were keeping their options open. This would have been less than a week before they signed to Polydor." As Roger Armstrong commented in *England's Dreaming*, "We had a studio holding time to record 'In The City'. When I got round to Ted's flat, he said, 'They've just cancelled; they're signing to Polydor this afternoon'."

A keen, New Zealand-born A&R man with a nose for what was happening in London, Chris Parry had approached The Sex Pistols but ran into what Jon Savage described as "problems pushing the deal through his immediate superiors". After the same fate met his discussions with The Clash, Parry wasn't about to let The Jam slip through his fingers, too. "After watching some second-rate punk band in a West London pub," he remembers, "Shane McGowan, who was one of the earliest Sex Pistols followers, said there was this band called The Jam, playing Saturday night at The Marquee. I should go and check them out. So I did and I liked them immediately."

The night was January 22 in front of a reported audience of around 500 – probably the most crucial gig The Jam ever played. Parry knew he had to be quick, since Island Records were rumoured to be sniffing around. Unfortunately, a hastily booked demo session had to be abandoned due to an IRA bombing in Oxford Street on 29 January and was rescheduled for a few days later. "I didn't hang around," Chris recalls, "and rapidly put them in a studio behind Oxford Street to get the feel of what they were like. Rick Buckler was a bit uneven and all over the place, playing more colourfully than he could pull off. I worked on him to get it more straightforward. Foxton was quite adequate and Paul was good, too."

In The Jam, Parry encountered three very different individuals: "Paul was very sure of himself. He told me over a pint of beer, 'I'm going to be an important figure. I just know I am. It's my destiny.' He had a bit of a temper and used to get angry. He was a little volatile. He was quite young, you know. He came through quite quickly. Rick was pretty easy-going, quite an even-tempered guy. Bruce could be moody."

Parry then organised a more formal recording test for the band at Polydor's Stratford Place Studios, which was spread across three days – February 9–11. "We ran through the material," says Chris, "which was pretty much everything that was going to be on 'In The City'. It was quite obvious that what I call the Polydor demo session was very good. All that was needed then was to record it properly." There followed a meeting at the company's offices about a possible recording deal and, sure enough, The Jam signed to Polydor the next day – February 15, 1977.

★　★　★

"The best period in my life" is how Paul Weller described 1976/early 1977 in The Jam's 1982 *Solid Bond In Your Heart* tour programme. There was now less friction within the band. There were occasional confrontations – when Bruce accidently broke Paul's treasured Hofner bass in the back of their cramped van one night, he received a black eye in return – but serious tensions seemed to have been smoothed out by the excitement of knowing they were on the verge of 'making it'. There was a high price to pay, though. Their rise to the top would require an immense physical and mental effort: from the moment the band linked up with Polydor until the day they played their last live concert nearly six years later, The Jam barely took more than a week off from recording or touring.

Just prior to that crucial Marquee gig, they played another support slot at the 100 Club on January 11. *Melody Maker* reckoned they played with "fire and skill" – a memorable quote lifted from early Jam handbills – and their first proper live review in *NME* described them as having "the outward trappings of a punk band, with guitarist/vocalist Paul Weller wearing a stiff stand-up collar of the Eton variety," and referring to the drummer's ubiquitous, Sixties square sunglasses, "Rick Buckler wearing what appeared to be masochistic goggles as used by those under sunray lamps." The review continued: "Their musical ability was considerably in advance of that displayed by most young bands that I've seen." It also noted their penchant for The Who songbook – 'So Sad About Us', 'Heatwave' and 'Much Too Much' – and soul favourites like Arthur Conley's 'Sweet Soul Music', Wilson Pickett's 'Mustang Sally' and Larry Williams' 'Slow Down', but recognised that their real and "exceedingly promising" talent lay in well-received originals like 'Sounds From The Street'.

The *NME* journalist was John Tobler. "They were a bit punky and played 'In The City', which I thought was good," he says now. "I went to see them in the dressing room and was surprised to discover that they came from Woking, which was where I lived." It's a reflection of The Jam's hometown anonymity that Tobler hadn't heard of them before. "Later, I interviewed them for Radio One," he adds. "Paul wanted to make his point and the others were pushed aside to some extent, simply because Paul had more to say. His greater urge to be a star was such that the others were really quite surprised by the progress which they'd made. It was obvious that Paul was the leader, quite apart from the fact that he was the singer, the writer and the guitarist."

Another early champion of the band was *NME*'s Tony Parsons, one of the journalists enlisted by that paper to chronicle punk. Impressed with The

Jam's performance at the Roxy on February 24, he criticised the audience's élitist nature: "Three months ago, it wasn't cool to say you liked The Damned. Now the black sheep of the New Wave are The Jam. It makes me puke, that kind of bullshit is just as vacuous as peace signs and half-hour guitar solos."

In that same issue, Polydor announced they had signed The Jam. Compared with sums paid for both the Pistols (£40,000) and The Clash (£100,000), it was a paltry figure. "It was a pretty crummy deal: £6,000 on signing and a 6% royalty rate," confesses Parry. "I said to John Weller, you need to get going quickly. I'll find you a decent lawyer and we'll sort this deal out once we get success. Don't worry about it. We signed the deal on the understanding that we'd be renegotiating."

Parry nurse-maided the contract through, since John Weller is reported to have overlooked the fine-print. As Chris admits: "John didn't know very much apart from looking after them in a personal way, so it was easier for me to impact on the band directly and quickly and he'd go along with it." Such was their parochialism that no-one connected with the group even had a bank account, as Parry discovered when he proudly handed John the advance. Chris laughs: "John exclaimed, 'I can't take a cheque.' So we went across to 399 Oxford Street, where Polydor banked. The money came across the counter in ten pound notes, John stuffed it in his pocket and went away a happy man! Crazy. But then we got them an accountant and a lawyer."

The Jam's contract had initially been for one single – Polydor were cautious – but the label took up its option before the first record was released, and ninety days after signing, the band's lawyer re-negotiated a more attractive package that covered four years and as many albums. "He sorted John out with a decent contract and then the royalty rate went up to about 13%," Parry remembers. Weller had never had any money – that is to say, a capital lump sum – and when his first royalty cheque arrived, the story goes that he offered to give it away. It is unlikely that his father, as manager of the band's finances, would have allowed such a magnanimous act – indeed, John squabbled frequently with his strongly principled if slightly naïve son. Eventually, £1,200 from the advance was spent on a totally inappropriate PA, while Paul's share was invested in several Rickenbacker guitars – his semi-acoustic 330 models and Foxton's 4001 bass were now Jam trademarks.

Parry rushed the band into Polydor's Stratford Place Studios to work on their début album. "I was keen on production but I needed an experienced engineer and brought in Vic Smith," Parry adds. Smith was a veteran of the recording industry who'd been present at The Beatles' infamous Decca audition in 1962 and had worked on projects as prestigious as The Rolling Stones' *Honky Tonk Women* in 1969. "The session just rolled pretty rapidly," Chris continues. "It was a small studio. Like many new bands, they had an album's worth of songs and were already playing them. We just wanted to capture the feel of what The Jam were about, not polish it. Paul wanted it rough and ready. He always liked Rickenbacker guitars, but they're really difficult to tune, so he ended up throwing them across the studio. We must have gone through every one in the country!"

Eleven days later, interrupted only by the band's growing live commitments – they played two weekly residencies, Wednesdays at the Red Cow in March, followed by Tuesdays at the Nashville Room in April – the LP was completed, to be fanfared by a single. On April 29, The Jam's first record reached the shops.

★　★　★

'In The City' began with an angry, stabbing three-chord guitar riff, then Foxton's pounding, descending bass-line kicked in after a few bars, before Buckler's snare-drum roll signalled the start of the song proper. It mirrored the live Jam sound – music that was harsh and energetic, but still rooted in melody, Weller's voice blustering and hoarse but still tuneful. A middle eight began with the sound of plectrum scraping against strings to create an atonal burst reminiscent of the second half of The Who's 'Anyway Anyhow Anywhere'. The lyrics owed more to 'My Generation', although proclamations like "I wanna tell you, About the young idea" and "But you'd better listen man, Because the kids know where it's at" were clumsier than Townshend's considered prose. The comparisons didn't stop there, either: the title of 'In The City' (and part of the melody) were borrowed from a 1966 Who song (the B-side to 'I'm A Boy'), a surf-styled number written by drummer Keith Moon and bassist John Entwistle.

Writing in U.S. magazine *Trouser Press*, Chris Burciago summarised the song perfectly as "the first in a long line of Jam anthems praising the power and vitality of youth . . . Weller may be writing a Sixties Mod anthem but he knows what time it is." Paul was keener to emphasise the line about "a thousand men in uniforms", telling *Moron* fanzine that the song was "about an innocent victim of police brutality; about the police beating up and killing for no reason." It wasn't – or, at least, that wasn't the main thrust of the lyric – but this is a poignant example of Weller's desire to take the political initiative offered by The Clash's Joe Strummer. The single's B-side needed less explaining: 'Takin' My Love' was a more aggressive version of the band's earliest-known recording, punked-up with perhaps Paul's most blatant debt to that tense, staccato R&B guitar style popularised by Wilko Johnson.

Voted 'single-of-the-week' in *NME*, 'In The City' was the fourth punk/ new wave hit. 'Anarchy In The UK' had been followed in February by The Stranglers' '(Get A) Grip (On Yourself)' and, at the start of April, The Clash's 'White Riot'. All four singles had hovered around No. 40, but The Jam were the first to appear on the BBC's long-running music programme, *Top Of The Pops* – an opportunity they rarely missed throughout their career. Weller's reaction to fame might best be described as cautious. There was the famous anecdote about him being more excited about finding a Who badge than signing to Polydor. "He'd be on the telly," remembers Steve Carver, "and five minutes afterwards, he's knocking on the door saying, 'Are Steve and Pete coming down the pub?' It was weird for my mum and dad! I watched the first *Top Of The Pops*, put my coat on and walked down the pub. Paul came running up and said, 'thanks for coming round for me, you bastard'. I didn't know he wasn't in the studio! He was shy about it, though. If you went round his house and watched *Top Of The Pops*, he'd sit behind you, chewing his fingernails. You'd go, 'Whatcha reckon, Paul?' 'Well, I'm not struck on the song, really,' he'd reply."

The course of punk was moving rapidly, and by the end of April, début albums from The Stranglers and The Clash had joined *Damned Damned Damned* in the racks. In *England's Dreaming*, Jon Savage is critical of The Jam's role in this radical musical mêlée. "Punk was politically riven as it interacted with the world outside," he wrote. "If The Jam and The Stranglers were going to coast in the slipstream of The Sex Pistols, then it was not surprising if they were judged on the same radical criteria and found wanting. Despite the element of novelty in both groups, there were also strong traces and/or ideological conservatism which made them a satisfactory bridge between the mainstream and punk's all-out assault." If the Pistols were the cornerstone of that "all-out assault", that didn't stop guitarist Steve Jones from borrowing the main riff from 'In The City' for the band's final single proper, 'Holidays In The Sun'.

Savage is right: there was no doubting Weller's musical conservatism. In an early issue of *48 Thrills*, Paul commented that, "if a group haven't got things right musically, people won't listen to them anyway. Right from the start, you've got to have rhythm and melody. You've got to have a good tune, whether you're Perry Como or the Pistols!" Many would argue that he was quite correct, of course – and, for someone who'd still to reach his nineteenth birthday, very sensible, too – but this view didn't exactly sit well with punk's disdain for technical and/or musical ability. Punk was about clearing away the tired musical detritus, instigating a musical revolution that upturned preconceived notions of talent; about shaking up those institutions which not only controlled the music business but which governed this land. "A good tune" wasn't on the manifesto.

There's a common misconception that The Jam were initially dismembered by the press. In the April 23 edition of *Melody Maker*, Brian Harrigan was one of the first journalists to scrutinise them in fine detail. "The Jam are the first band to make sense, for me, of the distinction between new wave and punk," he wrote. "The common denominator is the youth of its exponents, the simplicity and energy of the music, and a burning enthusiasm. The Jam underline this stance by coming on as Mods. Yup, they wear snazzy clothes, have their hair razor cut and even ride about on scooters. The Jam are finding the same solutions to their problems and the same means of expressing themselves as people like The Who and Small Faces did a dozen years or more ago."

The *NME*'s Nick Kent was equally receptive, delivering a sideways snipe to what he perceived as the hypocrisy-riddled punk ideology in the process: "I'd rather see The Jam any day than any number of attitude fetishists, if only because they've bothered to put the music first – and, as such, they will survive long after the 'I'm So Bored With . . .' merchants have scurried back to their parents' houses in Wanstead." Kent's statement seems to have been entirely borne out by Weller's prominence in the mid-Nineties, compared with Joe Strummer's marginal role in rock music, ever since The Clash fizzled out in the mid-Eighties.

In The City, the album, followed in mid-May. "Just the stage act we were playing at the time, which we just put down on vinyl," was how Weller accurately summed it up in *Creem* magazine in 1981. Clocking in at just over half-an-hour, the twelve songs were played at a furious pace – attracting such adjectives as "hurried", "bleak", "chaotic", "intense" and "highly charged". Weller's manner was serious and angry, his voice sometimes strained and never relaxed. Vic Smith and Chris Parry created an incredibly 'live' production – the sound isn't dissimilar, for example, to the best-known early live bootleg of the band, from a September '77 100 Club gig. But buried beneath this dense, sometimes impenetrable sound were definite peaks and troughs in Weller's songwriting.

Older compositions like 'I Got By In Time' (which included a verse about the passing of Paul's close friendship with Steve Brookes) and 'Non-Stop Dancing' (inspired by Weller's visits to those Bisley Pavilion Northern Soul all-nighters) had a tuneful Motown feel; while cover versions of Larry Williams' 'Slow Down' (no doubt discovered via The Beatles' 'Long Tall Sally' EP) and 'Batman Theme' (beefed up by The Who on their 1966 EP, *Ready Steady Who*) were pedestrian. 'Art School' was punchy three-chord punk, which Weller probably named after the education of Townshend, Ray Davies and John Lennon – punk = Sixties beat – and 'I've Changed My Address' echoed the message of The Who's 'Much Too Much', of giving a girlfriend the shove when marriage beckons.

Inspired by what Weller described as "urban politics", those lyrics which seemed to be plundered from The Clash's political agenda have rightly been criticised for being trite – but they are no more so than those of most of The Jam's contemporaries. 'Bricks And Mortar's lament about the faceless urban development was inspired by a series of upheavals endured by Woking town centre. 'Time For Truth' launched a direct attack on the Labour government of the day, its jibes at "Uncle Jimmy" prompted by Prime Minister James Callaghan's visit to Woking in December '76. The song also latched onto the death in police custody of suspect Liddle Towers in late 1976, after the coroner's verdict of 'misadventure' led the news media to demand a full enquiry. Towers became something of a *cause célèbre* (punk band The Angelic

Upstarts wrote their first single about him), although Weller's calls to "bring forward them six pigs/We wanna see them swing so high – Liddle Towers!", lacked political finesse, to say the least. And suffice it to say that lines like "Whatever happened to the great empire?/You bastards have turned it into manure" left much to be desired.

One of the album's highlights was 'Sounds From The Street'. Influenced by the vocal harmonies which had crept into some of The Who's mid-Sixties music courtesy of surf fan Keith Moon, it was a celebration of British youth which, like 'In The City', centred on London's nascent punk scene – of "young bands playing, young kids diggin' ". When Weller sang, "I know I come from Woking, and you say I'm a fraud/But my heart is in the city, where it belongs," it was difficult not to believe him.

In The City harboured one true masterpiece. From its opening power chords, the claustrophobic 'Away From The Numbers' was compelling. There was none of the unifying message heard elsewhere on the LP; instead, Weller vowed that "this link's breaking away from the chain". Too much could be made of lines like "I'm gonna break away and find what life is" – after all, Paul has never left the security blanket of his parents' support – but there does seem to be a grim determination to look beyond existing boundaries, onwards and upwards, and away from the 'numbers', Sixties Mod slang for the throng. Together with 'Sounds From The Street', the medium pace of 'Away From The Numbers', helped by a dreamy middle-eight, perfectly contrasted with the rest of the LP's breakneck delivery.

The album's stark, striking music was mirrored in its packaging, a variation on the monochrome design used for the 'In The City' single. This juxtaposed a photo of the black-suited band, with the distinctive Jam logo sprayed with an aerosol can, graffiti-like against a white tiled backdrop. The concept came from Bill Smith, Polydor's art director, who was on the same wavelength as Paul and responsible for all The Jam's sleeves up until 1981.

"That was a definite attempt to get away from the prevalent day-glo imagery that other bands, specifically The Sex Pistols, were using," Bill remembers. "The graffiti on the backdrop gave it that subterranean feel and we shot it with harsh lighting so it looked intensely black-and-white with that hard-edged look. For the back cover, we smashed the tiles up with a hammer. It was a time of showing what you were using, very DIY. Jamie Reid was doing the same for the Pistols, cut-and-paste and tear techniques. The torn, taped-on photos on the front of the single was based on that."

Despite the album's contemporary fury, reviewers inevitably drew parallels with the past – not only The Who but The Kinks and even The Flaming Groovies, an American band who shared a similar penchant for mid-Sixties melodies. An interview with *NME* declared, "All change and back to 1964", predicting that "The next big deal is: The Jam". Journalist Steve Clark caught Weller in an optimistic, opinionated mood. "We're the black sheep of the New Wave," he commented. "We're not into drugs. We don't need it . . .

We might when we're 30 or something. We might have to. In that case, we'll give up." Clark compared Weller to Townshend, Marriott and Lennon, speculating that "Paul Weller will in years to come . . . be regarded in the same light."

Despite the favourable media coverage, a long shadow loomed in Polydor's press release, which proudly proclaimed that the band "hold a strong and loyal conviction for Queen and Country. Anarchy in the UK holds no sway with The Jam." It was a portent.

In that same May 7 interview with *NME*, Weller reacted to what he perceived as the paper's sanctimonious left-wing stance by stating that the Queen was "our best diplomat" and worked harder than "what you or I do or the rest of the country". On May 12, he went a stage further in *Sniffin' Glue*, publicly aligning the band to one political party. "I don't see any point in going against your own country," he declared. "All this 'change the world' thing is becoming a bit too trendy. I realise that we're not going to change anything unless it's on a nationwide scale. We'll be voting Conservative at the next election." Coupled with the unequivocal image of the Union Jack flags draped over the band's speaker cabinets on stage, the entire affair was misconstrued by the weekly music press, who came to a hasty conclusion: The Jam were right-wing.

In fact, the imagery was unconnected with Weller's genuine political stance, which had yet to develop beyond a sense of conviction about the rights and wrongs of the world into any concise set of views. No-one had criticised punk heroes and late Sixties Detroit legends MC5 for decorating their turbulent stage performances with the Stars And Stripes. The Jam were merely mimicking the pop-art stylings of mid-Sixties Who, whose *My Generation* album cover depicted bassist John Entwistle clad in the garish red, white and blue of a Union Jack jacket. Decked out in identical attire, The Jam went a stage further when they blatantly copied the American cover of the same Who album by posing in front of Big Ben. Unfortunately, the right-wing National Front had hijacked the image as their emblem.

Weller had already voiced his opinions on the political stance of his songs in *48 Thrills*: "I think they have got some social meaning. We'd like to see change. I don't think people realise how close we are to a police state. The Labour government will want everything state-owned soon. It's getting to be like 1984 already. We're against things like fascism and communism but I don't want to get too involved in direct politics. The important thing is the music."

It's difficult today, after four terms of Tory rule, to envisage the political climate of 1977. Labour may have been in power but they seemed to offer few solutions and were relentlessly chastised by critics on both sides of the political divide. Prime Minister Callaghan encountered what seemed to be insurmountable problems with the country's national debt and his subsequent attempts to involve the International Monetary Fund were filibustered by MPs in his own party.

Labour had clearly lost control and the Conservatives capitalised on this unrest by creating the most radical manifesto of post-War politics – and selling it to the nation. As much as Weller's comments were designed to aggravate, his pledge to vote Conservative was in keeping with his upbringing. His family was typical of working-class households who switched their political allegiance to the Tories in the '79 election and beyond. They were hard-working, self-sufficient and dissatisfied with what was propagandised as Britain's declining moral fabric, from rising crime to national industries riddled with pay disputes and strikes.

At eighteen years old, the youthful Weller was merely absorbing a working class consensus that Labour were no longer the answer to the country's ills. As Paolo Hewitt noted in *Beat Concerto*, many of Paul's middle-class contemporaries were university graduates well-versed in political theory. The Clash's Joe Strummer and The Stranglers' Hugh Cornwell were aware of political philosophers like Marx and Lenin and indeed adopted far-left socialist views. If Weller identified more closely with the more accessible, patriotic yet socialist images painted by George Orwell, then he hadn't yet forged this into a clear political perspective. But what he did see was "rising unemployment, people boxed-up in impersonal council blocks and, worst of all, a small group of rich, powerful people controlling other people's lives through education, work and leisure."

Rock music has never been a comfortable bedfellow of right-of-centre politics and it was no surprise when Paul's stunt backfired: The Jam were vilified in the press, not least with allegations of far-right National Front sympathies. Worse still, Paul's "vote Tory" quip is still his most famous quote and remained a constant thorn in his side throughout the Eighties, when cynics used it as ammunition against his very public socialist convictions. Weller attempted to dismiss the affair by commenting that he "wouldn't vote for any of those cunts" and that "I was 18 and wanted the trendies to hate us and I succeeded". He confessed: "I sort of muddled in politics. I just really followed The Clash. I didn't know what I was talking about." At the time, Jam HQ attempted to minimise the damage and, accompanied by a statement that the band had nothing against the Queen, the Union Jack props were quietly folded away.

Before the backlash started, however, Weller also went on record in *Strangled* fanzine as supporting the forthcoming Queen's Silver Jubilee festivities. Three celebratory shows had been booked for the second week of June 1977, including an all-day family event at Chelsea Football Club's Stamford Bridge ground, organised by the local Council together with the Jubilee committee. The Jam would play for free as the finale to "a day of carnivals, steel bands and parades", supported by one of Paul's favourite new bands, The Boys. But such was the controversy surrounding punk that the event was thwarted when the GLC refused to grant a music licence. "When the audience learned The Jam weren't appearing," wrote

Miles, "a large part demanded their money back . . . the police had to be called to disperse an angry crowd." In fact, Polydor had offered The Jam's services to 14 boroughs but the response had been cautious. The two remaining Jubilee gigs, at Tower Hamlets' Poplar Civic Hall on June 18 and Wandsworth's Battersea Town Hall nine days later, only fuelled the fire of controversy surrounding the band's supposed Tory sympathies. "We are all very patriotic," they announced, "and we believe strongly in the Queen. We want to be involved in the Jubilee." It was a far cry from The Sex Pistols' Jubilee statement: the release of 'God Save The Queen', with its anti-monarchial sneer and nihilistic cries of "no future".

Meanwhile, The Jam hitched up as support for The Clash's *White Riot '77* tour. With Buzzcocks, Subway Sect and The Slits further down the bill, it promised to be punk's first significant national convoy, after the frustration of The Sex Pistols' cancelled *Anarchy* dates in late '76. The Jam signed up to play three dates, which began on May 7 at the Edinburgh Playhouse, Manchester's Electric Circus the following night and then North London's Rainbow Theatre, before rejoining the tour eleven days later for the last dozen or so shows. The Rainbow event was filled with incident, as fans destroyed the seating, an act described by the *London Evening Standard* as "a riot". As Jon Savage wrote, "The *White Riot* tour was the first outbreak of pure punk mania . . . the fabric of existing theatres could not deal with this unleashed fury. However good-natured, Punk *looked* scary and it resulted in damage to venues built for staider times."

Behind the scenes, The Jam found matters were equally chaotic. Claiming they weren't given an adequate soundcheck (the sound quality at the Rainbow was, by all accounts, dreadful) and that The Clash's manager, Bernie Rhodes, was pressuring Polydor to "bankroll" the tour, Weller, Foxton and Buckler pulled out. Rhodes retaliated by bragging that he sacked the band for reneging on an earlier agreement to subsidise those bands who had not secured a recording contract – a situation complicated by Rhodes' involvement with Subway Sect. Out of their £100 per night fee, The Jam were also meant to 'hire' The Clash's PA but their £1,000 buy-on fee was apparently never paid. The whole sorry mess created animosity between the two camps, a problem exemplified by a sarcastic telegram from The Clash: "Maggie wants you all round for target practice tonight."

Desperate to organise nationwide dates to promote their album, The Jam announced on May 21 that they had signed with the Cowbell Agency to organise their live dates. Now with Primary Talent agency, Cowbell's Martin Hopewell is still working with Paul Weller to this day. "At a small level, the agent's job is to convince concert promoters or club owners or college social secretaries that they should book this particular artist," he explains. "I organised a six-act show down at the Royal College Of Art and eventually ended up chasing The Jam around the dressing room with a piece of paper in my hand, saying 'sign here!' "

Cowbell acted swiftly and The Jam's first national tour began on June 7, a week after their LP entered the charts. It was an important building block in their career, since the band hadn't had much live exposure outside London and the Home Counties. Thirty-six dates and seven weeks later, The Jam had covered most points on the compass. From Eastbourne to Falkirk, and Cardiff to Cambridge, they drove all over the country in a Mark III Ford Cortina, while their gear travelled separately in a Mercedes van driven by three roadies, an adventure which Weller has since recalled with fondness. The tour climaxed with what can accurately be described as a triumphant finale at the cavernous Hammersmith Odeon – "their first major concert in London and a remarkable milestone in the growing acceptance of the new wave amongst audiences", according to *Punk Diary*. Like most bands, The Jam may have preferred the intimacy of tiny clubs but that conflicted with the necessity of reaching a wider audience and they had enlisted the services of one of Britain's most prominent concert promoters, Mel Bush.

The Hammersmith set was also notable for the inclusion of two new songs, 'All Around The World' and 'Carnaby Street', both sides of a new Jam single which had entered the chart the day before the concert. (Two other tunes had been considered for the B-side – 'The Modern World', which had been aired, together with 'Art School', 'In The City' and 'I've Changed My Address', on a John Peel Radio One session on April 26 – and 'London Girl', the third fresh composition from that concert. In fact, there had been talk of a four-track EP.) Foxton's 'Carnaby Street' was an uneventful ode to the faded Mod Mecca of the Sixties, his first composition for the band. "There was an increasing awareness that Paul was the beneficiary of the songwriting," suggests Parry. "It dawned on the other two that they weren't going to make any songwriting money unless they wrote some themselves. Now, Rick wasn't going to, but Bruce felt he could contribute. It did cause problems, because Bruce was driven to put a song out."

Altogether more exciting was 'All Around The World', premièred on TV when The Jam performed on *The Marc Bolan Show*, and arranged to great effect by Chris Parry. Fanfared by a drum roll, this rallying cry for a "youth explosion" crashed in with an aggressive two-chord guitar attack, and Weller's and Foxton's call-and-response vocals. The lines, "What's the point in saying destroy/We want a new life for everyone" and "You can't dismiss what's gone before" drove another wedge between The Jam and the anarchic rhetoric of punk. Indeed, Weller criticised those acts who indulged in punk clichés, commenting to *NME*'s Tony Parsons that, "what does exist is the worth of the individual bands. That means something as long as they're true to themselves."

He was talking about integrity, a quality which Paul strived to achieve publicly throughout The Jam's lifetime, the contradiction between his later socialist stance and quips about voting Tory notwithstanding. It meant that the band battled with Polydor to release only one – or, at most, two – singles from each LP, usually coupled with non–album B-sides, in order to give their fans value for money. It meant that the group, at least in the early days, attempted to keep ticket and merchandising costs to a minimum. And it also meant that Paul probably took himself too seriously in this quest for moral uprightness and honesty – which meant that he came over as precious to some.

Both 'All Around The World' and 'Carnaby Street' were performed during a second visit to Radio One's Maida Vale studios on July 19, alongside energetic versions of 'Bricks And Mortar' and 'London Girl', before Parry tucked the band away in a rehearsal studio in Aylesbury – "a farmhouse in the middle of nowhere", according to *Our Story*, "just a portakabin and some derelict stables" – to firm up songs for their second album. But the sessions didn't work out and the fiasco was abandoned after a week.

Paul Weller's concentration was focused elsewhere. After the band played in Dunstable on July 9, he had met a girl named Gill Price, a lively, strong-willed Bromley-born South Londoner who was then working for a fashion designer. As Weller put it on the back of The Jam's live album, *Dig The New Breed*, "Dunstable and that hotel?!" The two quickly became inseparable. Paul Weller had fallen in love for the first time in his life.

5

YOU DO SOMETHING TO ME

Gill Price had a profound influence on Paul and, therefore, the atmosphere within The Jam. It could be argued that her effect was as immediate as Yoko Ono's on Lennon and The Beatles, though the results were nowhere near as disruptive. "All of a sudden, she was there," says Chris Parry. "It changed things because the band up to that time were three lads – and then it was two lads and Paul and his girl. He got more serious, too, more detached from the band, more into himself. It took the shine off the camaraderie between the band, who were not quite the same anymore."

Within a few weeks, Weller moved up to London to share a flat in Baker Street with Gill; Bruce and Rick stayed behind in Woking. To an extent, the new couple cut themselves off, but this wasn't some cosy 'love nest'; their relationship was always turbulent and they rowed frequently. Friends noticed a distinct change in Paul's outward demeanour after meeting Gill – ironically, he seemed more of a loner. "Some distancing between Paul and the others is beginning to show," suggested a report in the music press.

"At first, Gill was very quiet," remembers Rick Buckler. "I don't know whether she was in awe of the whole thing but she was quite shy. She was always affable. We saw less of Paul because he was with her more of the time. It became a bit of a joke because Paul was living with her and took her on the road as well, so they were never away from each other. It was like Siamese Twins. They'd always slope off somewhere if they weren't needed for an hour or so. They were almost inseparable."

It is tempting to claim that Gill was more than just a girlfriend to Weller. Prior to meeting her, his interests and experiences had been fairly narrow, to say the least, since he'd lived only for music and fashion, which he defined with rigid tastes that might be viewed by an outsider as a restrictive outlook bordering on tunnel vision. Gill later became a strong, vivacious personality who was known for being the life and soul of the party, with a gregarious nature that contrasted with Paul's relative shyness. Her influence on Paul is difficult to define, but she certainly broadened his horizons and made him more aware that, to use an old phrase, there was a whole world out there. "I think she influenced his appreciation of culture," admits a close friend of Gill's. "Apart from being a couple, they did obviously seem to have a good rapport. They liked going to the same places, they always went on holiday to Capri, and they both liked art. I don't think their tastes in music exactly coincided, though."

Meanwhile, The Jam Roadshow continued. On August 6, they travelled to the second French Mont De Marson punk festival, south of Bordeaux, the story of which paints a lively picture of life on-the-road and yet betrays the monotony and routine of endless touring. "We got invited to play in this bullring, put together by a shady-looking bunch," recalls The Jam's agent, Martin Hopewell. "The Clash were involved, and The Stranglers and The Damned. What happened was extraordinary. There was a charter flight and it was just two minutes before the food started flying around. Having survived that, we arrived at Biarritz Airport to be met by this coach, by which time people were getting the worse for wear. At one point, this trickle of liquid came running back towards me and I realised to my horror that someone was having a pee further up the bus.

"We arrived at Mont De Marson, a little village in south-west France, with a market square, at which point Paul and Bruce decided to have a dip in the fountain – fully clothed. Within two minutes, the gendarmes arrived in this old black van. The band were shoved in the back and it went screaming off down the street with John and me running after it. We arrived at the police station, and finally got to interview the chief-of-police with the lads sitting there looking very woebegotten, like drowned rats.

"On the day of the gig, they wanted to move The Jam to a different playing spot and we came to the conclusion that we shouldn't play. This did *not* go down well with the French organisation. The next day, we tried to collect the money from a very heavily unshaven bloke sitting in this back-stage room down a long corridor with gangster types hovering about the place with flick-knives. Could we have that money for the show we didn't play yesterday? And the most extraordinary thing was we got it!"

Their first trip to Sweden across September 24/25 was just as disastrous. At Ronneby, The Jam were pelted with eggs and chair legs after their first number. The stage was then invaded by the audience, as the band beat a well-timed retreat. Later, they were forced to cancel a subsequent date in Holland because much of their gear had been trashed.

There were no such problems in September when the band played their second energetic but low-key London show at the 100 Club in a month – "It's nice to be back, I feel like Frank Sinatra," croaked Weller – although the preview of their forthcoming second album wasn't very encouraging. Behind the scenes, the band were recording the LP at Island's Basing Street Studios in Notting Hill, West London, with a £20,000 advance from Polydor, but something was wrong. Maybe it was the "pokey" surroundings or the distraction of Weller's infatuation with Gill Price, but the project has never evoked fond memories.

Chris Parry explains: "John Weller had this new percentage deal with

Polydor, which meant he got quite a lot of money for the next album which, all of a sudden, had to be done rapidly. *This Is The Modern World* was rushed, and sounds it. Paul's songs were alright, but they weren't as well prepared, so the session wasn't as quick as *In The City* – and not as much fun either. The songs got more Beatley, but they also had more of their own sound. Paul got caught up with everything-on-a-Rickenbacker. If he'd just been more open-minded, we could have moved the session on more fruitfully, with more time and care. It didn't achieve its full promise." Vic Smith remembers an incident when Paul completely lost his temper: "The guitar suddenly disappeared off the mix," he recalls. "Then something catches my eye in the studio: it's Paul's guitar fifteen feet in the air. He'd just got so frustrated over not staying in tune."

Parry's frustration at Weller's awkwardness came to a head during The Jam's first trip to the States in October, to promote the US release of *In The City*. Paul's pangs for the absent Gill were exacerbated by an extraordinary loathing of the country, an odd reaction for someone so enamoured with much of its musical heritage. "Paul was not behaving very well," says Chris. "He was just being petulant. I don't think The Jam travelled very well, particularly Paul. He's actually very much a Little Englander. John was the same – they all were. Their horizons were restricted to Britain and they never felt comfortable in America." The visit was heralded by adverts celebrating their album's five-month UK chart run, which declared: "These three British subjects are the illegitimate offspring of Peter Townshend, Ray Davies, Keith Richard, John Lennon and Jimmy Page". The Jam were scheduled to play around sixteen dates in twelve days in the major cities, at such legendary clubs as the Los Angeles Whisky A-Go-Go and New York's punk epicentre, CBGB's, plus the Boston Rat's Keller and San Francisco's Old Waldorf.

"Well, we didn't play in San Francisco," adds Chris. "Everyone flew in to see them and it was going to be the big show, but The Jam blew out because there was some earth problem with the microphones. John was terrified that Paul might die of electrocution." Instead, the record company executives and media, curious to see this anachronistic-looking English trio, descended on a second CBGB's date, only to witness Weller inciting the audience to rip up the chairs before winding them up further by announcing that The Jam had split. Accompanying interviews and radio talk shows were also characterised by the singer's spiky remarks. In a sense, The Jam's attitude towards their US audience was understandable, what with the anti-American stance of the British punk scene, typified by The Clash's rallying cry, 'I'm So Bored With The USA'. Paul Weller and America only had a brief encounter and there were no tears shed when it ended.

The band returned to Britain on the eve of the release of their third single, 'The Modern World', on 21 October 1977. Faintly reminiscent of The Who's 1967 single, 'Pictures Of Lily', the song took its title from

Weller's Mod obsession, of course, but its lyrics reacted to the criticisms he'd attracted in the press. It began by slating those who thought the writer "knew nothing about the modern world" before climaxing with the final line, "I don't give two fucks about your review" – although for radio friendliness, the album version was censored on the single to "a damn", an ironic compromise bearing in mind the defiant nature of the song's message. The final irony was that it stalled at No. 36, although its punchy, power chords, nimble bass lines and snappy drumming created a tense atmosphere central to the early Jam sound. The hectic cover versions on the flip – Arthur Conley's 'Sweet Soul Music' and The Supremes' 'Back In My Arms Again' – hinted at a short supply of original material but reflected the prominence of Sixties soul classics in The Jam's live set, which also featured, on occasion, Lee Dorsey's 'Ride Your Pony' (described by *Melody Maker's* Brian Harrigan as "fast, crisp and raunchy") and Martha & the Vandellas' 'Heatwave'.

When The Jam's second album, *This Is The Modern World*, followed two weeks later, it was met by a tirade of abuse from the music press. Commonly dismissed as rushed and ill-advised, it caught the band in a state of flux. In half a year, the Jam sound had evolved considerably – and for that alone, the LP was an achievement. Weller once spoke of the album as their attempt to "cross over" into new wave – "the pop music of the Seventies", as he called it. They were patently keen to progress beyond the punk mould of *In The City*, as evidenced by the melodic rush of Paul's slower, more contemplative songs and the cover photo by legendary Sixties photographer Gered Mankowitz. This showed the group gazing out from under the Westway (the A 40, which heads out of London), with bleak-looking council blocks behind them, and Weller wearing a Who badge and Mod-ish arrows stuck on his jumper. It was the first notable photo session in which the band weren't dressed uniformly in suits. Together with two songs directly connected with the capital, 'London Traffic' and 'London Girl', this image continued the thread of 'In The City' and 'Sounds From The Street' by forging a stark, urban identity for a band patently keen to rid themselves of their Surrey roots.

Bruce Foxton's two contributions, 'Don't Tell Them You're Sane' and 'London Traffic', were trounced by the critics, not least for their uninspiring lyrics; if the latter's environmental message pre-empted the pro-public transport lobby by a decade, then it was disgraced by the banality of the music. Weller's songs were just as patchy but more intriguing. The immediacy of 'Standards' made it a popular live choice, with another sub-Who, power chord structure that was matched by an equally basic anti-system/law message ("You know what happened to Winston" referred to the main character in Orwell's *1984*), while 'Here Comes The Weekend' drew on the idea of the 'Weekend Starts Here' slogan from that celebrated mid-Sixties music show, *Ready, Steady, Go!* But the real strength lay in the love songs like 'I Need You (For Someone)' and 'Tonight At Noon', which revealed a softer side to his nature, spoilt only by their occasionally trite lyrics. One of the album's highlights was 'The Combine', an expression used by Ken Kesey in *One Flew Over The Cuckoo's Nest* to describe "the system" (its story of life in a mental institution also inspired 'Don't Tell Them You're Sane' and 'Standards').

Mr. B. Cain, who is thanked for the "teenage blue" phrase in 'Life From A Window', was journalist Barry Cain, who later set up *Flexipop* magazine. Old friend Dave Waller and Sixties beat poet Adrian Henri were also thanked for "foresight and inspiration". In Henri's case, it was an understatement: despite being credited solely to Paul Weller, 'Tonight At Noon' took its name from one of Henri's poems and the first two-and-a-half verses from another, *In The Midnight Hour*. Both poems were published in Penguin's 1967 collection, *The Mersey Sound*, alongside work by fellow Liverpudlians Roger McGough and Brian Patten. It was a logical influence on Weller, bearing in mind his interest in Sixties Liverpool and, quite unusually for a working-class lad with few qualifications, a fascination with poetry which he had retained from his school days. "It's adapted from a poem by Henri," was how Weller couched it. "I really admire his sort of poetry and I think it's time the band really started getting into ballads and acoustic stuff." To further complicate matters, the album ended with a song that was also entitled 'In The Midnight Hour'; this time a bludgeoning cover of the Wilson Pickett soul classic.

Dave Waller was luckier: he received a joint songwriting credit for the otherwise undistinguished 'In The Street Today', for his lines, "Murder on the terraces/Fools in high places/It's all so sickening/And we're so satisfied". These were taken from one of his six untitled poems, which were printed at the back of a Jam songbook in summer '77. "As in all cultures, which hopefully the NEW WAVE will evolve into (or maybe it has?), there are a lot of other Art forms," wrote Paul as an introduction, "not only music, but why not NEW WAVE painters, playwrights, authors and poets? One such person, and I'm sure there are a lot more, is DAVID WALLER, a very talented poet. I relate very deeply to his works. I hope you can."

Paul's support of Waller wasn't merely a random philanthropic act. Paul genuinely admired his friend's work. Waller's bleak portraits of decaying urban life in the face of capitalism/consumerism imbued many of The Jam's songs. But this was the first indication that Paul was both looking beyond the boundaries of rock music, and wished to use what influence he now had to help others. As 1977 wore on, Paul was beginning to reveal a sense of responsibility about his role as a pop star. Having turned down an unlikely support slot with Peter Gabriel, "on the grounds that they still desired to play the smaller clubs", The Jam ended the year with a month-long tour, which was warmly received, in contrast to the panning which had greeted the album. "We are as big as the Pistols," boasted Weller to *NME* writer Steve Clarke. "We're on our second major British tour and the Pistols haven't even done their first one yet."

The roadshow was interrupted by a well-documented fracas in a Leeds hotel with members of an Australian rugby club. After bumping into the club's manager, Paul allegedly lashed out at him with a glass. The team responded by chasing the band around the hotel, before Bruce was brutally attacked, leading to cracked ribs, and The Jam's entourage was escorted by the police to another hotel. Meanwhile, Paul was arrested and spent a night in the local police station before appearing before Leeds Magistrates Court, charged with causing a breach of the peace. The publicity created an aura of confrontational punk credibility around The Jam and their live wire of a frontman – Paul even recalled the debacle on the sleeve for their live album, *Dig The New Breed* – but it was an isolated incident. At a time when contemporaries like Sham 69 were attracting a violent element, Weller adopted an anti-violence stance which, on the whole, was reflected by the band's fans.

The Jam may have increased their earning potential as a live act, but in between this gruelling schedule of dates, the ambitious John Weller made huge demands on his boys, pushing them into interviews with the press and securing numerous TV and radio spots. The cracks that had been evident on *This Is The Modern World* were beginning to show more clearly, as Paul and the rest of the band grew further apart. For the next few months, the future of The Jam looked uncertain. It seems that the band survived only by the familial structure which cloaked the group; John Weller may have driven them hard but he also demonstrated both commitment and strong management. In essence, John pulled them through.

Weller even approached Glen Matlock to ask if he would be interested in joining The Jam. By that time, Glen had formed a new band, The Rich Kids. "I'd fallen out with the Pistols and people were getting wind of that," says Glen. "Paul and I spoke about it – I was maybe going to play rhythm guitar. I remember being down The Roxy and Bruce and Rick came up and said, 'We hear you're gonna join the band. Will you wear a suit?' I said, 'yeah'. They said, 'What, like ours, from Carnaby Street?' I said, 'You must be joking,' and that was the end of it! I tried to get Paul to join The Rich Kids after that, because we had trouble finding a singer. The Jam played a gig at The Marquee and we talked to Paul before he went on stage, winding him up by saying his band was crap. He thought about it, though."

★　★　★

1977 may have been the 'Year Of Punk' but for both The Jam and the scene in general, it ended with a feeling of anti-climax. Early 1978 was a curious time for the music scene, in fact, especially for those musicians who had surfed the punk wave and were now unsure which direction to take. Paul Weller was no exception. Always one to feed off the ingenuity and enthusiasm of his contemporaries, he sensed the uncertainty that hung in the air. For a moment, the music scene hesitated – and seemed to respond by looking back. *NME* reflected the mood by matching new acts with old styles: Whirlwind looked like '58 Ted, The Pleasers like The Beatles (1963), The Jam wore Mod suits (1965), Skrewdriver adopted skinhead stylings (1969) and Adam Ant had shades of '73 glam. The Jam were also seen as the catalysts for 'Power Pop', a new crossbreed invented by the press that was half beat group, half new wave.

The 'power pop' tag felt rather tame, though, a word that might also have described The Jam's next single. Issued on February 24, 'News Of The World' was Bruce Foxton's first – and tellingly his last – A-side. The energetic guitar break represented Weller's best guitar work yet, though, within the song's crisp production – a definite progression from the second LP. The song was catchy enough, and its "Punk rock! Power pop!" overture captured the prevalent mood swing in the music papers, but its attack on tabloid journalism was as two-dimensional as the music. Having already tackled insanity, traffic congestion and the press, Bruce then dealt with legal injustices on the flip, 'Innocent Man'. This was coupled with a third track, 'Aunties And Uncles (Impulsive Youths)', a charming, melodic song on which Weller sounded more relaxed than ever (an early working version featured occasional fragments of dialogue in the style of The Small Faces' "mustn't grumble" in 'Lazy Sunday'). Its lyrics seemed to imply a 'V'-sign, suggesting it was Paul's way of reacting to parental advice about his intense relationship with Gill.

It was the third Jam single to include "world" in its title, and the sleeve photo depicted the band strolling down Carnaby Street – talk about wearing your influences on your sleeves. Together with a video shot on top of Battersea Power Station, these images maintained a deliberate link with London but, collectively, they were further indications that the band was treading water. "It was an interim record," sighs Parry. "It was OK. But it was Bruce's effort to write a pop song and it didn't work 100%."

The session for the single also yielded an unreleased song, 'She's Got Everything', titled after an old Kinks song, which began with a "la-la la-la-la" intro in the style of The Who's 'So Sad About Us'. Weller's lyrics, though, revealed a thinly veiled ode to Gill Price.

In it, Paul confessed to being "not well-liked" and a "social failure", sentiments which returned many years later when he revealed that "maybe it's my complexes but I get the impression that most people dislike me anyway, so I always start the conversation from that point. It can only get better." He may have been racked by self-doubt on occasion but Weller, on the whole, was also headstrong, totally self-absorbed and driven by a belief in what he was doing, sometimes at the expense of an emotional contact with other people. Many of those who met Paul during his days with The Jam – especially women – describe him as shy and nervous and not particularly relaxed. Even allowing for the hectic, rollercoaster lifestyle that took hold of the band, it is safe to say that it took Paul Weller a long time to feel at ease outside of the security of The Jam's inner camp – it has been a gradual process, like the unwinding of what Paolo Hewitt envisaged as that "tightly sprung alarm clock".

The day 'News Of The World' was released, February 24, 1978, coincided with the first of four low-key London dates at the Marquee, the 100 Club and the Music Machine under the banner of 'The London Blitz'. Together with isolated dates in Brussels and a trouble-ridden show in Paris, these acted as The Jam's by now characteristic warm-up shows for a forthcoming tour, but nothing could prepare them for what was in store on their second visit to the States – their first fully fledged tour there. The band flew in on March 11 in high spirits, buoyed by Polydor's anticipation that this second trip would break the band in America, as it was backed up by extensive radio and TV coverage. There was even an *NME* reporter in tow to detail the entire first week of the twenty-four dates booked. The omens were good.

The first three concerts in the North-East were support slots to allow The Jam to climb the first rung on the promotional ladder – but therein lay the first obstacle. Playing bottom of the bill, to American AOR band Blue Oyster Cult in cavernous venues, was a far cry from the rapturous reception back home at the Hammersmith Odeon. As *NME*'s Phil McNeill observed, "Playing to a sell-out gymnasium of doped-up college kids, The Jam and their audience went for instant culture shock. Weller is positively surly." The band played scattered dates of their own across the Mid-West, Canada, and two nights at New York's CBGB's, before returning to the Blue Oyster Cult tour, playing third on the bill behind British art rockers Be Bop Deluxe, in Phoenix, Arizona. Finally, The Jam bowed out with some high profile West Coast concerts, but to perplexed American punks unaware of Mod fashion, The Jam looked like bank clerks. The US radio and media were just as bemused by this sullen, disgruntled and very British band. The tour wasn't a disaster – in fact, the final show in San José sold out – but neither was it the roaring success they had hoped for. "Taking the short-cut from small clubs to stadia had backfired," Bruce later admitted. "We just hadn't built a strong enough following in the States."

★　★　★

The Jam's third album was already looming on their return in mid-April. The project looked ambitious: in late '77, Weller had promised that "for the next LP, I'll have it like a play, with different people singing the lyrics so that everybody will understand". But in reality, Paul's creativity had dried up, aside from a few songs written in America. His energies were directed elsewhere. Perhaps swayed by Gill's background in fashion, he even talked of opening a second-hand clothes store – the first murmurings of a restlessness which stayed with him for over a decade, but also a reflection of his increasing apathy towards The Jam. Weller wasn't the only one: Bruce was caught drunk in a nightclub around that time, ruminating about leaving music altogether to open a guest-house!

Chris Parry's derogatory views on some lacklustre studio demos halted proceedings, and the sessions were aborted, creating what has often been heralded as The Jam's legendary, 'lost' third LP. The truth is less romantic. "John Weller wanted to make another album," Chris explains. "I wanted to see what was coming up, the beginnings of an LP. There were odd bits and pieces that Paul had written, but the finished works were mostly Foxton songs and they just weren't up to it. It wasn't really a lost album. Nothing stood out. I said, 'Look Bruce, forget about the writing – you're not a writer. Until Paul can write again, this project isn't getting off the ground.' That didn't go down very well, and I don't think Foxton ever forgave me. Buckler wasn't very keen either, because he felt it was holding everybody back and Paul just spent some time brooding it over."

Piecing together the band's abandoned work-in-progress is difficult, although there were some interesting working titles like 'On Sunday Morning' and 'I Want To Paint' (from yet another Adrian Henri poem and "pretty off-the-wall", according to Rick Buckler). "The songs just weren't up to standard," Weller later admitted. "It was a bad period for The Jam and a lot of the trouble stemmed from me. I was writing soppy songs or trying to be flash or arty – and I know that's not what The Jam are about."

When I asked Paul about the project in 1992, his memories weren't fond ones: "It was just . . . it was awful. We were all lost at that time – me especially because, as a writer, I had no ideas. I dried up." The sole product of these sessions to have emerged so far is a three-track acetate prepared for The Jam's next single: a rough-and-ready performance of the punky 'Billy Hunt', backed with Foxton's 'The Night' and Paul's peculiarly blatant solo love ballad, 'English Rose'. On June 1, during a special concert at London's Paris Theatre for the BBC's *In Concert* series, the band introduced 'Billy Hunt' as "our new single, out shortly". But it, too, was scrapped. Instead, Weller returned to Woking and the safe, comfortable surroundings of his parents – "an obvious attempt to touch base with those things which had made him," as Alex Ogg suggested, although the move was prompted by him having to leave his London flat because of a stalker. With only a week-long tour in early June to disturb him, Paul pondered The Jam's future. Their last two singles had consolidated their position rather than strengthened it, and a year into their recording contract, Polydor's attention was shifting towards cartoon punks Sham 69, whose 'Angels With Dirty Faces' reached the Top 20 in May, followed by a No. 9 hit, 'If The Kids Are United', in July.

Up against it, Paul Weller set about perfecting a batch of tunes that would be among the finest of his whole career. "I wrote the bulk of the songs in a couple of days and didn't have a chance to sit around playing them for a long time," he told *Trouser Press* in 1979. "Most of them just came together." It was a make-or-break situation. "There was a feeling that we were being written off," he told me in 1992. "You know, *In The City* was good and then it all dampened from there. And that spurred me into writing *All Mod Cons*. It was me proving myself."

The Jam were assigned a new product manager at Polydor, Dennis Munday, just as "the shit was hitting the fan," as he puts it. "When I took over, it was a heavy time when the so-called third album had been rejected – though I don't think they ever finished it. I walked into that!" An ex-Mod in his late twenties who had worked with jazz greats like Oscar Peterson, Count Basie and Ella Fitzgerald, Munday also took on Siouxsie & The Banshees and Sham 69 – but he took a particular shine to The Jam, and Paul Weller especially. "I remember the first time I saw Paul," says Dennis. "The band were in the press office – this was early '77 – and what struck me was that Paul was like a mirror image of me when I was 16: black mohair suit, the whole Mod bit. Déjà vu!

"I was fairly distrusted for a period. They assumed everyone was a company man. They were definitely on the defensive, until they got to know me. They were all anxious young guys. Paul wasn't so much reticent as shy. I think he always has been and still is now. He's only gregarious or out-going when he's on stage." Munday acted not only as a co-ordinator but as a mediator between band and record company. "A product manager is responsible for putting the releases together," Dennis explains. "Every month, there's a release sheet and a roster of artists and you link up with A&R and the managers, the market plans and the sleeve designs."

The Jam's turnaround began with another song salvaged from the wreckage of those abandoned sessions. Both the stark, jerky style and the lyrics of another of Weller's 'London' songs, ''A' Bomb In Wardour Street' – about escalating violence in the capital, with references to punk hang-out, The Vortex – echoed The Clash, but the furious bite of its "a-p-o-c-a-l-y-p-s-e" climax was like a blast of cold air compared with the limp production of their second album. Parry had other ideas for the next single, though. "I'd heard 'David Watts' live and thought it was really good, so I said, let's record that as well. They weren't too sure because it was a cover." The opening highlight of the acclaimed 1967 LP, *Something Else By The Kinks*, which Paul had bought in the States, 'David Watts' told the tale of "that abominable golden school-boy" and was a wider metaphor for teenage insecurity.

Both songs were recorded at Mickie Most's RAK Studios, but the band had difficulty choosing the A-side. In early July, they were invited to appear on Most's TV music show, *Revolver*. Parry picks up the story: "I had acetates of 'David Watts' and ''A' Bomb'. John said, 'Mickie Most is down there, let's ask him. Mickie, have you got a minute? These two songs, what do you think?'. We played them both and Most said, "David Watts', that's the one!'. John said, 'Fine – if it's good enough for Mickie, it's good enough for me!'."

That said, the single was actually issued as a double-A-side on August 11.

'David Watts' may have worked within the live context – it remained a stage favourite – but this was pure mimicry, reinforcing the suggestion that the band were weak on new material. It was a bold if unimaginative move for a group who'd been lampooned for their Sixties obsessions, reinforced by the Mod imagery of arrows on the single's sleeve. The treatment added little to The Kinks' original, substituting Ray Davies' subtly sneering tone for the laddish terrace effect – "oi!, oi!" – of Foxton and Weller's shared lead vocals. The single was promoted by what was billed as a "mini-tour of seaside resorts" (which included the decidedly inland towns of Swindon and Guildford). The five dates also introduced some of the new songs from The Jam's third album, *All Mod Cons*, which was rapidly reaching completion – without Parry's help.

"I was spending more time at Polydor setting things up," Chris readily confesses, "so I wasn't at the sessions so often, during *All Mod Cons* – and there was a problem, really, with me. Bruce made it clear I wasn't welcome. Paul's hand was forced, in a sense. He said, well, if you're not an engineer, we don't need you for this next album, so that was that." The band stuck with Vic (who reverted to his real surname, Coppersmith-Heaven), and the band and Parry parted company. "We had cut a deal, a management consultancy almost," adds Chris, "because John wanted me to work and stay close with The Jam. I was to help run their career, but I never took them up on it. I've still got the contract somewhere, and I'd have got a fair percentage of their income. But I saw Paul being moody, and they weren't going to travel very much. So I left Polydor to set up Fiction instead, with The Cure."

The rest of August was taken up with The Jam's first-ever appearances at rock festivals, trips to Belgium and Holland sandwiching another milestone in their career – a headlining slot at Reading Rock '78. Together with a line-up that shunned the festival's traditional heavy rock fare to reflect current trends, The Jam spearheaded the bank holiday weekend by head-lining on the opening day. Weller caught the aggravational mood between skinheads and long-haired music fans, a sign of the times, with his first words: "I don't care how long your hair is, how short it is, if you got boots on, if you got plimsolls on – this is music, this is what you've got to dance to, enjoy yourselves, this is 'In The City'."

⋆　⋆　⋆

October 6, 1978 was a landmark in The Jam's history – it was the release date of their sixth single, 'Down In The Tube Station At Midnight'. The song was a stroke of genius on several levels. Musically, its structure was far more intricate than anything Weller had previously written and a prolonged recording session helped make it their most sophisticated, too. The produc-tion had a biting clarity which separated Bruce's distinctive bass line from Weller's guitar, topped by the deft touches of an intro and outro of ambient train noises and a musical fade-in at the end.

The lyric, which had apparently been dashed off around the idea of a short play (remember Weller's quote), used a first-person narrative to tell a witty, unflinching story of inner city violence. The story dealt with a commuter who is attacked while travelling home on the underground, his vivid impressions of the assailants, and the final twist – when he realises that they have stolen his keys to dish out a similar treatment on his wife. Whereas before, his efforts had occasionally been clumsy, Weller's skill here lay in the minutiae of the song's graphic, three-dimensional images – "creating characters and painting vivid, detailed portraits over jagged chords and some great pop music," as Paolo Hewitt wrote.

The single also returned The Jam to the Top 20, despite some disapproval from Radio 1: DJ Tony Blackburn commented that "I think it's disgusting the way these punks sing about violence all the time. Why can't they sing about beautiful things like trees and flowers?" Weller felt strongly enough to phone the station, and defended the song 'on air' by emphasising its anti-violent message.

If 'Tube Station' is widely regarded as The Jam's most accomplished achievement, then the song also acted as a watershed, sealing their punk-flavoured past and creating a template for the future. On the flip, a poignant, respectful version of The Who's 'So Sad About Us', a staple of their early live set, paid tribute to the passing of drummer Keith Moon, who gazed out from the back sleeve. There were other sly Sixties throwbacks: the line "smiling, beguiling" was borrowed from The Yardbirds' 'Evil Hearted You', while the design of the sleeve lettering mimicked the logo of the Small Faces' record label, Immediate.

Mod references were also scattered across The Jam's third album, which followed in early November – from its title, *All Mod Cons*, to pop-art target labels and an inner sleeve picturing old Sixties ska, Creation and Tamla Motown records and other ephemera, spread out on a Vespa scooter schematic. Both The Who and The Creation had dabbled in pop-art imagery in the mid-Sixties, which fuelled Weller's interest in the genre. Its accessibility also appealed to him, in the same way that he could easily relate to the language and the images of poems of Sixties writers like Adrian Henri. "Pop Artists brought into art everyday images that ordinary people could relate to," Paul enthused. "I was reading somewhere about the pop artists, and their work was very similar to what we're doing. They were taking everyday things like washing machines and turning them into art. That's basically what I'm doing really – taking an everyday situation, like a tube station, an everyday experience, and turning it into art."

Pop Art might roughly be defined as a school of art based on modern popular culture and the mass media, which upended traditional Fine Art values when it came to prominence in the Sixties. That often meant using household images not normally associated with painting – Andy Warhol's Campbell's Soup tins, Roy Lichtenstein's adaptations of screened newspaper cartoon iconography. Pete Townshend's pop-art obsession reached its zenith with *The Who Sell Out*, their third LP; the sleeve depicted members of the band in mock-adverts for products like roll-on deodorant and Heinz baked beans, which matched musical segments between the songs.

The Creation took their pop-art more literally, singing about a *Painter Man*, and describing their music as "red with purple flashes", as well as decorating their stages with in-situ "action painting". Weller may have toyed with pop-art imagery: when The Jam sang about the "new *Art School*", the accompanying video featured "action painting" against a stage backdrop; there was a photo session where the bemused-looking trio posed with a saw, a shovel and a fridge; a pop-art vein ran through many of the band's subsequent sleeves; and there was 1980's experimental *Pop-Art Poem* and that aborted song title, *I Want To Paint*. But Paul never indulged himself to the extent of, say, The Television Personalities, an amateurish post-punk outfit whose use of Sixties images and reference points made them a fully blown, if highly enjoyable, pastiche.

All Mod Cons' packaging may have suggested an assemblage of Weller's pet obsessions, but the music was nothing of the sort, and is rightly regarded not only as The Jam's most consistent collection but also one of rock's most accomplished late Seventies works. Its breadth of songs and the intelligent and intricate manner in which they were structured – their poise – were a great leap forward from the band's 1977 sound. The range of lyrics was stunning. Weller took a leaf from Ray Davies' 'David Watts' technique and invented some characters of his own: the middle-class businessman of 'Mr Clean' (a vehicle for one of his strongest invectives) and the cleverly portrayed, down-trodden dreamer that was 'Billy Hunt' (re-recorded from their aborted single).

Parry retained a co-production credit for two of the album's earliest recorded songs. The first, 'To Be Someone (Didn't We Have A Nice Time)', was one of its masterpieces, with its vivid lyrics concerning a faded rock star which, like the title track, dealt with the trappings of fame and Weller's disdain for what he perceived as the fickle, transient nature of the music business. The second was the charming 'It's Too Bad' (which hinted at The Beatles' 'She Loves You' melody), one of three love songs, alongside the soaring ode, 'Fly', and the sentimentality of the acoustic 'English Rose', which was possibly slipped on at the last moment, since it wasn't listed on either the inner or outer sleeve. Or maybe he borrowed the idea from The Beatles' 'Her Majesty', the unlisted track on *Abbey Road*. What did appear on *All Mod Cons* was a "Thanks to . . . the Southend Kids for conversation", but the idea of using snippets of dialogue was dropped at the last moment. "Paul wanted me to take the credit off," says Dennis Munday, "but by that time, the sleeves had been printed."

Other tracks, notably 'The Place I Love' and the superb 'In The Crowd', suggested a more mature, introspective side to Weller's songwriting. Lyrically, the latter continued the theme of 'Away From The Numbers' and 'The Combine', Weller seemingly in an existentialist mood about his sense of identity and the numbing sensation of a throng of people – "the vacant heart of crowd culture", as Simon Frith called it in *Creem* magazine. Towards the end of the track, the music slowly blurred with distortion and backwards guitar, echoing The Beatles' psychedelia of *Revolver*, as a snippet from 'Away From The Numbers' drifted into earshot.

All Mod Cons was an important climb up rock's ladder for The Jam, whose prolific output since punk – three albums in a year-and-a-half – was matched only among their contemporaries by The Stranglers. The Sex Pistols and The Damned had already split up. Siouxsie & The Banshees and Manchester's Buzzcocks were still rising stars and The Clash had, after a long sabbatical, bounced back with the commercially successful but critically reviled *Give 'Em Enough Rope* LP, but the end-of-year-polls in the weekly music press showed The Jam were among the leading contenders. In *NME*, *All Mod Cons* was voted No. 1 'best album', Weller came second to Elvis Costello as 'best songwriter', and in the 'best band' category, The Jam were runners up to The Clash. Not only did *All Mod Cons* outsell The Jam's previous LPs – it peaked at No. 6 – but it also earned them the respect of the rock press, who finally forgot those Who comparisons. Only *Melody Maker* expressed doubts, commenting with spooky foresight that Weller might "catch up with the rest of us in 1990. Can you wait?"!

If the album showcased Paul's most lucid batch of songs, then he was less communicative in interviews, though he did admit to his increasing disenchantment with happy-go-lucky, laddish bands like Sham 69, who he dismissed as pretending to be teenagers. One journalist asked if this was a concept LP. "You could just take a character like 'Billy Hunt' and centre it around him," Weller replied. "The trouble is that there have been so many things like *Quadrophenia* and Sham 69's *That's Life* that I let it hang loose rather than connect it."

All Mod Cons was the first Jam album that Weller was genuinely proud of – it's no coincidence that posthumous compilations have avoided earlier material – and the twenty-year-old vowed never to lose sight of The Jam's direction again. The LP was given the usual promotional live support: *The Apocalypse Tour* played throughout November, with a set that finished dramatically with a 'thunder flash' effect to close ''A' Bomb In Wardour Street'. The dates culminated in a prestigious performance on the first of a three-day Great British Music Festival at Wembley Arena on a diverse bill. Brian Young of Belfast punk band Rudi was in the audience:

"None of us were Jam fans and I wasn't expecting much because The Pirates, Generation X and Slade had played and were dreadful, but The Jam were great. There was trouble between Slade skinheads and Mods outside. There was nobody there, that was the funny thing, but someone got stabbed. Generation X had Marshall amplifiers and real rock star poses and they died. And Weller had

99

an AC30 sitting on a chair but because of the tension, they were really aggressive. They really impressed me." The Jam's camp applied considerable pressure to win a headline slot – a profile-raising exercise aimed at attracting mainstream rock fans. The ploy worked, convincing punters and promoters alike that The Jam were now capable of filling large-capacity arenas.

Their next step was to embark on their first European tour in February 1979. The band were accompanied for part of their leisurely jaunt around Germany, France and Belgium – nine shows in seventeen days – by *Sniffin' Glue*-turned-*NME* journalist Danny Baker, who prepared a typically light-hearted feature based around the experience. One of the dates was at that legendary Hamburg haunt immortalised by The Beatles.

"I was with Paul Weller at the Star Club the night he broke up The Jam," claims Danny today, with a wry smile. "They'd played to the smallest audience I'd ever seen at a rock concert. Rick and Bruce thought it was hilarious. We went round and counted twelve people there. Later, in the hotel, Paul was pissed off. I'd known him a long time, from *Sniffin' Glue*, so I sat down with him and said, what's up? He was drunk: 'It's all over. Punk's fuckin' had it, we know that, but if I carry on, it's a sham!'

"This is good copy, I thought, so I got out a tape player, and Paul talked about what had gone wrong. He asked as many questions of me as I did of him, telling me why The Jam had to split up. But the punch-line of the story, and why I remember it so well, is that when I got the tape home and put it on, all I had was 'tall and tanned and young and lovely' – I'd had a directional mic and there was muzak playing in the bar. So I made up what I remembered of what he'd said for a piece in the *NME*. I saw him about three weeks later. 'You bastard!' he said, 'you made all that up,' but we laughed about it."

The Jam returned to Britain in early March, just in time for the release of their next single, 'Strange Town'. On top of a stomping Northern Soul beat and a clipped rhythm guitar style heard on old Motown records, Weller returned to a familiar theme. The 'Strange Town' in question represented his continued fascination with London, with its references to A-Z Guide Books and Oxford Street and the city's impersonal, impenetrable nature, but its description of a visitor's sense of alienation and anonymity – "I'm really a spaceman from those UFOs" – may also have reflected Weller's experiences of being away from home while touring, especially his dislike of America. " 'Strange Town' is quite a vague idea," Paul remarked, when I interviewed him in 1992, "because one verse is about something and the chorus is about something else."

'The Butterfly Collector' on the flip confirmed that The Jam were in their prime. Based loosely on the The Kinks' 'Shangri-La', the song had a subtle, low-key atmosphere, particularly so on the verses. This only emphasised its vicious lyrical snipe at the rock groupie, inspired by a liaison with Sex Pistols cohort, Sue Catwoman. "It's about a girl I used to know during the punk days," Paul admitted, "who used to like to have a piece of everyone. I exaggerated a lot of the song – you have to exaggerate the truth, otherwise people don't get to see it. And I guess the title comes from the John Fowles book, *The Collector*." Both songs were linked by one of Paul's poems that was reproduced on the rear sleeve; Weller's interest in prose soon manifested itself as the first of several extra-musical ventures, a book publishing company.

Polydor were still keen that The Jam crack the States, so another venture was organised in April to promote the delayed continental release of *All Mod Cons*. Despite some prestigious slots, such as headlining at the New York Palladium, The Jam were again greeted with abject indifference by audiences and the media alike. Weller's bolshie attitude, both on-stage and off, alienated journalists, and while The Police and The Clash, for example, made serious inroads into the American heartland that year, The Jam made little impression. The whole, miserable affair cost thousands of pounds – Bruce even phoned home and threatened to leave on one occasion – and the band shied away from repeating the experience for some time.

It must have been some relief when the band returned to learn that tickets for their next UK tour had completely sold out. Originally to be titled *Jam 'Em In* but finally promoted under the banner, *Jam Pact Spring Tour '79*, the month-long jaunt throughout May reflected the group's growing popularity in Britain. "The Jam's concerts at the Rainbow are a pair of rousing successes," recorded *Punk Diary*. "They play their two nights to a sold-out house of parkas, rude boys and a scattering of punks. The encore ends with three covers – 'David Watts', 'Heatwave' and 'Batman'."

By now, The Jam had attracted an army of fans, who followed them around the country – and who built up something of a bond with their idols. "I remember one occasion at Townhouse Studios," says producer Vic Coppersmith-Heaven, "when I had this strange feeling of a presence behind me. I stopped the tape, turned round and there were about forty fans sitting in absolute silence, whom Paul had sneaked in to watch the proceedings." The most celebrated of these devotees was "Southend mod" Grant Fleming and it was a reflection of the Jam camp's wish to forge a close contact with their fanbase that he was chosen to write the programme notes for this tour. Later, he even supported them with his own band, Kidz Next Door.

Fleming was also cited as a key player in a London-based Mod Revival, which hit the headlines of the music papers, and eventually the national press, that summer. As early as March 1978, *Record Mirror* had reported on the band's Southend and Stratford entourage: "The Jam's fans are in the process of reorganising their transport and, in the true spirit of Mods, are planning to get scooters complete with all the wing mirrors . . . They're all as much into the complete Sixties fashion as they are into the band. The Jam fans are so keen to keep to the Mod style, they buy their suits from jumble sales, the originals from the period." By early 1979, expanding Mod strongholds in

Essex and North and South London melded into a scene which gravitated towards pubs like the Wellington in Waterloo.

That The Jam would be heralded as the scene's figureheads was an inescapable fact. To the Class Of '79, Weller personified cool, and the band's sound provided a template for the best of a new crop of bands, notably Romford's Purple Hearts and Catford's The Chords. Both won tacit approval from Weller, both signed to Polydor (Chris Parry's imprint, Fiction, in the Purple Hearts' case) and both secured support slots with The Jam – The Chords played at the band's Rainbow concert on May 11 after Paul had been impressed by their performance at the Wellington a couple of weeks earlier. Meanwhile, Arista even created a 'Mod' label, I-Spy, to sign two of the most talented 'revival' acts, Secret Affair, fronted by the outspoken Ian Page, and The Jam's old Woking friends, Squire. Both had also played on Jam bills: Squire at the Guildford Civic Hall in 1978 and Secret Affair in an earlier incarnation as power pop act the New Hearts on *The Modern World* tour.

Then there were the Merton Parkas (named after the classic Mod garment, and their South London home of Merton Park), who'd evolved out of an R&B act, The Sneakers, in much the same way as The Jam had progressed from their days covering Chuck Berry and Dr. Feelgood songs. On June 19, 1979, Rick Buckler sat in for their drummer, Simon Smith, at Ronnie Scott's for a set which included 'In The Midnight Hour'. The band, who centred around two brothers, singer/guitarist Danny Talbot and Mick on organ, had signed to Beggars Banquet and spent the summer recording their début album.

"Danny met up with Paul Weller and got a bit pally, and that's how Paul got to know Mick," remembers Simon Smith. "We'd just done some recording, which wasn't up to scratch. We wanted more of a live sound and hoped Paul was going to produce our *Face In The Crowd* album. Danny asked Weller and I think he gave it consideration, but their schedule didn't allow enough time. Also, the photographer Andrew Douglas was working with The Jam, and did the sleeve photos for *Face In The Crowd* on Brighton beach, so he helped link us together."

Despite his connections with the Mod Revival's major players, Weller distanced himself from the movement. Maybe he was wary of his "youth spokesman" tag, foisted on him by a music press eager to extract some meaning from punk's fallout. Paul also knew the pitfalls of being aligned with a particular scene – punk – and the resultant backlash, and having just shedded their Who comparisons, he wasn't about to commit commercial and critical suicide by reinstating them. This is quite apart from the fact that most of the Mod Revival bands were musically second-rate. Weller made his position clear in the Dutch magazine *Musical Express* in mid-1980. "*All Mod Cons* was a definite breakthrough in England and a lot of Mods started to come to our concerts," he explained. "I don't consider myself as any leader. I'm not really interested in the whole revival thing. It's a bit pathetic.

Have a look in the English music papers – there are ads telling you how to dress as a Mod and look like a Punk. Skins aren't supposed to like the same music as Mods but we make records for everyone. The music of the so-called 'Mod' bands is often a load of shit, middle of the road pop songs without balls. The Chords and The Purple Hearts are quite good but Secret Affair are shit."

A year later, his caution hadn't dissipated. "Despite what's been claimed, that New Mod thing was nothing to do with us," Weller commented in US magazine *Creem*. "It really came out of a few pubs down the East End of London . . . I thought [it] was alright. It gave a bit of new blood to the music. People said it was all very contrived, but I don't think it was from the kids' point of view – it's not their fault all those poxy shops filled with crappy clothes started up."

Those "poxy shops" also created a whole wardrobe based around and endorsed by the band, which must have profited them financially, in addition to a flourishing trade in straightforward Jam merchandise – which contradicts Paul's comments. Those Carnaby Street shops from which they had bought their clothes soon marketed a whole range of Jam-related products, creating new designs which the band then wore on stage. There was a roaring trade in so-called Jam shoes – the 'Gibson', the 'buckle casual', the bowling shoe and the dire 'stage shoe', a style travesty which was striped like a pair of old trainers – and many of their suits and other outfits came from the street's retail outlets like Merc, Melanddi's and Shellys Shoes. But as a rule, Weller distanced the band from the Mod Revival, which eventually petered away – at least publicly – while The Jam grew ever more popular.

★ ★ ★

While parka sales rocketed, the band began a five-month touring hiatus, punctuated only by a couple of one-off dates in June 1979: an incongruous performance in a massive marquee headlining the final night of Lancashire's week-long Saddleworth Arts Festival and, at the other end of the spectrum, a lunchtime publicity event at the opening of old friend Steve Brookes' music shop, Abacorn Music, in Brookwood just outside Woking.

On August 17, The Jam had their third consecutive Top 20 hit with 'When You're Young', a punchy dose of social realism à la 'My Generation', which mixed Weller's continued obsession with the spirit of youth with a growing cynicism and disillusionment of life's unfolding realities. It was crystallised by the line, "The world is your oyster, but your future's your clam", a poignant lyric from the first Jam single to be released after the Conservatives' election victory in May. Musically, 'When You're Young' was classic, stock-in-trade Jam, a spiky sound which bordered on the anthemic, radio-friendly but jagged enough to separate it from slicker new wave offspring like The Police and The Pretenders. The B-side, 'Smithers-Jones', was the strongest Jam song Foxton ever wrote – but also his last, aside from a forgettable instrumental on their last LP – with a melody which echoed The Who's 'I Can't Reach You'. The finishing refrain, written by Weller – "Put on the kettle and make some tea" – closely resembled a line from The Kinks' 'Shangri-La', another reference to the song from their 1969 LP, *Arthur*.

The single gave the band some breathing space to finish off their next album at Townhouse Studios. This time, the pattern was different. Instead of preparing the songs as demos, or being given the chance to refine them on the road, Paul wrote many of the tunes in the studio, knocking them off from the seed of an idea or a lyric one night and presenting complete songs to the band the next day – a challenge which Weller apparently relished, as the band got into the routine of demoing, rehearsing and recording. The work-in-progress of four songs, heard on the Jam retrospective, *Extras*, revealed how they had been written in a very complete form.

"What's interesting about them is that the arrangements on those early demos – just me on guitar – are almost exactly the same as they ended up on record," Paul told me in 1992. "When we first kicked off, we would always demo the stuff together. And then, as I got more confident as a writer, I took myself more seriously and had more set ideas about what the bass should do – or drums. And this isn't taking away from Rick or Bruce – they'd stamp their own identity on it. But I wanted the time to work out the ideas on my own before presenting them to other people."

On one occasion, searching for inspiration, Weller stumbled across an interview with The Creation's Eddie Phillips in a 1966 edition of *Record Mirror*, in which he mentioned two of their new songs. One of them, 'Private Hell', gave Paul the title of a song that he then wrote on the spot, a bleak tale of a woman's mid-life crisis that began with the words of the other Creation title, 'Closer Than Close' – a "horror story about the mundane: the death of communication, life without meaning; the hidden dangers of fulfilled expectations", as Chris Burciago wrote in *Trouser Press*. Despite the enforced hurry, the sessions dragged, due in part to Vic Coppersmith-Heaven's laid-back attitude, and the band's increasing sophistication in their use of overdubs and other studio facilities.

Weller took time out to tell *NME*'s Nick Kent in September that their forthcoming album was "about three close mates, who get split up when the civil war occurs: one joins the left, one veers off to the right while the third one doesn't feel any particular affiliation whatsoever. He's the abstainer. After the war's conclusion, three splintered comrades plan to meet up again." A Jam concept album set in the future Britain of the Eighties, it promised to be their most ambitious move yet.

6

ABOVE THE CLOUDS

"Tuesday night I reorganize my record collection; I often do this at periods of emotional stress . . . I pull the records off the shelves, put them in piles all over the sitting room floor, look for *Revolver*, and go on from there, and when I'm finished I'm flushed with a sense of self, because this, after all, is who I am."

(*High Fidelity*, Nick Hornby, 1995)

"Pop music, along with radio, TV and cinema is your art! All created especially for you. Great eh? Pop(ular) music is viewed by the select classes as –
a)   cheap and vulgar
b)   mindless entertainment for the mindless working classes, but
c)   very profitable."

(Paul Weller, *Jamming!*, 1981)

"The key single was 'The Eton Rifles'. To me, that was patently going to be a hit," says The Jam's product manager, Dennis Munday. He may have worked for Polydor but Dennis was disillusioned with the company's complacency. " 'When You're Young' didn't really happen – No. 17 for a band that had been around for that long. They were getting so far and couldn't get any further. I was getting pissed off with Polydor's general attitude towards The Jam, that we're only going to sell X amount of records so that's it. We'd had problems with Polydor's promotion department. They didn't get on with the guys. They were a generation apart – one of the guys, Tony Bramwell, had worked with The Beatles. So John Weller phoned me up and said, we want it changed.

"I'd worked with Clive Banks, one of the best independent pluggers. I played 'The Eton Rifles' to Polydor and got the stock response. They said that Radio One won't play it because of the political content and the line that says, 'went to bed with a charming young thing'. I played it to Banks who said, 'It's going to be hard work but we'll get it on the B-list and work through it.' At least that's positive, I thought. There was a meeting with Polydor's MD, A.J. Morris, where I sacked the promotion department and brought in Banks. And the single took off, The Jam's biggest hit to date. It broke through that barrier and launched them. 'The Eton Rifles' was a decisive point."

Introduced by a barrage of dissonant guitar and a thundering bassline, 'The Eton Rifles' reached No. 3 in the charts in early November 1979. Paul explained the song's inspiration to *The Story So Far* magazine: "I saw this TV programme and thought it was a good title. But the actual song is just a piss-take of the class system. I mean, I'm a very class conscious person. I realise it's a joke and it shouldn't really exist in the 1980s but it still does . . . It's also obviously a piss-take of these trendy socialists and fascists as well." Parodying part-time political activists, the song's message was later underlined by the behaviour of some Eton schoolboys, who taunted demonstrators on one of the numerous 'Right To Work' marches against rising unemployment.

The B-side to 'The Eton Rifles' was the sprightly 'See Saw', which Paul had originally given to Glasgow band and fellow Polydor act The Jolt. Signed by Chris Parry in 1977, The Jolt were actively encouraged to follow in The Jam's wake and supported them in Scotland that year. Taking note of Weller's Mod leanings, they donned suits and covered the Small Faces' 'Whatcha Gonna Do About It', before recording a version of 'See Saw' for their 'Maybe Tonight' EP, issued in early 1979. It was the first example of Paul helping out a new band, a philanthropic act that would be echoed over the next few years in various extra-curricular projects – and make a few quid out of the publishing royalties to boot.

Just as *All Mod Cons* had revived The Jam's fortunes a year earlier, 'The Eton Rifles' was a crucial turning point in their career as a singles band. While The Jam's star was definitely in the ascendant, their punk contemporaries had either waned or else changed their musical style – or both. Sham 69, Polydor's other major 'New Wave' act, for instance, reached No. 6 in August 1979 with 'Hersham Boys', but they faded from view within six months. The Stranglers' 'Duchess' was also a hit that August, but they would take two years to better its success. Buzzcocks had their last Top 40 hit, 'Harmony In My Head', in July, while newcomers The Ruts never repeated the Top 10 success of June's 'Babylon's Burning', and The Skids' last Top 20 hit was 'Working For The Yankee Dollar' in November. Bands can't be defined by chart positions, of course, but the times were changing and the new wave was getting rusty. Acts like The Clash, Siouxsie & The Banshees, Stiff Little Fingers and a new-look Damned were still successful. But as a Top 10 singles act, The Jam's only real competitors – and musically, the two were a world away from Weller & Co. – were The Police, who topped the charts that September with 'Message In A Bottle', and Elvis Costello & The Attractions, whose Motown-styled 'I Can't Stand Up For Falling Down' made No. 4 in February '80.

Setting Sons finally arrived in November. The idea of a concept album was a logical step for Weller, bearing in mind that those musicians whom he most admired – Ray Davies, Pete Townshend, Marriott/Lane, Lennon/ McCartney – had all had similar ambitions around the same juncture in their respective careers. Inspired by a Dave Waller poem-cum-short story, the LP told the tale of three characters based loosely on real people – a businessman, a revolutionary and someone with Weller's left-of-centre political views – who survive a modern-day English civil war. Its observations of the nation's past, present and future owed much to George Orwell's faintly patriotic vision, portrayed in his essays. "I like his version of socialism," Paul later told *Smash Hits*, "and I also think he had a lot of just basic common sense. Or he realised that the working class had that common sense and that's what he was striving for. And also the quote: 'If liberty means anything at all, it means the right to tell people what they don't want to hear'."

As it transpired, Weller's grand conceptual scheme for the album dissipated as much through lack of time as through any creative timidity, and only a few of the songs stuck with the theme so graphically illustrated on the front. Gazing out from the cover was the image of a striking bronze sculpture by Benjamin Clemens, *The St. John's Ambulance Bearers*, which stands in the Imperial War Museum and which painted the perfect picture of the solemn and sometimes bleak imagery of Weller's songs inside. The ironic use of British iconography – a British bulldog and a Union Jack deckchair on Brighton beach – on the inner sleeve was a bold move which invited misinterpretation, bearing in mind the previous furore surrounding Weller's past comments about voting Tory.

The songs provided a snapshot of the *Setting Sons* characters at various stages in their lives, beginning with the youngsters of 'Thick As Thieves' (one of the few songs written prior to the sessions). Next came the adult world of the businessman of 'Burning Sky', whose sentiments are presented in the form of a letter; the ambitious, dramatic anti-war epic, 'Little Boy Soldiers' (featuring Bruce Foxton on cello); and the 'Citizen Smith'-styled caricature of 'The Eton Rifles'. "But it was incomplete," Paul admitted when we spoke in 1992. "There were a few tracks that fitted into this idea, but I never got round to finishing it. Other stuff like 'Girl On The Phone' and 'Private Hell' – they're just songs that needed to be written."

It would be foolish to read too much into *Setting Sons*' theme, but there's a nagging coincidence between the idea of three friends growing apart and the increasingly separate lives of Paul, Bruce and Rick – each had his own individual circle of friends and they tended not to socialise together away from the band. "Quite nostalgic," is how Paul summarised the album, "kind of looking back". Whatever the case, *Setting Sons* succeeded not via any grand notions or concepts, but because of Paul's developing strengths as a songwriter. One of its highlights was 'Wasteland', a wistful, summery love song decorated with a gentle recorder melody that was once described as "The Jam's consummate English pop track". 'Girl On The Phone' hinted at

Weller's discomfort with his increasing fame ("She says she knows everything about me"), while taking a sideways swipe at the press. "It's like, when anyone tries to sum you up," Paul explained to me, "they think they know what you're about, and they know bits and pieces – but no-one knows what you're about because I don't know myself."

'Saturday's Kids' was a clever picture of suburban teenage life littered with incisive references which anyone might relate to, expanded from a poem which had originally joined several of Paul's literary efforts in the back of an *All Mod Cons* songbook. "It's a documentation of that lifestyle," Weller later commented. "It was actually written about my schoolfriends – all the people who still go down my local pub." With a studio deadline approaching, it was Rick's idea to re-record Foxton's 'Smithers-Jones' with the 'Jam Philharmonic' orchestra. And the dearth of new songs was emphasised by the album's finale, a hurried rendition of their old Motown favourite, Martha & The Vandellas' 'Heatwave', with the Merton Parkas' Mick Talbot guesting on piano – a wasted opportunity given the thought which had gone into the rest of the album.

What bound the material together more than any specific theme were the threads of cynicism and irony that ran through the lyrics. It's as if, despite his fame and influence, Paul felt he was still ultimately powerless to change what he saw as an "overwhelming wall of establishment". "Unflinchingly portraying lives and emotions set within a typically British context," wrote one reviewer, "*Setting Sons* offers no solutions, paints unbelievably bleak scenarios fuelled by Weller's despair at the fragility of relationships, the futility of protest, the harrowing lives people are forced to live." *Setting Sons* was the archetypal Jam record – dynamic, urgent, snappy and energetic – which may be one reason why Weller spent the rest of the group's life-span trying to escape from it. "I thought *Setting Sons* was a bit too slick, a bit too polished," he confessed in *Creem* magazine in 1981. "I don't think it's a really true sound." Maybe this reflected Weller's continued search for a social truth.

In early November, The Jam played two secret gigs at The Marquee and The Nashville under the guise of John's Boys and The Eton Rifles (and some adverts used the pseudonym, La Confiture), their traditional warm-up dates prior to a major tour. The support act for their next, month-long string of dates was Guildford's The Vapors, who had been spotted in a local pub by Bruce, who then agreed to co-manage them with John Weller. This ultimately reflected badly on The Vapors, who were dismissed as Jam copyists after charting with the novelty new wave hit, 'Turning Japanese'. As *Setting Sons* remained in the Top 5, most of the concerts sold out – and The Jam's popularity was confirmed when they swept the boards of the *NME* readers' poll a few weeks later. The groundswell of the Mod Revival was making its presence felt. "When I first saw The Jam in May '79," remembers journalist Pat Gilbert, "they had a punk/new wave audience. By the end of the year, you couldn't move for parkas!"

The band also made some headway during their next visit to America, undertaken in late February 1980, after a quartet of secret warm-up gigs in England. The pinnacle of their US trip was a sell-out performance at the 3,000-capacity New York Palladium, a show which *Rolling Stone* reviewed as "a Who-ish volley of impulsive rhythm and staccato bursts, all topped by Weller's angry young man howl". They may have tasted success on this grass roots level but instead of building on The Jam's enthusiastic, committed cult following Stateside, US Polydor clashed with the band by issuing the unsuitable 'Heatwave' as a single at a time when the American charts were full of AOR rock and cod-new wave.

The tour wound its way from the East Coast to the West, before the band ended up one evening at Hollywood's Sunset Marquee hotel in LA. The post-gig party was characterised by the usual, alcohol-induced high jinks, with tales of personnel being thrown into the pool in the early hours and damage to rooms caused by the crew's inebriation. In fact, the band had been socialising and drinking more on tour, especially Bruce, and the stories linked to their alcoholic excesses are legion. But they had reason to celebrate that night. John Weller received a call from England earlier that evening and passed on the good news: at home, The Jam's new single had just entered the charts at No. 1. It was official: they were now the most popular band in Britain.

That single, 'Going Underground', was the culmination of everything Paul Weller had strived for since their days fumbling around on stage at the Woking Working Men's Club. Its anthemic chorus was guaranteed to win favour from the band's increasingly loyal fanbase, with a simple, witty and effective lyric which made reference to the atomic bomb, an all-too-real threat in the light of the invasion of Afghanistan by Russia in December '79, but the song's lyrics also suggested a nihilistic rejection of society. Polydor at last devised a useful marketing incentive, in the shape of a double-pack single which added three live tracks. With 200,000 advance orders, the single was guaranteed to enter the charts at No. 1, the first time this had happened since Slade's 'Merry Xmas Everybody' in 1973. "Near to tears when 'Going Underground' goes to the top!," was how Paul later expressed his reaction on the sleeve of *Dig The New Breed*.

The release had been planned as a double-A-side, coupled with the more experimental 'Dreams Of Children', which mined the same fluid, faintly psychedelic seam and mirrored the oblique lyrics of earlier songs like 'In The Crowd'. The intro was taken from an earlier song, 'Thick As Thieves'. "When we finished off *Setting Sons*," Paul explained, "I got the engineer to play the whole album backwards and there was just one little piece of music, of backward vocal, that I liked. 'Dreams Of Children' was built around that, more-or-less made up on the spot." The technique reflected Paul's growing love of British psychedelia, especially '66-era Beatles and early Pink Floyd ("I'll tell you a guitarist I really do like, and that's Syd Barrett," Paul told *Trouser Press* in 1981).

Cutting their American visit short, the band flew back to perform on *Top Of The Pops*, on which Paul wore an apron – pop-art fashion – much to the bemusement of the viewers. There were also two victorious Easter dates at the Rainbow in front of an ecstatic audience as part of the venue's fiftieth anniversary celebrations. The second night was especially memorable for a poignant, enthusiastic cover of the Four Tops' 1966 Motown classic, 'Reach Out I'll Be There'. As with the December Rainbow concerts, Mick Talbot augmented the line-up on Hammond organ. Even though, as Merton Parkas drummer Simon Smith remembers, "he was discreetly hidden at the back, so they had this predominant organ sound but you couldn't actually see anyone," Weller had patently struck up a friendship with the pianist after the *Setting Sons* sessions, which would later blossom into something more substantial.

The euphoria that surrounded 'Going Underground' led to an unprecedented demand for The Jam's old singles, which were duly reissued – six even re-charted. This meant that by the end of the year, The Jam had placed more singles in the U.K. Top 50 than any band since The Beatles, whose record they now equalled. It was a vindication of Weller's vision and his desperate urge to be 'the best'. But the atmosphere created by this enormous success placed a huge burden on Paul to deliver the goods a second time. Taking stock, The Jam avoided the temptation to follow their No. 1 with a tour. Instead, they worked on their next album throughout the summer of 1980 at Virgin's Townhouse Studios in Shepherds Bush, West London. An interview in June mentioned that nine numbers were finished, with a target of fourteen, Weller commenting to *Making Time* fanzine that "I want to get some really good dance rhythms and experiment . . . I'm trying to get a more live sound."

★ ★ ★

The Jam had now developed into more than just a band. A whole apparatus had grown up around them, as Jimmy Telford – who later played keyboards with the band – remembers. "Kenny Wheeler was a big fat roadie who used to tour with The Kinks and Led Zeppelin in the Seventies," says Jimmy. "Hard bastard. He's a Londoner; him and John got on well. Dave Liddle was the ex-hippie guitarist, a bit of a casualty but still all there. He was nice enough. He ran around tuning the guitars. There was an insularity, a common bond, because they were all from around London. Kenny thought he was a fourth member of The Jam – he handled security and also acted as Paul's personal minder. They used to call the audience 'Muppets' because of the way they waved their arms about like Kermit!"

These were people recruited by John Weller, who effectively ran the whole show – and despite the disintegration of The Jam and even The Style Council, this set-up hasn't changed significantly to this day. The family atmosphere surrounding The Jam was quite literal. In addition to Paul's ever-present parents (and, unlike most managers, John went to every gig), younger sister Nikki ran the band's fan club from the Weller's Balmoral Drive address. For a while, she even dated Pete Carver, who not only helped Gill Price sell the merchandise on tour, but acted as a chauffeur for the band for several years.

Paul's apparent level-headedness about The Jam's runaway success is easy enough to understand: he had always derided the hollow, transient lifestyle associated with being a pop star. And his day-to-day working environment, with his parents close to hand, hadn't really changed, which must have helped him keep his feet on the ground. But what was quite amazing was his continued commitment not only to The Jam – "from now until September, almost every day is mapped out touring and recording," he admitted that spring – but also to a series of outside projects. He didn't put his foot on the break, he changed up a gear. If Weller's temperament was one of ever-changing moods, then he ploughed this emotional energy into new ventures and ideas.

The first was a publishing company, inspired and conceived by Paul's old friend Dave Waller. The decision was the logical progression both of Weller's continuing love of poetry and the desire to expand on the publication of Dave's poems, tucked away in that Jam songbook in '77. "Maybe a book will follow," Weller had written then. In an interview in *Zig Zag* a year later, Paul had mooted the idea again, stressing that he felt a responsibility to use his earnings creatively.

Riot Stories Ltd was inaugurated on January 25, 1980, with Paul and Dave listed as co-directors. Waller was also the author of Riot Stories' first book, a primitively produced A5 collection entitled *Notes From Hostile Street*, with a poem on each of its thirty-six pages, which was followed by an A5 "mixed bag of poems by a variety of writers" entitled *Mixed Up Shook Up* (1980). Paul assembled and designed another publication, *In The Car*, based around the idea of a pop-art magazine which mixed writing with hand-drawn sketches, which was followed in 1981 by a fanzine, *December Child*, again including Paul's poems. One of them, *Ten Times Something Empty*, was written in 1979 in the form of a numbered list – No. 5 read, "like a tired suburban station, in early morning/Your face at the window of a passing train/Bound for Waterloo". Another was *In The Land That Lies Between Us*, an unfocused but emotive piece of prose which attacked imperialism and the attitudes which breed war: "How great, the way the mighty beast extends/The Hand of friendship (careful to wipe it afterwards)." Weller also contributed a poem to a pilot issue of *Pacemaker* fanzine in 1981.

These efforts weren't the embarrassing indulgences that might have been expected of a rock star with artistic pretensions – far from it, in fact. Worse poems appear on a regular basis in such hallowed publications as the *Times Literary Supplement*. Paul's interest in the medium eventually led to him participating in the so-called Poetry Olympics at the Young Vic in London's

Waterloo on November 30, 1981, sharing a bill with celebrated Liverpool poet, Roger McGough – one of his first solo outings outside The Jam. This was also the first time Paul had been exposed to the new strand of post-punk poets.

Meanwhile, Dave's job was to sift through piles of poems sent in by young hopefuls, which led to a publication of a collection of verse by Aidan Cant and, in autumn 1981, *Jambo* by David Ward, "a small illustrated book of poems which link together into a running commentary of his lifestyle". But Riot Stories relied principally on mail order (especially through The Jam's fan club) until the publication in 1982 of Terry Rawlings' slim Small Faces biography, *All Our Yesterdays*, which reached a wider audience. In November 1982, Paul wrote to Peter Doggett of *Record Collector* magazine: "The only other things planned for Riot Stories Ltd are a book on the Jam and a book about stylists. Though not the rock'n'roll ones, that is the stylists who always hated/ignored/weren't interested in R&R, y'know. The Stylists cults like the Mods, Skinheads (original 69 versions not these horrible little present day fascists), Suedeheads and up to today's 'Soul Boys'."

Sadly, that project was stillborn, and Riot Stories' activities dissipated after Dave Waller died from a heroin overdose in Woking's Wheatsheaf Hotel in August 1982 – above the very pub in which the friends used to socialise. The tragedy had a profound effect on Paul: he had already turned his back on the excessive drinking which characterised The Jam's life on the road and this only strengthened his resolve to shun the physical excesses commonplace in the music business. "Dave had this romantic revolutionary idea in his head all the time about how the world should be," says Rick Buckler – and that influence can clearly be heard within the political strain of Weller's lyrics. Paul had always admired Waller's rebellious streak and his genuine writing skills, and as a tribute, the musician later wrote 'Man Of Great Promise' – a song which he occasionally performed again in the mid-Nineties.

As for Riot Stories, the imprint was later exhumed for two biographies relating to Weller, 1983's *Beat Concerto* (The Jam) and 1985's *Internationalists* (The Style Council). Sandwiched in between these glossy paperbacks was another black-and-white effort, *Spongers*. Compiled by Dave Potter with drawings by Gill Thompson, this A5 collection of poems written by unemployed young people "isn't a book of dole queue whines," as the back cover explained. "It isn't a book by lazy sods who don't work." And *Spongers* didn't contain very good poetry, either, compared with Riot Stories' earlier publications. Like some of Paul's other endeavours aside from his own career, Riot Stories acted as a channel to direct Weller's energies and ideas while never really fulfilling its potential.

★ ★ ★

Sessions for The Jam's next album were interspersed with the odd live performance scattered across the globe. They appeared on Spanish TV and at a Dutch festival in May 1980, followed by three impromptu British dates in June, culminating in a depressing experience at Loch Lomond Festival in Scotland that was marred by mud, rain and violence. July witnessed the band's first clutch of dates in Japan where the group were instantly accepted by a country which seems to have worshipped Paul Weller ever since – his popularity there has at various times exceeded that at home. After a fleeting visit to LA, the band played a couple of dates in August to road-test some new material. Both gigs were characterised by incident: the first, at Aylesbury Friars, invited more Townshend comparisons when Paul broke the neck of his guitar against an amp, and after the second, at the Turku Rock Festival in Finland, The Jam's entourage made a speedy getaway as the event dissolved into a riot, and the equipment and stage were thrown into a nearby river.

While The Jam were in Japan, a row ensued over the choice of their next single. Paul wanted 'Start!' but Polydor preferred another new song, 'Pretty Green' – and Dennis Munday was caught in the middle. " 'Going Underground' was ten out of ten – a hard act to follow," says Dennis. " 'Pretty Green' played safe. It would have been a typical Jam single whereas 'Start!' wasn't – and that, to me, would expose them to a much wider audience. There was a heated debate and it was left to the last-possible moment to decide: two sleeves waited at the printers. I always admired that about Paul – he never played safe."

Polydor were right to relent, and in August, Weller's intuition led to The Jam's second consecutive No. 1. 'Start!' had originally been titled 'Two Minutes' (from the line, "If we get through for two minutes only/It will be a start!"), and dealt with the importance of human contact – of connecting socially – and whether that could be achieved through a pop record. Critics focused instead on 'Start!'s musical debt to 'Taxman' from The Beatles' *Revolver* album, which had been on permanent rotation on The Jam's tour bus during their last American visit. Its stripped-to-the-bone production, the bass riff and the harsh, trebly guitar (especially the whining, backwards-sounding solo), were patently lifted from George Harrison's proto-psychedelic album opener. Weller was defensive about the accusations of plagiarism: "Apart from the first notes, the rest of the bass line is quite different," he countered, and has since added that listeners weren't meant *not* to notice the resemblance between the songs.

'Start!'s bass pattern also underpinned the B-side, 'Liza Radley', Weller's 'Eleanor Rigby'-meets-Syd Barrett, with the help of Foxton's accordion playing. It was one of Paul's last 'character' songs. "A piece of nonsense, really," was how he later described this haunting acoustic ballad, "just me playing around being quasi-psychedelic, English whimsy. Just images, words plucked out of nowhere."

Sound Affects, The Jam's fifth LP, followed in late November – but not before more arguments with Polydor. Dennis Munday explains: "There was a big problem. The Jam had booked a tour and Paul didn't want to finish the album until the new year because he didn't feel he had enough songs. Polydor weren't having a great financial year and weren't happy to lose it. The shit hit the fan and I got a phone call to go upstairs. The MD said, 'Is he playing games with us?' 'No,' I said, 'He's having problems writing the album.' Then he suggested that I see Kevin and Lol – I was working with Godley & Creme – to write some songs for The Jam! I just laughed. They're good songwriters, but an album of five Weller songs and five Godley & Creme songs doesn't bear thinking about. I don't think I ever told Paul!"

In fact, the album was finished on time – it had to be, because the band were committed to a sell-out UK tour beginning in late October. *Sound Affects* was named after Weller found a *BBC Sound Effects* record lying around the studio, and it appeared with a striking pop-art sleeve which mimicked the generic BBC design, each photo linked to a lyric on the album. The subtle title change ("Effects" to "Affects") switched the emphasis from passive to active, though. "It's in the lyrics of 'Start!' as well," Paul explained, emphasising his awareness of the potential power of music.

Sound Affects was an album of peaks and troughs rather than one of consistency. In contrast to the comfortable production of *Setting Sons*, it had a stark atmosphere influenced by the atonal style of the rawest post-punk acts like Wire, Gang Of Four and Joy Division, but there was also the odd funk bassline and acoustic track. It was a strange mixture, constructed from "scraps of images", and was the first tell-tale sign that Paul was expanding the band's traditional sound. Paul summed up the mood change when he later revealed, "I was drunk one night at The Venue, and someone said, 'What's the album sound like?' And I replied, a mixture between *Revolver* and Michael Jackson's *Off The Wall*."

Three songs harked back to old school Jam. The first track, 'Pretty Green', began with a thundering one-note bass-line, before Weller launched into a tirade against a society which revolved around money, where "power is measured by the pound or the fist". The abrasive 'But I'm Different Now' was built upon the guitar riff reminiscent of another *Revolver* song, 'Dr. Robert'. Backed by a horn section, the jolly 'Boy About Town' was a vibrant Mod anthem, perhaps inspired by a free London commuter magazine of the time, *Girl About Town*. The song was another of Paul's 'London' tributes: "It's just me being blown about up and down Oxford Street," he commented. Incidentally, a rougher demo version of the song was released on a flexidisc, free with *Flexipop* magazine, backed by *Pop Art Poem*, a clever DIY collage of psychedelic effects with Weller's deadpan spoken word verse improvised over the top. Originally known as 'Go Native', it was based around a poem that had been written for his *December Child* fanzine. "I played all the instruments on it. They're all slowed down and speeded up to get that weird effect," Paul later revealed.

Indeed, many of the tracks on the album avoided a straightforward tune for a more vague, psychedelic atmosphere built around layered instrumentation. "I hadn't written many complete songs," he later admitted, "just a few ideas and chord sequences, so much of it was made up on the spot. That's how you get more musical moods and colourings." The result of these experiments could be heard on the intense 'Set The House Ablaze', the quirky, soundtrack-styled group composition, 'Music For The Last Couple', and 'Scrape Away', an attack on the decline in people's ideals as they age. The excellent 'Dream Time' was psychedelic punk, based around another of Paul's poems; and the low-key, enigmatic feel of 'Monday' and 'Man In The Corner Shop' shared this poetic feel, the latter dealing with aspects of human nature like hardship, jealousy and inequality.

If Weller felt a growing conviction about the injustices of society, then he also seemed frustrated by his own inability to change them. "I wish that there was something I could do about it," he maligned in 'Set The House Ablaze', a title which mirrored the revolutionary theme of the poem on the back sleeve, *Mask Of Anarchy* by Percy Bysshe Shelley – the doomed poet who encapsulated the idealism and passion of the late 18th/early 19th century Romantic movement. "His stuff is really striking," Weller later commented of Shelley in *Smash Hits*. "A lot of it still makes sense today."

Another source of inspiration was Geoffrey Ashe's *Camelot And The Vision Of Albion*. The idea that "we had lost sight of our purpose and our goal as human beings, that material goals had hidden our spiritual ones and clouded our perception" ran through much of the album. There was also the influence of George Orwell's story of fighting against fascism, *Homage To Catalonia*, which reflected the author's growing interest in democratic socialism. Paul's songwriting was clearly in a state of transition. "The songs from the *Setting Sons* era are more like complete short stories," he told *Allied Propaganda* fanzine, "whereas these are based more on my thoughts. The idea was to get extracts from a conversation."

Another song, 'That's Entertainment', used more direct language to create what is still Weller's most vivid snapshot of English life. 'That's Entertainment's sardonic title and gritty images of everyday life painted a depressing picture of a decaying Britain which mixed the suburban boredom of 'Saturday's Kids' with the urban commentary of 'Tube Station'. In short, the song was a masterpiece – and heralded as such, much to the bemusement of Paul Weller, who claimed to have dashed it off after returning from the pub one night. In fact, it was based on a poem, *Entertainment*, by a young writer called Paul Drew, which had appeared in *Mixed Up Shook Up*, suggesting a certain degree of plagiarism on Paul's part.

"A deceptively artless listing of the elements of Weller's day," enthused *Trouser Press*, "it's a celebration of the commonplace, the pleasant as well as the not-so-pleasant . . . Weller's limited voice has rarely sounded better or more sincere, and Foxton works small miracles with his harmonising. To hear this is not just to experience the power The Jam wield in Britain but to understand where that power came from." The band resisted the temptation to issue it as the follow-up to 'Start!' But when 'That's Entertainment' was chosen as a single in Germany, however, demand was so strong that it became Britain's best-selling import single to date. It's a telling indication of the song's encapsulation of English life that it was later covered by two quintessentially British acts, Morrissey and the Wonder Stuff.

Sound Affects may be Weller's favourite Jam album today, but none of the band was happy with Vic Coppersmith-Heaven's flat production – and Paul was also frustrated by the producer's slow, laborious methods. In the past, Weller had supported Vic, intervening when Polydor, after hearing a couple of unsatisfactory takes of 'When You're Young', had suggested introducing an American producer. But the album had to be recut on numerous occasions in an attempt to compensate for the disappointment of the final masters. "In hindsight, we should have said the mixes weren't up to it," admits Dennis Munday. "That gave Polydor the opportunity to get rid of Vic, helped by the fact that the album had cost so much money." It was the last time Coppersmith-Heaven worked with The Jam.

★ ★ ★

At a time when Paul Weller was being groomed by the music press as post-punk's working class hero, *Melody Maker* arranged for him to visit his idol, Pete Townshend, at The Who's offices in Wardour Street, presenting the results under the headline, "The Punk And The Godfather". This meeting of the great Mod minds was an ingenious idea and might well have been beneficial to both parties. Having survived the death of their drummer, Keith Moon, The Who could still pull enormous crowds, but Townshend's musical creativity had been in sharp decline since the mid-Seventies. His energies had been redirected into movies: The Who documentary, *The Kids Are Alright*, and *Quadrophenia*, which had fuelled the Mod revival after its launch the previous autumn.

Weller might also have benefited from nurturing a mutual admiration society. If the same stunt had taken place in the mid-Nineties, there might have been talk of a musical collaboration, but the concept of bridging the generation gap was less fashionable then. The pair talked for a couple of hours about issues such as politics, songwriting and the question of cracking the American market, and an edited transcript duly appeared across four pages in *Melody Maker* in October 1980. But as it transpired, Paul and Pete seemed to have little in common. "If you lot are planning to continue, then change your set," Weller told him bluntly, referring to The Who's reliance on old material. "You're a tougher nut than I was," responded Pete. The journalist was Paolo Hewitt, who later lamented that Townshend's "wider philosophies clashed with Weller's dogmatic approach". "I disagreed with him about a lot of things," Paul told *Trouser Press*, "which was strange. I always thought there was some kind of affinity between us." Maybe the similarities were superficial: Townshend had a Bohemian art school background and his literary interests led him to become a commissioning editor for Faber & Faber, whereas the working-class Weller had the most rudimentary of school educations and shunned intellectual thought for more direct, plain-speaking behaviour.

Meanwhile, the *Sound Affects* tour swept through Scandinavia, Holland, Belgium and Germany before returning for the second leg of their British dates. Shane McGowan joined them on stage to sing 'Heatwave' at London's Music Machine on December 12. Shane and Paul had remained friends since punk's early days and McGowan's band, The Nips, had already supported The Jam on several occasions. A few months later, Weller produced The Nips' catchy, Mod revival-mocking *Happy Song*, issued in October 1981, and he is thought to have contributed guitar to the B-side, *Nobody To Love*. Two of The Nips' other songs bore a strong resemblance to The Jam: *Gabrielle* to *Strange Town* (it's uncertain which was written first) and *Infatuation*, which was an affectionate rewrite of *I Got By In Time*. The Nips even auditioned for Polydor, as Dennis Munday reveals: "It was at a time when I was semi-A&R. I tried to sign Shane. I offered him a singles deal, 10 K, and his manager said they were looking for 60 K. I said, 'Shane's got this reputation for drinking'. He said, 'no, no, no, he's given it up'. The problem was, about two weeks before this, when The Jam had played Guildford, Shane had turned up and was carried out on a stretcher, drunk!" McGowan later made his name with The Pogues, of course.

Paul had been invited to guest with other artists, too. During the *Setting Sons* sessions, he played the needling guitar riff on *And Through The Wire* for Peter Gabriel's eponymous third LP. "In my opinion, *the* two English rhythm guitarists are Pete Townshend and Paul Weller," wrote Gabriel. They had met at Townhouse "when we were in Studio 1 and The Jam were in No. 2 finishing off their next album. He was great – very self-effacing. I just love watching him play, he's like liquid energy." Weller also played piano on the Purple Hearts' 'Concrete Mixer', an unissued song later exhumed on a compilation LP, *The Beat Generation And The Angry Young Men*, which was put out on the Well Suspect label, run by London Mod club organiser Eddie Pillar.

Another project was the infamous 'England I Miss You Now' by Oi! punk band The Cockney Rejects. The track featured Paul singing about the passing of an old, semi-mythical England, a theme in keeping with some of his ideas behind *Sound Affects* – but the lyrics are open to misinterpretation. Never officially issued, the song was bootlegged in the early Nineties, prompting Paul to write to *Boys About Town* fanzine. Bearing in mind the Oi! movement's somewhat ill-founded reputation for fascist leanings and violence, Weller was not best pleased: "It was a Cockney Rejects demo that Pete Wilson and myself fucked around with one day in Polydor Studios," he explained in his letter. Wilson was a Polydor in-house engineer and producer of Sham 69, who often supervised Paul's demo sessions. "They asked me to write a song for them which never happened but I rewrote the words (or at least some of them). Their original lyrics were all 'We love the Queen Mum' bollocks . . . I couldn't understand how they could feel rejected yet cling on to the very thing which rejects them (i.e. this country's ruling classes and establishment). So I rewrote them and probably sang a guide vocal for them. Who knows? Who cares? It was fucking 'orrible as far as I can recall."

★ ★ ★

On February 14, 1981, The Jam played at The Cricketers pub in Westfield, just south of Woking, advertised as a Valentine's night charity gig by The Jam Roadcrew. "Every mod who could get on a scooter was there," says Steve Carver. "It was a disaster – just mud, blood and beer at the end. It was terrible and there were massive fights." It wasn't the first time the band had made a pilgrimage to their home town. A year earlier, almost to the day, they had played a packed-out fund-raising event for free at the Woking YMCA Centre (organised via the band's bank manager, who was also chairman of the Christian association), and another benefit gig in nearby Guildford to raise funds for the Sheerwater Youth Club on July 22, 1980. Weller had never openly shown any fondness for Woking during The Jam's first two years of success, or inclination to support it – quite the contrary, in fact. He had gone on record as saying he owed the town nothing.

Nevertheless, The Jam played two further 'secret' gigs in quick succession after the riotous Cricketers event. Their return to the Woking YMCA Centre raised £800 and was helped by support sets from The Purple Hearts and a young band called Department S who had evolved out of a ska/mod band called Guns For Hire, and who were soon to chart with their first single, 'Is Vic There?'. "We were out all day down the pub on a complete bender," laughs Pete Carver. "They were so shitfaced. I remember Bruce and Rick were playing 'The Eton Rifles' and Paul was playing 'Away From The Numbers'!" The following night was February 17 and, hangovers in tow, The Jam visited another of their old haunts, the Sheerwater Youth Club, with warm-up sets from two bands with whom Paul was potentially interested in working – all-girl trio Dolly Mixture and Scottish would-be funk group The Questions.

The last of these homecoming shows was filmed for an episode of BBC 2's arts series, *Something Else*. Steve Carver, who acted as the interviewer, explains: "Paul scripted and narrated this brainchild about making a TV programme and they wanted some groups on. It was Paul's big class statement, so he got all these herberts from Guildford and we followed them around for a day." Drawing loosely on the concept behind *Setting Sons*, Weller chose three teenagers to compare working class, middle class and upper class lifestyles, views and aspirations. Steve: "It was like wannabes. There was a geezer who worked in a timber yard, down the pub, getting pissed with his mates. He wanted to have a laugh but more money. Another went to grammar school, an obnoxious bloke who wanted to be upper class, and the third kid, who went to Charterhouse public school, was easy-going."

The programme allowed Paul to draw his various strands of interest together – music, poetry, politics – by including a couple of the writers involved with Riot Stories. "There was these bleak, miserable 'Among the rotting corpses'-type poems by Ann Clark, a punk poet, and an Irish guy, Aidan Cant, another doom and gloom merchant," adds Steve. "We filmed around Woking: all the cemeteries and the school we went to." There was even room for some pop-art imagery, with relevant Jam lyrics splattered across the screen. Weller had to leave Steve to finish off the editing because his girlfriend was ill: "Gill was in hospital and he said, that's it, I'm off," he explains, an illustration that Paul's sense of priorities were in order. Weller's bitterness about the injustices of Britain's class system ran deeply. "I think he saw it straight away," Steve Carver concludes. "It riles me because whenever reporters come down to Woking, they say, 'What's Paul's gripe? It's a lovely town.' Obviously, they didn't see the bits where we lived!"

Around this time, Weller also contributed a sleeve-note to a compilation album of the cult Sixties Mod band, The Action. Issued in 1981, *The Ultimate Action* was the first release for Demon's Edsel label, a pioneering archive project in a reissue market which has since blossomed into the most significant growth area of the music industry. Back then, the idea was still a novelty, and was aimed at a growing, male-dominated scene fascinated with the hidden recesses of pop's past, which centred around musty second-hand shops and record fairs. Paul Weller was a part of that scene.

"So many great records are made and yet so few bands ever really receive the recognition they deserve," he wrote. "Usually, these are lost to most people but kept alive by the 'cultist record collectors'. Out of the bands who never quite made it from the mid-Sixties, there's The Creation, Birds, John's Children, Artwoods, Eyes, etc., all of whom made at least a couple of outstanding singles . . . Practically all these bands were influenced by the Mod scene although it's apparent The Action were more so. The Action were one of the few bands to not only capture the Tamla/soul sounds, but actually shape it into their own style and sound." It was no coincidence that Paul wanted The Jam to move in a similar direction, fuelled by his widening interest in soul music.

The 1980 end-of-year readers' polls had confirmed what Paul Weller already knew: The Jam were the most popular contemporary band in Britain. In one survey alone, they won 'best group', 'male singer', 'guitarist', 'bass', 'drums', 'songwriter', 'single', 'album' and 'cover art'. Despite the band's reservations, *Sound Affects* sold over 100,000 copies and would have topped the charts had it not been for Abba's *Super Trouper* album. In 1981, The Jam could easily have graduated to the rock stadium circuit and played half-a-dozen high profile concerts as a platform to launch themselves properly in the States.

Instead, Paul Weller hesitated. Uncomfortable with the level of rock celebrity he was now attracting, he grew increasingly acerbic in interviews, attacking the vacuous glamour of the emergent pop cognoscenti on the one hand, and tiring of the narrow-mindedness of some of his audience on the other. It was the beginning of the end of The Jam.

7

BITTERNESS RISING

"And there was this other soul music that had been around since the Sixties. Uncommercial. Rarer and bursting with a rawness, an energy and a driving beat that just took you to another place. Northern soul."

(*Nightshift*, Pete McKenna, 1996)

"What the world needs now is a new breed of young groups. A lot of crap needs to be cleared away and only the young hipsters can do it. These groups must have: a) intelligence; b) raw sexual energy; c) a clear vision of pop(ular) music; d) a love for life; and e) determination. Girls and boys alike, it is up to you."

(Paul Weller, *Beat Surrender* tour programme, 1982)

"I was creatively quite exhausted," said Paul Weller of 1981, the first year since signing to Polydor that The Jam didn't issue an album. "*Sound Affects* was quite hard to finish, so I needed that year off." He wasn't twiddling his thumbs, though. Between February and July, the band played sporadic dates across Europe, Britain, Japan and America, culminating in the 'Bucket & Spade Tour', which included a short trip around England's seaside resorts. The music press were inevitably drawn to the trouble which erupted at The Jam's Paris show on February 26. The concert was interrupted on several occasions as scuffles broke out between visiting Britons and local French skinheads. One hundred people were arrested in the worst violence of The Jam's history. Weller made no attempt to disguise where his sympathies lay, cursing the French "animals" and tying a Union Jack flag to the microphone – a pledge of allegiance to the band's fans rather than some hollow patriotic gesture.

More significant in a political sense was a one-off benefit concert for the unemployed on April 27 at the Royal Court Theatre in Liverpool, one of the country's most depressed areas. After the sense of impotence expressed in the lyrics of *Setting Sons* and *Sound Affects*, Weller now saw a way forward. The Jam's pulling power could be translated into direct action: to focus awareness on specific political issues while also raising proceeds for those causes. Weller's troubled conscience and pent-up frustration were now given a release valve, although despite his growing socialist convictions, he was cautious about aligning himself with left wing campaigns, *en masse*.

The highest-profile pressure group at that time was Rock Against Racism, a coalition of sympathetic musicians and far-left activists which had been born from the embryo of a letter written in response to Eric Clapton's racist remarks on stage in 1976 – and as the culmination of Britain's tightening immigration policies over the previous twenty years. Their main target was the National Front, the extreme right-wing organisation. Loosely connected to the Anti-Nazi League, RAR organised shows which attempted to fuse black and white cultures by booking both punk acts and reggae bands, as well as two well-publicised events headlined by The Clash.

Although The Jam later played an RAR benefit, Weller was cynical about the movement at first, and his sentiments lay elsewhere: "You very rarely get black kids going to Rock Against Racism gigs anyway," he pointed out with some accuracy to *Allied Propaganda* fanzine. "I think all these banners are pretty silly, but CND is a bit different and we're talking about organising a CND gig ourselves. There is no real political bias and, no matter who you are, you surely don't wanna get blown to pieces and we should get that threat out of the way for a start," he declared. He patently believed in the potential power of The Jam's performances: "One of the best things about being in a band, you can bring people together who otherwise would never have met, even if it's just to see us at the Rainbow. What other medium gets through to so many people so effectively? You can discount TV, radio and the papers so music is the only channel through which change is gonna come about."

Enlivened by this fresh political fervour, Weller created The Jam's most uncompromising musical statement ever. Issued in late May 1981, 'Funeral Pyre' was a fiery, discordant single – and their first to be produced by engineer Pete Wilson, who had grown increasingly involved with the band. The bleak sleeve featured a morbid, black-and-white picture of naked, dismembered corpses around a 'funeral pyre' in the style of Edvard Munch's famous but disturbing 'symbolist' painting, *The Scream*. The lyrics' colourful metaphor attacked what Weller perceived as the hate and greed among those in power, convincingly communicated by brutal guitar and Rick Buckler's persistent drum rolls. The glimmer of a tune had to fight its way from beneath a sea of distortion. "To have a hit single that didn't have a pretty guitar phrase or a chorus, represented what we sounded like live," Paul explained when we spoke in 1992. "I was always conscious that we'd get too pop, especially when we started having No. 1's. You see, a lot of groups go the whole way and get more diluted. I wanted to make sure we go the other way and maintain our popularity but not choose the easy route."

It was a brave statement – and the single stalled at No. 4, a modest reflection of The Jam's enormous popularity. But coming after their longest-ever break between singles, and carrying a writing credit that read, 'Words:

Paul Weller, Music: The Jam', 'Funeral Pyre' suggested a disquiet within the band. The B-side, 'Disguises', was a menacing cover of The Who's effects-laden, psychedelic track from their *Ready Steady Who* EP, but it also hinted that Paul was struggling to write new material. " '81 was an 'orrible year for songs!" Paul later admitted on the sleeve for *Dig The New Breed*. 'Funeral Pyre' also jarred a British music scene by now charmed by the so-called New Romantics, though. Reacting against the anger and social realism of punk, synth-based acts like Spandau Ballet, The Human League, Visage and Duran Duran, and punk-turned-dandy Adam Ant, injected a new glamour into pop. Weller hated its saccharine flavour and drew parallels with the early Seventies glam rock he also disdained.

The New Romantics attracted several labels, such as 'Blitz Kids' after London's Blitz nightclub, or Futurists, inspired by the forward-looking emphasis on synthesiser-driven sounds. Weller may have detested the movement, but its overlap with London's emergent club culture began to fascinate him and eventually led to a change in direction for The Jam. In June 1981, he wrote an impressive page-long article on 'The Other Side Of Futurism' in the style magazine, *The Face*, in which he explained the futuristic aspects of books like *1984*, *Brave New World* and *Clockwork Orange* – linking their very different but equally harrowing prophesies to his growing socialist views. And prompted by his friendship with DJ and Department S singer Vaughn Toulouse, he frequented clubs like Le Beat Route on Greek Street, which played old soul classics together with a grittier brand of contemporary American funk than had been popular in the UK.

To Weller, it felt like an updated version of Sixties Mod culture, in the fusing together of new sounds and new styles. The clubland of the late Seventies was factionalised. There were mainstream, chart-dominated discos, as there are today, with their handbags and pink neon, aimed fairly and squarely at the post-pub high street brigade; there was a thriving black club scene in most of Britain's major cities, which traded in reggae and/or jazz-funk and imported soul; and there were gay clubs, which served up a diet of camp rock (Bowie, Roxy, etc.), camp disco (Donna Summer *et al*) and, well, camp anything, really. But at the start of the Eighties, these disparate environments began to overlap.

One particular record crystallised this cross-fertilisation between club-minded pop and Britain's fertile jazz-funk scene. Issued in July, Spandau Ballet's 'Chant No. 1' was a collaboration with Britfunkers Beggar & Co., who'd already broken through to the mainstream with 'Somebody Help Me Out' that February. Spandau's intense blaze of horns and syncopated funk riffs had a profound effect on Weller, simply because it broadened his horizons. UK funk/soul groups had been prominent since the late Seventies (Kandidate, Hi Tension, the Olympic Runners, Heatwave, The Real Thing, etc.), but they would have meant little to Weller at the time. After investigating the most successful (and white) jazz-funk acts of the period (Average

White Band, Spyro Gyra, Shakatak), Weller had found them too bland for his seasoned palate.

Pure jazz-funk was still popular in the early Eighties (Atmosfear, Level 42), but Paul was more interested in those acts which mixed the jazz-funk rhythms with soul tunes. Light Of The World led the way, followed by Funkapolitan, Central Line, Anglo-French collective Incognito, Freeez, who had charted with 'Southern Freeez', and Defunkt, who tasted cult status in autumn 1981 with the infectious 'The Razor's Edge', a club favourite in the style of Seventies act War. One of the most ingenious records of the era was 'Papa's Got A Brand New Pigbag' by Pigbag, an instrumental record packed with bright horn riffs and percussion which bridged the gap between post-punk and jazz-funk – and a Top 5 hit in spring 1982.

Within this climate, The Jam's spiky, lads' guitar rock ran the risk of sounding outdated, and Weller's train of thought was obvious when he spoke to Adam Sweeting: "I've been listening to Michael Jackson a lot; I like the guitar styles on his album, *Off The Wall*. Maybe Gang Of Four started that interest in disco. It was the first time I'd seen a white band with that sort of disco rhythm section. Andy Gill's a really good guitarist; his playing is half Wilko Johnson and half funk." Paul also became infatuated with the songs of Sixties and early Seventies soul pioneers like Curtis Mayfield, Norman Whitfield, Smokey Robinson and Marvin Gaye – artists whose work often combined a danceable groove and a social conscience within the lyrics. Weller patently wanted to incorporate his love of both soul and Eighties funk into The Jam's music – but his wishes would eventually lead to the band's downfall.

Weller's first attempt at integrating funk into The Jam's rather rigid style wasn't a great success. Issued as their next single in October 1981, 'Absolute Beginners' was a clumsy, disjointed collision of horns, guitar and an un-comfortable rhythm section. It masked the mystical, if somewhat preten-tious lyrics, of a genuinely charming song, which took its title from Colin MacInnes' quintessential novel about late Fifties London, whose central character embodied the Modernist lifestyle of jazz, clean living, independ-ence and scooters – in roughly that order. "I hate 'Absolute Beginners' now," Weller told me years later, describing the song as a "stop-gap". And accord-ing to Polydor's Dennis Munday, he wasn't that keen on it then: "Paul came in to my office one afternoon," he remembers. "He said, 'Listen to this, what do you think?' and played 'Absolute Beginners' – or 'Skirt', as it was first called. I said it sounded OK. 'It's fucking shit!,' he said and threw the tape in the bin and walked out!"

'Tales From The Riverbank', which backed 'Absolute Beginners', was more satisfying, and is one of the strongest and most enduring songs Weller has ever written. Indeed, Paul has since regretted that it wasn't the A-side. The song had grown out of two earlier prototypes, 'Not Far At All' and 'We've Only Started', its lyrics harking back to Weller's memories of the Surrey countryside. "It makes me think of Woking," said Paul. "It was written about my childhood." The song echoed late Sixties eeriness, reflecting another major influence on Paul's tastes, English psychedelia, which was enjoying a renaissance. New psychedelia centred around Piccadilly's Groovy Cellar, but if the story is true that Paul was refused entry because of the club's strict dress code, then it helped explain his lack of enthusiasm for this brief revival within a revival.

Two of his genuine commitments were confirmed by a string of concerts towards the end of the year: soul music and his aim to play fund-raising events for the Campaign For Nuclear Disarmament. As Robin Denselow noted in his story of political pop, *When The Music's Over*, Weller's unequivocal support of CND signalled his sudden and, to many observers, unexpected entry into organised political movements. The move coincided (or was maybe prompted by) CND's "rebirth" in 1981, as Denselow puts it. "Britain's anti-nuclear lobbyists were concerned at the changes in defence policy that would follow the election of the new Conservative Government," he explained, "particularly at suggestions that Cruise missiles would be shipped to Britain . . . The growth of Youth CND was particularly rapid, and within two years it was claimed that membership had risen from 2,000 to 8,000, and that 500 people a month were applying to join. Pop music was an important part of the process."

The turning point for Weller had come "when I got some leaflets and saw I could take some action, using what I'm best at". The idea of Youth CND particularly appealed: in Weller's eyes, it symbolised the younger generation seizing the initiative to fight against those forces which most threatened their lives – and Paul's enthusiasm was fuelled further after he became acquainted with YCND's mastermind, the teenage Annajoy David. She recognised Weller's pulling power: as Denselow explained, it made her job easier with school kids, because "if you throw in a quote from him, everybody wakes up".

On October 23, The Jam guested at a CND benefit at The Rainbow headed by Gang Of Four. Vaughn Toulouse joined them onstage for a brief set consisting of 'Going Underground', 'Sweet Soul Music' and a cover of Sandie Shaw's 'Long Live Love'. The following night, The Jam performed two sets from the back of a float as the climax of a CND rally on the Thames Embankment. In addition to Vaughn, the band was joined by two horn players – trumpeter Steve Nichol and saxophonist Keith Thomas, who went on to augment The Jam's line-up for nearly a year. The pair helped Weller to fulfil his aims for The Jam, by shifting the emphasis away from his guitar and giving him the confidence to tackle some of his favourite soul material. Covers of Chairmen Of The Board's hit, 'Give Me Just A Little More Time', and Eddie Floyd's 'Big Bird' were aired to great effect over four consecutive concerts beginning on December 12 – two at North London's Michael Sobell Centre, two at the Hammersmith Palais. Although the former were spoilt by poor sound, the events embodied Weller's new vision of the band's shows, which resembled a modern day Soul Revue with a socialist backdrop – CND literature was circulated, as Northern Soul was played between the sets.

In fact, Paul hired two Northern Soul DJs to provide the recorded entertainment, both of whom returned for the British leg of their spring tour in 1980 – Tony Rounce and Ady Croasdell, a record collector/dealer and later the muscle behind Ace Records' acclaimed Kent reissue label. Ady had known Weller for a couple of years. "I'd heard that Paul went to London shops like Rock On, and Rocks Off on Hanway Street, to buy soul records – Tamla Motown to start off with," says Croasdell. "I sold records through those shops so I knew he was getting interested in more obscure soul, and being a fan of his, I got talking to him at a Members gig. I got the impression he was a little possessive of his fans. If you liked The Jam, he'd like you to only like The Jam and not go off to see The Members! He wanted to be the best, definitely. I sold him a lot of Northern Soul bootlegs and reissues and, later, Kent LPs – reasonably cheap but good.

"At some stage, he must have said, 'Do you fancy DJ'ing on our tour?' I wasn't a DJ, I was just a collector, but I said, 'Yes, but do you mind if I bring my mate along?" With his distinctive bleached flat-top, Tony Rounce had a regular DJ'ing spot at Le Beat Route. "Paul wanted to take a DJ on the road for continuity," Tony explains, "not just to play Sixties records but records that seemed quite contemporary, providing an overview of music a Jam fan might like to hear before the show. I worked every English concert after that."

Tony was ideally situated to observe The Jam camp from the inside. "John Weller's bark was worse than his bite," he remembers. "People were quite frightened of him because John's a stocky geezer and talks with a gruff voice. He'd been a bit of a lad in his earlier life. But he was an absolute pussycat, a very nice man who thought the world of his son – a justifiable belief in Paul's talent. John was an unseen guiding force, and pulled The Jam through in the early days. By the time I worked with them, they were confident enough to stand on their own feet, but I don't think there would have been a Jam for as long if John hadn't been there to push it along. They were a family bunch of people who kept a fairly tight ship, in terms of who they employed."

★　★　★

"Nothing will be achieved all the time we remain separated," Paul proclaimed on BBC 1's *Nationwide*, about his support for CND, "but together we can win!" He may have sounded idealistic and naïve, but if this was, as some critics claimed, "another fashion and another pose", he kept it up for six years. He later said of the campaign that "of all the movements, it's really pro-life" and wrote a feature in *Melody Maker* stating that "CND is the most important political movement in the world at the moment". And in January 1982, The Jam contributed the apt 'Little Boy Soldiers' to the first of the era's

CND/anti-nuclear fund-raising albums, *Life In The European Theatre*. Paul patently believed in the cause: his problem was convincing his audience.

December 1981's quartet of concerts also allowed Weller to champion up-and-coming acts by giving them support slots. The line-ups changed every night: from all-girl trio and would-be pop sensations Bananarama, Department S and Ruts DC to power-pop outfit Reaction, Scotland's Mod pop-turned-indie funk act TV21, and Keith Thomas's Second Image. The audiences' response was mixed – and Bananarama, in particular, were badly received – which frustrated Weller. He wanted to break out of the ritualised rock gig scenario, but it was perhaps wishful thinking to expect his fans to follow suit without question, bearing in mind The Jam's patchy track record for support acts. But it was the first sign that he felt straitjacketed by what he viewed as the narrow-mindedness of the band's followers – a feeling of desperation which would lead to the bizarre sight during The Jam's last gigs of the Eton Rifles Dance Troupe. This featured Bananarama prancing around the stage amidst a barrage of abuse from the crowd.

★　★　★

The gigs also allowed Paul to introduce several acts signed to two new record labels, Jamming! (Zeitgeist) and Respond (The Questions, The Rimshots) – both of which were created with Weller's initiative and involvement. Collectively, the projects were the culmination of Paul's long-held desire to invest in new talent – he had told *Trouser Press* in May 1979, for instance, that "I'd like to channel money back into music". He resurrected the idea in an interview at the start of 1981, citing Sham 69 singer Jimmy Pursey's aborted 'Pursey's Package' label from 1979 as a "bodge of a job" to be avoided. It is impossible to believe that Paul wasn't inspired by the idea of creating his own Apple Records, The Beatles' idealistic label which succeeded in signing a few worthwhile acts, and scoring a few hit singles before declining into little more than a rich men's plaything. Despite the wealth of unsigned bands around, though, both Jamming! and Respond opted for artists who, on the whole, had already recorded and, more unfortunately, were perceived to be second division.

The more autonomous of the two was Jamming!, an independently distributed label run single-handedly by Tony Fletcher as an offshoot from his fanzine of the same name. Despite his tender age – he was only seventeen when the label started – he had been a good friend of Weller's for several years. "I went to school in Kennington in South London," he explains, "and was into Sixties Who and loved the imagery of *Quadrophenia* even when I was twelve, but I was one of those kids who was changed by punk. The Jam's 'All Around The World' just altered my values – it was so ugly, rough, violent. I started a fanzine when I was thirteen, which was initially called *In The City* – if it wasn't, I could claim that *Jamming!* was just a good name because of the Bob Marley song!"

Tony sums up why The Jam appealed to so many teenagers of their day: "There was a definite mod image – they were sharp. Secondly, I couldn't help it with these songs, which just hit me – brash but melodic. And there was no doubt about what Paul's lyrics meant. 'Away From The Numbers' was my favourite song for years. It said a lot to any kid who didn't conform. Naïve though they could be, the lyrics really spoke to us – 'Saturday's Kids' patronised the kids but then they wanted patronising. I liked The Clash but they went and won the punk battle for America and The Jam won it for Britain."

In The City had evolved into *Jamming!* by the time Tony wrote to Weller in summer '78. "I got a letter back from Paul within days saying, 'Sure, I'll do an interview.' I was embarrassed – the fanzine wasn't very good and we did it on a school Roneo machine. But he said, 'It's great that young kids are doing something. Give me a call.' I went to the studio the next week." Tony was only fourteen but the pair hit it off immediately. "I never asked Paul why he befriended me," reflects Tony, "but he took me under his wing. It was a friendship with a definite element of big brother, little brother. I looked up to him. I wasn't the only person he dealt with in this way. To some extent, he's carried on doing it to this day. Paul's got a very strong, very real cult of personality. There was always a sense that he was leading. There was no doubt that he was in charge, and you wouldn't talk in complimentary terms about other bands, for example. Perhaps that attracted the fans, that his personality came across further than just being an image on a TV screen or on stage."

Since Tony spent much of his time hanging out with the band, he was almost a part of their organisation. "I thought it was great that your dad could manage a band – this team of older men running it. The Jam had the most unorthodox way of doing business but it seemed to work. When they went on tour, the entire office went with them and left the answering machine on. I mean, that just doesn't happen in management – if you've got a No. 1 record, you don't go off and abandon it. John Weller never missed a show, whereas most bands would ask why the hell he wasn't back in London making phone calls. The family aspect of the band probably helped create a family of fans who were very loyal to The Jam, which was second to none. They followed them round the country. It felt like you were following a team – you almost felt as if you'd take a bullet for this band. You really believed in them. The Jam always looked after the crowd and let them into the soundchecks."

Meanwhile, the idea of a record label kept cropping up in conversation. "It was summer 1980, and I was doing my 'O'-levels," says Fletcher. "I think that now The Jam were successful, Paul was making money but wanted to stay true to his intent. He said, 'I've been thinking of starting a record label. Do you want to run it?' I was pretty ecstatic at being offered. For a while, Paul kept talking about the label. Should it be called Jamming! or stay separate from the fanzine, or should we do it with Polydor? It took close to a year – eventually we agreed to call the label Jamming! because it had a recognised name. Then people assumed that Weller owned the fanzine – but that was never the case."

Tony was given his own office within the suite which The Jam rented in Nomis Studios in West London. "Paul's girlfriend made me a cup of tea on my first day," he remembers. "Gill was running the Jam office upstairs – a lot of the time, there was only us around. She was very friendly. Paul and Gill were very much in love and always a close couple. Gill had to share Paul with the world at large which most girls don't have to do with their boyfriends. He also came to be seen as something of a sex symbol, which wasn't easy for her.

"That first day, I was sitting there making a few calls – on one hand, I was king of the castle, but on the other, I was still nervous. John Weller opened the door, saw me and said, 'What the fuck are you doing here?' I replied, 'Erm, didn't Paul tell you? We've set up this label, Jamming! Records.' 'He never told me nothing. He's gonna lose a fucking arm and a leg on this one! What the fuck's he doing?' Then he walked off. I don't think I have to comment on that – there's an awful lot in there! Remember that we'd spent a year setting this up." Paul may have shown a commitment to investing in young talent – to channelling his energies into projects outside of The Jam – but he was patently wary of informing his father.

"The way Paul set up the label seemed a good idea at the time," Tony continues. "He said, 'I'll pay for the first record, and the money earned you can use to run the label; I'll have sixty per cent and you'll have forty.' Nobody told me that you're not worth anything unless you own fifty one per cent. I wish I'd known more about business because it didn't make sense for a number of reasons, the biggest being cash flow. It was daft. There was very little money laid out – about £1,400 – but that takes ages to recoup. He hadn't set up any overhead budget: they would pay the phone bill but there were still overheads like postage. It was set up the wrong way. It was a recipe for disaster because when I needed to spend five hundred pounds recording the second single, I had to ask him for the money. We set up distribution deals with Rough Trade and Pinnacle but they'd take ninety days to pay you."

Jamming! was launched with a single by Belfast's self-proclaimed "first punk band", Rudi. They had already issued two singles and contributed to a compilation EP on Northern Ireland's foremost independent label, Good Vibrations, since mid-1978. After the success of Good Vibrations' other notable band, The Undertones, Rudi participated in an episode of the TV programme, *Something Else*, devoted entirely to the Belfast music scene. But just as the dynamic trio were attracting genuine publicity, Good Vibrations went bust, and despite a liaison with producer Pete Waterman, who secured them a publishing deal, a record contract wasn't forthcoming.

Rudi's phone rang one day in the summer of 1981: it was Tony Fletcher, who had interviewed the band for his magazine. "Out of the blue, he called up and said, I'm starting a label," remembers guitarist Brian Young. "Tony was an absolute Weller fanatic and I suppose that's why he called his magazine *Jamming!* He had one of Weller's own Rickenbackers. The neck had got broken, so Paul gave it away in a competition at a gig. Tony had bought it off the winner, got a new neck and played it in his band, Apocalypse. He and Paul were really friendly. When they were recording *Setting Sons*, Fletcher had taught Bruce Foxton how to play the cello.

"Tony wanted a band to start the label whom he both liked and who'd shift records. Our records were getting played more and more, so Tony knew our name would sell. Weller would never have chosen us; as far as he was concerned, we were a dodgy Northern Ireland punk band. It was an ordinary shoestring independent label – we never got a wage and had to pay our own way over from Ireland." Rudi set about recording their first single for Jamming!, 'When I Was Dead'. "Paul booked us into Polydor's Stanhope Place studios, Marble Arch, under a false name – supposedly doing demos for Polydor," says Young.

This was common practice, in fact. Dennis Munday recalls auditioning a couple of Paul's recommendations from Southend – The Cards and The Leapers – although neither signed to the label. "We recorded three songs for the single," continues Brian. "Paul and Pete Wilson produced it, but we couldn't use Paul's name because we were terrified of Polydor finding out it had been recorded there. Weller showed us things we'd never known, like how to do harmonies." Issued in September 1981, 'When I Was Dead' was a dynamic new wave effort – both energetic and melodic but slightly dated, though it was well-received. " 'When I Was Dead' sold over five thousand copies, got good reviews and went in the indie charts," Young remembers. "Then we played with The Jam at the Hammersmith Palais in December, which went really well."

"We recorded Rudi's single and had copies in the shops ten days later," says Fletcher. "Now, Paul had no idea you could get a single out that quick – and neither did I. There was enormous media attention prompted by Weller's involvement. The week we released the first Rudi single, my name seemed to be everywhere! Everything felt right. There was a naïveté in my running of the label, particularly on the business side. For example, nobody – not John Weller, not Paul – told me about VAT. I just spent all day on the phone rabbiting to anybody who called: direct line printed on the record sleeve, just talk, talk, talk, spread the word, sell the records, talk to Paul about putting out another one."

"Another one" meant a single from Zeitgeist. This unusual Cornish six-piece group had already released singles on their own label and on Human Records, which reflected the experimental sound of post-punk – but a scheduled album, *Underwater*, had been aborted. Like other rhythmic independent acts of the time (A Certain Ratio, Fire Engines, Higsons), Zeitgeist dabbled in a punk-funk hybrid – 'militant funk' – with its trademark percussion, trumpet and sax. Following their proclaimed wish to play "Eighties soul", they covered The Temptations' socially aware Motown classic, 'Ball Of Confusion', as their first Jamming! 45, issued at the end of that year.

" 'Ball Of Confusion' got lots of airplay," Tony recalls, "but Paul didn't have any idea about business. It's rare that pop stars know how records sell. He'd say, 'What's happening? We're on the radio but we're not selling.' If a band gets airplay, you need records in the shops the next day – posters, advertising, a few gimmicks. But we were clueless. Paul always thought, for as long as I knew him, that 'Going Underground' went in at No.1 purely because there were so many Jam fans, not because Polydor pulled every trick in the book."

Paul was also vague about some of the realities of life, simply because he had never had to face up to them. "When we started the label, I was on the dole – seventeen pounds a week," says Tony. "But then the dole were saying, 'When are you going to get a job?' Up until now, there had been no question of getting a wage – I had no contract and didn't even get my bus fare. So I told him, 'Paul, I'm going to have my dole cut off.' Now, this guy is like Britain's No. 1 pop star. He said, 'Well, whatever you get on the dole you can take from the label.' But that then added to the cashflow because no-one budgeted in seventeen pounds so we were out of cash within two months – the little tin was empty!"

In contrast to Jamming!, Respond was funded by Polydor, who were responsible for the records' manufacture and distribution – and it was seen as a reward from the label for The Jam's success. Respond was inaugurated on September 3, 1981, at the 45–53 Sinclair Road address of Simon Napier-Bell's Nomis Studios near Shepherd's Bush Green, which Paul has inter-mittently used as a base ever since. Both Paul and John Weller were listed as directors.

The label's first signing was a Cambridge-based all-girl trio, Dolly Mixture, who melded a post-punk quirkiness with melodies reminiscent of Sixties girl groups – aptly, their one-off début for Chrysalis in 1980 was a cover of The Shirelles' 'Baby It's You'. They were a band of contrasts. "Dolly Mixture wrote with urgent teen conviction because, like their heroes The Under-tones, they *were* teenagers," wrote Saint Etienne's Bob Stanley for a recent compilation of the band. "On stage they giggled and wore floral dresses, but not so long that you couldn't see their dirty great work boots."

Dolly Mixture came to Weller's attention after supporting The Jam during the summer of 1980 and at Hammersmith Odeon later that year, and appeared in Paul's *Something Else* documentary footage at Sheerwater Youth Club. However, they dealt more closely with Paul's father, as bassist/singer Debsey remembers: "His parents were wonderful. His mum was just so outgoing and friendly and young and bouncy, chatting all the time, cheeky. I think it was John Weller who suggested fixing up some studio time at Polydor." After some demos, the paperwork was drawn up. "We had this meeting with Paul and Polydor," recalls Debsey. "It was about the contract, which was dreadful, and Paul was saying, no, it shouldn't be that and that. He was really on our side."

The Damned's Captain Sensible produced both Dolly Mixture's Respond singles – the offbeat 'Been-Teen' (November 1981) and the melodic summer pop of 'Everything And More' (March 1982). "It was funny seeing these two punk greats chatting awkwardly about our record," says Debsey, referring to Weller and Sensible. "I don't think they'd ever met. They were being very polite. Weller was all smart and Captain was all scruffy. Weller was always so well dressed and groomed – and skinny. We always felt really messy with him!" (Incidentally, Dolly Mixture sang backing vocals on 'Happy Talk', Sensible's surprise novelty hit in June 1982, giving them a taste of success in sharp contrast to the sales of their own releases.)

"Once we were on the label, we didn't have as much contact with Paul," Debsey admits. "He was elusive and he was busy doing his own thing. I wondered, to be honest, if he knew what he was doing sometimes – I had a feeling he was grabbing at bands. He was encouraging and a good fella, but I just wondered what he really thought. We used to get such snatched comments from him or treasure something we'd heard that he'd said about one of our songs. I think he was shy. He was terribly nice with us but awkward – and we were shy as well. We always wanted to impress him, of course!"

Respond's second release came from funk-pop band, The Questions. As sixteen-year-old school boys, this Edinburgh four-piece had recorded two Beatles-influenced singles, 1978's 'Some Other Guy' and 1979's 'Can't Get Over You', for the city's Zoom label, which made its name for discovering Simple Minds. After a couple of line-up changes and a musical rethink, The Questions settled upon the trio of bassist/vocalist Paul Barry, guitarist/keyboardist John Robinson and drummer Frank Mooney. Their listed influences in late 1981 mixed contemporary white pop (Spandau Ballet, Skids) with American funk (James Brown, The Jacksons), a blend which is evident on their clumsy, Weller-produced Respond début, 'Work 'N' Play', in February 1982.

The label's other signing was an unlikely choice – a rockabilly band, The Rimshots. Rudi's Brian Young is critical of Paul's A&R acumen. "No offence, but Weller's taste was almost like the kiss of death," he laughs, "the Midas Touch in reverse. Any band he picked was guaranteed to flop. The Rimshots only got on Respond because Paul was drunk one night, when he went to see them. They supported us at The Venue one night, and couldn't figure what they were doing on the label either!"

★ ★ ★

Four days after The Jam's four London 'soul revue' dates, the band played a secret, unpublicised gig at the Golders Green Hippodrome, North London, on December 19, 1981. Tickets were restricted to members of the band's fan club and the concert was recorded for broadcast on Radio One, giving the nation a chance to hear several new songs from The Jam's forthcoming album – 'The Gift', 'Precious', 'Ghosts' and 'Town Called Malice'.

These were among the five or so songs that had already been completed; during November and December, the group had started recording with Pete Wilson in Oxford Street's AIR London Studios, owned by ex-Beatles producer George Martin. By coincidence, The Jam found themselves in a studio adjacent to Paul McCartney, who was recording with Michael Jackson, and the two Pauls posed for a Linda McCartney photo which eventually appeared in *Smash Hits*. It would take another fourteen years before the pair collaborated musically for the *Help* project.

The album sessions were split into two definite halves. "I wrote almost all the rest of the tracks over Christmas," Paul later told me. "I came back with about six songs I'd finished at home." Weller seemed preoccupied with creating The Jam's best-ever collection. Driven to progress beyond what he perceived as the shackles of The Jam's orthodox rock sound, he worked hard during the day and played hard by night, absorbing London's nightlife and reflecting its influence in his music. Weller was under considerable pressure. The Jam had only issued two singles in 1981 and, as Alex Ogg noted, Paul had to endure the "burdensome psychoanalysis" of a music press which hung onto his every word.

Weighed down by the sole songwriting responsibilities, Weller "gagged under the weight of expectation". A gulf widened between him and the other two members, and tensions emerged in the studio. Paul later expressed his frustration that Bruce and Rick failed to capture the feel of his demos. Something had to give; and taking a break from the sessions one day, Weller suddenly collapsed at a pool table, suffering what was described as a mini-breakdown. "I just felt detached," he later explained, "as if I was in a dream and that I would slip away."

"I saw the pressure which Paul came under," admits Tony Fletcher. "Although he always wanted his lyrics to be observed, he never thought it would get that intense. He was still young. It was incredibly hard to deal with and I saw it get to him. Paul McCartney looked younger than him in that photo of them together. Paul was ill, and he was drinking too much. Eventually, he got shingles, which is unusual in your early twenties. He was suffering and, in retrospect, I don't think he had a way out. Even bringing in the brass for *The Gift* was a big step. Here was a band that represented white Bulldog England back in '77. It shifted. Now, they had black jazz-funk guys playing with them."

As The Jam were enjoying a clean sweep of the end-of-year readers' polls in the music press, the LP was quietly completed. Early in the New Year, fan club members received a Christmas flexidisc featuring 'Tales From The Riverbank'. "It's a re-recorded version we did originally for the LP," wrote Paul in the accompanying letter. "I suppose the main difference is the added brass, which is how we've been doing it live." On the subject of the band's horn players, he commented that "I think they're the only other instruments we can add without losing any of our own sound". But despite his attempt to shore up The Jam with additional members and a new direction, plus the optimistic tone of his letter, Paul Weller suspected that the album would be their last – and he wasn't the only one. "I can remember being at AIR London and listening to a playback of *The Gift*," says Dennis Munday, "and Paul definitely wasn't happy. Thinking it was their final album – and he almost certainly knew that – maybe he thought, 'I want it to be the best'."

8

EVERYTHING HAS A PRICE TO PAY

"I used to throw up before I went on stage. I'd be *physically* sick. I drank a lot – I wouldn't be staggering around but it eased me a bit. Since I've given up drinking so much, I get less nervous. Maybe I'm a little more confident now."

(Paul Weller, 1982)

"My admiration goes out to P. Weller for turning left. It shows that progress is possible."

(Joe Strummer, 1987)

"Pop stars are generally one of the most self-centred, unhealthy, big-headed bunch of wankers around, so why should I wish to be associated with people like that?"

(Paul Weller, *Jamming!*, 1981)

Whatever the foreboding behind the scenes, The Jam's return in early February 1982 was triumphant, both commercially and creatively. The double-A-sided 'Town Called Malice'/'Precious' was the band's second single to enter the charts at No. 1, and both songs were performed back-to-back on *Top Of The Pops* for the first time since The Beatles' 'We Can Work It Out'/'Day Tripper'. And as their most blatant acknowledgements of Paul's love of soul, both songs successfully integrated black influences into The Jam's sound. "I got heavily into soul at that time," Paul later told me. "I'd always listened to stuff that was before '68. Anything after that, to me, just didn't count. Then I dropped that kind of tunnel vision. I started to get into more contemporary music as well. Michael Jackson's *Off The Wall* was the album that really opened it up for me. Soul was getting tougher as well. D-Train's 'You're The One For Me' was a big influence. Great sound. I hate all that insipid, wimpy stuff. I felt a lot of Seventies soul/jazz-funk was too soft. I like more abrasive, real sounds."

Against a Tamla Motown backdrop, 'Town Called Malice' was another superb slice of social realism. As with Paul's lyrics on 'Private Hell' and 'That's Entertainment', the song questioned the mundanity of life's day-to-

135

day chores by creating vivid images of "lonely housewives", "disused milk floats" and "Sunday's roast beef" – stylistically similar to the poems of Dave Waller and Aidan Cant published by Riot Stories. Weller confessed that he had "always wanted to do a song with that Motown beat", citing Madness's 'Embarrassment', a hit in November 1980, as an influence. If 'Town Called Malice' echoed mid-Sixties soul, then 'Precious' acknowledged mid-Seventies funk – classics like Brass Construction's 'Movin'' – with a respectful nod towards 'Papa's Got A Brand New Pigbag'. Driven by Paul's rhythmic wah-wah guitar and the stabbing horn riffs of Thomas and Nichol, this poetical love song was also given an extended 12" treatment (the standard format for contemporary soul records since the late Seventies) to complete the dance package.

The songs may have summed up Weller's influences in one neat package, but they also divided his audience. The Motown-like melody and backbeat of 'Town Called Malice' was soulful, true, but the song itself was quintessential Jam. 'Precious' was nothing of the sort. This classy stab at white funk attracted comments like "what's all this disco rubbish?" from the band's less adventurous fans – but if anything, there was still too much of The Jam's huffing and puffing and not enough groove. Weller was breaking out, but not everyone wanted to escape with him. I wonder how many Jam followers bought D Train's 'You're The One For Me', which charted that month?

With 'Town Called Malice' lording it at the top of the charts for three weeks, the band kept their feet firmly on the ground by playing a benefit concert organised by Rock Against Racism in late February at the Polytechnic Of Central London. The band's five-song set followed a Jobs Not YOPS/Right To Work march to protest against the Youth Opportunities Scheme (YOPS), later reinvented as the Youth Training Scheme (YTS), which the Conservative Government were introducing as a form of vocational training – a poorly paid substitute for the old apprenticeship scheme (and with no guaranteed job at the end of it). The demonstration culminated in three thousand people crowding into the Royal Festival Hall to be addressed by Labour MPs, and Weller's support was ample confirmation of his growing socialist sympathies.

Paul made his position clear in an interview with *Record Mirror*: "It's just like punk never happened," he scoffed. "I think there should be music with some kind of sensibilities, some kind of consciousness, instead of this showbiz crap like Adam Ant wants to bring back. He just makes me puke . . . I don't have an extravagant lifestyle. I haven't got any mansion, just a two-roomed flat, I haven't got a car and I do my own shopping." At the pinnacle of The Jam's success, then, Weller was adopting a hard line that pre-empted American punk's 'straight edge' ethos – of cutting out stimulants and maintaining a clean lifestyle that was almost puritanical. "I did a bit of clubbing last year and that's my lot. There's a duty not to . . .

Rock can destroy you if you let it. Like, I don't take drugs anymore, I've even given up drinking."

Tony Fletcher remembers the stark change in Weller's demeanour. "Everybody involved with The Jam could knock the beers back, the girls included," he grins. "Paul would come in and complain of enormous hangovers. After a few black-outs, he said, 'This is fucking mad, I'm too young for this.' And he quit drinking during the last Jam tours, which made an enormous difference. Paul was different once he was sober. He did get very serious and dour. In retrospect, he was changing his life."

An equally uncompromising stance was revealed in the lyrics on *The Gift*, issued on March 12, 1982. Many of the songs led a tirade against those in power – the ruling classes, heads of state and industrial bosses – and their effects on the less privileged. But if there was one word which ran through the music, it was 'unity' – an ironic, idealistic quest, bearing in mind the fraying relationships within the band. The key songs ended both sides; the title track had an evangelical lyric concerning "the gift of life", and a together-we-can-be-strong message which brought to mind the uplifting, spiritual tones of socially minded early Seventies soul. Its guitar riff was lifted from The Small Faces' 'Don't Burst My Bubble', but the song's message was sadly buried beneath a murky production.

"Trans-Global Express" was just as cacophonous, but its use of dub and psychedelic techniques made it even more powerful. Adapting its title from the name of an old railway company which Kraftwerk had borrowed for an album, this semi-instrumental was built around the riff from the World Column's funky Northern Soul classic, 'So Is The Sun'. "I had a lot of songs written upfront," Paul later told me. "There was only a couple of experimental things, like 'Trans-Global Express', which was done on the spot." You had to read the words on the inner sleeve to understand the song's message, which was in essence a revolutionary call-to-arms to "see the hands of oppression fumble, and their systems crash to the ground".

"I suppose the overall sound/effect is quite soul-influenced," Weller had suggested in that fan club letter, "but not necessarily Tamla Motown. I really wanted to try and create a 1980's brand of soul." The packaging, as ever, was ingenious; the album was sold in a striped pink 'gift' bag (a similar pattern to the 12″ 'disco' cover for 'Town Called Malice'), with a photo of a Northern Soul dancer on the inner sleeve. (Such was Paul's perfectionism that he had the sleeve altered at the very last minute, to remove some scribbled lines on the design, and twenty grand's worth of covers had to be scrapped.) But the band were growing apart, evidenced by the stark black-and-white live photo on the back cover, which ominously showed Weller at one end of the stage and Bruce and Rick at the other.

There was a hollow ring, too, about the title of the album's opener, 'Happy Together', one of the genuine masterpieces on an otherwise disjointed affair. Another was composed in the studio: 'Ghosts', a gentle ode to those who have lost sight of themselves, urging them to "lift up your lonely heart and walk right on through". Equally charming was 'Carnation', which dealt with the greed and avarice of human nature. 'Running On The Spot' was more upbeat and its ringing guitar riff and ingenious production remoulded The Jam's musical shape, with some excellent backing harmonies towards the end.

But in trying to forge a new vision for The Jam, Weller sometimes sounded pretentious and affected. The main culprit was the ironically titled 'The Planner's Dream Goes Wrong', which punctured the myth of urban development's "dream life luxury living" with rundown high rise council blocks; the song's appealing melody was spoilt by the stapled-on ethnic flavour of Caribbean steel drums. And Bruce Foxton's clumsy funk instrumental, 'Circus', was as unimaginative as its title, chosen because AIR London's studio overlooked Oxford Circus. Despite the conversational style of the album's lyrics, few songs put across Weller's point in an accessible way. There was no doubting Paul's efforts or intentions – technically, his voice had improved, for example – but the overall impression was of something incomplete.

Dennis Munday agrees. "But the problem was not so much with Paul," he argues, "as that his writing had transcended The Jam's and Bruce and Rick's style. They were a great rhythm section but there was no way The Jam could have developed. *The Gift* is a good album but it's not a great album. Paul had become a far better songwriter and he couldn't write for Bruce and Rick anymore."

To promote the album, there was the inevitable tour – under the *Trans-Global Unity Express* banner – which took in Britain across March and early April, before a string of dates around mainland Europe, followed by Canada, America and Japan. After *The Gift* sold healthily in the States, extra shows were added in Los Angeles and New York, which kept The Jam on the road until mid-June. "I hope this tour is the fucking shake-up," scrawled Paul angrily in the programme. "I hope it is the knife to slice through the increasing apathy. Most music at the moment is pure 'showbiz' and pure crap. If I thought all that a group could accomplish was appearing on *TOTP*, I'd fucking jack it in tomorrow. We've got so much inside us, we've just gotta let it come through. And forget your prejudices, forced upon us by social conditioning. Forget them! Find your own values. I want my music to reach people emotionally to maybe show 'em just how much power we have inside us." Quite apart from his obvious frustration, it was the contrast between Paul's strident message and the genial notes from the other two which stuck out like a sore thumb. "Well, another year!" began Foxton, before chatting about the tour and the album, ending with a question, "but just how much can one take alcohol-wise?" "I'm really looking forward to playing a live set again," said Rick. "And not forgetting yourselves, it will be a great tour."

"We got to travel on the tour bus," remembers DJ Ady Croasdell, "which was just the hardcore of The Jam and a dozen people. The atmosphere was good, quite good fun. They had a few in-jokes. I remember a story that Paul had put a turd in a plastic bag and nailed it underneath a desk at a Conservative Party Conference! The group weren't tense between each other, I wouldn't say, but there was no great camaraderie. I never saw them row but they weren't big mates, either. It was business-like – this is the job – and travelling between the gigs is boring. Rick would go off and read a book. Paul, me and one of the bouncers, Joe Awome – a really nice lad – played cards with Brian Hawkins, who did the merchandising."

Rudi were the main support act on some of the tour's major dates. "By the end of the tour, we were getting encores," says the band's Brian Young. "On the last night in Leeds, our new single 'Crimson' was 'single-of-the-week' in *Sounds*. Guitars were like a bad word by then so we'd brought in a keyboard player. 'Crimson' had airplay everywhere." But while the sales of their second Jamming! single were healthy, Brian found the situation between members of The Jam unusual. "We thought they'd be good mates but the three of them hardly spoke to each other throughout the whole tour. They didn't even knock about together – three separate camps, really. Paul would be dead sensible after the gig and have a cup of tea, and Bruce ended up with us because he liked a couple of drinks and playing pool. Paul was a nice fella, but we could see the change since we'd first met him, in the people he surrounded himself with – 'yes' men. After the gigs, Paul would have his entourage with him. What surprised us most was that Rick and Bruce weren't included. Live, they were very much a three-piece and we couldn't understand how there was nothing at all offstage. I found that very strange."

"Gill Price was on the tour bus," adds Ady Croasdell. "It was funny because she liked a drink and a laugh and we'd get legless at nights – she wanted a cockney knees-up, 'C'mon darlin', let's have a giggle' – but Paul wasn't that bothered. He wasn't a drinker. He took the touring and the music seriously and he'd have a laugh but it was straighter than I thought it would be – you expect sex, drugs and rock'n'roll and there wasn't any of that! They often rowed – Gill blind-drunk and Paul stone cold sober! But the night would usually be over by ten-thirty, and there was little night-clubbing, though Bruce was up for going out more than the others."

Footage from the Birmingham Bingley Hall concert, which was later edited for release as the *Trans-Global Unity Express* video, illustrated that despite an energetic performance, The Jam were not at their best on the tour. For all Paul's convictions, the band lacked subtlety and finesse and Weller's playing was clumsy at times. There was also a memorable moment when Paul reacted to Bruce's close harmony on 'The Butterfly Collector' by freezing him with a look-that-could-kill.

Weller's idealistic political ambitions also heightened his frustration. The Pet Shop Boys' Neil Tennant, then a *Smash Hits* journalist, summed up the dilemma: " 'All I want you to do tonight is think about what we're saying.' Paul Weller sings with anger and passion but what *is* he saying? Pull together? No nuclear war? Us against Them? What does 'Trans-Global Unity Express' ('our overall message') mean to *you*? Pop stars can only introduce, in a loose way, a few ideas that might otherwise pass some of their audience by. More important is the atmosphere of shared motivation which they can generate. And The Jam can generate this like few others."

The backlash had started: "A Jam gig is a fairly joyless spectacle," maligned Barney Hoskyns in *NME*. Referring to Paul's recent penchant for sportswear (and, therefore, that of The Jam's audience), he commented that "The Lonsdale sweatshirts are eloquent symbols of its rigour and sobriety. By using [R&B] as the basis for social anthems, they kill off the humour and narcissism of its live performance." Whereas the message of Elvis Costello's recent soul-styled album had been *Get Happy!*, there weren't many smiles from the stage at Jam concerts. Hoskyns also observed that despite Weller's pleas for racial and cultural unity, The Jam's audience was dominated by white working-class males, "chanting the encores like possessed football supporters".

It wasn't surprising that Paul became disenchanted. "I think the music press and the trendy London scene put Weller off Mods," says Ady Croasdell, suggesting that his fans didn't embrace the shift in Paul's soul tastes from the Sixties into the Seventies. Weller's obsession with youth may have dovetailed neatly with many of The Jam's fans being so very young – 90% of their audience was under 21 – but his increasingly sophisticated, twenty-something tastes weren't mirrored by his followers. "Paul certainly didn't want to be seen as a square," says Croasdell, "and fourteen-year-old kids in parkas probably embarrassed him. Although The Jam were good with the fans, I think Weller wanted them to develop with him – and, basically, they didn't."

The live soul covers were warmly received, though. The highlight was undoubtedly their version of Curtis Mayfield's spiritual, humanitarian anthem from 1971, 'Move On Up'. This mainstay of The Jam's 1982 live set was occasionally accompanied by a soundcheck favourite, James Brown's soul classic, 'I Got You (I Feel Good)', while Ray Charles' 'Hit The Road Jack' was sometimes tagged on the end of a new song, 'Pity Poor Alfie'. Similarly, Sam Cooke's 'Chain Gang' was segued into 'Just Who Is The Five O'Clock Hero' from *The Gift*.

There had already been talk, as early as mid-1981, in fact, of a Jam covers EP. It made sense: performances of Sixties songs were scattered across their records, in addition to the soul favourites which were now creeping into their live set. By early 1982, Weller had firmed up four songs for a proposed single – 'Move On Up' and 'I Got You (I Feel Good)', plus Edwin Starr's powerful 1970 Motown anthem, 'War', and The Chi-Lites' early Seventies 'floater', 'Stoned Out Of My Mind'. The songs were recorded around February '82 at Fulham's Maison Rouge Studios as part of the band's first self-produced sessions but they were unhappy with the results, and the EP was scrapped.

'I Got You (I Feel Good)' eventually appeared on the posthumous Jam rarities collection, *Extras*, which also unearthed covers of The Beatles' *Revolver* track, 'And Your Bird Can Sing' ("that's just me with Pete Wilson playing the kit," said Paul) and The Small Faces' 'Get Yourself Together'. There were also confirmed recordings of The Beatles' 'Rain' and The Kinks' 'Waterloo Sunset' and 'Dead End Street'. Also in the archives, according to Polydor's Dennis Munday, are versions of Gene Vincent's 'Be-Bop-A-Lula', Eddie Cochran's 'Summertime Blues', Sam Cooke's 'Wonderful World', Muddy Waters' 'I Got My Mojo Working', Ben E. King's 'Stand By Me' and The Small Faces' 'My Mind's Eye'. The band had also performed John's Children's Marc Bolan-penned 'Desdemona', featuring Department S's Vaughn Toulouse on vocals. These demos allowed Paul to act out his musical fantasies as a diversion from the monotony of recording.

The Jam's rousing treatment of 'War', meanwhile, was chosen for the 12″ edition of a new single, 'Just Who Is The Five O'Clock Hero?', issued in Germany in early June but imported in sufficient quantity to guarantee a Top 10 UK hit. "The *real* heroes are obviously the geezer who *has* to go out and do a nine to five job," said Weller – who'd never done a normal day's work in his life – explaining the idea behind what was one of the strongest cuts on *The Gift*. "So the nurses and the miners are the real heroes because they keep the country going – and not pop stars."

After The Jam's roadshow ground to a close, there were plans to play another CND benefit concert, a No Nukes Festival in the summer, at Queens Park Rangers' Loftus Road football stadium in Shepherds Bush. Unfortunately, permission was refused by the local council, but this hiatus gave Paul and Gill a chance to go on holiday to Italy in July. It allowed Weller a breathing space to reflect on The Jam's future – and all he could see was a tireless single/album/tour treadmill. He knew he fronted the most popular band in Britain, and that fact fixed him forever under the spotlight. He was well aware that he only had to pick his nose and the music press wrote a review – and this degree of scrutiny made him uncomfortable. Weller also realised that The Jam had reached the stadium-level status of the rock giants he despised. He knew that the band was a secure commercial proposition for the foreseeable future, and this burden of responsibility rested uneasily on his shoulders.

Meanwhile, pop was also witnessing a sea-change away from punk-derived, guitar rock, but Paul felt he was swimming against the tide of his audience's conservatism, and wasn't convinced that Foxton and Buckler were capable of following him upstream. Two of the bands Paul most admired, The Beatles and The Small Faces, had disbanded in their prime – or close to it. As Weller was lying on that beach in Italy, the decision presented itself: he had to disband The Jam.

The decision hadn't come out of the blue, of course. "We had a conversation, 1980 maybe, when we were discussing the longevity of the band," recalls Dennis Munday, "and Paul said, 'I don't want it to go on forever. It's alright while we're making good records and we mean something. If we don't, then I want us to stop. And I *will* stop it.' He didn't want to end up like The Who, who were a pale imitation of their former selves." Tellingly, the first person to hear the news on Paul's return to England was John Weller.

★ ★ ★

Dennis Munday was one of the first people to learn of Paul's decision from John. "I wasn't surprised," he admits. "I realised in the last year something was wrong but couldn't put my finger on it. I don't think the decision was that hard for Paul. I think he realised that, at the age of thirty, lyrics like 'golden faces under 25' and 'Life is a drink and you get drunk when you're young' might have a hollow ring. Youth-orientated music is just that: you've got to move on. Paul told me he didn't want to be restricted by a specific format. His musical horizons broadened and he was listening to all sorts of stuff. You could hear the changes coming in the last couple of years, with songs like 'That's Entertainment'. Once it got beyond, say, *Sound Affects*, he had to compromise. What brings it home is 'Funeral Pyre', which harked back to the old Jam. Paul was faced then with two options: he either carried on within those narrow parameters or broadened them. You can hear it in 'Absolute Beginners', and you can also hear that Bruce and Rick are not on the same wavelength – he was going in a direction they couldn't follow. They recorded cover versions of 'War' and 'Stoned Out Of My Mind', and I think Paul used a drum machine."

Bruce and Rick were dealt the blow later that month, during the recording sessions for their next single, a lush ballad poignantly entitled 'The Bitterest Pill (I Ever Had To Swallow)'. Buckler recalls the moment as if it were yesterday. "We'd just arrived at the studio," he explains. "John Weller sat us all down in the reception area and Paul just came out with it. He said he was leaving the band, and there were a couple of seconds of absolute silence as it sank in. Bruce tried to persuade Paul that maybe we should give it a rest for a while – go off and do your solo thing but don't officially break the band up. Give it time to make sure you're making the right decision. But Paul was adamant and had obviously been thinking about it for some time. In the last few months, before we knew we were going to split, Paul had certainly become a lot more moody. Mind you, he'd been like that anyway, when he was with Gill. They had their own little world, which they buzzed off into. We hadn't really taken much notice."

Buckler doesn't seem bitter about Paul's decision: "He was obviously dissatisfied with the way the band were going. He said he didn't want to be on this treadmill of having to write to order to fulfil a recording, go out on tour and then be back to square one again – we had an incredible workload. He looked uncomfortable. In his mind, I think he was searching for a new direction and The Jam's format wasn't going to be part of that." One of the keenest opponents was Paul's dad, as Rick explains: "John didn't want us to split. In fact, Paul was the only person in the world who was going to split the band. Everybody was trying to persuade him not to be so hasty – the record company, the agents. But I think that once he'd got the bottle to announce it officially to us, there was no going back. I have to say it was a bit out of the blue."

Tony Fletcher was kept in the dark, too. "I had no idea Paul was going to break up the band," he admits. "But when we were recording our Apocalypse single in August, Paul played us 'The Bitterest Pill', which had just been finished, and one wag in our group said, 'That's a great solo single, Paul.' He gave us all a really odd look, which I think said a lot."

Both the other Jam members were understandably devastated by the announcement, and it has been widely reported that Bruce in particular took the news badly. Foxton later stormed off the set during a protracted video shoot for the single, and later announced he wouldn't play any farewell gigs. "All the enthusiasm had gone and I just couldn't come to grips with the fact that we were splitting up," Bruce later admitted (and Dennis Munday was used as a double to model the back of Foxton's head in the video). The Wellers reacted to this move by informing Bruce that Glen Matlock would take his place. The ex-Sex Pistols bassist wasn't actually approached – but the ruse succeeded in luring Foxton back.

There was no hint of portent in a fan club letter sent out late that summer. Within its very positive tone, Paul even spoke optimistically of America: "The USA tour was a success," he wrote. "It was really encouraging, loads of young kids coming to the gigs, really enthusiastic. I think most kids there are getting bored with the usual crap they get shoved down their throats and I reckon things could really change." To their fans, The Jam's future seemed bright. Paul described the next single as "an exercise in dramatic writing (I think). Actually, I wanted to write a song without any politics or 'heavy' theme, so this one is just a straight tearjerker. It's very different for us, very slow and with violins (!). I think people will be able to appreciate it on two levels, either seriously as a real soul ballad or a bit tongue in cheek. Some of the words are outrageously dramatic."

There was also talk of an EP of out-takes from *The Gift* sessions and a live album was slotted in for November – "not just a straight live concert, but more of a retrospective. With songs from all different periods and one special!

A song from 1975!! It's a recording of us in a club in Woking, not good quality but very, very interesting."

When 'The Bitterest Pill' finally arrived in early September, Paul's sense of humour was lost on many fans. How could The Jam create such a straightforward pop song – with lush string accompaniment, too? It is easy to sympathise with Bruce's complaint in *Our Story* that "it was just becoming the Paul Weller show". Paul was friendly with The Belle Stars' Jenny McKeown, who sang backing vocals on the single – and Paul and Jenny were pictured together on the cover of *Melody Maker*. Vaughn Toulouse posed on the single's front cover; and Vaughn's friend, Lee Kavanagh (who sang on Department S's hit, 'Is Vic There?'), was seen kissing Paul in the video. The song echoed the big Sixties productions of singers like Dusty Springfield.

Flipping the single over, 'Pity Poor Alfie' might have pointed a way forward for The Jam. Crashing in with horns, the song's groovy, swinging vibe brought to mind the theme tune to Britain's best-loved Seventies cop series, *The Sweeney*. It then segued into 'Fever', Little Willie John's R&B classic popularised in 1958 by Peggy Lee's jazz–pop hit.

On September 20, The Jam fulfilled the commitments of their *Solid Bond In Your Heart* mini-tour. The two horn players were ditched in favour of a keyboard player, Jimmy Telford of Scottish band Everest The Hard Way, and backing singers Afrodiziak, featuring future Soul II Soul vocalist and solo artist Caron Wheeler. The band were forced to cancel some continental dates after Paul contracted shingles – a sure sign that he was feeling the strain – but despite the tensions within the band, the concerts were their most enjoyable for some time now that the end was in sight.

Life on the road had ground Weller down, though. "Part of the problem was that big tour of America," suspects Jimmy Telford. "They were about to break but I think Paul got pig sick of Bruce and Rick. I detected an element of self-destruction at times, because he didn't really adhere to all that superstar shit. He almost didn't want to be that big. He liked his cult position. He could quite easily have been a massive superstar. He just needed to keep the band together, even if he'd sacked Bruce and Rick and kept the name The Jam. Bruce was difficult but he knew their position was under threat. From their point of view, there was an axe swinging above their heads."

Now that the split was accepted as inevitable within The Jam's camp, the plan was to announce, in early October, the dates for a farewell November/December tour before the world learnt of the decision. Paul was scheduled to break the news after the group performed on the first episode of Channel 4's *The Tube* on November 5, but there was a leak, allegedly via a member of The Chords. The rumour began in the gossip page of *Sounds*, and spread to *Record Mirror* and London's *Evening Standard*, and on October 30 the band reacted with a hand-written press release. Paul's comments were typically forthright and serious-minded:

"Personal address to all our fans – At the end of this year, The Jam will be officially splitting up as I feel we have achieved all we can together as a group. I mean this both musically and commercially . . . I'd hate us to end up old and embarrassing like so many other groups do. I want us to finish with dignity . . . The longer a group continues, the more frightening the thought of ever ending it, because that is why so many of them carry on until they become meaningless. I've never wanted The Jam to get to this stage. What we (and you) have built up *has* meant something, for me it stands for honesty, passion and energy and youth. I want it to stay that way and maybe exist as a guideline for new young groups coming up to improve and expand on. This would make it even more worthwhile . . . thank you for all the faith you have shown in us and the building of such a strong force and feeling that all three of us have felt and been touched by. Here's to the future, In love and friendship, Paul Weller."

The hand-out was followed by a letter to 'Jam Club' members, in which Paul revealed that "I have been thinking about it for some time now (at least for almost a year) . . . There are other reasons . . . being the writer and the kind of 'figure head', there is a constant pressure to write the next LP . . . it adds a bit of edge to my work, but at the same time I have never been able to sit back and *enjoy* what we have done, it's been like this for six years but I don't think I could take another six years . . . it would do me nut in." When The Jam finally appeared on *The Tube* to perform a short concert, it was clear who felt most comfortable about the split – both Bruce and Rick looked unhappy, whereas an unusually relaxed-looking Weller spoke optimistically about future projects such as his new plans for Respond.

Details soon emerged about a farewell Jam single – although Paul hadn't been able to decide between two new songs, 'Beat Surrender' and a title already familiar to Jam fans as the banner from the previous tour, 'Solid Bond In Your Heart'. "I remember sitting down with Paul in a hotel room in Weymouth and he played me the two songs," remembers DJ Tony Rounce. "He said, 'I dunno, whatcha reckon for the single? It's really between these two, waddaya think?' I said, 'Solid Bond' is far and away the single. He said, 'Well, I'm saving that.' I thought, 'Who are you saving it for!? Somebody on Respond? A rainy day? For Christmas?' "

Issued in late November, The Jam's final single was almost guaranteed to top the charts in the wake of the announcement, and sure enough, 'Beat Surrender' became their third and final single to début at No. 1. Introduced by a piano riff, the song had a yearning melody and Northern Soul feel built around an anthemic chorus. There was a conspicuous absence of guitar – and without the instrument, a naked-looking Weller shuffled awkwardly from foot to foot on *Top Of The Pops*, vaguely trying to dance before deciding it probably wasn't a good idea. Instead, piano and horns were in the driving seat, which set the template for Weller's next musical endeavour.

'Move On Up', 'Stoned Out Of My Mind' and a radical reworking of Edwin Starr's 'War', with vocal backing from Afrodiziak, constituted the bonus disc of a double pack edition of the single. More unusual was the offbeat, low-key B-side, 'Shopping', an obvious title from the fashion-conscious Weller but actually a laconic look at consumerism. Paul's deadpan vocals matched the song's lazy atmosphere in what represented his first serious dabblings with jazz – Rick played with brushes – and the logical progression from 'Pity Poor Alfie'/'Fever'. On the front sleeve, Gill Price reflected the song's apt title by modelling with a white flag, while Paul contributed a pretentious sleeve proclamation, with key words highlighted in pop-art colour, under the guise of The Boy Wonder – the first of several sleeve-writing pseudonyms he would create.

Several extra dates had to be added to satisfy the unprecedented demand for The Jam's hastily arranged 'Beat Surrender' tour. The band's line-up was swelled by the return of a two-man horn section, Kenny Witton and Colin Graham, in place of Thomas and Nichol (who later emerged in the successful soul act, Loose Ends). The excitement during those last dates reached fever pitch. In Glasgow, the band received a standing ovation *before* the gig, and they played an unprecedented run of five nights at Wembley Arena. "I remember the obsessive devotion of the audiences," says Tony Rounce. "Paul could have gone out there and sung 'Old McDonald Had A Farm' for two hours. I had the thrill of introducing a few gigs towards the end. I'd never seen 10,000 people at Wembley from a stage point of view. The adrenaline rush was incredible. You're standing there and it's like, you're the Christian and there's 10,000 lions there. I can see why John Weller used to get so wound up. Paul asked some fan called Greg, who ran the band's American fan club, to introduce them at Brighton." The Jam finally bowed out with an emotional concert at the Brighton Centre – a possible indulgence on Paul's part bearing in mind the town's Sixties Mod connotations.

There was more Weller rhetoric in the tour programme, as he confidently skirted over The Jam's break-up after asserting their achievements: "Anything that is good (bloody good) must come to an end if it wishes to remain good and here endeth the first chapter. I'm ready for the next bugger . . ." What followed was ostensibly a manifesto for Paul's future. Bruce, in contrast, seemed gutted: "For me it's kind of difficult to realise that this is the last tour The Jam will ever play. The End!" he wrote, before soberly concluding that "individually we will be pursuing various projects next year". Rick, as ever, kept his message short and undemonstrative: "Thanks for all your support over the past years. I'm going to miss you."

After six years, as many albums and a clutch of classic singles – and their years prior to that "playing every shithole in Surrey" – The Jam had finally broken up. To their many thousands of fans, with whom they had struck a quite unique bond, it was the end of an era. The atmosphere among the audience on that last evening in Brighton had been reserved – disbelieving, almost. The last song The Jam ever played live was 'The Gift' – it was a poignant finish – and a stunned, mournful hush had descended over the venue as the crowd filed out through the exits, clutching their tour pro-grammes, their jackets and their memories of one of Britain's finest-ever bands.

"I was quite relieved about The Jam splitting up," admits Dennis Munday. "The pressures, particularly on Paul, were enormous – too much – trying to live up to that 'spokesman for a generation' tag, trying to deliver three singles and an album a year and tour as well, especially at his age. The problem is that Polydor expected every record to make No. 1. Even when 'Absolute Beginners' sold 300,000 copies or whatever, they looked on that as a failure. That's hard to live up to.

"As you mature, you find you don't have as much in common with some people. 'Thick As Thieves' summed it up. It's called growing up, it's natural, and when you're in a pop group, even more so, because you're living with each other. You don't see your girlfriend as much as you see the people in the band – and it's hard work. The only negativity would have been in keeping The Jam going. I've read articles that claim he had another year. Well, he didn't. I hate to think what the seventh Jam album would have been like. Instead, they went out with a No. 1 album and a No. 1 single."

★   ★   ★

The overriding impression of The Jam's final chapter is that, behind the scenes, the Wellers ran roughshod over the rest of the band. For example, Foxton and Buckler had wanted the last show to be in Guildford, because of its proximity to Woking, but were overruled. Paul was interviewed alone by the BBC on Brighton pier in the hours leading up to their farewell performance, much to the irritation of the other two. The Jam's big selling official biography, *A Beat Concerto*, published in a collaboration between Riot Stories and Omnibus Press almost a year later in autumn 1983, was written by a friend of Weller, *Melody Maker*-turned-*NME* journalist Paolo Hewitt. Much to their chagrin, the book made scant mention of the band's rhythm section, drawing only on the briefest of interviews. And although both Bruce and Rick were asked to sift through a mountain of live tapes, neither was directly involved in choosing the tracks for the scheduled live LP.

The Jam's recorded history didn't end on that emotional night on December 11, and the fallout of their popularity continued well into the New Year, spurred on by the arrival of *Dig The New Breed*. Taking its title from an old James Brown classic, *Dig The New Breed* was issued in early December not only as a fitting epitaph for a band whose tours were as important to their fans as their records, but also because The Jam still owed Polydor another album. The disc was tastefully packaged in the style of an old black-and-white Sixties

LP, the uncluttered white back cover leaving room for three very different farewells: Paul's written in dramatic pop-art prose; Bruce's serious and emotional; Rick's honest and straightforward.

Dig The New Breed was a solid, representative overview of The Jam in concert, spanning their whole career. There was no sign of the promised material from 1975, and with only one 1977 recording and two-thirds of the selections taped in the Eighties, the LP was weighted towards their more recent shows, reflecting Weller's low opinion of their pre-*All Mod Cons* work. The album's highlight was a blistering cover of 'Big Bird', a rock/soul/funk workout that substituted the graceful power of Eddie Floyd's '68 Stax sound for grittiness and aggression, creating a 'Trans-Global Express'-like anthem that stood alongside 'Move On Up' as The Jam's most successful foray into soul.

The end-of-year readers' polls were a predictable landslide, The Jam fending off the new pop brigade of Culture Club, Wham! and Duran Duran. And when Polydor re-promoted the group's singles back catalogue for a second time, post-Jam euphoria pushed the first twelve 45s back into the charts, together with the year-old 'Town Called Malice' and the first UK issue of 'That's Entertainment' – an achievement which won them a place in the *Guinness Book Of Records*.

A year after the announcement of the split, Polydor compiled the inevitable retrospective: the double-album *Snap!* was a tasteful collection of all their singles, plus selected album tracks and B-sides. 'Funeral Pyre' was remixed "as nobody was completely happy with it" and "it was decided to use the demo version of 'That's Entertainment' because it had a certain quality that was never captured again". Roughly translated, this meant that Paul was dissatisfied with the results after Bruce and Rick had gotten hold of the song. The album came with a free live EP, which included covers of the Small Faces' 'Get Yourself Together' and Curtis Mayfield's 'Move On Up' – the perfect indication of Paul's tastes of the period.

Snap!'s artwork was designed by a friend of Weller's, Simon Halfon, using simple devices such as dynamic *sans serif* typefaces and bold, symmetrical blocks of colour. This distinctive style was a cross between pop-art and the cover art of Fifties and Sixties jazz albums (like David Stone Martin's work for Verve and Reed Miles' designs for Blue Note). Halfon had co-designed the *Beat Surrender* cover and has worked closely on the packaging of Paul's music ever since.

A Beat Concerto (extracts from which were printed on the sleeve for *Snap!*) was also packaged by Halfon. But by drawing on his circle of friends, Weller had cemented the divide between himself and both Foxton and Buckler, who had never disguised their animosity towards Paolo Hewitt. In Bruce and Rick's version of events, *Our Story*, they criticised the journalist for being "omniscient" – in other words, he pretended to know things even though he wasn't there – and Bruce questioned Weller's authorship of some Jam songs by commenting that many of them "stemmed from Rick's drum patterns or from me". After the split, Weller reacted by shunning any contact with either ex-Jam member – and incredibly, he hasn't spoken to them to this day.

What is really fascinating, though, is the degree of bickering, back-biting and plain immaturity which seems to have emanated from the whole affair. (During the course of researching this book, for example, I found those interviewees who were close to Paul Weller were often willing to dismiss Foxton and Buckler – it sometimes felt as if the pair were "untouchables".) Compared to the "acrimonious split" suffered by many bands, The Jam's parting of the ways was by all accounts relatively civilised, but perhaps that was only possible because their bassist and drummer relinquished what little responsibility they might have had. And yet people still felt it necessary to make snide remarks about them, with comments like, "they were the finest rhythm section in Woking", and still felt the need to take sides – and, in most instances, that was Paul's.

But what of Wellers' role in all this? "I've been meaning to contact them and it has been playing on my mind recently," he admitted in *Boys About Town* fanzine in 1991. "I wouldn't play with Bruce or Rick again, it's nothing personal. That was then, this is now. We were the right people for The Jam. But outside of that, I don't think we'd be any use to each other. We made The Jam sound together and it worked. We became limited within the framework and I think that stopped us progressing, but more as musicians. I wanted to go a different place with The Jam and didn't feel we could go there together. But I would definitely like to get in touch with them again and I will do. It's crazy not to see someone for eight or nine years after spending so much time together."

But Weller has never picked up the phone to ring his ex-colleagues. In fact, he consciously avoided them, according to Rick. "Just after the band had split, I went down to Solid Bond, the studio he had," Buckler remembers. "I was in and out of London so I was passing and thought I'd pop in. I went there about three times and he wouldn't come out and say hello. Obviously, I gave up in the end. Why bother?" Maybe there was a pang of guilt on Paul's part. After all, despite Dennis Munday's protestations on the pair's behalf, Polydor passed on their option of signing "the other two" as solo artists. Foxton's stab at a solo career with Arista Records nose-dived after a minor hit with 'Freak' in mid-1983. A year later, he found himself without a record contract. Intermittent projects kept him busy throughout the Eighties, before he returned to the first idea that had been mooted after The Jam's split – he joined up for a long spell with old friend Jake Burns in reconvened Irish punk band Stiff Little Fingers. And Rick's attempts at maintaining a career with his group Time UK were met with studied indifference from all but the keenest Jam die-hards.

The truth is that The Jam's rhythm section were a tight, proficient unit who lacked the ability and imagination to diversify as musicians. Funk drumming and bass playing were quite different techniques to those within rock and the pair struggled to adapt – Bruce's solo on 'War' sounded awkward, for example. And Paul was right that the pair lacked his musical vision. Speaking about Paul's next venture in their book, *Our Story*, they explained, "It wasn't that we thought it wasn't any good, it was more that the music was just not our style. It just wasn't the sort of thing we enjoyed listening to".

Foxton and Buckler were able back-up men rather than artistes or auteurs, but then neither were they ever encouraged by Weller to develop on anything other than his terms. In this respect, Paul's attitude seemed petty and selfish; the fact that he knew he *was* The Jam should have made him more aware of the potential difficulties which Bruce and Rick would face. But given the opportunity to help Rick out, he declined. "When I started Time UK," Buckler explains, "I rang the Wellers' office and asked for a list of The Jam's fan club members so I could write to all them and let them know what I was doing. And the office said, no, because it's all part of the Style Council's fan club and we're not going to let you use it. It was all part of Paul severing connections completely."

A neat comparison would be with the band which has most inspired Weller. When The Beatles split, John Lennon and George Harrison – and Paul McCartney, after 1971 – consciously 'looked after' Ringo Starr, because they knew he had the toughest route to solo success. Paul's attitude, in contrast, smacked of using people in a way which conflicted with his talk of unity, love and justice.

When confronted in *Highlights And Hang-Ups* with his ex-partners' reluctance to participate in this 1994 documentary, Weller looked bored. Shrugging his shoulders, he looked cold to the touch. "Well, I don't really expect anything from them," Paul replied. "I don't feel they owe me anything and I don't owe them anything either. I suppose part of me finds it quite sad that they feel that strong about it, especially after such a long period of time. But I don't know why they feel so hurt because we started a band when we were kids, we made it, we had a lot of success. I didn't want to go on. End of story."

Bearing in mind that Paul spent six years in the same band as these people, it is difficult not to criticise him for just closing his mind to the whole issue. Weller's unwillingness to face up to this responsibility tallies with the fact that he has been able to rely on his father, and the closely knit group of allies who John Weller has woven around Paul, to deal with many of the confrontational decisions necessary in such a high profile career. If a situation presented itself which forced Weller to step outside of the emotional bubble in which he has existed for most of his life, he has resisted it. "I liked Paul," says keyboardist Jimmy Telford. "He's difficult but he's essentially a good guy, well meaning in intentions. I always thought Paul was really straight in his dealings but he did tend to leave the dirty work to his dad."

In Weller's defence, the whole band had drifted apart – and the rigmarole of occasional correspondence and the Christmas card cycle was probably never going to change that. If Paul felt responsible, then it was because he had carried the burden of responsibility of The Jam – and, therefore, Bruce and Rick, too – for many years. Once free from the shackles, there was never the temptation to go back and inspect the ball and chain again just to make sure. He was far too busy enjoying his new-found freedom. He was far too busy enjoying his next musical project, The Style Council.

9

ALWAYS THERE TO FOOL YOU

style *n.*   **1.** the correct way of designating a person or thing
             2. a superior quality or manner
council *n.* **1.** a body of people formally constituted and meeting
             regularly
             2. an ecclesiastical assembly

"Respond Records hopes to help towards destroying Rock Music and Rock Culture."

(Paul Weller, *Flexipop*, 1983)

"In the jazz world, you meet all kinds of cats, on absolutely equal terms, who can clue you up in all kinds of directions – in social directions, in culture directions, in sexual directions."

(*Absolute Beginners*, Colin MacInnes, 1959)

Paul Weller has spoken of 1983 as his most creative year. "Once you've reached a peak, you have to climb another mountain," explains Dennis Munday. "Paul wanted the freedom to do what he wanted. The Jam reached a peak with 'Going Underground' and it was very difficult to maintain that." Dennis took a more active role in Paul's career after The Jam's split. "I hated the last Brighton gig," he admits. "Once Christmas '82 was over with, we got back to work and it felt like a breath of fresh air. Splitting The Jam up made a big difference to Paul – it had taken its toll and I could physically see the weight off his shoulders as he became freer and more easy-going. He dearly wanted to get out of that yearly routine of singles/album/major tour. Suddenly, he didn't have the pressure of writing a specific type of music under the oppressive atmosphere of The Jam." Referring to Chris Parry's description of Weller as a 'little Englander', Dennis adds: "It went beyond the bounds of Dover."

While The Jam went through their very public divorce and the nation's music press reacted with gushing memorials, Weller was busy behind the scenes developing ideas for his next projects. He knew what he wanted to avoid. He didn't want to be tied to an orthodox band. He didn't want to be shackled to an intensive recording and touring schedule. And he definitely wanted to drop The Jam's punk guitar sound, as he explained to *Go Go* fanzine in 1986: "I was getting more and more frustrated with The Jam towards the end. I thought the musical side was limited. The following was all-lads-together types. I didn't like that aspect. I grew sick of the whole rock sound, all those loud guitars and crashing drums. The whole attitude of rock stinks. I'd sooner play a Himalayan nose flute. The Sex Pistols were the last really good rock band."

To obtain the creative freedom he was looking for, Weller did a number of things. First, he shunned the possibility of forming a fixed line-up of musicians. Nor did he follow another traditional rock route of embarking on a solo career. Instead, he concocted the idea of a loose collective of musicians which would be based around a central nucleus, and which could change according to the environment. "I had this whole thing planned for months," Weller explained in The Style Council biography *Internationalists*, "so to me, it was just a case of doing it at the first opportunity. I want to work with people who aren't into the star thing and who don't whine, people who just get on with it. I want people who look good as well." These last barbed comments seemed to be barely disguised jibes aimed at Foxton and Buckler.

Initially, Paul couldn't decide between two names for his new project – it was very nearly called the Torch Society, probably inspired by the legendary Northern Soul club in Stoke-on-Trent, The Torch. This was instead used for the band's fan club, and the 'flaming torch' emblem, also derived from the Northern Soul scene with its 'keeps on burning' motto, appeared on their early releases. Instead, he chose The Style Council – "a friend of mine thought of the name," Paul revealed. It spoke volumes about Weller's attitude at the time: he was already known for his neat, fastidious Mod dress sense, but by stating his case so boldly, he was bound to irritate those who took the words literally – which seems to have been part of the plan.

In keeping with Paul's growing love of soul music, he chose to push the guitar into the background to allow keyboards to play a more prominent role – and for that, he needed someone he could trust. In autumn 1982, Paul had phoned Mick Talbot; the two of them had got on well when Mick had guested on *Setting Sons* and a few of The Jam's London shows. Above all, Mick had a relaxed demeanour, which helped to create a new environment at polar opposites to the deadly serious atmosphere which had surrounded The Jam. "Mick had a great sense of humour," Dennis Munday recalls. "He was laid back. With Mick, Paul had somebody he could lean on, which he never had with the Jam – he'd taken the full brunt. Life became much lighter and easier and a lot of that was down to Mick as a personality."

Mick and Paul actually shared a lot in common, both musically and socially. "We're the same age," explained Weller in *Internationalists*. "We know records of the early Seventies when both of us were skinheads and suedeheads. And I wanted that particular organ sound because I've always liked the Small Faces, who used it." Talbot's role in The Style Council was invaluable. Besides his laid-back temperament, he also contributed to the band's music, collaborating on the occasional song with Paul and writing several tracks – mainly instrumentals – himself. It should be stressed that while Weller patently led the band, The Style Council was far from being a solo project, but the public never took Talbot seriously as an equal partner. It was assumed that he was there because he wouldn't argue with Paul.

Born in the same year as Weller on September 9, 1958 in the south London district of Merton Park, Mick had his first musical experience singing in a play at school when he was six. In his teens, Talbot formed an R&B band with his brother Danny, The Sneakers, which then evolved into the Merton Parkas around 1978. Mick kept his job as a shipping clerk by day and played gigs around London by night, with a set which included soul covers like 'What'd I Say', 'Tears Of A Clown', 'Do You Love Me?' and 'Band Of Gold'. "I never got into the punk thing at all," Mick told *NME*'s Adrian Thrills in summer 1979. "I liked the energy but I couldn't take the non-musicality of it all . . . The only band I ever really liked then were The Jam. They were a younger version of what the Feelgoods could have become. Mainly, I just carried on listening to a lot of blues stuff, Bo Diddley and Muddy Waters."

"In 1979, The Merton Parkas got a recording contract and a short while after this I met Paul," Mick explained in *Internationalists*. "There was some talk of him doing some production for us but it didn't come about." In autumn 1980, The Merton Parkas disbanded after a backlash in the music press against the Mod Revival. Mick joined the soul-influenced Dexy's Midnight Runners in time for a European tour, at the end of the year in which the band had topped the charts with 'Geno' and issued the critically acclaimed album, *Searching For The Young Soul Rebels*. When three members split from the group, Mick followed them into The Bureau, an eight-piece soul/jazz-influenced outfit who issued two promising singles and a foreign-only LP in 1981. Neither made much impact, and The Bureau were defunct by the end of 1981. When he received the call from Weller, Talbot was on the dole.

Weller's second move after The Jam's demise was to create a more permanent base from which to work. Having re-signed to Polydor, he bought the lease to the company's studio in the basement of Stanhope House, Stanhope Place, London W2 – off Bayswater, opposite Hyde Park and a few yards from Marble Arch. Paul had always liked the ambience of the studio, and The Jam had posed on the spiral staircase at the back of the building for the cover of *Beat Surrender*. After some necessary improvements, Paul created Solid Bond Studios – later described as "a typical recording studio with offices and a games room, but always a friendly meeting place". Not only could he record whenever he felt like it, day or night, the offices could be used by his father, who was still his manager, and his sister Nicola, the 'studio secretary/manager', who helped run the day-to-day business with Paul's girlfriend Gill Price. Gill also helped out with the accounts.

On January 5, 1983, Weller guested with a young duo by the name of Everything But The Girl – Ben Watt and Tracey Thorn – during their first proper London gig. The evening had been organised by Tony Fletcher's *Jamming!* magazine as part of the ICA's annual rock week. "Paul said he wouldn't mind playing with them," says Fletcher. "I thought, yeah, what a winner – his first show after the split. That was a mad event because the word got out via *The Evening Standard*." Ben explains: "Paul rang us up. It was just after The Jam split up and no-one really knew what he was going to do. I remember speaking to him in a phone box, *(adopts accent)* 'S'Paul 'ere. I really like wot ya doin'. It's really great and we should jus' do summing.' The first thing we agreed to do was at the ICA." The couple were then studying at Hull University. "We were both huge Paul Weller fans," admits Tracey. "I remember going down the end of the road and Ben was inside the phone box, gesturing – it's Paul Weller! We were standing there in our overcoats, freezing!"

"Pete Wylie's Wah! Heat were the headline and King were the support," continues Ben, "and we were offered a slot in the middle. We only played for twenty minutes." Halfway through the set, they introduced Paul Weller, who hadn't been spotted since the last Jam concert. "It was quite a shock," laughs Tracey. "The whole audience collectively fainted." Weller duetted with Thorn on covers of the bossa nova jazz classic, 'The Girl From Ipanema' and Peggy Lee's 'Fever', and played guitar on a version of The Jam's 'English Rose' (which the couple had already recorded) and Cole Porter's jazz standard, 'Night And Day'. "He played in the set and we came back for the encore and sang 'Fever' again," adds Ben. Because news of Paul's impending appearance had leaked out beforehand, the hall was packed and subsequent music press reports claimed that Weller had expressed interest in producing the next Everything But The Girl single. The event was a reflection of Paul's desire to branch out – to defy preconceptions and follow his instincts, wherever they might take him.

★　★　★

Back in the summer of 1982, Tony Fletcher's own band, Apocalypse, became the third act to release a record on his Jamming! label. They supported The Jam on several occasions and had roped Paul into producing their début single. Built around a faint reggae rhythm and topped by a trumpet riff, 'Teddy' showed genuine potential, in a style reminiscent of The Jam's 'Pity Poor Alfie'; while the other side, 'Release!', was edgy, Jam-like power pop. "When we were recording that single, there seemed to be a lot on Paul's mind," reflects Tony. "He cancelled the session twice. He wanted to blow the thing out. He put us off for a month and that's when he went on holiday – we didn't realise that he was thinking of breaking up The Jam. We were looking for a reggae feel so he suggested we contact The Specials' Jerry Dammers. We said, 'How can we get Jerry Dammers?' 'I dunno, call him up!' That came from someone who was successful so young – the world does tend to work that way for you. It didn't happen. We said, 'We'll wait for you to come back,' and he spent a week with us."

Two months after the single appeared in September 1982, Apocalypse re-recorded 'Teddy', "to replace the original 7″, which we are no longer happy with", in a dub reggae style – without Paul's help. This might have aggravated Weller, but Tony Fletcher blames other factors for Paul's growing disenchantment with Jamming! "There was a decision about whether to issue a Rudi or a Zeitgeist single – we couldn't do both. The Jam crowd understood Rudi, who were a proper rocking band, better than Zeitgeist, who were a bit arty. But I was impulsive, so I plumped for Zeitgeist's 'Over Again', which wasn't very good – so I definitely take my share of the blame. I was very much a hands-off A&R person and let them get on with it. Paul hated that last Zeitgeist single, which pissed him off beyond anything about Apocalypse re-recording 'Teddy'. He probably thought, 'Why am I putting my money into this if I don't like it?' "

It was a make-or-break time for Jamming!, which had very nearly signed The Alarm (but lost out to IRS) and also toyed with the idea of working with Department S. "There was talk of putting some money behind another Rudi single but Paul pulled the plugs, tied in with the fact that he was splitting up The Jam," adds Tony. "He called me over the Christmas period that year and said he wanted to stop the label. Paul said, 'There are reasons the label's not really working and you can have the label. I want to do Respond in a different way.' He was nice about it on the phone – Paul always was diplomatic. I was like, OK, I wonder if a major label will finance it? I had loads of ideas. Apocalypse was happening. There were good things around the corner. Looking back, there wasn't really much of a musical vibe to the label. But Jamming!'s six singles were all indie hits – that's not a bad track record."

For Rudi's Brian Young, it was a bitter disappointment. "John Weller had arranged a national headline tour for us with an agency, shortly after the spring '82 Jam dates," he remembers. "It had gone well, so Paul and John Weller had a chat with Tony and had decided they were going to put money into both Jamming! and Rudi, because Jamming! was easily outselling Respond. They would do everything to push our next single, 'Love Is Electric', to make it a hit. We were actually booked into Abbey Road Studios. Then, just a couple of days before, we had a phone call from Tony that Jamming! had to fold. For Rudi, that was the final kick in the teeth. We were told everything was going so well and then Weller knocked it on the head. There was an awful lot of bad feeling, too, between Tony and Paul. Tony was badly disillusioned for a long time and they fell out over it. He did so much to set the label up and then to have it taken away when it was about to succeed really annoyed him."

Fletcher now has mixed feelings about Jamming! "I was running around working with Paul but felt like people were earning big money and I never took more than seventeen quid a week," he recalls. "I put so much time into the label that my fanzine, *Jamming!*, only came out once a year for two years. At the same time, Paul was taking us on tour, producing us, being a mate, all of which was great. He'd say, 'What are you doing this evening? Do you fancy going down Le Beat Route?' But his attitude to money was weird. You might go down there and Paul would be, 'Well, get them in then.' He felt everybody should buy their own round, but I had no money whatsoever. That's a combination of making it very young and having that parental stability."

A hint of bitterness still rankles Tony to this day, when he recalls the final blow. "John Weller came in one morning," he recalls, "opened that door the same way he had eighteen months earlier and said, 'You've got two weeks to get out of here.' Did his dad do the dirty work? Yeah, there's no real doubt about that. That stuck with me for a while, because it didn't help mine and Paul's friendship. It wasn't very straight and forty per cent of the company actually meant I was left with a couple of grand debts – which I didn't have. So I ended up in the shit all round the place."

Paul's other label hadn't fared much better during 1982. After singles from Dolly Mixture, The Questions and The Rimshots, Respond issued a bizarre post-punk dub 45, 'The Big Bad Wolf' by Urban Shakedown. A far superior, radical reworking of The Questions' 'Work And Play' arrived that October, but it proved to be the label's last release through its current deal. "Respond through Polydor failed abysmally," states Tony proudly. "They sold hundreds while Jamming! was selling thousands. After a couple of singles, Paul was aware of that and got more behind Jamming! When Rudi did 'Crimson', he put an extra sum of money into the label. At that point, Respond was no competition. It was the classic major label situation, thinking that a pop star, our major asset, wants to make some records by his mates, so we'll put them out."

The truth is that Weller hadn't been satisfied with either of his labels. While Jamming!'s singles far outsold those on Respond, Paul didn't like Zeitgeist, and Rudi were rooted in the guitar rock he was attempting to leave behind – and, in any case, Jamming! was run by Fletcher and Paul wanted overall creative control over his new venture. Despite Dennis Munday's chaperoning, Respond had been largely ignored by its host, Polydor, who seemed to treat the label merely as a pay-off to Paul. Like most artist-run labels, Respond had failed to score major chart hits – but that was about to change. Weller reacted to Polydor's indifference by sealing a new manufacturing and distribution deal with A&M and started scouting around for talent. He retained The Questions, scrapping proposed plans for their last single with the old deal, 'Someone's Got To Lose', in the process. Paul had made his first major decision after The Jam's split by amalgamating his labels into one – a revamped Respond.

*   *   *

Back in the late summer of 1982, Paul had advertised for budding young singers to send him demo tapes. One of the replies came from a lively seventeen-year-old from Chelmsford, Essex. Paul Weller had found the first (and last) star for his label – Tracie Young. "I used to look in the *NME* or *Melody Maker* in the ads for bands looking for singers," she remembers. "I nearly joined an electro band, City 19 from Basildon. I loved singing, and there was a section in the bits'n'pieces editorial in *Smash Hits*: Paul was looking for a female singer alongside The Questions for his Respond label that he was re-launching. He wanted singers between 18 and 24. I was 17, so I let it go. Then this advert cropped up again around September 1982, so I made a cassette of me singing an old soul tune, Betty Wright's 'Shoorah Shoorah', into my home stereo. After seeing The Q-Tips one night at The Venue in Victoria, I posted the tape as an afterthought. I didn't tell a soul."

"The next week, I got a call from Gill Price, saying Paul had my tape and liked it. So I went to see him at what became Solid Bond. It was a nice day so Paul said, 'Let's go and sit in the sunshine'. There was a raised-up square of garden in the corner of the grounds. It seemed funny. You have an image of somebody and 'sunshine' wasn't a word I associated with him! We went outside and he seemed more intimidated by being with a teenage girl than I was by being with this famous pop star. Then Paul said, 'Come in the studio and we'll hammer a few tunes out at the piano, a bit of a sing-song, see how we get on.' We did soul stuff like 'Band Of Gold' and 'Reach Out I'll Be There'.

"I left the studio with a demo tape of 'The House That Jack Built', written by The Questions. Paul said, 'This is the song I think we should be doing.' I have to say now that I didn't like it but I came away really excited. At seventeen, you don't look a gift horse in the mouth. The next thing I knew, we were recording this song and photo sessions were booked." Meanwhile, Weller had used The Jam's swansong single as an important springboard for the young singer: Tracie not only sang on 'Beat Surrender' but joined the band on *Top Of The Pops*. "Paul said, 'We don't actually need you to do backing vocals, but it'll be good exposure for you.' Some of the vocals are Afrodiziak, but I did the one-on-one harmonies with Paul," she adds. "I then read that The Jam were splitting up. I phoned and, typically selfish, asked if this affected my position. 'No, it's got nothing to do with The Jam,' Paul reassured me. 'This is my own venture.' So that all went full steam ahead."

So too did The Style Council, although details were slow to emerge. Rumours circulated that Paul's new project would be introduced on Sunday, February 20, at an under-eighteens gig at The Drill Hall in Central London, but while The Questions, Bananarama and Tracie played, Weller merely looked on. Instead, The Style Council was officially unveiled later that month, Paul describing Mick Talbot as "the finest young soul/jazz organist in the country". The launch was accompanied by stills from their first photo session in Boulogne, which revealed Weller had undergone something of an image overhaul. Gone was the dour countenance of The Jam and their very British persona; in its place was a cool, cosmopolitan look characterised by cream Macs, two-tone brogues, black sunglasses, a carefully poised cigarette and a wry grin.

The inspiration came in part from Paul having finally read Colin MacInnes' *Absolute Beginners*; he was drawn irresistibly into the book's exciting world of an exotic late Fifties London full of coffee bars, with a teetotal lead character and his love affair with modern jazz. That world didn't really exist, of course, but the idea must have felt like the perfect antidote to The Jam. But the old Weller attitude still lurked behind the new aesthetic: "I don't want to mellow out," Paul proclaimed. "I don't care anymore. I'm just going to do what I want to do and say what I want to say. I don't care if people think I've cracked or changed. I still mean it! I'm an angry young man."

The Style Council's remit had a decisive emphasis on packaging and presentation. With this in mind, Paul contacted a photographer, Peter Anderson. The Scotsman had moved to London in 1980, quickly securing regular work with *NME* – and for the next two years, his camera was one of the paper's busiest, which was how he met Weller. "I had an assignment with Paul just as The Jam had finished. We did a silly, tongue-in-cheek pastiche session where I photographed him as John Steed of *The Avengers*, with his girlfriend as Emma Peel, for the *NME*'s Christmas issue '82. That was the start of The Style Council's pastiche photographs. Up until that point, people imagined Paul and The Jam as serious and full of angst and no humour. But we got on well. It was how I liked to work; there was some brief to work to, but it had to be invented on the spot."

A few weeks after the shoot, Weller contacted Anderson again. "Paul seemed quite into the way I worked," he remembers. "The next stage was The Style Council proper and thoughts turned to what they wanted to do. We went off to France to take some photographs around January of '83 – somewhere in Brittany. My favourite from that session was on the back of the single, 'Speak Like A Child', and there were large fly-posters with the same image, which was Paul and Mick walking down a street in France with their overcoats on. Again, it had a feeling of pastiche, as if a fashion photograph met a still from an Alain Delon film. It wasn't specifically planned but that seemed to suit the way Paul and I both thought. The feeling I had, right from the beginning, was that there was a sense of fun about it all – even though we were in France in January, freezing cold, we were having a laugh. The photographs were still serious but with a great tongue-in-cheek element. A lot of people didn't get that about The Style Council, which is a shame. It got funnier as we went along."

Beneath this arty photo of Mick and Paul posing on a French street corner, music press advertisements listed details of their début single in six European languages: "A new record by new Europeans, 'Speak Like A Child' by The Style Council." Polydor set the promotional wheels in motion: on March 1, Weller outlined his plans for both The Style Council (known as TSC for short) and Respond to Radio 1's Richard Skinner, and both Tracie and Paul were interviewed on Manchester's Piccadilly Radio on March 7. Paul asked young bands to send in tapes to Respond, but "if it's rock music, don't bother. I just can't take those blaring guitars anymore. We've had twenty years of rock rebellion, it's got us nowhere." He also enthused about the soulful voice of Culture Club's Boy George, as well as the·Fun Boy Three (who, like Weller, cleverly melded politics with pop), and Scottish band and fellow Polydor act Orange Juice, who were currently cruising the Top 20 with their biggest hit, 'Rip It Up'.

It was Orange Juice's drummer, the Zimbabwean-born Zeke Manyika, who drummed on the single – as Dennis Munday remembers, "all the bands used to come in the office so he would have known Zeke through Orange Juice". Zeke was listed as an 'Honorary Councillor' on 'Speak Like A Child', the first song to be published through Paul's new publishing company. Formed in early February, Stylist Music took its name not so much from The Style Council but from a term used by élitist Sixties Mods – stylists. More importantly, this was another sign of Weller's new-found independence – although he had formed an earlier publishing company with The Jam, And Son.

Issued in early March 1983, 'Speak Like A Child' ushered in a new age for Weller. Maybe it was a coincidence but the 7″-only package in a plain black sleeve (coloured only by the band's name and the 'keeps on burning' logo) echoed the design for the Sex Pistols' début, 'Anarchy In The UK', so treasured by Paul and his friends back in late 1976. No–one was claiming that 'Speak Like A Child' was as revolutionary a statement as 'Anarchy' but, for Weller at least, it was the manifestation of a bold musical rethink.

It was also a wonderful pop record. Dennis Munday agrees: "One day, I phoned up out of the blue and Paul was recording. All I could hear was 'Speak Like A Child'. Whack! I said, what the hell's that? Paul replied, 'Oh, just something I've written. What do you think?' Even over the phone, I knew that was out of the box. Its *joie de vivre* summed up what the Style Council was about. That openness wafted over you. The only time The Jam ever made a track like that was 'Boy About Town' – light, airy, but with something to say. 'Speak Like A Child' wasn't just a disposable pop record."

The song had a faint Motown feel but its sound was fresh and modern – with Paul's funky bass line, Mick's smooth, high-pitched keyboards, the shrill brass and the synth-drum crashes. And Tracie's backing vocals were close to a duet with Paul in places. The B-side, 'Party Chambers', was driven by piano, topped with Mick's now-dated, squeaky synth. The single also introduced

160

The Jam's first-ever publicity photo from 1973.
L-R: Steve Brookes, Rick Buckler and Paul Weller.

Fire'N'Skill - The Jam on Stage in 1977. *(Erica Echenberg/Redferns)*

The Jam in Punk London in their stage uniform of black suits and white shirts. L-R: Bruce Foxton, Rick Buckler and Paul Weller. *(Ebet Roberts/Redferns)*

The band's energy on-stage was legendary. *(Stephen Morley/Redferns)*

Backstage '77: Weller changes into something more comfortable.
(Ian Dickson)

The Style Council *à* Paris in 1983. *(Peter Anderson)*

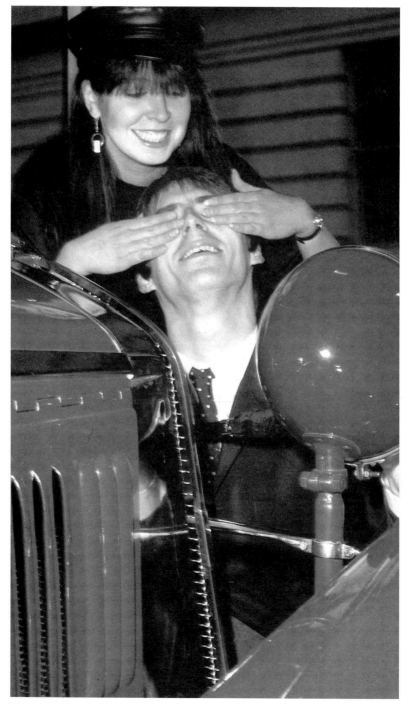

Is it Paul and Gill Price or John Steed and Emma Peel? December 1982.
(Peter Anderson)

(Virginia Turbett/SIN)

Father and son in Japan, where Paul has always enjoyed immense popularity. *(Pennie Smith)*

Happy times - The Jam at the height of their popularity in May 1980. *(LFI)*

Weller as the petulant, spikey-haired young punk.
(Erica Echenberg/Redferns)

(Derek D'Souza)

The Rickenbacker guitar, an image forever associated with Paul.
(Ian Dickson)

Mick and Paul in Hyde Park, summer 1984. *(Peter Anderson)*

Do not adjust your wing mirror. Weller and that Mac in 1983. *(Peter Anderson)*

(Peter Anderson/SIN)

Paul and Dee, together on the set of the video *Shout To The Top. (Peter Anderson)*

Weller going wild in the wood, 1985. *(Peter Anderson/SIN)*

(LFI)

Paul Weller was one of the driving forces behind Red Wedge, a loose cooperative of musicians whoose aim was to publicise left-wing views. *(LFI)*

Two of punk's great songwriters: Paul Weller and Elvis Costello onstage at London's Apollo Theatre, December 1983. *(Derek D'Souza)*

The Style Council played the enormous Artists Against Apartheid Festival at Clapham Common in 1986. *(LFI)*

Weller in the mid-Eighties with his new highlights, the result of spotting some grey hairs. *(LFI)*

The Paul Weller Movement helped re-launch the musician's career in the early Nineties. *(LFI)*

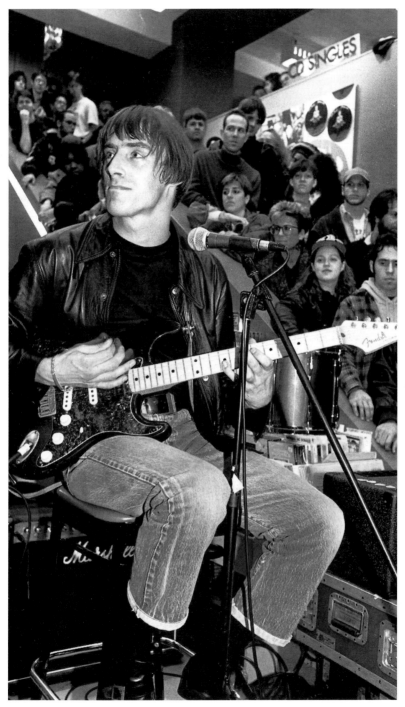

A packed-out personal appearance at Tower Records in New York.
(Ebet Roberts/Redferns)

Paul and Dee. *(Pabbix UK)*

Paul duetted with Bobby Gillespie during a Primal Scream soundcheck in late '94. *(Pennie Smith)*

Paul celebrating his birthday with Dee C. Lee and his father John, at the Ivor Novello awards in 1994. *(LFI)*

L-R: Paul McCartney, Noel Gallagher, Paul Weller - alias The Smokin' Mojo Filters - and actor Johnny Depp. *(Brian Rasic)*

The new Clapton? Paul's return to the guitar has earnt him comparisons with some of the rock greats. *(Steve Gillet/Redferns)*

Paul and his down-to-earth nature in 1995. Nearly twenty years into his career, he is more successful than ever. *(Tim O'Sullivan/FSP)*

the Cappuccino Kid, a fictional sleeve-note writer that came to symbolise both The Style Council's most self-indulgent excesses and Weller's very real attempt to inject humour into the band. This "geezer we bump into around the cafes and restaurants of the West End" was in fact journalist Paolo Hewitt, with a little help from Paul: expressed in ornate, mock-19th century prose, the Cappuccino Kid's thoughts were sometimes amusing, sometimes impenetrable, often pretentious.

But Paul's idea was not to take the idea too seriously, a sentiment made obvious by a tongue-in-cheek promotional video for 'Speak Like A Child' with footage of the group, along with Tracie and Paul's sister, Nikki, dancing aboard an open-top double-decker bus. This *Magical Mystery Tour* meets *Summer Holiday* idea, which culminated with the crowd hopping and skipping across the Malvern Hills, was directed by Tim Pope, then known for his work with The Cure, who was responsible for most of The Style Council's early videos.

'Speak Like A Child' was well-received, reaching No. 4 after generally favourable reviews. "It was great to see Paul succeed," says Dennis Munday, "because there were a lot of people who'd have been quite happy for him not to. The record sold massively, over 350,000, without even a picture of the group on the front." Despite Paul's continued success, many of The Jam's fans hadn't followed him, dismayed and aggravated at the pretentiousness of it all. The cult of Paul Weller had persisted throughout The Jam because young lads continued to identify with him: he seemed to talk common sense, he was well-dressed and the music sounded great, they thought. To the doubters, The Style Council was a different matter, and the audience at the band's early gigs was quite different from The Jam's. That laddish, sweaty atmosphere was evaporating. Weller stayed true to his working class roots and shunned behaviour which he labelled as 'intellectual', but there lay an inherent contradiction. Weller's fascination with poetry, literature and socialist political thinking were, to an extent, the domain of the educated middle-classes – it was just that his approach was less academic.

A week after the release of 'Speak Like A Child', Respond returned with Tracie's first offering, 'The House That Jack Built', a week or so before her eighteenth birthday. The fact that the singer's surname wasn't used until much later helped to replicate the Sixties pop persona of stars like Lulu and Millie. "Go – '83," ran Weller's sleeve-note under the guise of Lord Jim – a name taken from the title of a Joseph Conrad book. "And there's no looking back – if this is to be the year of decision then who's to decide . . . from the influence of soul to the essence of pop – Respond Records asks you to try Tracie and then decide." Paul also produced the single for Solid Bond Productions, co-designed the sleeve with Simon Halfon and appeared in the backing band, the Soul Squad. He even interviewed the singer on a 12″ track, 'Tracie Talks'. Thanks to its association with Paul, the naïve pop charm of 'The House That Jack Built' gave Respond a Top 10 hit with its first release under the new arrangement. Things could not have been better. Or could they?

"When I got to the session, Paul and the engineer Brian Robson had recorded the backing track and I loved these synthesised strings," explains Tracie. "But after one day's recording, Paul said, 'I've had an idea' and stuck this horrible robotic drum section in, in place of this lovely guitar line on the instrumental. And it was faster. 'You've speeded up my voice,' I complained. He said, 'Who's gonna know? Nobody's heard you sing before.' I thought it sounded awful. On the first Respond tour, I was only singing a couple of numbers, but I deliberately made cock-ups so people would know I wasn't miming, because the music was on backing tape. People came up afterwards and said, 'You didn't sing on that record because your voice sounded so deep tonight'. It rankled with me." The situation was reminiscent of Paul McCartney's days with Apple Records in the late Sixties, when he launched and took control over the career of Mary Hopkins, a fresh-faced teenager who later resented her lack of creative freedom.

The B-side of the single, 'Dr. Love', was a Weller original named after an old Northern Soul classic by Bobby Sheen, which had earlier been given to Bananarama. Their version appeared that month, in fact, on their début LP, *Deep Sea Skiving*. Recorded in late 1982, Paul's demo still exists in Polydor's vaults. Apparently, Bananarama were also interested in 'Circus', Bruce Foxton's funky instrumental on *The Gift*, but Weller never wrote the necessary lyrics.

The set-up behind Respond was simple: Paul Weller ran the show. "All finances to and from the artists were down to Paul," Tracie explains, "but we all had access to A&M's facilities – A&R department, press, promotion. A&M paid for everything. Paul was keen on this philosophy that ran with Respond: it was about youth, about despising certain popular musical trends. I became brainwashed. I never forget saying I liked an Eagles record. The look I got was like I was condemned, without words being said, to the corner of the room," moans Tracie. To the twenty-four-year-old Weller, there was probably no greater crime than liking The Eagles. "Nothing was said directly, but I picked up attitudes I had to tune into if I was going to be part of this set-up. Looking back, it was farcical. The initial concept that Paul was trying to achieve – yeah, I applaud the ideals. But it was job security: I did what I was told and I said what I thought I should say to make sure I got paid my £50 a week." Like Tony Fletcher before her, Tracie was aware that ideals didn't pay the bills.

A Respond tour followed. "I hated the tour," states Tracie. "I wasn't ready. The concept was nice, of sending the Respond artists out to play a show together. The Questions had the larger set but didn't have the hit. I had the hit but didn't have the band. I did a couple of numbers live with The Questions. There was never a great deal of love lost between us. There was resentment that I had hit singles and The Questions hadn't. Why was I the one with my name at the top of the posters?"

★　★　★

Avoiding the temptation of a full-scale national tour to promote 'Speak Like A Child', The Style Council spent April 1983 appearing on a couple of European TV shows with backing singers Tracie and Claudia Konijin. The band's exposure in Britain was restricted to an appearance on comedy TV programme *Three Of A Kind*, performing the Isley Brothers' breezy, mid-Seventies soul classic, 'Harvest For The World', with Paul playing bongos, backed up by Tracie and The Questions. It reinforced Weller's collective vision both for his band and his label – the concept of a floating line-up.

The Council's first live appearance in the UK was at the 'May Day Show For Peace And Jobs' concert at Liverpool Empire Theatre, organised by CND in aid of Merseyside Unemployment Centre – though this still wasn't a fully fledged gig. The two songs were played using backing tapes – only the vocals and keyboards were live, as Paul admitted to the audience – but the aim was to re-emphasise their support for the campaign. This continued on May 7 when the group guested at Youth CND's open-air Festival For Peace concert in Brixton's Brockwell Park, South London, in front of an estimated 70,000 people. At the climax of a march from Victoria Embankment, they played on a bill which included Madness and The Damned. The event was turned into a disaster by bad weather, as disgruntled fans threw mud-balls at the performers. Out of tune, out of time and a general shambles, The Style Council played 'Speak Like A Child' and their forthcoming single, 'Money-Go-Round', before sloping off. It was suggested that their short set was a result of a direct hit on Weller's yellow jumper, but the singer responded by reiterating that they had only planned to play two songs.

For this second event, Weller and Talbot had been joined by several 'Honorary Councillors': two backing soul singers, Albaie Johnson and Breeze James, bassist Jo Dworniak from funk band I-Level, a sit-in reggae drummer called Pete, 'Spegos' on percussion, plus a horn section of sax and trombone. This was roughly the line-up which taped a radio session for David Jensen's *The Evening Show*, with one notable exception. The Style Council needed a drummer and Zeke was tied up with his commitments to Orange Juice.

"Paul asked me to find him someone who was young, who could play jazz music and who wasn't just a straight ahead rock drummer," says Dennis Munday. He knew of a jazz musician from Eltham, South East London, who was scarcely out of school. "I phoned him and left a message about the audition at Nomis Studios. His mum phoned me back and said, 'You're not taking the micky, are you?' But he went along and got the gig."

Born on May 31, 1965, Steven Douglas White was already a trained musician. "I began to play drums after I had been given a snare drum of my uncle's," he explained in 1985. "I got my first drum kit when I was 13. My dad used to take me to Ronnie Scott's. When I was 16, I decided to find a teacher. I enlisted the services of one of Britain's great jazz drummers, Bobby Orr, and the innovative fusion drummer Bill Bruford." White had been accepted to study at two American colleges but the "ignorance of the British education system prevented me from going". He kept busy with jazz gigs around London and spent three months "working on Difford and Tilbrook's musical, *Labelled With Love*". And then he got the call about the audition. "Dennis didn't tell me the name of them," Steve added. "I walked in and found out it was The Style Council. I was more over-awed with the fact that it was Mick Talbot, one of my heroes from when I was fifteen; I used to see The Bureau down at Deptford."

Issued on May 20, 1983, 'Money-Go-Round' was much more club-friendly than the group's début. This was a tense if slightly stilted funk jam which suited Weller's lyrical rap about the evils of capitalism and imperialism. The song "consisted of an unexpected attack on the financial and military status quo that questioned why there hadn't been a referendum on US bases, Cruise, and 'the real issues that affect our lives'," as Robin Denselow put it in *When The Music's Over*. "To follow 'Speak Like A Child', which was a huge record, 'Money-Go-Round' was a dangerous song because it was so political," Dennis Munday proffers. "Paul told me he wanted to issue this as the next single. I said, 'You're not going to get airplay. The content will put off Radio One, so it won't be a big hit. He said he didn't care – this was a statement he wanted to make. His political convictions were very strong and he meant it at a time when many people would have played safe. He took far more chances with the Council than he ever did with The Jam – and 'Money-Go-Round' is a prime example. To come out pointing the finger like this could have ruined his career. But he never took the soft option." As it transpired, 'Money-Go-Round' reached a respectable No. 11 in the UK, and the author's considerable royalties were donated to Youth CND.

"The song came from one of their earliest sessions, with 'Headstart For Happiness' and 'Solid Bond In Your Heart'," adds Dennis. " 'Money-Go-Round' started off as a jam session with Mick, Paul, Dee and Jo Dworniak. The producer Pete Wilson just pressed the 'record' button while it was happening. That's why it's got no proper start. Annie Whitehead dubbed an introduction on with a trombone. The lyrics were put on afterwards." The song was also Weller's first to be given the remix treatment, a technique which was still unusual for records other than those aimed at the clubs – although Bert Bevan's mix of 'Money-Go-Round' was only available on a European 12″.

On the B-side, the tuneful 'Headstart For Happiness' was a summery acoustic song that remains one of Weller's most endearing compositions and part of a new spirit of optimism which ran through his lyrics. It was in stark contrast to the grittiness of 'Money-Go-Round'. And the third track, Talbot's 'Mick's Up', was the first in a series of groovy, Jimmy Smith-inspired Hammond organ instrumentals. These paved the way for late Eighties acts like the James Taylor Quartet and Corduroy, who seemed to base their entire career around the same sound.

The sleeve of 'Money-Go-Round' underscored the Council's contrasting moods: on the one hand, Paul was earnestly reinventing Britfunk with a confrontational tirade; on the other, a photo of Weller and Talbot jumping out from behind a tree, included on the insert, continued their playful use of images. The back cover explained the verses and showed photos of a coffee maker, which also graced the front of the 7″. "That was done in Linda's Café, at the bottom of Edgware Road, just near the studio," adds Peter Anderson. "They used to deliver rolls to Solid Bond!"

'Money-Go-Round' was the first Style Council song to feature Dee C. Lee, a singer who divided her time between session work and forging a solo career. Born on June 6, 1961 of Caribbean descent (St. Lucia, to be exact) in Balham, South London, Diane Katherine Sealy grew up with her brother and sister, and worked as a model after leaving school, specialising in hands (false nails) and feet (platform shoes). Her break came when Wham! required a backing vocalist: Dee sang alongside Shirley (later of Pepsi & Shirley) on the duo's second and third singles, 'Young Guns (Go For It)' in autumn 1982 and 'Bad Boys', issued in May 1983.

"Paul was quite friendly with Wham!," explains Dennis Munday. "I can remember being in some café around the back of St. Christopher's Place, where we were all having a cup of coffee with George Michael. Paul quite liked Wham! in the early days." Animal Nightlife shared Wham!'s label, Innervision, which led Dee to sing on the hip, jazzy London outfit's first two singles, 'Love Is Just The Great Pretender' and 'Native Boy'. To Dee C. Lee, a confirmed soul girl, 'Money-Go-Round' was just another gig. Paul Weller, at that point, meant nothing to her. Legend has it that when Paul showed her round Solid Bond, she spotted some gold discs on the wall and asked, "Who's The Jam?" "Some crap group who recorded here," Paul apparently replied.

In late May, on the night of Paul's twenty-fifth birthday, The Style Council took part in a concert at London's Paris Theatre as part of The Respond Package Tour, broadcast on Radio 1's *In Concert*. Supported by Tracie and new Respond signings A Craze and Vaughn Toulouse's new dance act, the Main T. Possee, the group played an acoustic set which included a cover of Jimmy Young's 'Times Are Tight', a popular club tune which had been released in April.

By this time, Respond had notched up a second, minor hit with The Questions' neat funk-pop effort, 'Price You Pay', backed with a cover of Heatwave's 'The Groove Line'. Despite the fact that the music for the Main T. Possee's 'Fickle Public Speakin'' was written by Weller, who also co-produced the single and featured on the record together with Mick Talbot, the single was a flop. This was a shame, because this infectious funk rap was one of Respond's most worthwhile achievements, but this was another hint that something which had been touched by the Weller hand wouldn't automatically turn to gold.

In June, The Style Council visited Paris – the continuation of a love affair with France which had started earlier that year in Boulogne. The trip resulted in a new single, as well as reels of photos of Weller and Talbot posing in brightly coloured woollens in front of various Parisian landmarks. "I went to Paris a couple of times with them," remembers Peter Anderson. "The best picture to come out of that was a fly-poster of Paul's shoe, with the Eiffel Tower in the background, out of focus, with his hand and an ID bracelet – that you could reflect back to a Fifties French fashion photograph." The imagery perfectly matched the atmosphere of the resulting *À Paris EP*, issued in August – four tunes which, according to the cover, "all had a similar 'Blue Mood' and a certain French flavour about them". Indeed, the liner notes to the 7″ were completely in French, as were the adverts in the press.

The lead song, 'Long Hot Summer', was an appealing love ballad which suited its title perfectly, capturing the mood while the sun was still shining. The video followed suit, Weller bearing his chest as he and Mick punted down a Cambridge river – but the initial shoot had to be edited after one clip caused offence because of its supposed homosexual undertones. Steve White added some bongos but the song's smooth, modern production and the "shoo-be doo-be, doo-be doo-wap" refrain brought to mind the kind of bland soul stylings of Imagination – it *was* a lovely tune, though. A seven-minute version was performed on the music TV show, *Switch*, incidentally, one of the few occasions when Paul played bass on stage. But having criticised other chart groups, Weller had now created the ultimate in mainstream pop. His main defence was that he only occasionally returned to such a commercial sound. For every 'Long Hot Summer', there was a 'Money-Go-Round'. Also on the EP, 'Party Chambers' was reworked as a jazzy instrumental, giving Talbot free rein to mix Hammond organ and piano. 'Le Départ' was a ponderous piano instrumental (the sleeve humorously claimed that the piece was to be used as the theme for a new French film called *The Golden Lama* starring one Alain Mélon). And best of all was 'The Paris Match', named after the city's principal magazine. Poignantly accompanied by accordion, some sensitive guitar playing and Mick's piano, this mournful, beautiful ballad ranks among Weller's finest-ever compositions.

The idea behind *À Paris EP* was based on a series of Modern Jazz Quartet albums, where the famous foursome had visited different countries to record indigenous music. However, Weller's talk of a five-year plan to record different EPs around the world was another ruse – the idea of *The Postcard EP* taped in Switzerland using Alpine Horns and yodelling with a dance theme was appealing but highly unlikely. "I don't see myself as British anymore," Paul added. "We regard ourselves as European."

"People still weren't getting the humour," adds Peter Anderson. "There was something about the style/fashion angle they didn't understand. On the way back from Paris, we were in the bus, and suddenly it was suggested, 'Let's get out and take this photograph of Paul and Mick running through a red poppy field' – like a parody of a TV advert! 'Are they gay? Are they not gay?!' It was to take the piss out of people, really." The image turned up on the Japanese edition of *Introducing The Style Council*, a mini-LP in a sleeve based around the design of the *À Paris* EP, which compiled most of the band's songs to date. One of Weller's new-found freedoms was the ability to avoid the prolonged recording sessions necessary for an album – which is one reason why the band opted for singles in 1983 rather than keeping all the songs back for an LP. As a stop-gap, *Introducing The Style Council* did precisely that on the continent but was never officially issued in Britain.

Pressure was mounting for the band to play live shows and so a tour, dubbed as 'Council Meetings', was announced for October. During a five-date, two-week jaunt around Europe visiting Hamburg, Paris, Zurich, Amsterdam and Brussels, the band copied the traditional format for jazz gigs by performing two sets, with support slots from Tracie and DJ Vaughn Toulouse during the interval. Despite Paul breaking his arm in Germany while fooling around, which meant he couldn't play the guitar for the last two nights, optimistic reports from the gigs filtered back to the UK.

The band returned for a live TV appearance on *The Tube*, but chose rousing versions of 'Headstart For Happiness', a cover of Chairmen Of The Board's 'Hanging Onto A Memory' and a new song, 'My Ever Changing Moods', instead of their imminent single, 'Solid Bond In Your Heart'. The Jam had originally recorded this last song as their swansong. This later surfaced on *Extras* with a vibraphone intro lifted from Judy Street's Northern Soul favourite, 'What'. But Weller withheld it in favour of 'Beat Surrender'. 'Solid Bond' was also put forward as The Style Council's début release – indeed, Tracie remembered that "Paul gave me a tape to learn the harmonies" – but again, it was delayed.

'Solid Bond In Your Heart' was finally issued in November 1983. The song's uplifting shout-it-from-the-rooftops message was perfectly married to a Northern Soul feel – the synth strings, the "on-the-fours" beat from Zeke Manyika (his last contribution to the Council before concentrating on his solo album, *Call And Response*), and some driving saxophone from Chris Hunter. The video was an excuse for Paul and Mick to indulge in their Mod roots with a mini-*Quadrophenia*. The film was shot at Woking Football Club, with a plot "about two suedeheads, thirteen years later, who go for a reunion but no-one turns up". The video began with Weller pulling up on a scooter to meet Mick at their old haunt. Inside the club, the room suddenly filled with dancing people as DJ Gary Crowley, an old friend of Weller's, played the single – but it turned out just to be a dream. Weller returned to this nostalgic then/now approach many years later with 'Uh Huh Oh Yeh' and 'Stanley Road'. The other side of the single, 'It Just Came To Pieces In My Hands', was an edgy, primitively recorded solo guitar ballad, aside from some doo wop-styled backing vocals. Paul described the song's message as representing "blind foolishness of conceit".

Although a string of dates was announced for December, the British leg of the Council Meetings tour was postponed until the spring – presumably because the band had recording commitments. The Style Council only played one further concert before the end of '83, when they participated in 'The Big One'. Organised by actress Susannah York together with CND, this 'Theatrical Show For Peace' at London's Apollo Theatre on December 18 raised funds for various peace organisations, and featured a variety of rock acts, as well as drama sketches. Among the Council's five songs were 'A Gospel', a rap performed with guest Dizzy Hites, and an acoustic rendition of 'My Ever Changing Moods' with Elvis Costello duetting on vocals. As Robin Denselow observed, CND was being bolstered by pop music at a time when nuclear disarmament had become established as Labour Party policy. But political pop music was being helped in return: CND provided a forum where music and protest could continue.

Despite his political commitments, Weller's shifting personal perspective was never far from his mind. Interviewed in *19* magazine towards the end of the year, Weller revealed how he felt the burden of establishing himself beyond The Jam had lifted over the past year. "I think I am happier nowadays," he pondered. "Probably it's because I'm more in control of what I'm doing. I'm generally more confident, and I equate happiness with having confidence. Also, I'm not tied down to release dates or to months of touring. Like, in our last year with The Jam, one tour lasted four months. It just done me in. It's the little things that please me like the record sleeves. We have more freedom and time, now, to pay attention to the details. I don't mind making a fool of myself now. What I can't stand is indifference. A lot of things we do are meant to wind people up." There seemed to be one inescapable fact: Paul Weller was having fun.

Judging by early reports, The Style Councils' forthcoming album would be ambitious. "It's a double LP – one side romantic, slightly sad, a bit moody," Paul revealed, "the second side more funky; the third with today's pop songs; and the fourth remixes of the singles." He then stressed, "With The Style Council, it's not important that we're all playing on every track. There's no ego behind the records, as such. The album's feel will be *romantique* in a funny and pretentious way." This same humour was also apparent on *What We Did On Our Holidays*, a video EP issued that Christmas compiling their promo films to date – the sight of Paul stroking his skinny chest in

'Long Hot Summer' was enough to make anyone laugh. But 1983 was an important year for Weller, during which he put some serious ground between himself and his past. Although the spectre of The Jam continued to haunt him throughout The Style Council's career, it might easily have crushed him in those early months. Instead, Paul entered 1984 with everything to play for.

★   ★   ★

The year started off well. In February, The Style Council issued what stands as one of Paul's strongest songs and most eloquent lyrics, the sprightly 'My Ever Changing Moods'. The title implied some admission on Weller's part of his own temperament, but the mood swing in question had as much to do with Paul's observations of the changes in public attitudes and social policy under Thatcherism as his own personality – it was about "how the important issues in life are obscured by trivialities," he observed. The Conservatives had won the General Election on June 9, 1983 for a second term in office, after the sense of national euphoria which swept the nation in the wake of the Falklands War. But by 1984, unemployment had soared, while 20,000 (mostly) women demonstrated outside Greenham Common to protest about the proposed location there of US Cruise missiles. Once again pledging his support for CND, Weller was seen on TV lending his name to the campaign.

With 'My Ever Changing Moods', Weller also created what might be described as The Style Council's sound. In 1983, Paul had dabbled and experimented with different ideas, finding his feet and exploring new possibilities, but their fifth single forged a more distinctive approach – Weller discovered a less abrasive guitar tone he was happy with, for example, and returned to the instrument for a heart-lifting solo, while the tune itself had that yearning, personal quality which characterises his best songs. It still felt modern, though: producer Pete Wilson played bass synth and Paul's soulful vocal style meant it was easy to imagine contemporary artists like Culture Club's Boy George or George Michael singing the melody. Despite its lyrical edge, this was 100% pop music, horns and all. Not only did the band notch up another massive domestic hit but having signed a deal with Geffen in America, Weller enjoyed his first taste of Stateside success when it made the Top 40 there.

'My Ever Changing Moods' was joined by 'Mick's Company', another of Talbot's organ workouts. The delicate acoustic B-side, 'Spring, Summer, Autumn', was a Weller composition disguised by the tongue-in-cheek pseudonym of Jake Fluckery, a play on the name of folk singer Jake Thackray. A cover of Chairmen Of The Board's 'Hanging On To A Memory' had been planned as B-side and artwork was even prepared, depicting a young child with a guitar (which might possibly have been Paul) and the slogan, "features excerpts from two hips from Amsterdam", but the idea was shelved. Another of the songs aired at concerts in late 1983 was 'Up For Grabs', written about

Sixties playwright Joe Orton – Paul had cited John Lahr's Orton biography, *Prick Up Your Ears*, as one of his favourite books. This song too had been slated for the single, but a studio recording never materialised.

When The Style Council's début album, *Café Bleu*, followed in March, it proved to be the culmination of Weller's widening horizons. In one fell swoop, he expressed his love of a whole range of musical genres which he'd felt hadn't been possible in The Jam. For all its strengths, the album sounds positively schizophrenic today. From rap to jazz, soul to acoustic ballads, Hammond organ instrumentals to guitar pop, love songs to political diatribes, it created a *potpourri* of sounds and textures. Eclectic and ambitious, *Café Bleu* was very much in keeping with the mid-Eighties music scene's anti-rock stance and, if Mods were magpies, then Weller had rummaged through the nooks and crannies of music past and present.

Like the 12″ edition of 'My Ever Changing Moods' and in keeping with the album's title, *Café Bleu*'s tastefully designed sleeve carried a blue-tinted photo of Mick and Paul outside a Parisian café – as did the novel A5 lyric booklet inside, prefaced by an affected four-page story from the Cappuccino Kid. The French connection was taken a step further by a quote on the rear sleeve from "18th Century French visionary", Jean Paul Marat, a propagandist and heroic martyr for the extreme left-wing who died in the French Revolution, and prophesied the invention of weapons which would, "with a flick of the finger, tear a million of you to pieces". This patently reflected Paul's continued commitment to CND.

The whole package was the product of intense attention to detail, as Peter Anderson explains. "Paul and Simon Halfon would have ideas – Paul's concept usually, and Simon laid it out. Then I took the photos and Paolo Hewitt was involved in the blurb. It felt adventurous. Paul's complete conviction led to quite strange images. He had to fight against the authorities at Polydor – they always wanted his face on the front to 'hard sell' and he was steering away from that. Photos weren't duplicated, if possible. The 7″ would be different from the 12″. For me, it was satisfying because there was a wide use of photographs; posters, adverts, record labels. The attitude was, let's have a shot of the top of a cappuccino cup and put it on the label, or a picture of a Perrier bottle. There was an identity which linked them together."

The music was just as thoughtfully packaged. The double-album idea of four distinct themes across each side hadn't materialised. Instead, they were squashed into two: the first half of *Café Bleu* introduced the jazzier, more atmospheric music, and the second was brasher, more upbeat and less moody. It felt like the difference between winter and summer. Of the thirteen tracks, five were instrumentals and Paul sang only six of the remainder. This endorsed his earlier statements about avoiding a central player – although it was clear that Weller was in charge. Only twelve titles were listed on the sleeve, though; Weller's eloquent attack on Britain's class system, set to a beautiful tune and accompanied only by some jazzy guitar, was added at the very last moment. "Paul said he'd written and recorded 'The Whole Point Of No Return' and wanted it on the album," Dennis Munday explains. "But by that time, the sleeves were finished – in those days, they took ages to print. And we couldn't scrap, I don't know, 100,000 covers."

The instrumentals were an adventurous ploy on Weller's part, and added light and shade rather than suggesting that he had run short of lyrics. They ranged from the sublime (the smoky jazz guitar of 'Blue Café') and the clear-cut jazz (like the straight-ahead bop of 'Dropping Bombs On The Whitehouse' and the perky Latin jazz fusion of 'Me Ship Came In!') to the dancefloor-friendly (a swinging Northern Soul-meets-Hammond organ affair, 'Council Meetin' '). Weller was honest about his aims: "the jazz tracks were just us attempting to sound like someone else," he later told me. Instead of filling the album up with old singles, three of the band's strongest tunes were re-recorded: Paul, Mick and Dee C. Lee shared verses on a fuller-sounding 'Headstart For Happiness'; 'My Ever Changing Moods' was slower with more audible lyrics; and 'The Paris Match' was given over to Ben Watt and Tracey Thorn from Everything But The Girl, who lent the song a bluesy torch singer vibe.

"We'd kept in touch with Paul throughout this period," says Tracey. "He was sending us songs. I remember we really liked 'Headstart For Happiness'. He was keen for us to collaborate. He writes furiously. And he changed his mind a lot. He'd get into one idea and then go, 'no, no, no'." As Ben puts it, "There'd be another letter three days later." Tracey: "He was impulsive, but full of ideas and enthusiasm and a lot of drive and that's inspiring when you're working with someone. I could see he was being influenced by stuff he was hearing, because we played him 'Eden', which we were working on, and the records do have things in common. He was absorbing influences around him, soaking up what was going on. We then agreed on 'The Paris Match'." Ben's guitar technique was totally different from Paul's: "That fascinated him, I think, when I was playing that chordal style, hitting the strings on the offbeat."

The range of musicians on the LP was as broad as the music itself. Chris Bostock, from Northern Soul-styled pop band Jo Boxers, played double bass on the gentle summer pop swing of 'Here's One That Got Away'; Animal Nightlife's saxophonist Billy Chapman helped out on some of the jazz tracks; and other guests included session musicians like trumpeter Barbara Snow and saxophonist Hillary Seabrook. Dee C. Lee also sang on the neo-funk anthem, 'Strength Of Your Nature', which echoed Heaven 17's skill at mixing dancefloor rhythms with the latest technical developments in synths and drum programmers – with a melody borrowed from Lee Dorsey's soul classic, 'Working In A Coalmine'. As Weller's first (and one of his last) rap explorations, 'A Gospel' dated more rapidly than the rest of the album but its revolutionary theme was delivered with style by Dizzy Hites, a London-based singer whose previous claim to fame was his minor novelty hit with 1982's 'Christmas Rapping'. Incidentally, Dizzy later recorded his own version of Weller's poetic rant at Solid Bond Studios, aided by Steve White on drums and issued as 'The Gospel!' on EMI in early 1985.

Steve White, in fact, was the most significant musical addition to the fold: he was pictured on the back sleeve alongside Weller and Talbot. The band's nucleus had effectively grown into a trio. *Café Bleu*, meanwhile, may have received a mixed reaction – Polydor, as ever, had been cautious, and the album was slated by the rock-based music paper *Sounds* as "dispensable dross" – but it only narrowly missed out on the No. 1 spot and spent eight months in the charts, a longer period than any of The Jam's albums. The Style Council wasn't Paul Weller's plaything, as some cynics had thought. They had already proved themselves to be one of the most vital and creative forces within the British pop scene of the mid-Eighties.

10

ALL THE PICTURES ON THE WALL

"I like arrogant people."
(Paul Weller, *Internationalists*, 1985)

"This Changing Man"
(headline on Paul Weller article, *Melody Maker*, March 1984)

"The best concert I've ever seen was by a gospel group. There was nothing theatrical about that. It was just their voices. It makes you realise what power there is inside you. That's the same thing we do."
(Paul Weller, Dutch magazine *Style*, autumn 1984)

"The Style Council represents all I believe in and hold dear to me. This group and its ideals is the sum total of my life. That's why it contains so much beauty and strength. I think we are a soul band, not in the colour of skin sense, but in the spiritual sense."
(Paul Weller, *Internationalists*, 1985)

During a break between songs at The Style Council's Chippenham Gold-diggers concert on March 10 1984 – their first full-length show in Britain – the ghost of Weller's past came back to haunt him. A rowdy chorus of "We are the Mods, we are the Mods, we are, we are, we are the Mods" hung in the air like an embarrassing fart, a throwback to the laddish singalongs of the Jam days. Weller was visibly irritated. "This song means more than any clothes or tribes," he spat, before breaking into 'Money-Go-Round'. It was a poignant moment. Weller was quite clearly prepared to jettison Jam fans who didn't appreciate his new project. Broadcast on both radio and TV, the concert also showed how far Weller had progressed in such a short space of time, and how well the band had taken to playing live; the performance had a loose, vibrant quality that was rarely captured on vinyl.

With The Style Council, Paul Weller shifted his perspective both musically and lyrically, but many of his fans were antagonistic. "He had just come out of a hugely successful rock group and realised he had the opportunity to indulge a side of him that liked completely different things," suggests Everything But The

Girl's Tracey Thorn. "He seemed sick of being the angry spokesman for every-one's causes." Paul had tired of being, as Ben Watt puts it, "tied into a three-piece rock band that he had to play and rehearse with every day. He wanted to do something more current and more flexible. He sensed there was a shift away from punky pop music. Perhaps there was a more interesting scene happening at a roots level."

The jazz flavours which ran through *Café Bleu* hadn't happened by acci-dent. Both Weller and Everything But The Girl were part of a groundswell who were showing interest in jazz, a genre which had been marginalised in rock circles since the mid-Seventies. In Weller's case, he was rooting himself in the original Modernist music. One of the music press buzzwords of 1984 was 'New Jazz'. There was a danger that journalists were lumping a number of unrelated acts under one banner to give the impression of a scene. However, there was a flame of truth behind the smokescreen of media hype, since many of the acts collaborated with each other and shared the same producers and studios.

But jazz was a misleading term for this new vanguard; in reality, there was just a changing tide of acceptance for jazz styles within pop. Sade was definitely the most successful exponent of the genre. Her best-selling *Diamond Life* album offered a palatable cocktail of soul, jazz and pop. In the same building as Sade, Everything But The Girl had recorded their début album, *Eden*, which wove a subtle jazz backdrop of Latin and Bossa Nova behind Tracey Thorn's haunting voice. Simon Booth's Working Week formed out of the ashes of 'New Jazz' pioneers Weekend, and followed two ground-breaking jazz-fusion 12"s with the soul-jazz album, *Working Nights*. Of more substance than Sade was Carmel, whose moody jazz-blues vibe was closer to the true torch singer spirit. And Jerry Dammers injected a variety of jazz influences into the Special A.K.A.'s three-years-in-the-making LP, *In The Studio*. If there was a 'New Jazz' scene at all, then it revolved around trendy, Fifties fashion-styled nightspots like The Wag and The Mudd – London clubs which Weller frequented. These nightspots felt like a natural progression from jazz-funk and contemporary soul clubs, and were promoted by sophisticated style magazines like *The Face*. Two bands in particular were championed by this hip 'jazz' cognoscenti. Latin dance act Blue Rondo A La Turk epitomised designer club chic, but deemed even cooler were Animal Nightlife. Fronted by the camp Andy Polaris, they created a smooth, club-friendly sound reminiscent of Chet Baker's graceful jazz vocal on the classic 'Do It The Hard Way' – pop with a swing in its step. Weller appeared keen to immerse himself in this new vibe and he returned the favour of borrowing saxophonist Billy Chapman by singing backing vocals on Animal Nightlife's breezy tropical pop hit from August 1984, 'Mr. Solitaire'.

Together with The Style Council, these acts strove for some degree of musi-cal sophistication – the love of percussive Latin rhythms, say, or the smoky atmosphere of jazz ballads. But there the similarities ended. Weller didn't feel any more a part of 'New Jazz' than he had identified with the Mod Revival. Both Paul and Mick openly supported those acts which they liked; indeed, Paul voted *Eden* as one of his favourite LPs of the year in *The Style Population*. But Weller wasn't about to reinvent The Style Council as a some hard be-bop combo. Jazz was merely one of the many flavours of their music – and, in any case, it had all but disappeared within a year of *Café Bleu*.

★   ★   ★

The 'Council Meetings' concerts in mid-March 1984 were the first oppor-tunity for many of the band's British fans to experience The Style Council in the flesh. Preceded by that concert at Chippenham Golddiggers, the one-week tour mirrored the unorthodox format which European audiences had witnessed the previous year. Still wary about committing himself to extensive live tours, Weller said he wanted to avoid a grandiose comeback by quipping that "there will be no big build-up or mystique; you only end up with enigma on your face if you do!" There was another attempt at humour in a press release, credited to Dick & His Two Swingers, which read something like, "You've had thunder flashes, laser lights and blood capsules. Now I think it's time for a new approach to live stage presentation, and levitation could be just the answer."

If these light-hearted comments upstaged The Jam's earnest stance, then Weller was still quite serious about the tour's aims. The Style Council took an impressive army of ten musicians on the road, including a new bassist, the teenage Anthony 'Bert' Harty, Animal Nightlife saxophonist Billy Chap-man, and vocalist Jayne Williamson (who later sang with the Brand New Heavies as Jayne Ella Ruth), plus two musicians from Tracie's Soul Squad – percussionist Steve Sidelnyk and pianist Helen Turner. Their live set included covers of The Impressions' uplifting 'Meeting (Over) Up Yonder' and Funkadelic's 'One Nation Under A Groove' (the ultimate late Seventies club anthem). The Council played the first half-hour of each show, fol-lowed by a performance from up-and-coming socialist songwriter Billy Bragg – described by some as a one-man Clash-meets-Bob Dylan – and The Questions, before Weller & Co. returned for the final hour-and-a-half of the evening. Aside from the Newcastle date, when a box of Paul's singles and Mick's suitcase were stolen from the band's tour bus, the trip was an unmitigated success.

The dates were followed by a second jaunt around the continent – including dates in France, where a bizarre promotional film was broadcast starring the band. According to Iain Munn's self-published diary of The Style Council's activities, *Mr. Cool's Dream*, *The Style Council À Paris* was split into several scenes, set in a second-hand record shop (where Mick interviewed Paul about the band), a French wine cellar and a restaurant. This light-hearted curio seems to have bridged the gap between Tim Pope's lively promotional videos for their singles, and The Style Council's later venture into cinema, *Jerusalem*.

The band then jetted off for four gigs each in Japan (where they were mobbed by adoring fans) and America, which emphasised Weller's wish, as Dennis Munday put it, "to look beyond the bounds of Dover". A film of the show in Tokyo was issued in August as a video, *Far East And Far Out*, which showed them relaxed and patently enjoying the adulation. While the three-piece horn section added a new depth to their sound and Jayne Williamson's voice was impressive, it was Weller who really shone. Often singing without his guitar, he managed to perform without resorting to the posing commonly adopted by lead vocalists. Where Paul had often looked gruff and uncomfortable on stage with The Jam, now he even smiled a few times. *Far East And Far Out* documented The Style Council at the pinnacle of their live abilities.

The US dates were also warmly received. Album sales were encouraging, too, though *Café Bleu* was renamed *My Ever Changing Moods* there to capitalise on the single's popularity. And when 'You're The Best Thing', one of the strongest tunes on *Café Bleu*, was chosen for the band's next single, its Stateside popularity prompted an invitation as the second white group ever to appear on America's legendary music TV show, *Soul Train*. The band declined, commenting with self-deprecating irony that "it's against our principles"; to their mind, the show was nothing more than a black US version of *Top Of The Pops*. Later, however, Weller admitted he'd liked to have done it.

Issued in May, 'You're The Best Thing' was firmly in the 'Long Hot Summer' mould; only the backing music was more intricate, from Paul's delicate guitar to Billy Chapman's saxophone. With its Impressions-like falsetto chorus, this lush, soulful ballad constituted Weller's most blatant stab at a straightforward pop song so far – and it worked beautifully. The catchy tune gave the band another Top 5 hit and seemed to be on permanent rotation on the radio throughout that summer.

'You're The Best Thing' was part of the double-A-sided *Groovin'* EP, but the song's success inadvertently dwarfed its companion, 'Big Boss Groove'. This modern R&B tune strutted along, driven by Mick's strident piano playing, a horn section and a finger-clicking soul backbeat – and a harmonica solo from Paul. The song's lyrics reiterated Weller's rallying cry that "together we can be so strong", as the supposed method of overthrowing those in power. Such blatant sloganeering didn't stand up to close scrutiny but as a tool for attacking what Weller perceived as the hypocrisy of politicians and other leaders, the rhetoric was effective enough. It neatly echoed the socially aware strain of early Seventies soul, displacing the trouble-ridden black ghettos of America's inner cities to Britain's own battle lines, from Greenham Common to the troubled clashes between the police and the pickets during the Miners' Strike.

This was no empty rhetoric, either. On May 26, The Council reaffirmed their support for unilateral disarmament of nuclear weapons by playing a Youth CND benefit concert in Coventry, as part of a tour of military bases –

enthusiastically described by Paul as "the best TSC gig to date", perhaps because he felt he now had a stronger motive than merely playing good pop music. On July 7, they played two sets at a miners' fund-raising show in Liverpool Mountford Hall, interspersed by performances from two other bands of a left-wing persuasion, Bronski Beat and Madness. The rousing encore saw The Style Council and Madness team up for a performance of Smokey Robinson's 'It's Time To Stop Shoppin' Around'. In September, the group played a second miners' benefit, this time at London's Royal Festival Hall, where they shared a bill with Wham!, Working Week and Everything But The Girl, together with comedians Alexei Sayle, Rik Mayall and Nigel Planer. And on the first date of their 'Council Meetings Part Two' in Wolverhampton in October, they raised money for a CND initiative against a missile base in Barrow-In-Furness. For Weller, these endeavours were the most logical way to channel his beliefs into something positive.

★   ★   ★

Given the group's level of success, Weller found it difficult to keep abreast of both The Style Council *and* Respond, but the label had been steadily active. Tracie had scored another Top 30 hit back in July 1983 with her second single, 'Give It Some Emotion'. This pleasant Motown-influenced pop number was backed by a joint Weller/Young effort, 'The Boy Hairdresser' (named after an old Joe Orton play), and 'Tracie Raps', another of her chats with Paul.

But Tracie Young wasn't happy. "I was absolutely choked because Paul did exactly the same as before," she remarks. "He gave me a demo cassette sent to him by two songwriters, Chris Free and Lucy Barron – alias A Craze. He said, 'Have a listen. I don't think much of the girl's voice, but they're good songwriters.' I particularly liked 'Give It Some Emotion'. It had a lovely, laid-back guitar rhythm. But Paul then re-recorded the backing track and it was horrible. I didn't like it and told him so and we had a huge row. I stormed off into the bathroom and slammed the toilet door behind me so hard that the handle fell off and I couldn't get out! An hour later, Paul knocked on the toilet door. 'Are you coming out?' 'Nope!' 'Why not, Trace?' ' 'Cos I'm locked in, that's why!' He had to open it from the outside. Yes, we did argue, but inevitably, I backed down because I was the novice. I didn't know my way around the studio or the music business, so I bowed to his better judgement. 'Give It Some Emotion' was a reasonable hit, but I felt a pattern was being set and that my image was being made for me. I then started to panic." Weller may have given Tracie a lucky break in her career, but it appeared to be on his terms.

The Questions also enjoyed their second minor hit with the faintly ABC-like 'Tear Soup' in September '83. A Craze were also signed to the label and issued the delightful 'Wearing Your Jumper', a soft, summery ballad featuring Mick Talbot on jazzy Wurlitzer. The single stood head and shoulders above the heavy-handed, synthesised backing tracks of much of Respond's output but fared less well commercially, despite the potential selling point of Weller's production credit. However, the label's flagging profile was given a welcome injection with the arrival in October of a sampler album, *Love The Reason*. "Business is a polite word for dipping your hands in shit," wrote Weller on the sleeve. This may have fitted in with Weller's socialist viewpoint, but the comment seemed out-of-place on a Respond product from the head of the company.

In some ways, Respond never surpassed the LP, which mixed selections from the label's modest back catalogue with a number of exclusive songs. Backed by The Questions, Tracie tackled Sister Sledge's mid-Seventies nugget, 'Mama Never Told Me'. A Craze donated the catchy 'Keeping The Boys Amused' and there were two new artists: the Stax soul-styled Big Sound Authority who had evolved out of lead singer Tony Burke's West London Mod Revival band, The Directions, but who were picked up by MCA after delivering the promising 'History Of The World'; and a charming acoustic folk ballad, 'Peace, Love And Harmony', from the mysterious N.D. Moffatt. Long thought to represent some absurd Paul Weller disguise, Moffatt was certainly never heard of again.

During 1984, Respond entered a slow but inevitable downhill slide – though the label's many critics might have argued that this decline began on the day it was inaugurated. Nevertheless, the potential was there to capitalise on a year in which two-thirds of Respond's first batch of singles charted in the UK, a record that may only have been beaten by Apple. But the release schedule quickly developed into a two-horse affair starring The Questions and Tracie. February's excellent 'Tuesday Sunshine' thankfully steered The Questions away from attempting to be a hard-line Britfunk outfit and towards writing solid, soulful pop music – and they were rewarded with a near-Top 40 hit, with a little help from Steve White. They followed the single in May 1984 with an appealing ballad, 'Building On A Strong Foundation'. It didn't deserve to flop, but the same couldn't be said for their last single in September, the bland cod-funk of 'Belief (Don't Give It Up)'. The Questions' début album, also titled *Belief*, dribbled out in October and featured Steve White on one song, 'Someone's Got To Lose', but as a collection of songs, it fell woefully short of expectations.

Tracie wasn't having much luck either, although preparations for her album boded well. "Prior to a second tour," she explains, "I said I couldn't play with backing tapes any more, so we put together a band, with a drummer, Steve Sidelnyk, who was a lot of fun, a guitarist, and a bass player, Kevin Miller – and Joe Jones, who was playing keyboards for The Questions. Then we got another keyboard player, Helen Turner, who played for The Style Council."

As soon as the LP was underway, however, there were problems. "I wasn't happy about Paul's decision to exclude the first two singles, which I thought jeopardised my career," sighs Tracie. "I felt he was giving me a career and then playing with it, using me as an experiment. No other non-established artist would try a move like that and expect an album to sell." It was after the sessions were completed that Tracie really clashed with Weller, though. "I was unhappy arguing so much about which should be the first single off the LP," she continues. "We recorded the album, made up mostly of some songs Paul gave me, plus a couple by The Questions. I felt the title track, 'Far From The Hurting Kind', was the best choice. Paul wrote it, so I didn't anticipate any objection. But I came up against a brick wall. He said it would make me look like some silly Northern Soul pastiche, and felt it was utterly the wrong choice. He wanted another of his songs, 'Nothing Happens Here But You', which I dug my heels in over. I was as obstinate as he was. I felt I should be allowed some guidance in my own career. The single which was eventually released was 'Souls On Fire', the only one neither of us vehemently opposed – which was a stupid reason."

Issued in March 1984, the brittle, synth-funk of 'Souls On Fire' was indeed a disappointment. Weller returned to his pseudonym of Jake Fluckery on guitar, and Paul and Tracie shared a writing credit; on the B-side, the singer tackled A Craze's 'You Must Be Kidding'. If it all felt like some cottage-industry Motown, then the single's title wasn't very apt: Respond was starting to sound formulaic and bland and Tracie's no-frills pop needed a serious injection of charisma if it was to survive. And that's what happened after a chance meeting on an aeroplane.

Tracie picks up the story: "I bumped into Elvis Costello flying back from recording *The Tube*. We had a brief but friendly conversation about songwriters and what I wanted to do. He said he would write me a song and, frankly, I didn't take that as meaning much. But sure enough, this tape arrived, '(I Love You) When You Sleep'. It was difficult to work with in its present arrangement – we had real problems and almost gave up, but I liked its unusual, quirky lyric." According to Tracie, her mentor didn't take too kindly to this outside interest. "I wasn't allowed to speak to Elvis directly. All communication went between Elvis and Paul, and then Paul to me. I presume their paths must have crossed in the past. Paul wasn't willing to relinquish any area of control, not for one moment. The Questions seemed different. Because they were writing their own songs, he gave them more control. I felt my situation was bordering on manipulation."

'(I Love You) When You Sleep' was a refreshingly novel, sweet-sounding ballad with a melody which swooped and dived. As a single, it should have curbed Tracie's slow but gradual descent into anonymity – but it didn't. Another of the album's highlights was an obscure cover. "I was a big Martha Reeves fan," explains Tracie, "and found this tacky album, done in recent years, in a bargain basement. There was one great song, 'Thank You', written by General Johnson of Chairmen Of The Board, with archetypal Sixties orchestration and very uplifting. It was so joyful. I played it to Paul and said I didn't want to mess around and be creative, I wanted to just sing it. Nope, came the reply. Money was getting tight so we couldn't have a brass section. It was a sadly understated record. And I was very disgruntled with the whole album."

With hindsight, it is easy to sympathise with Tracie's frustrations. *Far From The Hurting Kind* was a genuinely worthwhile collection – even if it was never going to take the music scene by storm. Weller's name was written all over the LP, from songwriting to guitar playing, production and sleeve design. Aside from 'Dr. Love', Tracie tackled several other Weller songs: The Style Council's soft ballad, 'Spring, Summer, Autumn'; the exclusive 'Nothing Happens Here But You', a swinging, summery tune (and Paul was probably right about its potential as a single); and the frantic soul stomp of the title track, which should be filed alongside the Jo Boxers' 'Boxer Beat'. Perhaps the album's most touching moment, though, was another ballad, The Questions' evocative 'I Can't Hold On 'Til Summer'. But the impetus of her early hits had subsided, and although *Far From The Hurting Kind* made the Top 75 for a couple of weeks, it swiftly disappeared from view.

The same might be said of Respond itself – and the label parted ways with its parent company, A&M, towards the end of 1984, but not before issuing its most adventurous single. September's 12″-only 'Never Stop (A Message)' was credited to the mysterious M.E.F.F. – alias the Mighty Eltham Funk Federation, Steve White's first recorded venture away from The Style Council. A dedication to legendary drummer Art Blakey hinted at the record's jazz leanings; 'Never Stop' was a Latin dance-styled chant, with enough scope for a lengthy drum solo towards the end, while 'Nzuri Beat' was a freeform jazz drum/conga workout. But despite the appeal to hardcore fans of Weller's name in the production credits, the single was lost in Respond's final, overlooked batch of releases.

"I don't think Paul had a clear vision for the label," Tracie concludes, "and I don't mean that disrespectfully. He couldn't relinquish control at all, which was a tragedy because he didn't have the time to devote to it. He couldn't steer the ship himself properly, but he would not let anybody else take over the helm. He eventually ran it aground. He wanted to be all things to everybody – and he couldn't." While Paul was patently a more shrewd and talented songwriter than any of the Respond artists, maybe his career might have met a similar fate without his father's managerial skills. Had John Weller run Respond, its course may have been quite different.

★   ★   ★

Supported by Tracie, and with the imminent release of a new Style Council single, the 'Council Meetings Part Two' convened in October 1984 for a brief trip around Britain and the continent. Their fan club magazine, *The Style Population*, reported that they had planned to stage a play, *Three Musketeers Go Wild*, in the middle of performances, "based on the fortunes of the two young ex-students trapped by the Youth Training Scheme who end up kidnapping the boss. But an accident to one of the actors postponed the play." And they weren't pulling the readers' legs, either. The scope of the band's set was just as ambitious, with room for solo endeavours: Dee C. Lee, who was one of several new recruits to the band's live squad, performed 'Don't Do It Baby' (her latest release after signing to CBS in late 1983) and Steve White aired M.E.F.F.'s 'Never Stop' and 'Nzuri Beat'. There was also a cover of Defunkt's 'The Razor's Edge' and two new songs. The first was a tribute to Paul's late friend Dave Waller, 'Man Of Great Promise'; and the second was the Latin-styled 'Have You Ever Had It Blue?'. This breezy tune was reported as having been written for a forthcoming musical film adaptation of *Absolute Beginners*.

A few days after the tour began, The Council's next single reached the shops, supported by confrontational adverts that proclaimed, "Make no mistake/this is all class war/fight back/Shout To The Top!" Those who expected a Marxist lecture were instead treated to arguably the band's most comfortable venture at combining their own sound with an authentic soul backbeat. Quite apart from the song's energetic vibe, 'Shout To The Top' worked because Mick's driving piano riff did all the legwork (like a faster 'Big Boss Groove') and the basic melody was mapped out using the strident, Philly-styled string arrangements of noted BBC theme composer John Mealing. Simple but effective, it gave the Council another sizeable hit. Despite his subsequent doubts to the contrary, Weller's first stab at producing his own record was an unmitigated success.

The lyrical message was there for all to see and hear in the title, the latest in a long line of Weller's pleas to "think big" and "stand proud" that dated back to his cover of 'Move On Up'. Weller still believed that socialism was a viable proposition to present to the electorate. This message was also evident on the sleeve: "No! To abolition of the GLC and the local councils. Yes! To a nuclear free world. Yes! To all involved in animal rights. Yes! To fanzines. Yes! To Belief." This was the first evidence of Paul's new-found support of animal rights activities. His girlfriend, Gill Price, had not only converted him to vegetarianism but opened his eyes to contentious issues like blood sports and animal testing.

Both the single's B-sides were less upbeat. 'Ghosts Of Dachau' was an anguished ballad, based around the theme of the Nazi wartime concentration camp, with Weller's vocal straining and uncomfortable. "I really feel this is one of the best songs I've ever written," he commented. "I went to Dachau in 1978, it's just outside Munich in Germany, and still the place haunts you." Nearly as haunting was 'The Piccadilly Trail', which conjured up images of loneliness, especially with its contemplative lyrics like "I'm so scared of the weeks ahead".

That month, The Style Council made a memorable appearance on *The Tube*, where they performed, among other songs, a full-on funk cover of

Defunkt's 'The Razor's Edge', after which Paul cooled off on-screen in a Jacuzzi with Jools Holland. The Style Council then acknowledged their enormous popularity in Italy by visiting the country again to play three outdoor concerts under marquees. In May, the band had performed at the St. Vincent Estate Show festival and the Italian leg of their European tour was voted as the year's best by the country's leading music magazine.

Weller may have led the life of a pop star but such distractions didn't seem to dilute his deeply rooted sense of political conviction, which manifested itself over the coming months with two fund-raising records of very contrasting natures. "A dispute about pit closures and the future of mining communities was seen by much of the media and the public in more simple terms," wrote Robin Denselow, "as a show of strength between a hard-line left-winger, Arthur Scargill, the miners' leader, and an apostle of market forces, Margaret Thatcher. The media, for the most part, reflected public opinion in their hostility to the miners, particularly as the bitterness and the violence grew."

By November, the ten-month-old strike had weakened and miners were gradually returning to work. But one of the miners' unlikeliest allies, from their standpoint at least, was pop music. Weller hadn't been alone in actively endorsing socialist views; acts like Billy Bragg, The Mekons and The Redskins played benefit concerts and campaigned. Paul took matters a stage further, hastily assembling a group of musicians to record a profile-raising single, 'Soul Deep', with money to be donated to an organisation known as Women Against Pit Closures, run by Mrs. Scargill. The project was to be credited to The Council Collective – effectively The Style Council with a little help from their friends Dee C. Lee, Dizzy Hites, Vaughn Toulouse and Animal Nightlife's Leonardo Chignoli, plus veteran US Motown star Jimmy Ruffin (whose father was a miner) and British soul singer Junior Giscombe, best-known for his hit, 'Mama Used To Say'.

'Soul Deep' was a clumsy electro-funk track which sounded hurried – which wasn't surprising, since the backing track had been laid down in one day, and the vocals the next – but it reached its goal of publicising the miners' cause. However, the idea was very nearly shelved. On 30 November, on the brink of the single's release, two miners were charged with murder after David Wilkie, a taxi driver in South Wales, who was ferrying strike-breakers to work, was killed by a concrete block which had been dropped on to his car from an overhead bridge. A press release was circulated on December 5 regretting the cancellation of 'Soul Deep' for "artistic reasons". This was almost certainly a smoke-screen for Weller's indecision. Eventually, the single was released and the sleeve-notes were changed: "The aim of this record was to raise money for the Striking Miners and their families before Xmas but obviously in the light of the tragic and disgusting event in South Wales, some of the monies will also go now to the widow of the man." Paul explained the delay in the music press: "We just wanted time to think about it. I still think the strike's got to go on and got to have support, but that kind of violence isn't going to help anyone."

Despite the predictable lack of airplay (some radio stations and shops boycotted the single, as did some club DJs), 'Soul Deep' made the Top 30 and sold a healthy 100,000 copies. That meant a donation of nearly £10,000 – not a sum to be scoffed at – helped by performances on *Top Of The Pops* and *The Tube* and a Radio One interview with Weller and Ruffin.

Buried away on the B-side of the record was 'A Miner's Point', an interview by journalist Paolo Hewitt with some of Nottingham's striking miners, which covered many of the critical issues – an intelligent device to communicate the salient arguments to purchasers ignorant of political issues. Another £1,000 was raised after Mick and Paul DJ'd at a party at The Wag Club in London's Soho, between sets from Madness, Bananarama, Orange Juice and Aztec Camera. This was one of a handful of pre-Christmas benefit parties around the capital organised by IPC Magazines to raise money for the striking miners' families. There was never a more pertinent example of that old tenet, actions speak louder than words.

'Soul Deep' was mixed with the help of Heaven 17's Martyn Ware, whom Weller had met while recording another charity single – and one which certainly inspired the Council Collective. The record, Band Aid's 'Do They Know It's Christmas?', was the brainchild of Ultravox's Midge Ure and the Boomtown Rats' Bob Geldof, who planned to raise funds for famine-hit Ethiopia. Through their numerous contacts, they coerced many of the country's most famous pop stars to offer their services – including the lead singer of The Style Council.

"Bob rang me and I thought it was a great idea," Paul later explained, evidently cautious about the idea of singing on a record with the likes of Duran Duran and Phil Collins. "The cause is the only one common thing between us, otherwise you'd have never gotten all these bands together." He wasn't the only one to receive a phone call towards the end of '84; a fair proportion of pop's glitterati gathered together for a moment's music and the record topped the charts, generating a substantial sum of money in the process. The single paved the way for a whole wave of charity records across the world – most specifically, USA For Africa's million-selling 'We Are The World' – and a year later, Band Aid was back in the Top 10.

Weller's role in Band Aid was minor, although he was called upon to mime Bono's lines on *Top Of The Pops*, and for the most part, he looked uncomfortable and bemused in varying measures during the proceedings. Perhaps he was sceptical of others' motivations – when many of the participants had never outwardly lent their support to other pertinent causes. On the day of the recording session, Paul had pulled up in a cab in the pouring rain while other arrivals required limousines or even helicopters, which didn't go unnoticed by the press – the cynical retort was that the stars turned out for Band Aid to boost their own careers. But The Style Council frontman was also an easy target. For a start, he openly expressed socialist views and yet he was, as Denselow observed, "a very rich, fashion-conscious pop star, who clearly benefited from the existing political and economic system, writing songs that attacked it".

But Weller was hardly a "Champagne socialist". He seemed to exist quite frugally, bearing in mind his considerable income, with a lifestyle which lacked the ostentation of many of his contemporaries. Projects like the Council Collective and The Style Council's ceaseless commitment to benefit events was surely proof enough of his convictions. On December 1, 1984, for example, the band had played a fund-raising show for animal rights groups at Margate's Winter Gardens, which had preceded two nights at London's Royal Albert Hall to tie in with the release of 'Soul Deep'.

Also, like many of his contemporaries, such as Billy Bragg and The Redskins, he was interested in democratic socialism, not communism, and consequently could live with the paradox of being a comparatively wealthy left-winger. It is true that Weller had failed to unify his political beliefs into a coherent philosophy. Nevertheless, he was sure of one thing – he supported the miners over the government and found Thatcher's policies repugnant.

★ ★ ★

Despite regrets about what Weller regarded as the worsening political climate, 1984 ended on a high note for the group. Among an assortment of future plans, there was talk of Paul writing and producing a record for Jimmy Ruffin, who was then recording for EMI (although this came to nothing). And a "TV documentary" would include "stuff from our favourite books and plays, and we want Kenneth Williams to be in it" – a concept which, as it transpired, was closely married to their next album. In America, The Style Council were voted 'best new band' by college radio stations in their New Music Awards, and 'Shout To The Top' was chosen for the film soundtrack of *Vision Quest* (alongside Madonna); and *Café Bleu* stayed in the Australian charts for thirty weeks, despite the fact that Weller had never set foot in the country. The band responded by treating fan club members to a festive flexidisc: poorly recorded live takes of 'It Just Came To Pieces In My Hand' and 'Speak Like A Child' which were purportedly "bootlegged from the bootleggers".

The most immediate priority, however, was recording The Style Council's next album – although plans to begin work in January were scuppered when Paul was appointed joint president of the United Nations' International Year Of Youth, together with actress Julie Walters. One of Weller's first imperatives in his new-found role was to help the National Youth Trade Union Rights Campaign, in their fight against Government plans for new legislation around Easter. Set up in 1981 by members of the Labour Party Young Socialists, the NYTURC claimed that this law would lead to the withdrawal of supplementary benefit from those unemployed sixteen- and seventeen-year-old school leavers who refused to join the Youth Training Scheme. As the youngest member of the band, Steve White had already visited the House Of Commons in August 1984 to support the campaign, and had been shocked to learn that around two dozen teenagers had died while on YTS placements.

Recording sessions for their next LP finally commenced in February, but the band took a break to attend a YTURC demonstration against the Government's attempt to create "industrial conscription". This culminated in a 50,000-strong petition being handed in to the Prime Minister at No. 10 Downing Street. Backed up by current celebrity signatures from the likes of Frankie Goes To Hollywood, Madness and Alison Moyet, pop music was knocking on the doors of power, not to campaign for broader social issues or against travesties abroad, but to oppose a specific piece of legislation. It was an unusual enough stunt to attract the media, and the envoy, led by Weller and Billy Bragg, was captured in the freezing cold on TV's evening news bulletins.

Later that day, The Style Council played a free concert across the river from parliament in front of five thousand young campaigners. After speeches from Labour MPs, the band were joined on the small stage by Billy Bragg for a celebratory performance of Curtis Mayfield's 'Move On Up'. From Weller's point of view, the day again showed that action spoke louder than words: he had put his lyrics into practice, and the proposed Government legislation was eventually withdrawn. The Council also appeared in a film which was made to publicise International Youth Year, together with other pop artists (Madness, Strawberry Switchblade, Jerry Dammers, Martyn Ware) and comedians (Julie Walters, Rik Mayall, Robbie Coltrane, Lenny Henry). If the documentary was aimed at making the public aware of the project, then it was wasn't very successful, since there is no evidence that it was ever screened. "The idea was for it to be shown on music programmes but so far that hasn't really happened," Weller admitted in the fan club magazine, *The Style Population*. It didn't bode well but Paul seemed nonplussed.

"I'm still a bit unsure about my involvement," he wrote. "I think it's more of a media thing in a way – I'm a sort of figurehead. I spoke at the first national conference in Sheffield, which was interesting. There are several different aims to it. There are lots of hiking clubs and Brownie groups, which is fine, but there's also the people whose interest is more political – that's more the side I'd like to be involved in. I think the aim should be to create a circulation of information among young people through these groups, then use it in a political way." He concluded by mentioning a National Lobby of Parliament planned for November, but the whole project seemed half-hearted. While Paul had been very effective in publicising political campaigns from within the world of pop music, his ability to stretch beyond that sphere was debatable.

By this time, *The Style Population* had evolved from a straightforward quarterly magazine into an arena for the widening political debate among the band's fans. The issues naturally tended to reflect Weller's – and most readers sided with Paul's left-wing – views but the phenomenon was unique among the pop bands of the time. Even in the punk days, fanzines rarely dealt with specific political issues outside the sphere of music, let alone carried informed debates on subjects like the European Space Programme or the location of Trident nuclear missiles.

Weller's recommended reading, as listed in *The Style Population*, included such cornerstones of left-wing thought as *The Ragged Trousered Philanthropists* and *Britain's First Socialist*, as well as more contemporary publications like *Scargill And The Miners*. In the same issue, Mick Talbot discussed the possibility of a memorial concert in Japan in the summer to commemorate the fortieth anniversary of the dropping of bombs in Hiroshima, with proceeds going to hospitals for people who were still suffering, but the idea never came to fruition.

Within this climate, it was no surprise that The Style Council's next record had a confrontational stance – and sure enough, the rousing 'Walls Come Tumbling Down' had a snarl and a bite that Weller hadn't demonstrated since The Jam days. To those fans who had grown disillusioned with the group's tuneful ballads or the eclecticism of *Café Bleu*, the single felt like a warrior returning. There was no ambiguity here, aside from the bizarre sight on the sepia-toned front cover of a Noel Coward-like Mick Talbot wearing make-up. "You don't have to take this crap," Weller barked gruffly, above a solid, Northern Soul bedrock of horns, organ and a driving beat. "You don't have to sit back and Relax". The last word alluded to the 'Frankie Say Relax' T-shirt craze which followed the enormous success of Frankie Goes To Hollywood's single a year or so earlier.

Succinct and hard-hitting, 'Walls Come Tumbling Down' also took a pot-shot at the "public enemies No. 10", with a revolutionary cry which preached that "we can actually try changing things". The band then took this message of solidarity to Warsaw in Poland to shoot a promotional video. Sporting a fancy 'wedge' haircut and dressed strikingly in pink and black in the bleak surroundings of a city suffering a level of poverty and oppression almost unimaginable in Britain, Weller's socialist rhetoric somehow sounded empty. True, the Poles had just cause to rise up against "those in authority" – and in Lech Walesa, they had a figurehead to guide them – but they didn't need to hear it from a Western pop star who could have no conception of their frugal lifestyle.

The B-sides were credited to the Council Folk Club. 'The Whole Point II' succinctly expanded upon the anti-"lords and ladies" message of that late addition to *Café Bleu*. This disdain for the upper classes was echoed by 'Blood Sports', a scathing attack on hunting which was written for a fund-raising compilation album. The song's songwriting royalties were donated to a defence fund for two members of the Hunt Saboteurs Association, who were being held in remand for anti-fox hunting activities.

Britain's animal rights movement had expanded considerably during the

Eighties, both in terms of numbers and in its willingness to take direct action against all forms of animal abuse – from vivisection and fox hunts to the fur trade. While organisations like the B.U.A.V. (the British Union for the Abolition of Vivisection) witnessed an upturn in membership applications and the country's percentage of vegetarians gradually rose, more militant collectives like S.E.A.L.L. (the South East Animal Liberation League) and the A.L.F. (the Animal Liberation Front) made the headlines. While the tabloid newspapers raged against demonstrators who pulled stunts like throwing red paint across butchers' windows, the Government adopted a hard line against terrorist activity. In fact, during this period, the police devoted more officers to the animal rights issue than to any other extremist group apart from the IRA. A pop star who publicly donated money to imprisoned demonstrators was treading on dangerous ground.

The anti-fox hunting lobby was swept along by a tide of public support which wasn't enjoyed by the anti-vivisectionists' more drastic measures. Nineteen members of S.E.A.L.L. were arrested following their part in a well-publicised raid on the animal testing laboratories at Wickham in October 1984. One of the defendants was Style Council bassist Kevin Miller's wife Sally, who was a mutual friend of Gill Price and Tracie – so the singer recorded a special dedication to accompany the release of her next single. "We wrote a set of lyrics to Paul Hardcastle's '19' one night," remembers Tracie, "altering them to suit the circumstances of the trial. Sally helped me research the facts through the government documentation we had about vivisection statistics."

The result was '19 – Wickham Mix', featuring a joint songwriting credit to Paul Weller, although he had nothing to do with the actual recording. "I didn't even want him in the studio, when I was recording it," Tracie explains. "I was like a little girl trying to please her daddy, I suppose. But I used the music from 'Soul's On Fire', which was a joint effort between myself and Paul." Fronted by a straightforward cover of George McCrae's Seventies soul side, 'I Can't Leave You Alone', the single marked Respond Records' return to Polydor in July 1985, and was credited to her full name, Tracie Young. It was a make or break time for the singer, having ventured out from Weller's protective shirt tails. Despite a supporting cast of Style Council and Respond regulars, however, the single flopped – and the same fate awaited the bland 'Invitation' in October. Sandwiched between them was a lame cod-funk effort from Vaughn Toulouse, 'Cruisin' The Serpentine'. All three releases in Respond's new schedule sold poorly.

During the summer of '85, optimistic reports outlined Respond's future projects. A solo Mick Talbot disc was planned, possibly to be produced by Matt Bianco's Mark Reilly, alongside a Steve White jazz EP, and there was even talk of two Style Council records on Respond: an album featuring cover versions of their favourite songs, and a soundtrack LP for *Business As Usual*, a new film about trade unionism. Tracie was enthusiastic about a "new album, which is nearly completed", planned for early 1986. But Paul was busy with The Style Council, and without the cache of his name at the helm, the label was cast adrift. With John Weller's managerial clout behind her, Tracie remained at Polydor for another year. She recorded two singles under the new arrangement – drafting in Steve White for a Style Council tune, '(When You) Call Me', and 'We Should Be Together' – but the album's worth of songs was scrapped.

In early 1986, Paul wrote an obituary in *The Style Population*: "We gave Respond a good three years now and it's really exhausted its purpose and use. It's got such a lousy reputation that we feel it's no longer worth putting out any more records." It was an accurate epitaph. During a period when Paul Weller commanded more critical respect than ninety per cent of his contemporaries, Respond's output was met with corresponding derision. There has always been a stigma attached to artist-run labels, ever since the failure of The Beatles' Apple label, although it is fair to concede that much of Respond's output was sub-standard and uninspired. While some releases shared the melodic strengths and lyrical acumen that helped make The Style Council so appealing (which isn't surprising, given Paul's multi-faceted involvement with many of them), it spoke volumes about the cult of Paul Weller that critics and fans alike weren't prepared to accept from Respond artists what they were quite happy to lap up from the man himself.

★　★　★

On June 8, 1985, The Style Council's second album went to No. 1 – a crowning achievement for Paul Weller. To him, *Our Favourite Shop* felt like the best LP he had ever made. "This record is so important to me," he wrote in *The Style Population*. "I've spent so much time over the lyrics. It's also more organ and guitar-based. I've never believed so positively in any record as I do this one. For me, everything feels right. I don't say we'll never match it again but it will take some doing."

The eye-catching gatefold sleeve design was the visual embodiment of the album's title, picturing Paul and Mick immersed in a 'room' chock-a-block with clothes, books, records, photos, magazines, instruments and other trinkets. The collage reflected the pair's tastes in fashion, music, TV and film, comedy, politics, literature and, in Mick's case, sport. The idea felt like an extension of the inner sleeve for The Jam's *All Mod Cons*. After all, who else but Weller would have chosen a Rickenbacker guitar, a clutch of soul LPs, a CND beret, a Gaggia coffee maker, a poster for *A Hard Day's Night* and a Tony Hancock book? The cover opened out to reveal a black-and-white photo of the pair in a pose disarmingly similar to that of Lennon and McCartney on the wall of the 'shop'; indeed, the record slotted into the middle of the sleeve in the style of the *Beatles For Sale* LP.

"People complained that *Café Bleu* was a jumble of styles," explained Paul, "that there were so many things going on it got confused. But it wasn't confusing to us – it just wasn't what people are used to, that's all. Though there's still loads of styles on *Our Favourite Shop*, it's more coherent and more confident. We took more time over it, too. I don't think we had ever previously rehearsed songs before we recorded them."

Whereas *Café Bleu* felt like a lucky dip into Weller's varied musical tastes, *Our Favourite Shop* forged these flavours into a more cohesive sound – which was odd, bearing in mind the involvement of over twenty 'Honorary Councillors'. The most notable of these musicians were Camelle Hinds, who was now their unofficial bassist, and Dee C. Lee, who sang on six songs. The other acute difference between the LPs was *Our Favourite Shop*'s absence of jazz influences, aside from the occasional guitar lick or Latin vibe.

With vague plans for a twenty-track LP, the band had recorded intensively over a ten-week period, before whittling the project down to thirteen songs and the Latin jazz title track instrumental. Weller expanded on its theme: "The subject matter of the album is Britain today, what we see around us. We didn't set out to make an overtly political album, we just chose the best songs." And unlike The Jam, the political rhetoric wasn't accompanied by angst-ridden music.

Nevertheless, over half the lyrics were of a clear-cut political persuasion, making the LP Weller's boldest statement of intent to date, backed up on the cover by quotes from the likes of the outspoken intellectual and Labour MP Tony Benn, radical US comedian Lenny Bruce and Oscar Wilde's *Man Under Socialism*. In hindsight, *Our Favourite Shop* represented the pinnacle of Paul's use of overtly political sentiments in his music. Thankfully, the songs weren't tarred with a staunch party-political brush and while a few dealt with specific issues, many of the lyrics painted broader strokes. The pair explained their political beliefs as part of a dialogue about the songs on the cassette version of the album.

The album's opener, 'Homebreakers' – one of four Weller/Talbot compositions – eloquently highlighted the plight of a family ripped apart by unemployment and poverty, and was spoilt only by Talbot's mediocre vocal technique. The pair also collaborated on 'Internationalists', one of the LP's cornerstones, using a variation on the Modernist/Stylist terminology to suggest, as Paul put it, "someone who doesn't identify strictly with their own country". Powered by Weller's wah-wah guitar, this urgent soul-rock workout updated The Jam's 'Trans-Global Express' by reiterating the need for worldwide unity and, ultimately, some form of revolution to somehow rid the world of inequality. "A song about the power we all possess if we choose to unite and rise up to fight capitalism and oppression," was how Paul summarised it with an idealistic naïveté. "I thought of the old socialist song, 'The Internationale', when I wrote it."

At the other end of the spectrum was 'Luck', a bouncy pop ditty which evoked summery images. And the final Weller/Talbot song was 'The Lodgers', the theme of which was evident from its subtitle, 'She Was Only A

Shopkeeper's Daughter' – the lodgers in question being the Conservative Party, of course.

Some of the album's most unsettling lyrics were accompanied by the softest music. After learning about the plight of those who had died on Y.T.S. schemes, Steve White wrote some new lyrics for 'Have You Ever Had It Blue?' The result, 'With Everything To Lose', portrayed a sadness which was amplified by a mournful melody. And 'A Stone's Throw Away', Weller's evocative ode to the universal nature of struggle, was dramatised to great effect by its naked string orchestration. The album's real gem, however, was Paul's heartfelt memorial to his old school friend Dave Waller, 'Man Of Great Promise'. Back in 1978, in the songbook for *All Mod Cons*, Weller had included a tribute to his friend: "Dave, your words fill me with new hope for the modern world, whilst your words on decay and destruction have the foresight of a person a 1,000 years old. There are those who are held in high esteem who do not deserve it in light of you." The letter was signed "Your loyal and devoted friend, Weller P. (fan club No. 0001)". Weller had pondered over releasing 'Man Of Great Promise' as a single but decided against it – maybe he was too emotionally bound up with its subject matter. Equally beguiling was 'Down In The Seine', described by Talbot as an "aggressive, European-flavoured waltz", and inspired by Scott Walker's interpretations of Belgian *chansonnier* Jacques Brel. "There is a good musical tradition in France, especially with jazz," Weller remarked to *Go Go* fanzine. "The French have a very distinct melodic sense as well. I like stuff by some European writers, Brel – and even Brecht's stuff, a German writer around in the Twenties and Thirties."

The album's main pitfall was an unfortunate experiment with comedian Lenny Henry, whom the band had met on several occasions, both on his various TV shows over the years (he sang 'You're The Best Thing' with them on an episode of TV's *Saturday Live*) and via his work with the International Year of Youth. Lenny's rap on 'The Stand Up Comic's Instructions' mimicked the racist bigotry of Northern comedians – the twist, of course, being that Lenny is black – but the song's novelty rapidly wore off.

Another of the LP's least convincing ventures was 'Come To Milton Keynes', an unprovoked attack on the Bedfordshire 'new town' notorious for its faceless linear plan and 'artificial' architecture. The song's lyrics suggested a reality of drugs, violence and "losing our way" behind a façade of "luscious houses" where the "curtains are drawn", the idea being to create a musical pastiche which matched the supposed artificiality of Milton Keynes itself. "Every piece of tackiness we could think of was thrown in," commented Paul, explaining its quirky mix of horns and strings and the snatches of the *Sale Of The Century* theme, 'Viva Espana!', 'Robin Hood' and a cricket commentary voice.

'Come To Milton Keynes' was banned from some TV and radio stations after complaints from enraged local residents – some of whom were Style

Council fans. The local branch of the International Year Of Youth – of which Weller was president – reacted by inviting the musician to visit the town but he refused, presumably embarrassed about the degree of the backlash. The adverse reaction was wholly justified: not only had Weller never visited Milton Keynes but the town's similarities with Woking, by then a booming Eighties equivalent of a 'new town' itself, were considerable. Woking, therefore, might have made for a more logical target – but the songwriter chose not to soil his own doorstep.

To add insult to injury, 'Come To Milton Keynes' was chosen as the band's next single at the end of June. The Style Council had made their first significant mistake – as one of the weakest possible selections from *Our Favourite Shop*, this was their first single to miss the Top 20. Within a few weeks, Weller confessed his regret about the decision in *The Style Population*. An exclusive instrumental mix of 'Come To Milton Keynes' was donated to a compilation album, *Sons Of Jobs For The Boys*, which was aimed at raising awareness about unemployment on Merseyside – so at least something productive came of the song. A more sensible choice might have been the B-side, '(When You) Call Me', which was a simple, gospel-tinged love song marred only by a heavy-handed synth drum. 'Boy Who Cried Wolf' was issued throughout the rest of the world, where Milton Keynes held no significance, as the second single from *Our Favourite Shop*. Despite some now-dated synth sounds and an insensitive production, the song's plaintive melody carried it through, helped by backing vocals from Tracie.

Our Favourite Shop was heavily promoted with hefty exposure throughout TV, radio and the press and nearly lived up to the humorous boast of the advertisements, which proclaimed it "the second and finest LP from probably the best pop group in the world". The album sold well across the globe, especially throughout Australasia, Europe and Japan. But it failed to make any headway in the States, where it was renamed *Internationalists*, despite the ground that had been made by *Café Bleu*. Any number of reasons may have lain behind the LP's modest Stateside sales, but one factor was certain: Paul Weller wasn't willing to endure a lengthy stint slogging around the backwaters of America to rectify the situation, and The Style Council remained largely unknown outside of the major East and West Coast cities for the rest of their days.

★　★　★

During their *Internationalists '85* Tour of the UK, the first leg of which played through June, The Style Council again attempted to stage their play, *Three Musketeers Go Wild*, as another technique of avoiding the standard gig format, but the project fell through a second time. Instead, they performed two sets, the first devoted to *Our Favourite Shop*, plus other new songs, and the second to more established material. Out went the brass: "We dropped the horn section because I think there was a danger of us getting stuck with that

191

sound," explained Weller. "We like to feel we're adaptable and that we can change the line-up. It's important to keep that, otherwise you end up being just like any other band." In came the dramatic *A Word From Our Leaders*, which consisted of a slide show projected on a large screen while an audio tape played interviews with Prime Minister Margaret Thatcher and other political leaders, accompanied by a manic drum rhythm and saxophone solo.

Weller noticed a change in their fans during the tour: "The audiences looked very different as well – still quite a varied age range, a lot more girls though (not teenybop kinds), which is nice. I don't like 'lads bands'." This last comment was a thinly veiled swipe at his past musical life with The Jam. "We were asked to reform for a lot of charity gigs," he revealed. "It doesn't annoy me when they ask, I can understand it, but it doesn't interest me."

The dozen or so dates were followed by a string of open-air concerts. On June 22, The Style Council headlined Glastonbury Festival to a wet and muddy fifty thousand-strong audience – the first occasion they'd topped an outdoor bill and played in front of such a large crowd. Then it was off to a festival in Denmark and two in Belgium, the second show in front of an even bigger gathering – 120,000 spectators.

But these shows were nothing compared with the events of July 13. That was the day of Live Aid, the biggest pop music phenomenon the world has ever seen. The idea had grown out of the Band Aid record, organised by Bob Geldof and Midge Ure. Having assembled a stellar array from the world of mid-Eighties pop for 'Do They Know It's Christmas?', they convinced the most famous names in rock to perform on one bill. Statistics suggested that ninety-five per cent of the world's televisions tuned into Live Aid, as the marathon event was beamed live across the globe, where numerous other countries staged their own supporting shows.

Live Aid was launched at noon to a packed-out Wembley Stadium with a set from Status Quo, featuring Paul's old mentor Rick Parfitt. Twenty minutes later, The Style Council played a four-song set. Weller was expected to make a political statement but this didn't materialise – which might be explained by Weller's later admission that he had suffered from extreme nerves during the whole performance. The event was a milestone in the history of musical protest, which was elevated from minor league gigs and the odd free festival to the world stage in one fell swoop. Live Aid publicised the horrors of African famine far more effectively than even Bob Geldof imagined, and led to a number of other high profile shows – including the Nelson Mandela Seventieth Birthday Tribute to campaign for the release of the world's best-known political prisoner. Weller's statement in 'Walls Come Tumbling Down' that "We can actually try changing things" had come true: pop music *was* a powerful weapon of enlightenment and, in Live Aid's case, a fund-raising tool to the tune of $140 million worth of contributions.

Weller seized the initiative after Live Aid by helping to create Red Wedge, a pressure group which sought to inform people about a broad spectrum of left-wing issues. But Paul had more immediate problems on his mind. After an ill-advised Japanese tour playing huge stadiums with various other acts – The Associates, Go West and Culture Club – The Style Council flew straight to Australia for Weller's first-ever visit to the country. Soon after they arrived on August 11 for a week's break before their first concert, the trouble started.

A British daily newspaper ran a story on the incident with the headline, "Wrecker girl stuns a star. Rock star Paul Weller was left to foot a whopping £2,600 bill after a girlfriend wrecked his hotel suite. The young woman ripped wallpaper, smashed a stool and left burns and blood stains on the carpet during the Style Council singer's recent tour of Australia. Ex-Jam star Weller paid for the damage at Melbourne's Regency Hotel." The tabloid press have a poor reputation for accuracy and the true nature of the events is confused. Some sources suggest that Paul's girlfriend, Gill Price, flew out to meet him in Australia, only to be met by a member of the band's security with a return ticket and a message not to contact Paul again. Later, rumours circulated that Gill had signed a declaration never to speak about her relationship with Paul and, in return, the Wellers bought her a house. One fact was definitely true, though: Paul Weller had broken up with his long-standing girlfriend. It was probably pure coincidence but this split corresponded with the start of a slow but steady decline in the musical quality and the commercial success of The Style Council until they eventually disbanded four years later.

11

TIME PASSES . . .

"We are socialists and try to lead by our actions."

(Paul Weller, *Internationalists*, 1985)

"I still come from that modernist approach, and I always will do. That's my attitude. And that's another reason why people should be supporting contemporary black music. It fits in with the whole Modernist philosophy. The Sixties are nice to listen to, but I don't think you can make them a way of life anymore. You've got to look for something new."

(Paul Weller, *Go Go*, 1986)

"I don't always see myself in terms of age but I did notice a couple of grey hairs. Outraged, I immediately had blonde streaks put in. What next! Dentures? Baldness? Gout? Age . . . What a swine!"

(Paul Weller, aged twenty-seven, 1985)

Dee C. Lee's role within The Style Council had steadily increased ever since her first guest appearance with the band on 'Money-Go-Round'. But throughout the summer of 1985, it was evident that she was now treated as a fully fledged member. Rumours soon emerged in the gossip columns that Dee and Paul were an item, and within a few months, the pair admitted that their relationship went beyond mutual professional admiration. The couple's romantic involvement didn't directly affect the day-to-day running of The Style Council, but the atmosphere within the band was definitely changing. Mick and his girlfriend Shane Chapman became parents – a boy named Gene – which led to a shift in his priorities. Suddenly, the thought of lengthy spells away from home on tour seemed less appetising.

Paul himself had never publicly expressed an interest in having children – far from it, in fact. Around 1984, there was another tabloid story. "No kidding! Weller's sex snip ruled out," ran the headline. "I want a vasectomy because I am sure I never want any kids and I haven't got any paternal instincts at all," Weller explained. "The kind of person I am and what I do is far too selfish to devote the amount of time to kids . . . So I was trying to

194

have the operation – you know, the little snip – but the doctor said I was too young." He was also drawn on the subject of marriage: "I can't see the point of it. A piece of paper doesn't mean you are going to stay with someone. It's like having a contract with a band. If people are going to leave, they are going to leave."

Before the decade was out, Paul Weller would not only have married Dee but they would also have the first of two children. And within a year of Paul's split from Gill Price, *The Sun* newspaper printed a report in June 1986 that the new couple had "secretly bought a £300,000 house together. The beautiful, three-bedroom Victorian cottage is in North London's exclusive St. Johns Wood, with a forty five-feet garden. Built in mid-1880s, it has been restored to include all-original features." Weller also learnt to drive and bought a Ford Granada – it was a picture of conventional domesticity that Weller would have balked at a few years earlier. And it eventually contributed to the break-up of The Style Council.

For the moment, though, Paul's love affair with Dee manifested itself in his active support of her career. In September, she featured prominently on a re-recording of 'The Lodgers' from *Our Favourite Shop*, receiving a full credit for the first time and appearing next to Paul and Mick on the cover photo backstage after performing on Channel 4's *Soul Train*. This was probably Weller's first serious attempt at writing a modern soul tune, which worked well as the backdrop for another anti-Government tirade – 'the lodgers' in question being those at No. 10 Downing Street. But the song had already been given a 'Club Mix' (alongside a more appealing treatment of Mick's instrumental, 'Our Favourite Shop') on the 12″ edition of 'Come To Milton Keynes'. Four months after the album's release, the band expected their fans to accept a third variation as their new single with the caption, "presented to you by public demand". Admittedly, 'The Lodgers' sounded more robust with the addition of a horn section (and Camelle Hinds' bass in place of the original synth), but a complete absence of new songs was masked by twenty minutes of live recordings from their summer tour.

Away from The Style Council, Dee had struggled to make any impact as a solo artist. Her records were only remarkable for the fact that she wrote most of the songs – an unusual situation among contemporary British soul singers. One of her best compositions was 'See The Day', a Bacharach & David-like ballad which she performed on the next leg of the *Internationalists '85 Tour* in Italy and Germany in September. In mid-October, 'See The Day' was issued as Dee's next single and gave the singer a surprise Top 5 hit – though its progress might have been helped by her live rendition of The Style Council's 'Luck', as well as 'The Paris Match', "performed by the Council Quartet". Weller also contributed an exclusive composition, 'Just My Type', under his Jake Fluckery pseudonym, to Lee's début album, *Shrine* (issued in early 1986), but for the most part, Dee kept her solo endeavours quite separate from the Council's – and, perhaps as a result, she was unable to sustain her profile.

Instead, she played a more prominent role rounding off *Internationalists '85* with three sell-out nights at Wembley Arena in early December. "We shall be joined by a 12-piece string section, 4-piece brass section and Yes! Even a conductor," was the announcement. It was The Style Council's largest indoor UK show to date.

★　★　★

While the personal lives of the band were changing, Weller busied himself with plans for an ambitious new tour which seemed to embody the very core of The Style Council's *raison d'être*. The project, which was given the banner of Red Wedge, represented the culmination of Paul's socialist initiatives to date. By late summer 1985, the wheels had already been set into motion and a press release was issued voicing the project's aims and ambitions:

"Red Wedge is the name of a whole host of musicians, actors, celebrities and assorted people, whose purpose is to bring left-wing ideas to other people. Set up by the Labour Party, it is a direct result of the wonderful Billy Bragg's Jobs And Industry tour of early this year. Red Wedge makes no bones of its intentions – we want the Tories OUT and a Socialist Government IN. Red Wedge is aimed at young people and hopefully carrying young people's aims . . . One of the Council's Wembley shows in December will be for Red Wedge and this is only the beginning. Action speaks louder, now get involved!"

Bragg was fast emerging as the most potent political force British pop had ever seen. Fusing the aggression (and the disregard for musical technique) of punk and both the political tradition and one-man-band style of the folk movement, he sang about issues like civil rights, the right-wing press, the trade unions and the Falklands war in a plain-speaking style which won him many admirers. By 1985, he had already notched up two Top 30 albums, which were followed that year by two uncompromising hit singles, the 'Between The Wars EP' and 'Days Like These'.

It was a reflection of Bragg's impact that, early in 1985, the musician had been summoned to the House Of Commons for a brainstorming session with no lesser figure than the Leader of the Opposition, Neil Kinnock. The Labour head was keen to discuss the issues which affected young people, in an attempt to recover from their landslide defeat in the 1983 general election. "Eager to restore the party's credibility with young voters, he began to explore ways in which Labour and pop music might get together," according to Robin Denselow in *When The Music's Over*. The result was a coalition between pop and politics. Weeks later, Bragg announced details of his Jobs For Youth tour, alias the Jobs & Industry Campaign – a groundbreaking concept because the singer would be joined on the road by Labour MPs whose role was to chat with his audience. "How should we dress?" the later shadow cabinet member Robin Cook had asked. "Whatever you feel natural in," was Bragg's reply. The concerts were a cautious success from Labour's point of view – petitions were signed and MPs chatted awkwardly with the gig-goers – and party leader Neil Kinnock wanted more.

On July 23, 1985, a meeting was held at the Labour Party's South London HQ, where MPs, actors, journalists and pop stars – including Bragg and Paul Weller – discussed how they could best promote left-wing issues. Also present was CND's Annajoy David, who commented afterwards that "we need to inject people with a new enthusiasm for socialism". There was some hesitation about Bragg's suggestion for a name; some felt it too rooted in old-style Labour. But in September, Red Wedge was born, with a loan of £3,000 from Labour and the National Union of Public Employees to get off the ground. The official media launch followed on November 21, 1985, with a dour assembly in the House Of Commons, which began with a speech from Kinnock. He announced with some satisfaction that a Red Wedge package – a fluctuating collective of musicians not dissimilar to the concept behind The Style Council itself – would tour Britain early the following year.

Some observers were surprised at Weller's involvement; after all, he had adopted a revolutionary attitude in many of his more recent songs and had criticised Labour for being what Bragg called a "staid political party with often middle-of-the-road ideas". "The Labour Party is potentially great," Paul had written as early as 1982, "the idea behind it, but I don't even think they consciously abuse it, they just ain't got a fucking clue, really." But Weller had been affected by the impact of Live Aid, which had proved that, collectively, pop music *could* achieve tremendous results. It's also likely that Bragg's involvement persuaded Paul to join Red Wedge: the pair came from similar backgrounds (Billy was the working-class son of an East London warehouseman) and shared a radical far-left political outlook.

Bragg was realistic. He sensed that communicating a range of specific broad-left ideas as part of the entertainment package was far more constructive than spouting revolutionary rhetoric. Weller had felt uncomfortable with his "spokesman for a generation" role, ill at ease at expressing his views in interviews, but Bragg was a born public speaker – and together, they forged a mutually beneficial relationship which saw Billy as the mouthpiece of Red Wedge and Weller as the tour's major musical attraction. Bragg was aware that, with the pulling power of The Style Council, its profile would be much higher. Despite Red Wedge's assurances that "we're not saying 'Vote Labour' ", the party's direct involvement meant that the tours amounted to a travelling recruitment campaign – if not a fully blown party political broadcast. Leading pop musicians were, for the first time in Britain, advocating people to vote for an established political party at the next general election – or rather, vote to get rid of their rivals in power, which amounted to the same thing.

With the organisational engine of The Style Council's road crew and security behind them, the Red Wedge tour began on January 26, 1986 in an old Manchester theatre, the Apollo. At the press conference, Weller commented that "if you ask us all questions, you'll get different answers, but we all want to get rid of the Tories". Paul also talked of wider ambitions for the project, "because we hope to be involved in drawing up the Party's youth and arts programmes". The five or so concerts which followed proved to be a great success musically – as did a second round of gigs in March – and represented good value for money. For a small entrance fee, each show lasted well over two hours, which not only featured several main acts – The Style Council, Billy Bragg, The Communards, plus reggae artist Lorna Gee – but a host of often surprising guest appearances.

On various nights, audiences were treated to Jerry Dammers (who played with The Style Council), Junior, Lloyd Cole, and Tom Robinson, plus members of Prefab Sprout, The Smiths, Madness, Working Week, The Kane Gang and Spandau Ballet. The Style Council's set sometimes featured a rendition of Sly Stone's funk classic, 'Thank You', and Gil Scott-Heron's anti-apartheid anthem, 'Johannesburg', while Dee C. Lee performed her own interlude, backed by Weller and Talbot. Each performance then climaxed with a finale of the artists involved – a medley of cover versions like Dennis Edwards' 'Don't Look Any Further', Curtis Mayfield's 'People Get Ready' and 'Move On Up' and Jimmy Cliff's 'Many Rivers To Cross'. Red Wedge also hosted a concert at the Hammersmith Odeon as part of a Farewell Festival for the GLC (Greater London Council), headed by future Labour MP Ken Livingstone, which was about to be abolished. Despite the broad cross-section of artists huddled together on one tour bus, there were apparently no quarrels. "I think that's because all of us were doing it for a fundamental reason," explained Weller. "That's why we don't get ego clash. That's why it all went so smoothly."

The effectiveness of the Red Wedge shows in raising their audiences' awareness of political issues was less certain. And the day events were often quite shambolic. In the evenings, Labour politicians circulated in foyers and each punter arrived to find a brown paper bag on their seat, which contained a selection of pamphlets relating to such issues as the Anti-Apartheid Movement, unemployment among young people, CND and women's rights. A proposed tie-in album never materialised, but a Red Wedge video was later issued; footage from the Newcastle City Hall concert was interspersed by interview clips explaining the reasons behind the project. Weller also promoted the scheme on TV's *Club Mix* programme, stressing that they were "not on a missionary crusade", before joining funk group Black Britain, who had supported The Style Council at their Wembley Arena shows, on guitar for their cover of the Beginning Of The End's early Seventies hit, 'Funky Nassau'. "Their attitude's good," Paul commented.

Red Wedge encountered considerable flack from various quarters. Conservatives were naturally dismissive and American rock svengali Miles Copeland launched a scathing attack on Paul Weller. "He is a small businessman, and when he goes to negotiate his deal, and talks to his banker, and thinks what he's doing with his money, he thinks in a Conservative, free-enterprise mentality," said the manager of Sting and owner of I.R.S. Records. "He talks about the class struggle, and perpetuates the myth that people are different." Weller reacted to Copeland's criticisms by denying that he was a hypocrite and adding that "I wouldn't get questioned if I was an author. It's just that people think that pop music should be about frivolity. I'm not a tax exile. I spend my money in a constructive way." Weller frequently had to defend his position, in fact, against cynics suspicious of how a wealthy pop star could relate to the poor or unemployed. He responded to such an accusation on Piccadilly Radio: "I know where I come from and what I've come from and the fact that I've made money now doesn't really affect the way I feel".

A more damaging swipe at Red Wedge came from within the ranks of the left-wing – albeit those whose hard-line views clashed with Kinnock's increasingly moderate position. Elvis Costello, for example, was sceptical about both the name and what he described as "the biggest badge you can wear", referring to Billy Bragg's lyric that "wearing badges is not enough in days like these". Discontentment about Red Wedge among the militant, hard-left was voiced by SWP (Socialist Workers Party) member Chris Dean, alias *NME* writer X Moore, who described the project as a "very good but fanciful idea", before dismissing it as "a tidy way to sell out socialist principles in favour of electoral success for Kinnock".

Dean's own band, The Redskins, pledged to "sing like The Supremes and walk like The Clash", but ended up sounding like a punky version of early Dexy's Midnight Runners, with a hint of rockabilly. The socialist skinhead band had called upon Steve 'Boy Wonderful' White to play on their mid-1985 hit, 'Bring It Down! (This Insane Thing)'; and Jam trumpeter Steve Nichol had played on their 1983 single, 'Lean On Me/Unionize!' The Redskins were the product of a grass roots socialist music scene which had evolved in the early Eighties – of which Billy Bragg was also a part.

The press labelled the scene 'agit-pop', a play on the term agit-prop, short for agitational propaganda. Although not directly involved in this hard-left groundswell of activity, Weller could effectively bridge the gap between humble miner's benefit gigs and large, media-saturated events like Live Aid. The fact that he could communicate on both levels was to be commended. The agit-pop scene also nurtured the so-called ranting poets (Attila The Stockbroker, Seething Wells, alias journalist Stephen Wells, Benjamin Zephaniah), comedians (including Porky The Poet, alias radio DJ Phil Jupitus, who bowed out of live work after supporting The Style Council on their Renaissance Tour in late '87), fanzines (*Wake Up*) and anti-fascist groups (Red Action). Red Wedge may have expected their collective support; it didn't get it.

In the wake of the first Red Wedge tour, Paul's position had been realistic: "Really, this country needs a new political strategy, based on a modern form of socialism. It doesn't matter a fuck what you're singing about, it's your actions that count. So I don't feel we have to make political songs. The most important thing for us is to turn up at the anti-apartheid rally, for instance, and play there to show our support. I think that's about all that pop music can do."

That Artists Against Apartheid Meeting was held on South London's Clapham Common on June 28, 1986. The British wing of the A.A.A. had been launched in April by The Specials' Jerry Dammers to campaign for the cultural boycotting of South Africa until apartheid had been lifted; Dammers had actively supported this cause ever since 1984's Special AKA anthem, 'Free Nelson Mandela'. As Robin Denselow revealed, one of Dammers' first moves with the A.A.A. was to draw up a draft contract "for artists to show their record companies and lawyers" – which is why messages like "The Style Council are anti-apartheid" and "This record is not for sale in South Africa" appeared on their later albums.

Dammers then organised the enormous, eight-hour free festival on Clapham Common. The stellar, suitably multi-cultural cast included Hugh Masekela, Elvis Costello, Billy Bragg, Sting, Boy George, Sade, Peter Gabriel and Gil Scott-Heron – whose 'Johannesburg' was also the highlight of The Style Council's brief set in front of an estimated quarter-of-a-million people, while their rousing 'Move On Up' was later captured for posterity on a fund-raising video, 'Freedom Beat'. The impact of the event should not be underestimated in helping the publicity drive which led to the eventual release of Nelson Mandela.

The campaign's attention turned on Paul Simon later that year, after he flouted the boycott with his infamous collaboration with South African musicians on his best-selling *Gracelands* album. Weller signed A.A.A.'s open letter to Paul Simon, presented to the musician on his visit to Britain in April 1987, calling on him to apologise to the UN General Assembly as the culmination of perhaps the most confused political debate to have raged in recent times.

Two months after the petition to Simon, Bragg & Co. returned under the banner: "Red Wedge and Neil Kinnock invite you to attend the Red Wedge Election '87 press conference at Ronnie Scott's Club". The back of the invite read, "Move On Up. Go For Labour", a motto based on Red Wedge's slogan, "Move On Up! A Socialist Vision Of The Future", itself borrowed from Curtis Mayfield via The Style Council. This was the start of the first pop music campaign in British election history. A hastily booked tour entailed a dozen gigs, which built up to the eve of the election on June 12. Although the venues were smaller than before, the organisers singled out marginal constituencies, and the dates were well-attended, lured by the Red Wedge mainstays, plus The The's Matt Johnson, and The Blow Monkeys (whose optimistic duet with Curtis Mayfield, 'The Day After You', was banned from radio in the election run-up). Guests included The Housemartins and ex-members of The Beat, who joined Bragg for a version of their old favourite, 'Stand Down Margaret'. Meanwhile, a second tour of comedians led by Ben Elton and Lenny Henry played elsewhere.

Critics dismissed the operation as "style socialism by humourless blokes", describing it as an unhappy compromise between apolitical pop fans and hard-left militants. But Red Wedge's main aim had always been to reach beyond the *Militant* paper-sellers and preach to the unconverted, to young people who might otherwise not have voted – and, in this respect, it succeeded. Red Wedge was part of what observers across the political spectrum admitted was an impressive campaign. In the 1983 election, nearly half of those aged under twenty-six hadn't voted at all, whereas in 1987, Labour's greatest improvement was among eighteen- and twenty-four-year-olds. Sadly for all concerned, it was all to no avail – the Conservatives won their third term in office.

As Neil Kinnock commented bravely that Labour must embark on a fundamental re-appraisal, everyone involved with Red Wedge felt equally disillusioned. Billy Bragg's response was quite philosophical, but The Style Council's founder reacted more strongly. After June 12, the revolutionary stance of his lyrics subsided and political issues were confined to a small proportion of his new material – before disappearing altogether. "We really hate that tag 'political group'," Paul moaned in *The Independent* in early 1987. "I don't like the way it sets us up as some kind of spokesmen. That's just crap . . . We are musicians who've got political ideas and attitudes which we put into our work. I like quite a few older political songwriters, like Sly Stone, Curtis Mayfield and Norman Whitfield and you know we wear those influences very much on our sleeve."

On April 25, 1987, The Style Council played a twenty-minute slot at a large CND/Friends Of The Earth Rally in Hyde Park to commemorate the first anniversary of the Chernobyl nuclear disaster. An estimated crowd of 80,000 marchers packed the park to hear the likes of Billy Bragg, while The Style Council's set included the otherwise unheard 'Love, Peace And Unity'. This was followed by a concert on July 19, when The Council and friends The Jazz Defektors pledged their support for the Nicaraguan Solidarity Campaign by performing at the Brixton Academy on the week-end marking the anniversary of the Central American country's revolution. Monies raised were then donated towards the organisation's publicity drive, aimed at highlighting America's funding of the Contra army there. 1987 also witnessed the group's appearance at an AIDS Benefit concert at London's The Barbican, alongside Erasure, house music star Darryl Pandy and The Communards.

The Style Council played their last benefit in March 1988 at the Hackney Empire in North-East London. Together with Sinead O'Connor and Ben Elton, they joined the Fight Alton's Bill campaign against the Liberal MP's proposed anti-abortion legislation. But for the last year or so of the group's life, Paul Weller was for the most part conspicuous by his absence from such events – and has rarely lent his support to such causes since then.

In 1991, Weller reflected on this withdrawal from political issues in *Boys About Town* fanzine. "With The Style Council, more than The Jam, we got dragged into that political arena too far," he admitted. "We'd go anywhere in the world, Australia for example, do a press conference and get journalists asking us what we were going to do about Maggie Thatcher and the state of the nation. It was mainly due to our lyrics and getting involved in projects like Red Wedge. It is one thing for a writer to write something, but it shouldn't make them a spokesperson for that subject."

★   ★   ★

Away from the political limelight of benefit gigs and free festivals, The Style Council were strangely quiet during 1986. The end of March finally witnessed the release of the two-year-old 'Have You Ever Had It Blue?', a jazzy, tropical pop song with wistful lyrics which had since been rewritten as 'With Everything To Lose' for *Our Favourite Shop*. The single was lifted from the soundtrack to Julien Temple's stylised musical adaptation of Colin MacInnes's vivid tale of late Fifties London, *Absolute Beginners*. Instead of the monochrome, first-person style of the book, which allowed the author to paint vivid pictures of outlandish characters as they passed through the narrator's life against a canvas of race riots, Temple stapled the plot onto an extended pop video. If the novel was stylish glistening chrome, then the film was tacky dayglo neon.

Weller had been offered a bit part role in the movie as Dean Swift, the sharply dressed modernist, but declined after he learnt that filming would take three weeks – "The band could record an album in that time," he quipped. Likewise, Temple had refused Paul's offer to write the whole soundtrack because he wanted to involve a variety of artists – and talk of Weller re-recording The Jam's 'Absolute Beginners' proved to be more fiction than fact. However, the Palace Pictures film did feature 'Have You Ever Had It Blue?' and Mick Talbot's laid-back jazz instrumental B-side, 'Mr. Cool's Dream', with arrangements by jazz legend Gil Evans.

As it transpired, only a few bars of 'Have You Ever Had It Blue?' were heard in the movie, much to Paul's disappointment. The single was a Top 20 hit, though, and the film's dancers, The Jazz Defektors, performed in the accompanying video. Paul and Mick became friendly with the troupe, and having offered them a support slot at their Brixton Academy gig, they mixed their 1987 LP, *The Jazz Defektors*, at Solid Bond Studios – where one track was also recorded.

Weller retained his love of the novel, writing the introduction to a reprinted edition in the early Nineties, but he was sceptical about the film. "I didn't really like it, maybe because I know the book so well," he told *Go Go* fanzine. "You could make a great film out of it, almost like a documentary.

Have you ever seen *Alfie*? The kind of technique they used . . . narrating sometimes as well. It would have been quite interesting, because most of the book is narration first person. They just blew it!"

The Style Council's only other release that year was a live album, *Home And Abroad*. Together with an accompanying video, *Showbiz*, this was drawn from their *Internationalists '85* concerts. It was an accurate document – no more, no less – but there was an air of indifference about the package, from the minimal artwork (aside from a novel, Japanese-styled 'obi' paper ribbon) to the unadventurous track-listing – which failed to include any of the band's soul covers, for example. It was a half-hearted stop-gap between studio albums which lacked the loving care and attention afforded to Weller's previous in-concert LP, *Dig The New Breed*. And it was also redubbed extensively in the studio, a sure sign that Weller was unhappy with the raw material.

The band were, in fact, buried at Solid Bond working on a new LP. Sessions were interrupted at various intervals; Paul sang 'Harvest For The World' with David Grant at a sickle cell anaemia charity auction ball in London, where Dee C. Lee sang 'That's What Friends Are For' with veteran soul singer Madeline Bell. "It's a good cause that genuinely needs funding," Weller put it simply. "That's why I got involved." He also mentioned in *The Style Population* that "we're trying to set something up with General Johnson who used to be with Chairmen Of The Board – that'll be great." The idea made sense: Weller had in the past performed two of the early Seventies soul group's songs.

The project arose because Chairmen Of The Board were enjoying an unprecedented renaissance in America. They weren't to be found in the national charts but over in North Carolina on the eastern seaboard, a strange phenomenon had hit the holiday resorts of the wealthy – beach music. Rumour had it that Chairmen Of The Board wouldn't accept offers to play in Britain because they were earning too much money every night playing concerts at home. Norman 'General' Johnson was tasting a new lease of life, together with other veteran soul acts like The Drifters and The Tams.

It was The Tams who scored with the superb, Sixties-styled tune, 'There Ain't Nothing Like Shaggin' ', reflecting a new dance craze that was sweep-ing the East Coast – the shag – and beach music was adopted by the Northern Soul scene over here. Just as appealing was Chairmen Of The Board's 'Loverboy', issued by EMI in September. There were various mixes of the song but The Style Council's involvement was stamped all over the single: the cover carried the message "remixed by Paul Weller", Mick Talbot added a keyboard solo and the sleeve was tastefully designed by Simon Halfon.

Clues as to Weller's musical direction have often come from his listen-ing habits so his enthusiasm that summer for young soul singers like Paul Johnson, Steven Duntaine and Pat Knight hinted at the direction The Style

Council might take. The band also recorded versions of club classics like Willie Clayton's 'Love Pains' and David Sea's 'Night After Night' (although they didn't appear until 1993's rarities collection, *Here's Some That Got Away*). And at a time when the mainstream music press was fast losing interest in him, Weller gave an in-depth interview to *Go Go* fanzine in August 1986, in which he talked of his current record-buying tastes – "In America, there's a brilliant music scene with all these little independent soul labels" – and described a shift in his songwriting. "When I was 18, I wasn't interested in singing tender songs," he revealed. "All that anger and frustration you don't know what to do with was channelled through our music. I'm twenty-eight now, ten years on, and I'm not so frustrated!" Weaving the two strands together, it might have been possible to predict the approach of The Style Council's next LP.

Sure enough, the first evidence of their forthcoming material revealed a definite shift in their sound. In September, the band performed two new tracks on a TV special entitled *Rock Around The Dock*, staged on the River Mersey: 'It Didn't Matter' was a laidback love song and 'Angel' was a soaring ballad which had originally been recorded by one of America's leading soul singers, Anita Baker. The most striking aspect about both tunes was the backing music, which mimicked the glossy, sophisticated production of new American soul. It was obvious that Dee C. Lee's tastes were rubbing off on Paul.

When 'It Didn't Matter' was chosen as the next Style Council single for release in January 1987, it was a disappointment. Weller's voice sounded hollow and disinterested, and the sterile backing music was flat and dreary, which wasn't helped by the song's lumpish rhythm. In trying to recreate the high-tech production values of cutting-edge American soul, as created by backroom boys like Jimmy Jam & Terry Lewis, Weller ended up with a bland song which lacked the character and the melodic strength which had rescued previous ballads like 'Long Hot Summer' and 'You're The Best Thing'. The B-side, 'All Year Round', was even weaker, despite borrowing its tune from the far superior 'Big Boss Groove'. More interesting was a tender performance of Lionel Bart's 'Who Will Buy', from the musical *Oliver!*, but this was restricted to a Japanese import of the single.

'It Didn't Matter' was universally trounced by the critics. Outside of specialist soul publications, few journalists were sympathetic to the sounds which were filling up the US R&B charts – let alone Weller's clumsy attempts at emulating them. Rap music was actively promoted in the weekly music press, and while soul veterans like James Brown, Aretha Franklin and Marvin Gaye were treated with awe, leading American soul artists like Luther Vandross, Freddie Jackson and Alexander O'Neal received scant attention. While hip-hop acts like Public Enemy would be lauded by *NME* that year, The Style Council were given their last-ever front cover by the paper a day after 'It Didn't Matter' was released. The press were far more interested in the Sixties soul feel of the 1987's biggest musical sensation, Terence Trent D'Arby. For the first time in his career, Paul Weller had fallen out of favour. For nearly ten years, he may not have been the darling of the press but they had always dealt the star a fair hand. But from this point on, he was ridiculed mercilessly by the critics, who delighted in the backlash to the extent that Weller withdrew from being interviewed by the mainstream music publications.

The same indifference greeted the band's new album, *The Cost Of Loving*, in February – and with some justification. Packaged as a DJ-friendly double pack which played at 45rpm, the album contained only nine tracks because they tended to be longer than before. "There are still another seven or eight songs 'in the can'," Weller revealed in *The Style Population*, many of which finally surfaced on the rarities CD, *Here's Some That Got Away*. The album suffered from a crisp, antiseptic feel, which was the result of Weller's single-handed production. There was little of the earthiness or anger of their earlier records and Talbot had dropped the electric organ – a key ingredient of the band's earlier musical brew – for the cleaner sound of the Rhodes piano and the synthesiser. "The actual musicianship on this LP is probably our best so far, certainly the most confident", Paul explained, but there was none of his undiluted enthusiasm which had accompanied *Our Favourite Shop*. Some of the songs were excellent, though. The majestic 'Heavens Above!' resurrected the spirit of early Seventies Marvin Gaye (especially his acclaimed *What's Going On* album), with its soaring melody and gliding rhythm, which moved up a gear halfway through by breaking into a jazz-funk jam. 'Right To Go' was an effective hip-hop track featuring a young London rap trio, The Dynamic Three, which picked up where 'A Gospel' had left off in 1984. The song's original title, 'The Right Must Go', spelt out the song's message more clearly – and the lyrics urged people that they must register to vote in the forthcoming general election. The anti-Thatcher lyric of 'Fairy Tales' was set to a beefy R&B feel and the title track combined a lovely tune with a funky backing beat.

The problems lay with the slower songs, which congregated on the second disc. 'Walking The Night' and Anita Baker's 'Angel' were sickly smooth. Slightly less grating was 'A Woman's Song', which was added at the last moment (it wasn't listed on the sleeve). This ornate ballad was based around an old nursery rhyme but Dee C. Lee's vocal on this and other songs sometimes sounded brittle. Collectively, the album felt bitty and incomplete. This was unfortunate because the band patently considered the LP as a whole, rather than as individual components – and they dithered over which songs should be chosen as singles. 'It Didn't Matter' had been a last-minute choice and while the title track was issued in Japan and 'Heavens Above!' came out in America, Britain were dealt the graceful but uncommercial ballad, 'Waiting'. The song may have been one of the LP's genuine highlights but as a single, it flopped: issued in March,

'Waiting' was the first Style Council 45 to evade the Top 40. Something was definitely amiss.

The LP's most striking aspect was its anonymous plain orange sleeve, which featured nothing else but the album title and the band's initials, both of which were barely legible. It was Weller's 'Orange Album' in the style of The Beatles' 'White Album' – much to Polydor's consternation. Weller has commented that "I like music with bollocks" but *The Cost Of Loving* had nothing much swinging between its legs. Nor was it that successful: despite reaching a respectable No. 2, the album quickly fell out of the charts.

'Walking The Night' featured backing vocals from John Valentine of The Valentine Brothers, whose most famous song, 'Money's Too Tight To Mention', had given Simply Red their first hit. They were fronted by Mick Hucknall, who was fast earning himself a reputation as one of Britain's most talented white soul singers. His voice was ideally suited to Simply Red's slick, soul-pop approach. Paul Weller's rather sharp tone, in contrast, did not sit comfortably with *The Cost Of Loving*. In fact, his vocals gave the impression of ramming a square peg into a round hole. They didn't fit.

12

HAS MY FIRE REALLY GONE OUT?

"As Dee said to me the other day, The Style Council are probably as big as they're ever going to get now, unless we compromise. There's no way we're going to do that, so I'm not worried about becoming bigger – if we slide, we slide."

(Paul Weller, *The Style Population*, 1986)

"When is a pop group not a pop group? When it's The Style Council."

(Paul Weller, 1992)

Weller was playing into the cynics' hands: for all his efforts at injecting some humour into his image and his music, *The Cost Of Loving* sounded like the product of someone who was taking himself too seriously. The light-hearted nature which had enlivened their earlier records was saved instead for *Jerusalem*, a half-hour feature film starring the band. And if fans and critics alike were baffled by the LP, then this joke of a movie was lost on all but a handful. The concept had been in the pipeline for some time. It had first been mentioned as far back as late 1984 when it was reported that The Style Council were negotiating with Channel 4, as well as "some of the better film makers around town". This *Magical Mystery Tour*-type film would feature the band, together with their family and friends, but have no direct bearing on their music.

In early 1985, *The Style Population* reported that the band were "set to start on their first film in April. It will be a forty-five to sixty-minute film and feature songs off the new LP. Both Mick and Paul will act (hee-hee) in it alongside proper actors. The script is being written between them and Paolo Hewitt and the plot is apparently a 'modern day parable' about how our culture and rights are being taken away by bureaucracy and Thatcher's monetarist policies." That summer, Paul mentioned the idea again: "We also hope to make a short film sometime to accompany our LP. It tells a modern day fable about Unity amongst people and the power they have if they come together."

In summer 1986, they finally received the necessary funding (it cost a modest £140,000) and filming commenced that August. Although they still hadn't thought of a title, Weller explained his plans to *Go Go* fanzine that month: "The story . . . well, if you've seen our sleeve-notes, it's gonna be based around that style. It should be quite funny. It won't be us going up north talking to unemployed kids, it will be a little bit surreal." As *The Style Population* grandly reported at the end of that year, "after three years of ideas, promises and near misses, the fabled film is ready." Like many of Weller's ventures, the idea was probably inspired by The Beatles. Paul's curiosity about Joe Orton, for example, would have been ignited by *Prick Up Your Ears*, the playwright's rejected screenplay for the Liverpool band. The Beatles' cinematic endeavours varied from the cunning documentary-style musical fantasy of *A Hard Day's Night*, a format which *Jerusalem* essentially mimicked, to the zany humour of *Help!*, which *Jerusalem* also tried to emulate. The result was closer to the unfocused indulgence of the Fab Four's TV movie, *Magical Mystery Tour*, although its surreal nature and its attack on British society owed more to, say, Derek Jarman's futuristic 'punk' movie, *Jubilee*.

The location filming was eventually completed inside of three weeks. Paolo Hewitt contributed the screenplay, which duplicated the pretentiousness of his Cappuccino Kid sleeve-notes. The Communards' Richard Coles handled the narration and the band themselves provided ample evidence as to why pop stars shouldn't attempt to act. The meagre plot began with The Style Council being tried for crimes against the state (with no sense of irony about the film itself, it must be added), and their subsequent quest to discover 'the truth' was a good excuse for numerous costume changes and supposedly witty asides. Drummer Steve White summed it up neatly: "The film is a fantasy trip through the English countryside, following the adventures of The Style Council on clockwork Vespas. Featuring four songs from the LP, the film is funny, serious, commentative – *Carry On* meets Lindsay Anderson!"

White's mention of scooters (though they were actually Lambrettas) referred to the film's most memorable scene, when the band drove into a quaint old English village (Aldbourne in Wiltshire) to hear a reading of the film's inspiration, William Blake's *Jerusalem*, by 'the Queen'. The fact that the head-of-state was played by a black actress was a clever touch which was calculated to provoke – and as planned, it infuriated tabloid newspapers like *The Sun*. But the film brought to mind the fairy tale of the Emperor's New Clothes: behind the movie's ostentatious designs, maybe the whole scheme was an elaborate hoax or in-joke by the band at the expense of the audience?

Jerusalem is the most famous work of the early 19th century poet and mystical visionary. The poem was later turned into a hymn, but despite recent misinterpretations of its meaning, such as its use at Conservative party conferences as a patriotic statement, Blake's message was one of revolution. *Jerusalem* tells of how "England's green and pleasant land" has been corrupted by the power-wielding classes which have fed off it.

In his biography of the poet, Peter Ackroyd described *Jerusalem* as "Blake's own powerful religious vision, in which he relates spiritual myth to chronological history, and translates Judaea and the Holy Land to England. It is the context in which he launches a fine polemic against commercialism and war, industrialism and science, all seen as aspects of the fallen 'Vegetated' universe . . . He attacks the precepts of rational morality and the moral law that names 'good' and 'evil'."

In its own fumbled away, The Style Council's *Jerusalem* also ridiculed the state of the nation. Weller described the movie as "a journey, an Odyssey. It's us travelling through a surreal England. There are comments in the film, but they're not done in a sledgehammer way. They're quite oblique." The capital letters emphasised in the film's title (*JerUSAlem*) also stressed another angle: "It's having a go at America," added Paul, "but mostly it's anti-British. It's hitting out at the nationalism of the British Empire and modern-day hooligans."

Jerusalem was shown as a second feature for two critically acclaimed films of the time, *Mona Lisa* and *Down By Law*, before being picked up by Palace Video, a wing of the company behind *Absolute Beginners*, for a home video release. Incidentally, the film's delicate theme tune, 'Francoise', could be found on the B-side of 'Waiting'. The film also took the place of a support act on the band's 'General Election Tour', which began on Valentine's Day 1987. The group's performances were mediocre, though it is worth noting the inclusion of 'Everlasting Love', a ballad sung by Dee C. Lee (not to be confused with the old Love Affair classic) which was never issued. Many of The Style Council's regular musicians were absent. Weller later dismissed the concerts as one of the year's low-points and their line-up was radically overhauled for some live dates in the summer, but there was a sense, in the wake of the LP, that the band were losing interest. As one critic put it, The Style Council "sounded as clinical as their white uniforms".

Also conspicuous by his absence was Steve White, who had grown disillusioned with the band's lack of activity the previous year and had left to concentrate on his new sideline. Having played what Steve called some "small intimate" gigs as a duo with a Hammond organist in the summer of 1986, he teamed up with the tenor sax virtuoso Alan Barnes, who "did for me only what I have ever known with the Style Council". The pair formed the Jazz Renegades, who premièred at the Soho Jazz Festival at the London Palladium in October 1986, the first in a string of dates in both Britain and Japan through to the end of that year.

★ ★ ★

Angry at the widespread criticism of *The Cost Of Loving*, Weller responded by pledging himself to several new projects, including a series of singles which would stand apart from any forthcoming LPs. "This will be our Plan A for 87/88," Paul explained, before speaking soberly about the relationship between the band and their audience: "We are the judges, you are our jury. We create what we feel at the time and always hope it is our best. The Style Council is an idea, a concept (careful!) and a way of life. In between times, we shall be writing and recording two LPs, one of our own tunes and one of a venture, talked about for a while, of an LP of covers of some of our favourite tunes."

Few of these ideas came to fruition, partly because of live commitments. European dates were followed in April 1987 by the band's first Japanese dates for three years, which signalled the brief return of Steve White. There were also a couple of fleeting visits to Italy, first for a tour and then for some open-air shows. Paul also took time out to interview one of his heroes, Curtis Mayfield, backstage at Ronnie Scott's jazz club for the soul legend's *Curtis Live* video.

As for Weller's stated ambitions, the only non-album single turned out to be 'Wanted'. Issued in October, it was subtitled 'Waiter, There's Some Soup In My Flies' in another bizarre attempt to bemuse the band's audience. As for the tune itself, 'Wanted' was a straightforward ode to unrequited love, but its forlorn, yearning lyrics were disguised by its breezy melody. The song had a more upbeat, endearing feel than most of *The Cost Of Loving* LP, the title track of which was re-recorded for the B-side. This much slower reworking had been commissioned for Lezli-An Barrett's well-received motion picture, *Business As Usual*, a pro-union/anti-Thatcherite drama starring Glenda Jackson, Cathy Tyson and John Thaw.

To promote the single, the band embarked on their *Renaissance Tour*. There was more of a sense of enthusiasm about the Council's stage demeanour than the lacklustre shows from the spring, and their set aired three new songs – two beautiful, atmospheric ballads with hints of Elvis Costello's 'Shipbuilding' entitled 'It's A Very Deep Sea' and 'Confessions 1, 2 & 3', plus the otherwise unheard 'Cover Me With Love' sung by Dee C. Although the band had declared a wish to play smaller, more intimate venues, this may well have been a reaction to their dwindling popularity – the two Scottish dates were cancelled, allegedly due to poor advance ticket sales. It was a portent. The Style Council would only ever play one more full-length British concert in their lifetime.

The new material represented work-in-progress for the band's next album. "Songs so far have a very rich melodic sound," revealed Weller in *The Style Population* before the year was out, "some very jazz, in a melodic sense, though not necessarily in style. The others are more funky and lyrically, for me, some of the best I've done – very complex ideas but simple methods." Rather than writing *Jerusalem* off as a fanciful extravagance, the band were, incredibly, planning an even more adventurous cinematic scheme. "We still want to make a feature film and are now looking for backers," wrote Weller, with not a hint of irony. "We'd also like to do a musical/play and will be meeting young playwrights in the next few months." Again, both schemes were stillborn. Instead, and far less imaginatively, the band's back catalogue was recycled with three EPs – *Café Bleu* featured pointless extracts from their début LP, *The Birds And The B's* sampled four of Weller's more sublime, acoustic B-sides and, best of all, *Mick Talbot Is Agent '88* assembled his Hammond organ instrumentals.

Nothing was then heard of The Style Council until the arrival of a new single, 'Life At A Top People's Health Farm', in May 1988. Weller described this oddity as an update of Bob Dylan's mid-Sixties rant, 'Subterranean Homesick Blues'. True, it shared Dylan's ramshackle collage of names and ideas – the witty, punning lyrics name-dropped public figures as diverse as Margaret Thatcher, *The Archers* and Leon Trotsky with images of dog tracks, bingo, gas shares and lettuce. But the song was a mess and the whining vocals were drowned among a clattering, murky collision of horns and crass drums.

Less abrasive was the flipside – the beguiling 'Sweet Loving Ways', which was a laid-back jazz-soul love song with relaxed guitar playing reminiscent of George Benson. The bare-chested, sun-tanned Weller and Talbot – thumbs up and wearing straw boaters – looked out from the sleeve with beaming grins as if to test people's patience. Weller was soon critical of the single, too: "I hate it," he admitted. "I listen to it now, a year later, and I can't think where I was at then. I've moved on since then so it's hard for me to think back to how I felt at the time."

Confessions Of A Pop Group arrived a month later. Clocking in at nearly an hour, this was by far The Style Council's longest album but also their least understood. *The Cost Of Loving* may have flummoxed many people but it still very nearly topped the charts. *Confessions*, by contrast, only reached No. 15 (their only LP not to make the Top 10) and vanished after just three weeks. For a start, there was definitely an image problem. Many of the band's recent singles – and the album cover itself – carried stark, black-and-white photos of the band which seemed to reflect their tendency for a rather antiseptic production.

The oblique, self-indulgent humour of advertisements for the LP didn't help, either. These felt at odds with the rather sombre atmosphere of the album's photos. And the fact that the band declined to chat about their new release only distanced them further from their audience – further evidence of a gulf which had grown after the demise of the band's fan club, The Torch Society, in autumn 1987. The music, too, was completely disconnected from the pop scene of 1988. Weller has stressed in the past that he has always been divorced from prevailing trends, but that is patently not true – his song-writing had already been affected by punk, rap, modern soul, new jazz and other, more subtle nuances of the day. But *Confessions Of A Pop Group* was an ironic title from a group who seemed to have shed the pop music of the period altogether.

The album title followed 'Life At A Top People's Health Farm' in a series of tongue-in-cheek names which seemed to confirm Weller's look of ennui on the cover. A sense of fun was evident from many of his lyrics but they sometimes came across as clever-clever. The combined effect of the refined music and Dan Davies' colourful fine art paintings, visually describing each song, was one of taste and sophistication. There was even a promotional function for both the LP and Davies' paintings, a cheese and wine bash at the respectable London venue, Hamiltons. "Don't you think you're heading for trouble?" the *Rock Of Europe* TV show asked Weller. "Yes, but that's all part of the fun," he replied. The band always acted as self-professed arbiters of style but maybe they had now taken the stance too far? Needless to say, the LP was less than favourably received by the critics.

Confessions was quieter and more reflective than *The Cost Of Loving* – and Paul's vocal technique had noticeably improved, but there was none of that old Weller passion. The album was divided in two: the first side was subtitled 'The Piano Paintings', and over five compositions, the group dabbled in classical music with lush string arrangements, gentle melodies and a meandering atmosphere – all of which somehow recalled Brian Wilson's feel on the Beach Boys' *Pet Sounds*. 'The Story Of Someone's Shoe', which dealt with the seedy emptiness of a one-night stand, was softened by vibraphone and the soothing harmonies of the Swingle Singers – "easy listening à la Michel Legrand," as Paul later described it, an influence which dated back to *Café Bleu*. 'It's A Very Deep Sea' and 'Changing Of The Guard' were both mournful lullabies whose sad lyrics were laced with regret and self-doubt – of "dredging up the past to drive me round the bendz" and "crying over nothing worth crying for". 'The Little Boy In The Castle' was a delicate piano instrumental. Then there was an ambitious, ten-minute-plus composition in three parts: in the central section, 'The Gardener Of Eden' cast a weary eye over today's ecological ravages in one of Weller's most sensitive lyrics, set to a mesmerising jazz tune sung by Dee C. Lee. This was preceded by an ornate harpsichord piece, 'In The Beginning', and the 'Three Piece Suite' (as it was subtitled) ended with another of Talbot's quiet piano solos, 'Mourning The Passing Of Time'.

Side two was more upbeat. Above a wonderfully warm melody, 'Why I Went Missing' sounded like a confessional – "There's plenty more I could have kissed/And those who wanted it – I could of resist/But I blamed myself for this out of town kissing". Just as charming was the jolly soul-pop of 'How She Threw It All Away' (with its shades of Earth, Wind And Fire's 'September'), but the album's real masterpiece was the title track which ended the LP. Nearly ten minutes long, this impressionistic attack on decaying society was underpinned by an incredibly funky bassline – it felt like a slowed-down, more sophisticated 'Money-Go-Round'. Put quite simply, *Confessions Of A Pop Group* was Weller's deepest, most complex album to date, with a breadth and diversity reflected by the wide range of instruments and guest musicians.

The whole package seemed very grown-up – but then that wasn't altogether surprising. On the sleeve, Dee C. Lee was seen tactically positioned behind the piano to disguise the fact that she was heavily pregnant. Dee and Paul had married in July 1987, and a month before the album's release in June 1988, she gave birth to a son, Nathaniel (known as Natty for short). "It means 'gift of God'. We really like old names," the couple explained, in what seemed to be the picture of domestic bliss. There were reports that Paul had bought his wife a £10,000 Jeep, when she passed her driving test. Mick also wished to spend more time with his family, which might explain why an autumn 1988 tour was cancelled – although Polydor claimed that Talbot was suffering from a rare virus which "could keep him out-of-action for two years".

To round off the *Confessions* album, The Style Council issued their *1-2-3-4* EP in July. This 'Summer Quartet' led off with the LP's most radio-friendly song, 'How She Threw It All Away', which was followed by the sublime, bossa nova feel of 'Love The First Time'. There was also a timely return for 'Long Hot Summer', and 'I Do Like To Be B-Side The A-Side', credited to the Mixed Campanions, was an update of Talbot's instrumental, 'Mick's Company'. But it was a reflection of the band's fading fortunes that the EP stalled outside the Top 40.

Within a couple of months, rumours were already circulating which suggested a split within the group. *The Sun* reported in August that "Paul Weller has killed off his band because he wants to spend more time with his family". "Paul and Dee want a complete break so they can be real parents to their baby," a 'friend' revealed. By the end of the year, Steve White had effectively left the band. The drummer had taken a less active role on *Confessions Of A Pop Group*, and with no prospect of any significant live work, he teamed up with the James Taylor Quartet. Across 1988 and 1989, he played over one hundred gigs with the Hammond organ club combo, as well as sitting in on their *Get Organized* album.

★   ★   ★

Weller's loss of focus as a songwriter coincided with the birth of the most significant development in recent musical history. Created in the gay clubs of Chicago in the American Mid-west, house music first arrived in Britain during 1986. At that time, the dominant forms of black dance music in the UK were the raps of early hip-hop and the robotic rhythms of electro soul, as well as the smoother, more traditional tones of modern R&B, of the kind which influenced *The Cost Of Loving*. House music was faster than these styles and was defined by two distinctive characteristics: its incessant rhythm was built around the offbeat hi-hat in a way which duplicated the late Seventies disco beat, and the tune was usually driven by a simple piano riff. Although it was instantly popular in the north of England, house wasn't fully accepted by southern clubs at first – until it mutated in early 1988 into acid house, a hybrid which retained the insistent beat but incorporated psychedelic bleeps and special effects in place of a traditional song.

Meanwhile, the catalyst of M.A.R.R.S.' ground-breaking No. 1, 'Pump Up The Volume', in September 1987 led to a minor revolution within the British music scene early in '88. Records like S-Express's 'Theme From S-Express' (April) and 'Superfly Guy' (July), Bomb The Bass's 'Beat Dis' (February) and 'Megablast' (August), Coldcut's 'Doctorin' The House' (February) and The Beatmasters' 'Rok Da House' (January) were all enormous hits on independent labels which borrowed elements from house music to differing degrees, by artists who were essentially DJs rather than musicians.

During the summer of 1988, the UK club scene blossomed into the so-called "second summer of love", fuelled by the spread in the use of the drug ecstasy. Acid house was always an anonymous phenomenon, a world of obscure 12″ imports and remixes which baffled all but the knowing domain of the house DJ. Some UK labels like ffrr, Champion and Cooltempo issued the most popular songs, before the market was flooded with acid house compilations. Paul Weller was initially suspicious of both the music and the lifestyle. Asked in an interview in *The Face* in mid-1988 whether The Style Council might dabble in acid house, he replied, "Nah. If we made a house record, we could call it Council house . . . that would be nice!" His major stumbling block was the lack of song structure to interrupt acid's seamless beat.

During the latter half of 1988, a more soulful strain developed – garage house, a throwback to the earliest house hits like Farley 'Jackmaster' Funk's 'Love Can't Turn Around' (August 1986). Actually, the term 'garage' had been around since the late Seventies to describe a rhythmic form of modern soul. There was now a boom of more tuneful house music – and Paul became intoxicated by records like 'Break 4 Love' by Raze (December 1988).

"I went mad on garage records," Weller later admitted. "I came from hating it to being totally obsessed by it. I liked it because it was rough and it sounded raw. Lyrically, it was also positive. Soul music in the Eighties had become really slick, I suppose because of the technology, and that's not where I'm at." Paolo Hewitt explained this development in one of Paul's later tour programmes: "Groups such as Blaze, Phase 2 and producers like Marshall Jefferson and Frankie Knuckles, quickly became favourites. Through their work, Weller had seen how contemporary R&B could be shorn of its increasingly slick nature and returned to its roots with a modern sound and feel. This was where he now wanted to take the Style Council."

Another of Weller's favourites was Joe Smooth's authentic house hit, 'Promised Land', a popular import before the single was given a full British release at the start of 1989. (Today, it remains one of the classic Chicago house tunes, together with Sterling Void's 'It's Alright', as covered by Pet Shop Boys, and Marshall Jefferson's 'Move Your Body – The House Music Anthem'.) A few weeks later, in mid-February, The Style Council were performing their own version of 'Promised Land' on *Top Of The Pops*.

Weller's decision to plagiarise a contemporary house record remains one of the most bizarre of his career – it was probably due to a combination of impulse, boredom and a genuine love of the song itself.

"I just thought it was a good song," Paul told *Fresh Air* fanzine later that year, describing the original as "a bit under-developed . . . It always sounded like a gospel song to me, the chords and the way the voices were. We didn't change it that much really, but we just made it more inspirational, more up." If the house beat was stripped away, 'Promised Land' shared the spiritual soul vibe of Curtis Mayfield's 'Move On Up'. But by opting for such a derivative rhythm, The Style Council added little to Joe Smooth's treatment.

There was nothing new about white British acts beating American black singers to the charts by covering their songs, of course. The Rolling Stones and, to a lesser extent, The Beatles made a habit of it in the early Sixties, but The Style Council were resolutely criticised in leading dance magazines like *Blues 'N Soul*. To cynics of Weller's recent conversion to house, it felt like the musician was cashing in. Nevertheless, the single sold well through specialist dance shops and was played on soul radio stations – and since garage house was still an underground phenomenon, these were usually the illegal ones. "To hear our record on one of the pirates is a real honour," Paul declared. "It's like we've made it. It means more than being on *Top Of The Pops*. The music we get our inspiration from is all that club stuff anyway." These stations also picked up on the single's B-side, 'Can You Still Love Me?' This sounded chunkier and more natural than 'Promised Land' but still mimicked the style of Chicago house with a melody not dissimilar to Colonel Abrams' massive mid-Eighties hit, 'Trapped' – itself an influence on house music. The single was remixed by Juan Atkins of Model 500, a pioneer of Detroit's emergent techno house sound who also worked with The Beloved.

"Look out for *The Singular Adventures Of The Style Council*," read the message on the back cover of the single. Healthy sales of this TV-advertised 'greatest hits' on its release in March affirmed the band's popularity – but by outstripping their most recent albums, it hinted that this status was rooted in the past. The LP was promoted two months later by an '89 Mix' of 'Long Hot Summer' – bearing in mind the song's theme, it was hardly likely to fulfil its potential in May. The strangest aspect of the single was the "brand new track" on the flipside, 'Everybody's On The Run', which shared the garage house vibe of 'Can You Still Love Me?' Mixed by New Yorker Freddie Bastone, alias house outfit Corporation Of One (responsible for the club favourite, 'The Real Life'), the song also featured a guest soul vocalist, Brian J. Powell.

"Brian comes from the gospel circuit and we got to know him through Dee's sister, who's involved in the church," Paul told *Fresh Air*. "He did a gospel TV musical thing around Christmas time. I was just impressed with his voice. He's done some backing vocals for Dee as well." It transpired that The Style Council had wanted this strident dance track as the A-side – and it even fronted the promotional editions which were sent out to club DJs – but Polydor had refused.

In fact, behind the scenes, there were growing tensions between the band and their label. During the sessions for *Confessions Of A Pop Group*, Polydor had apparently introduced a money penalty which would be levied for each day the album was late, although this clause was eventually removed. Other reports suggested Polydor had given Paul a one million pound advance for the album. According to *The Cover* magazine, Weller responded by "delivering the finished tape on a C90 cassette with a defiled mugshot of Polydor's A&R chief attached. Relations chilled." Paul had told *Just 17* magazine that his label was "bewildered by this album," saying, "This is going to be difficult, it's going to be trouble."

The plot thickened further when a mysterious single trickled out on the Acid Jazz label in February '89. King Truman's 'Like A Gun' was a pseudonym for The Style Council, as Dean Rudland, who was later general manager at the label, explains. "Weller must already have been pissed with Polydor and he's hanging out with the Acid Jazz crowd. Well, release this record! It's five mixes, mainly instrumental in the style of George Clinton/P-Funk, with Dee giving it her Dee-like wail. Mick is on keyboards, Paul on guitar – it's a Style Council record, no messing about."

Meanwhile, Acid Jazz boss Eddie Piller was managing the James Taylor Quartet, then featuring Steve White, who happened to be signed to Polydor – and therein lies a story. Having heard a rumour about the King Truman record, a senior record company executive accosted Piller on one of his visits to their offices, held him up against a wall and said something to the tune of, 'If you release that record, I'll fucking sue you!' Needless to say, the King Truman record was deleted fairly sharply.

★ ★ ★

The so-called 'acid jazz' scene had evolved around 1988 as an antidote to acid house, which had swept through clubland that year. Prior to that, the norm was 'rare groove' – obscure late Sixties and early-to-mid-Seventies funk, soul and jazz – which had provided the bedrock of London's more fashionable clubs and warehouse parties prior to the arrival of house. "Rare groove in '87 was massive, especially in the South East," says Dean Rudland. "But suddenly, all these people had nowhere to go. The younger kids got into acid house. Most of the rare groove DJs were playing house all of a sudden. The only choice was to go to an acid jazz club."

The growing interest in jazz and Seventies funk was strong enough to lead Ace Records, for example, to launch their reissue label, Beat Goes Public, with compilations by DJs like Gilles Peterson and Baz Fe Jazz. "They played pure acid jazz at the launch night for Beat Goes Public at the 100 Club – but the term hadn't been invented," says Dean. "Gilles and Chris Bangs were DJ'ing at the Special Branch do's, playing old funk and jazz records – funky

Lou Donaldson, Gene Ammons, Cal Tjader. And Marco Nelson, who later played bass with Weller, was DJ'ing with a warehouse crew, Family Function/Shake & Fingerpop, so Weller was hanging around with these people. Gilles's club at Dingwalls on Sunday lunchtimes started in '88 and quickly took off. He also had his show on Radio London and tried to think of terms to corner what this music would be called. They tried 'popcorn jazz', because it was based around James Brown's 'Popcorn' beat, but that never took off and then they came up with 'acid jazz', as a reaction to acid house. The start of the acid jazz scene, record-wise, was probably a white label with Coldcut-type cut-ups called 'Open Channel D' by the Night Trains."

There was now a ready-made audience for records which added a contemporary flavour to Seventies 'rare groove'. "There were two types of people involved in the acid jazz scene," says Dean, "old soul boys and old Mods." So it wasn't surprising that Weller was naturally drawn to it. Gilles Petterson was an old soul boy and Eddie Piller was an ex-Mod who had run several record labels, and so the scene was soon solidified with the creation of the Acid Jazz label. "It occurred to Gilles, Eddie, Marco and Chris Bangs, 'Why don't we make a record?'," Dean remembers. "The artists were there: the Brand New Heavies, the Young Disciples. Galliano, alias a North London Irish bloke Rob Gallagher, was rapping freestyle over instrumental records which Gilles was playing; one of these was 'Frederic Lies Still', over Pucho & The Latin Soul Brothers' version of Curtis Mayfield's 'Freddie's Dead'. That was the first record on Acid Jazz.

"The label then put out the *Illicit Grooves* album via Polydor in late '88 – and I remember that Weller went to the launch party at Dingwalls. There were two volumes: the first one had Galliano and the Night Trains." Just as the label's profile grew, so too did the clubs associated with it. "Scenes don't just happen, they evolve as something very good happens. Weller was definitely going down Dingwalls and checking out the club scene. Marshall Jefferson house records were being played alongside jazz like Art Blakey and Reuben Wilson. That created the whole atmosphere of acid jazz."

★　★　★

Paul's obsession with modern dancefloor grooves continued throughout the first half of 1989. "There's so much good music around now," he commented. "I was re-reading an interview we did last year and I didn't have any good words to say on anything. My enthusiasm for music has been rejuvenated. There's all these different terms out – garage, club – but to me, it's just soul music. One of the first records of last year, 'Reachin' ' by Phase II, I thought was fantastic, the real thing. I compare it to the early blues, Fifties and Sixties R&B." It emerged that The Style Council's next album would definitely be in this house vein, but Paul was also absorbing other forms of American black music. "I didn't like the Acid thing. I like what's

217

followed it – the deep house stuff. Some of the new hip-hop as well, people like De La Soul, musically they're so clever. I like some of the swing-beat stuff as well – Teddy Riley." During the spring, Paul and Mick produced a cover of Lamont Dozier/Odyssey's 'Going Back To My Roots' by seventeen-year-old Lisa M, for Zomba Records. "I wanted someone a bit different, someone who would make people sit up and say, 'Oh, look who's producing that'," the singer told *Just 17* magazine. "We approached them and they agreed. They were brilliant and so talented." Both 'Promised Land' and 'Going Back To My Roots' were engineered by one of Solid Bond Studios' in-house staff, Brendan Lynch, who was to play a crucial role in the development in Paul's future career.

Weller revealed he was working on various other projects: "There's supposed to be a Red Wedge album still in the pipeline. Three years later, it's still happening! We've done a hip-house track for that, with two girls called Trouble And Bass. They've got a DJ with them as well, who's really good. The J.B.'s did some horns on this track. It hasn't got a title at the moment. It's a cool groove. It's funk – jazz-funk, I suppose. It will probably be on our next album which will be out late summer." The song in question was eventually called 'That Spiritual Feeling', which finally surfaced on Paul's first solo release. When questioned about the content of their forthcoming Style Council LP, Paul replied, "It's gonna be a mixture of styles really, probably more instrumental than before. It's hard talking about these things, because I change my mind every time."

By this time, Paul had expressed his fondness for the music of the Blow Monkeys, who shared The Style Council's knack of writing intelligent lyrics within a graceful soul-pop context. And they too had incorporated house into their sound. The Blow Monkeys' lead singer and songwriter Robert Howard (alias Dr. Robert) was both camp and stylish – unusual traits for an Australian – and he and Weller forged a mutual admiration society which led to a long-lasting friendship.

'Sure Is Sure' was aired during a brief tour of Japan with guest singer Omar (later a star in his own right), before the group returned for a one-off concert at the Royal Albert Hall. It was The Style Council's first proper show for over eighteen months. "That was mainly because we were disillusioned with playing live," Paul explained. "We had some really lousy band members, so that put me off, and I've had a kid since then so I didn't wanna be away from home either. I'm glad I never went away on tour because I would've missed lots of things like him growing up."

The evening was July 4, American Independence Day. The previous night, Weller had DJ'd at Dingwalls, a reflection of his continued affinity with club culture. Despite the modest sales of their last few singles and a complete lack of advertisements in the music press, the Royal Albert Hall show easily sold out – helped by posters around London publicising the event as part of the Capital Radio Music Festival. In the wake of the singles compilation and the band's absence from the live arena, most of the audience had been expecting to hear a fair proportion of the band's old hits. Instead, The Style Council turned the concert into a house revue, coming on stage dressed in shorts and performing around twenty tracks, less than half of which had appeared on their records. The audience were stunned.

Three songs were taken from the slow side of *Confessions Of A Pop Group*, including 'It's A Very Deep Sea', which segued into the Beach Boys' 'California Girls'. Only four further selections pre-dated that LP: 'The Cost Of Loving' and 'A Woman's Song' from '*The Orange Album*', plus two of Mick Talbot's instrumentals. Their three recent house tunes were played – 'Can You Still Love Me?', 'Promised Land' and, with Brian Powell joining them on stage, 'Everybody's On The Run' – together with that new song, 'Sure Is Sure', and King Truman's 'Like A Gun'. But the rest of the tracks were a mystery.

The show bore no relation to the crowd's perception of the band and they responded by booing and shouting abuse. It proved to be The Style Council's last concert, but it wasn't the respectful farewell some might have hoped for. It wasn't that the music itself was poor – Weller had adapted himself well to house – but the songs lacked the stamp of Weller's personality. The whole spectacle felt like a karaoke – except that the audience didn't want to join in. After just over six years, a longer period than Paul's recording career with The Jam, one of the Eighties' most adventurous and ambitious pop groups had ground to an unseemly halt. Whereas The Jam had ended at the pinnacle both of their success and in terms of the respect which they commanded from both their fans and the rock critics, The Style Council did the opposite.

★ ★ ★

Audio bootlegs of that fateful night have shed some light on the material from the rest of the concert. The Blow Monkeys' Dr. Robert sang a tune called 'Now You're Gone', while bassist Camelle Hinds took to the microphone for 'I Can't Deny Myself'. 'Waiting On A Connection' was a vibrant modern soul tune which was recorded in 1988 for North London funk band Push due to Paul's involvement with the funk/jazz scene. This was shelved until 1993's Style Council rarities CD, *Here's Some That Got Away*, though the song was resurrected during the mainland European wing of Paul's first solo tour in late 1990. Since much of the new material was sung by Dee, it seemed likely that they were taken from her long-delayed second album – but nothing was forthcoming.

Despite reports that the next Style Council LP was to be titled *Modernism – A New Decade* (or *A Decade Of Modernism*, as the LP is sometimes known, or even *1990: A New Decade In Modernism*), the band were strangely silent. The scheduled single, 'Sure Is Sure'/'Love Of The World', never materialised and a press release was eventually circulated in August to announce that not only

219

had both the LP and the single been scrapped, but that The Style Council, after six years, had disbanded.

Modernism – A New Decade has since earnt the tag of Weller's "great lost album" but, needless to say, it lacked the musical ambition of such other shelved projects as *Lifehouse* (Pete Townshend) or *Smile* (Brian Wilson). Judging by those advance cassettes which exist, the songs were devoid of Weller's usual trademarks – there was none of his lyrical bite or even the musical adventurism of *Confessions Of A Pop Group*. But the musician has always been able to replicate a particular genre – and as a club-derived house LP, *Modernism – A New Decade* is a respectable effort. Its most distinguishing characteristic was the touch of Oriental-sounding flute work which lent the album a Far East flavour, and the lyrics, submerged as they were under a chunky house beat, relied on a simple gospel message of unity and love. "At the time, I really believed that garage house was the new Mod music," Paul later told *NME*.

The proposed track listing for the album kicked off with 'That Spiritual Feeling', followed by 'Everybody's On The Run', 'Love Of The World', 'Sure Is Sure', 'A New Decade', 'Can You Still Love Me?', 'The World Must Come Together' and 'Hope (Feelings Gonna Getcha')'. The last of these was aired that summer after Weller gave an advance copy to a London DJ. So too was Paul's collaboration with The J.B.'s, 'That Spiritual Feeling'. Marco Nelson (who had played bass at their Albert Hall finale) took a copy of this track down to Dingwalls, where DJ Gilles Peterson made a special announcement before playing it. Two of the songs were issued as B-sides, of course. Weller kept the first track back for his solo career and 'Sure Is Sure' has since surfaced on a bootleg EP, but the rest of the album has never materialised.

Behind the scenes, there had been a personality clash. "It was really that one person," Paul later told me, "the managing director at the time, David Munns. *Modernism – A New Decade* wasn't really an instrumental album as far as I was concerned. I guess they saw it that way because there weren't any 'real' songs, it was all house grooves. It totally baffled them, I think." Weller paused, before laughing: "It probably would have baffled everyone else as well!" There was another reason why the LP was rejected, because of the fact that the LP was made autonomously via his own Solid Bond Productions. "Polydor would have had to pay a lot of money to take up the album," Paul explained, "which David Munns wasn't keen on doing. But it was going to be our last album, anyway. We were going to split after that. We'd done enough. There was no enthusiasm in the band any more."

After a relationship with Polydor Records which had scarcely seen Paul Weller out of the charts for a dozen years, the label had unceremoniously rejected his last album. Paul had predicted the scenario three years earlier. "I wouldn't like to be forced into a position where I have to compromise

220

and make records just because that's what the public want to hear, or that the record company want to hear," he told *Go Go* fanzine in August 1986. "I'd sooner get out and do something else." And that's exactly what he did.

★ ★ ★

What is now strikingly clear about The Style Council is how Weller always felt haunted by the spectre of The Jam – it was almost as if he was twisting and disguising the Council's sound so that, eventually, the world might forget that the singer on, say, 'Promised Land' was the same angry teenager heard on 'Bricks And Mortar'. If his release from The Jam was akin to escaping from a prison sentence, then he seems to have felt as if he was on the run, musically, from The Jam's sound for the rest of the Eighties.

When I interviewed Paul about The Jam's *Extras* compilation in the summer of 1992, I suggested that The Style Council's more recent records were misunderstood. His reaction was surprisingly animated. "I think The Style Council were misunderstood from Day One," he complained. "The legacy of The Jam was so overpowering that we never really got off the ground. We had this constant weight behind us." But The Style Council were always more tongue-in-cheek, surely? "Some of it was and some of it wasn't," was Paul's reply. "Our thing was that it could be both – it could be anything – and I think that mentality was too wide for a lot of people. They like really precise things.

"With The Jam, you knew where you stood – you either liked it or you didn't. With The Style Council, maybe we'd have this really abrasive lyric but with a lilting Latin beat or there'd be real changes in mood all the time. And I don't think a lot of people got their heads around that. There wasn't one overall sound. I think a lot of people couldn't understand that it constantly changed. Also, most people are generally resistant to change. They feel more comfortable with what they know – we're all like that, I guess. But my thing was to try and change people's attitudes, especially those around me and what they felt I was about. And the press got really pissed off – well, we had a lot of fun winding them up, to be honest. But that's not to say that The Style Council wasn't serious – because it was. Musically, we were dedicated to it."

Paul was cautious about the degree of success of the group's floating line-up of guest musicians. "It was all hit-and-miss but, you know, no-one else was doing that then. I feel we were out of time – whether we were ahead of our time, I don't know, but we were out of sync, especially in the mid-Eighties. Everything else seemed really planned and the whole music scene was bland and marketed and controlled – and I hated it. We were reacting against that." And Weller's political profile also had its side-effects: "I think it was too strong and overshadowed the music because people spent all their time talking about politics, or the rhetoric which went along with it, instead of talking about what was happening musically. That's why I felt people missed out on what The Style Council were about. But I still feel like we're going to have our time. People will appreciate the music for what it is. Five years, ten years – whatever – they'll come round and make it all worth the wait!"

13

OUT OF THE SINKING

"There's not much else groups can do but play live and make records."
(Paul Weller, 1992)

"I need to have music to stabilise me. It stabilises my whole being and my whole mentality. When I finish a song and I think, 'yeah, it's a good song', it adds something to my life, it keeps me sane."
(Paul Weller, 1992)

"It was probably the first time I'd had the opportunity to stand still and take stock of what I was doing in life."
(Paul Weller, 1993)

Come 1990, the start of a new decade, Paul Weller's life was in a strange state of flux. For the first time that he could remember, he wasn't in a band. He didn't have a recording contract. He hadn't played a gig since that disappointing finale with The Style Council in mid-1989. He was constantly being ridiculed in the music press. And worst of all, he wasn't writing songs like he used to. The Eighties for Weller had been a time of finding himself – but now he wasn't sure where it had all taken him.

"After The Style Council, I felt totally unleashed," he told *NME*. "I had no record deal, no publishing deal. For the first time since I was eighteen, I was a free man. But I went through a period when I thought, 'What do I do now?' because I'd spent so many years doing the same thing – and when you haven't got anything to work towards, it can really throw you." Paul was also worried about his age – he was approaching his thirty-second birthday. "I guess it's because all the people I really liked made their best music when they were either teenagers or in their early Twenties," he admitted to Paolo Hewitt. "The longer they went on doing it, the blander it became."

Unsure about his own career, Weller busied himself helping out with his wife's new album, under the collective name of Slam Slam, together with friends Dr. Robert, DJ Hector and Marco Nelson (who had by now formed The Young Disciples). The project evolved out of plans for a Dee C. Lee solo album around mid-1987, which had been announced together with an

223

abandoned Red Wedge LP but scrapped after protracted problems in trying to escape her CBS contract. Dee shared Weller's uncertainty about her future career. "Slam Slam was basically me hiding behind a group name, with a lot of help from Paul and everybody," she later revealed. "I literally used to just go in and record what the guys had written."

The resulting album, *Free Your Feelings*, was a typical dance record of the period, its mix of mechanical rhythms, synthesised drum patterns and soulful vocals strongly redolent of the garage house tunes Paul had been buying. The LP was originally available on import from America, where the singles had created quite a buzz in clubland, before finally being issued in Britain in April 1991 by a seemingly reluctant MCA.

Weller either wrote or co-wrote seven of the ten songs, shedding some light on that farewell Style Council concert, which had premièred four of the tunes: 'You'll Find Love' and 'Tender Love' (both penned by Paul), 'Move (Dance All Night)' (a joint effort between Dr. Robert and Dee C. Lee) and Dr. Robert's 'Depth Charge'. Paul also contributed 'Something Ain't Right', 'Giving It Up', a co-composition with Mick Talbot entitled 'What Dreams Are Made Of' and a collaboration with Dee in 'Nothing Like It'. But most significant was Paul's dreamy jazz-funk number, 'Round And Round' – it would later surface on his first solo LP.

Coupled with the fact that Dee, Talbot, Dr. Robert and Marco Nelson all worked on Paul's subsequent ventures, the Slam Slam album represents a fascinating but uncomfortable stop-gap between The Style Council and what followed. Had *A Decade Of Modernism* been released, then *Free Your Feelings* would have been its logical successor. Instead, the Slam Slam LP crystallised the problems Weller was facing in making the difficult transition from a musical dead-end to his eventual solo comeback. He tellingly spoke of the record as having happened "without point or reason". It showed.

Equally baffling was The Style Council's low-key reunion in April 1990 for a Japanese satellite TV programme, *Hit Studio International*. Presumably prompted by a healthy financial incentive, the group assembled in a London film studio to mime to that aborted final single, 'Sure Is Sure', while Weller performed 'The Whole Point' live. Few of Paul's European fans would have been aware of the broadcast – but the event was notable for reuniting him with the estranged Steve White. "I didn't think me and Steve could have carried on after The Style Council," Paul later confessed to *NME*. "If he hadn't got in touch with me around that time, it might not have happened. Steve had left a couple of years before the band broke up – not necessarily with bad feeling but there was a vibe between us." According to White, Paul chatted to him at the TV studios about his future plans: "Paul said, 'I'm just going to do some demos. Do you want to come have a play on some stuff?' We went down to Solid Bond and did a couple of days of demos."

In the short term, though, Weller found himself adrift in a musical wilderness, contenting himself with the welcome distraction of family life – centring around the couple's son Nathaniel. "I didn't know anything about children so you have to discover these things," he later admitted. "It was a real culture shock because it was so different from anything else I had experienced in life, so it took me a while to get to grips with that. And then, for two years or so after he was born, I really wanted to see his first steps or see him crawl or say his first words."

The responsibilities of fatherhood seemed to have given Weller a healthy dose of real life. As Paolo Hewitt put it, "the situation demanded a new perspective". One of the problems inherent in being famous for most of your adult life is the inclination to be too self-absorbed – self-centred, even – as a result of continually being the centre of attention. Bearing this in mind, the process of rearing a child appears to have had a profound effect on the musician. "I've lost my cynicism," he told *Boys About Town* fanzine. "This is mainly due to my child. When you lose cynicism, life opens up for you. When I was younger, I just saw things as either right or wrong, there was no in-between, it was like tunnel-vision. Now it's like someone has taken those blinkers off me and I can see things for what they really are."

Paul Weller hadn't become a house-husband, though. During late 1989 and the first half of 1990, he made the short journey to Solid Bond Studios from the family's home near Holland Park, to write and record under the watchful eye of engineer Brendan Lynch. But something definitely felt wrong. Weller has since admitted that during the twilight days of The Style Council, he lost his thirst to write new material. While he was enduring the upheavals of setting up a home and family, his music had lost its bite, and the occasional flashes of inspiration in his songwriting were sanitised by a smooth, sophisticated production. The spark of creativity which had kept him active since the mid-Seventies had dimmed.

"There was no direction in my work," he later confessed. "It was like a lost time for me. Anything that I did write, I felt, well, I've already covered this. It's old ground. I could quite easily not have got back on track. I didn't feel inspired. It was like a downward spiral I was slipping down and I was getting more and more lost." The situation demanded a major re-think. Racked by self-doubt and confusion, Weller sat back and took a long look at himself. "I began to question why I was doing it," he explained. "Is it for the money? Well, no, it's not really. Is it for the ego? Not particularly. It took me two years to realise that I do it because I love music. So I've come full circle."

Because family life tended to keep him at home, Paul spent less time visiting nightclubs, and his penchant for garage house music slowly faded as a result – it lacked the same appeal in the living-room. Frustrated by his feeling of musical stagnation, Paul found himself rifling through his old record collection and stumbled across those bands which had inspired him in the first place – such as The Small Faces and The Beatles. In keeping with his more sophisticated palate, he was drawn to their post-psychedelic side rather than the primitive feel of their earlier recordings. In 1986, Weller had told

Go Go fanzine, "The Small Faces are still my favourite all-time band, but I don't know what you can do with that music anymore." Now he knew.

Slowly but surely, Weller's interest in house music was supplanted by a growing taste for the late Sixties sounds of bands such as Traffic and Spooky Tooth. In the process, he rediscovered his love of playing the guitar. This watershed didn't happen overnight, but somewhere between that infamous Albert Hall finale and late 1990, the creative limbo which had plagued him through those dark months gradually subsided. In effect, Paul Weller was reinventing himself.

This shift in his tastes tallied neatly with the late Sixties/early Seventies-inspired grooves emanating from labels like Acid Jazz and Gilles Peterson's spin-off label, Talkin' Loud. At their best, these acts fused elements of funk with jazz, house, soul, rap, R&B and even psychedelia – and their sense of adventure rubbed off on him. By now, Paul was friendly with many of the individuals involved – singer Brian Powell and Marco Nelson's Young Disciples, for example, were both signed to Talkin' Loud. And Steve White's latest project was a modern jazz fusion collection, *A Certain Kind Of Freedom*. This showcase for new jazz talent was a continuation of previous jazz samplers put together by Working Week's Simon Booth – *Acid Jazz And Other Illicit Grooves* and *The Freedom Principle*. The LP drew on the skills of both White and Mick Talbot, plus Paul Francis, a member of The James Taylor Quartet who would figure in Paul's initial solo venture. Meanwhile, Mick Talbot hooked up with Galliano, who had followed Gilles Peterson to Talkin' Loud. The whole atmosphere of these outfits was of a loose aggregation of musicians – and, in this respect, The Style Council had been ahead of their time.

By autumn 1990, Paul had a handful of new songs, which he felt were far more promising than before. He was fired up to write new material for the first time in what seemed like ages, but his confidence was still at an all-time low. Uncertain about launching himself as a solo artist, he decided cautiously to test the water. Only one course of action presented itself: Paul Weller had to go out on the road and win back his audience. After years of evading the issue, he also made an important admission to himself: "I didn't want to hide in a group anymore. Now it's just me." In reality, the differences were cosmetic. Since Steve Brookes had left The Jam in 1975, Paul Weller had enjoyed a free reign as band leader and all that this position entailed – creative freedom, idolatry, media scrutiny and overall control. This was just a different twist.

Opting to play a series of low-key dates across the country, he assembled a band under the banner of The Paul Weller Movement, with Steve White back on drums. Weller's long-time friend Paolo Hewitt lent his support as DJ on the first tour, but the other musicians were less familiar, recruited from acquaintances loosely connected with the acid jazz scene. Steve brought Paul Francis with him on bass, Jacko Peake doubled on sax and flute and

Max Beesley was brought in on keyboards and vibraphone – together with Damon Brown (trumpet, flugelhorn), Chris Lawrence (trombone) and Joe Becket (percussion).

"There's absolutely no concept behind it," Paul explained. "Basically, it's just a matter of finding myself musically, to get my self-confidence back. The last two years, I have spent a lot of time writing and recording songs, so I just want people to hear them. I've not been out playing like this for at least fourteen years. I have no new record to promote, no hit that will draw full houses and actually not even a record contract."

On November 1, 1990, Paul Weller played his first gig as a solo artist – and he chose the nerve centre of acid jazz, Dingwalls. In the audience at that sell-out show was Dean Rudland: "That night was the biggest event of the year. I worked at Acid Jazz from mid-1990 and that was so important to the Acid Jazz people, not so much the club crowd. After that gig, everybody wanted him back. He was building a repertoire. I saw him at Guildford Civic Hall, which was badly attended but very good – firing on all cylinders. He was finding that balance between the rock and the soul."

Weller then embarked on his first solo tour throughout November and early December, sweeping across mainland Europe before returning for dates around Britain. "Where once, in typical bullish manner, he had thoroughly denounced The Jam, he now began to see a more balanced picture," wrote Paolo Hewitt. This sense of freedom was reflected in Paul's live set. For the first time, he was happy to dip into his past, mixing Jam songs ('Precious', 'Pity Poor Alfie') with Style Council favourites like 'My Ever Changing Moods', 'Man Of Great Promise', 'Speak Like A Child' and 'Headstart For Happiness'. The crowds reacted enthusiastically to new compositions like 'The Strange Museum', 'Kosmos', 'Here's A New Thing' and a slow, soulful tune, 'Like Yesterdays'. These were joined by Slam Slam's 'Round And Round' and that 'lost' Style Council workout, 'That Spiritual Feeling'. Paul was reluctant at first, though. "The tour was put together, which I really didn't want to go on," he admitted. "I had no interest whatsoever, but I'm really glad I did it, because if I hadn't, I think I would have just kept on sinking."

Despite the patchy turn-out – many of the venues in the provinces were less than half-full – the dates were a cautious success, a fact reflected when Radio One broadcast the show at London's Town & Country Club. The brittle, antiseptic atmosphere of latter-day Style Council was replaced by a rootsy style played by a musician who no longer seemed afraid of unleashing the odd rock guitar solo or injecting some passion in his stage show. Weller's voice had progressed, too; during an energetic version of the Isley Brothers' early Seventies single, 'Work To Do', he sang effortlessly around the melody in the style of Stevie Wonder – a technique also borrowed by Acid Jazz star Jamiroquai.

In the wake of the tour, Weller was plugging away as usual at Solid Bond

Studios in February 1991, recording various demos in the back room. "Paul had quite a few ideas," Steve White remembers. " 'New Thing' was one of the tunes. 'Spiritual Feeling' was there, because that was one of the final Council tunes. But there was also 'Yesterdays', which never came out. We cut 'New Thing' with Pete Wilson producing and that originally was going to be a single. Paul got the Irakere brass section – Cuban brass – to play on that and I was playing with sampled tape loops."

Meanwhile, Marco Nelson's Young Disciples were in the main studio putting the finishing touches to their début album, a melting pot of soul, jazz and rap entitled *Road To Freedom* – and it was a fusion which captivated Paul. Snowed-in due to bad weather, he and Brendan Lynch struck upon a novel mix of samples and 'beats' (hip-hop vernacular for a drum backbeat), to accompany one of Paul's most encouraging new songs, 'Into Tomorrow'.

And who better to produce the single than legendary New York producer Jimmy Miller, who had worked with such luminaries in the Sixties as The Rolling Stones, The Spencer Davis Group and Traffic. Miller had come out of semi-retirement and flown over to Britain to work with various artists, most notably with Primal Scream on their award-winning *Screamadelica* album. According to Weller, Miller was brought in to work on the "final overdubs and mix. That didn't really work out."

"Jimmy had produced the first version of 'Into Tomorrow' but he fell asleep at the desk because he was so pissed – so Paul sacked him on the spot," is Damon Minchella's version of events. As bassist with Ocean Colour Scene, Damon was also recording at Solid Bond with Jimmy Miller as producer. The group were managed by their guitarist Steve Cradock's father Chris, who had booked them into the studio knowing that his son was a big fan of Weller's. Cradock, who would soon become an integral part of Weller's entourage, had previously fronted The Boys, a Mod band from Solihull, south of Birmingham. Throughout 1988, they had played Mod clubs and scooter rallies. "We used to do loads of covers," says Steve, "all the ones The Jam did!"

Cradock had befriended another Birmingham band, The Fanatics, who had dropped an obsession with The Velvet Underground after seeing The Stone Roses in 1989. Having married the harmonies of The Beatles and The Byrds with a modern independent – or indie – sound, the Roses had become 1989's band-of-the-moment. Weller had been wary of indie bands, dismissing them as "student rubbish", but he was impressed both by The Stone Roses' songwriting skills and, as an aside, their Mod-ish image. The ripples of influence of their début album, *The Stone Roses*, spread across the independent scene, inspiring many of the bands whom Weller has since championed and/or worked with – such as Oasis, The Charlatans, Blur and The Bluetones.

The most notable of these was Ocean Colour Scene, who were born when The Fanatics teamed up with Steve Cradock in autumn 1989. Having adopted a strong Sixties persuasion, the band were heavily tipped by the music press after two promising singles, 'Sway', and the minor hit, 'Yesterday Today'. In early April 1991, Ocean Colour Scene were in the process of laying down songs for their début album at Solid Bond. "Paul had bought our singles and was really into us," recalls Damon Minchella. "He heard we were in the studio so he came down to meet us. We got on like a house on fire, basically." Steve Cradock was especially chuffed: "I bought a scooter off Paul. He had a Vespa 50 and I thought, I'm having it!" (Paul had been given the scooter as a present from his mother around the time of The Style Council's *Our Favourite Shop*.) By that time, Weller had dispensed with Miller's services – though there was no animosity. "He's a great geezer, though, nice," Paul said. "He's got some great stories as well." Instead, Paul produced 'Into Tomorrow' himself with the help of Brendan Lynch, cutting the song live on Good Friday 1991 but retaining the guitar solo from the original demo, which had been played through a practice amp. "I wanted to get a record out," he explained when we spoke a year later. "I'd been offered a couple of deals, none of which I felt were right, and I wasn't ready to sign either. I only had a few songs, but I wanted to make a record. It was nice to be playing the guitar again."

After his untidy departure from Polydor, Weller was reluctant to jump into bed with the first record company who showed any interest. Instead, The Paul Weller Movement's 'Into Tomorrow' was issued on his own label, Freedom High, in early May. The song's spacious production and its rhythmic mix of horns, organ and funky drums echoed late Sixties acts like Julie Driscoll, Brian Auger & The Trinity. But its driving force was Weller's gutsy delivery – both in his passionate vocals and his vibrant guitar style. To many of Weller's fans who had been disillusioned by the last few Style Council records, 'Into Tomorrow' felt like a return-to-form. Its rough-and-ready edge had been conspicuous by its absence from his music since mid-Eighties songs like 'Internationalists' and 'Walls Come Tumbling Down'. A backwards guitar solo even hinted at '66-era Beatles, which had so influenced Paul over a decade earlier.

The single's other two tracks fitted more comfortably into the acid jazz mould. 'Here's A New Thing' was a jaunty Latin soul number topped with horns and flute and built on a funky bassline and the piano riff from Marshall Jefferson's house classic, 'Move Your Body'. "The hardest thing is letting go/But once you do, life starts to flow," sang Weller in his best Curtis Mayfield falsetto, "Here's a new thing . . . Gotta let go of the past." If that 'past' referred to his skeleton-in-the-closet, The Jam, then he had now stopped fighting against it. That was just as well, because the quarter-of-a-million sales which greeted The Jam's *Greatest Hits* in June led to a rekindling of interest in the band, prompting the creation of tribute bands like All Mod Cons and English Rose.

But the message was clear: Weller was striving forward. By the same token, he was also happy to resurrect 'That Spiritual Feeling' from 1989, a Style Council group composition with Talbot, Lee and Marco Nelson. This instrumental jazz-funk jam with James Brown's brass section, The J.B.'s, perfectly conjured up the atmosphere of early Seventies rare groove. With its soaring horn solos, electric piano and a shuffling beat, 'That Spiritual Feeling' indulged in fusion – acid jazz – in much the same way as *Café Bleu* had dabbled in Sixties jazz.

Paul summarised 'Into Tomorrow' as "me trying to get a grip on becoming a thirty-something and the great grey mass that lies between the simple black and white world of my youth". He had been struggling to recapture his musical focus, but his motivation was rekindled with this rhythmic mixture of R&B-fuelled aggression and a Small Faces-styled guitar riff. It was an important watershed in his career not only creatively but also commercially, since it put him back on the Top 40 map despite a modest promotional campaign. The packaging hinted at Weller's new mood – emblazoned across the cover and the labels was a multi-coloured Mod target, a design which also appeared on posters for another round of gigs under the banner, Live Part II. "I did a second tour in April," he explained, "which again I didn't want to do, but all the time I was finding my right direction. It was the best thing that happened to me because now, for me, I'm back on course."

The fourteen-date trip tended to avoid the usual towns and venues. By doing so, it felt as if Weller was stretching out beyond his core fan base and testing the water elsewhere – both to remind people he was still out there and, by the same token, to see if they were still interested. Still restless with the format, Weller rejigged the Movement's line-up: in came bassist Henry Thomas (who may forever be associated with his role in the early Eighties musicians' tutorial TV programme, *Rock School*), and the horn section was whittled down to Gerrard Pescencer (trumpet and flugelhorn). Two backing vocalists, Linda Duggan and Zeita Messiah, were also drafted in – though the move was later viewed as a mistake. "It was embarrassing," Steve White later exclaimed. "These two girls were kinda foisted on us. Originally, there was a need for some backing singers because the tunes were lacking without extra voices and the people in the band couldn't really sing."

Paul was still comfortable to air a cross-section of the old ('That's Entertainment', 'The Piccadilly Trail', 'Long Hot Summer', 'Carnation', 'Tales From The Riverbank') and the new ('Bitterness Rising', 'Into Tomorrow'). The set also featured an obscure early Seventies soul-jazz cover, Bobby Hutcherson's 'Ummh!' At the Brixton Academy gig on April 20, Weller learnt of the death of Steve Marriott, caused by a fire in his home the previous night. The Small Faces singer had been Weller's greatest icon for many years – live footage of the Sixties band reveals how Paul has not only mimicked Marriott's dress sense and vocal style but also his stage movements. As a tribute, Weller performed 'Tin Soldier', which was captured on a video of the concert issued that August. Viewed with hindsight, this film depicts a musician who was definitely undergoing a period of transition. The video featured only five new songs, but by reworking some of the best songs from his past, Paul was forging a style on which to build for the future.

"I didn't have a fucking clue what was going on," he conceded two years later in *NME*. "It was a ramshackle affair, really. But in retrospect, the tours were really constructive. You can find yourself on stage sometimes. It can bring something out in you – ambition, drive, motivation." The growing belief in his live ability is one of the factors in Weller's renaissance, and 'The Paul Weller Movement' soon evolved into plain old 'Paul Weller', almost as if the banner had acted as a prop or a stop-gap until he felt confident enough to play under his own name, with no frills attached.

Unhappy with his band, Paul dispensed with most of the musicians, sticking only with Steve White and Jacko Peake for the LP's recording sessions during the late summer and autumn of 1991. "There was a lot of foot-finding at the time," reckoned White. "It just takes a while to find a direction sometimes. I think it took a while for him to suss out what he wanted to do and what he was hoping to achieve – to settle on something that made him happy. So, as with his true style, he likes to try different things."

A self-funded single was all very well, but Weller knew that to rebuild his career properly, he needed the solid financial backing and comprehensive support structure of a major record deal. John Weller spoke to all the leading record companies throughout the summer of 1991, but his asking price of nearly half a million pounds immediately scared off all but the most dedicated parties. There was talk of a deal with Talkin' Loud and an album, tentatively titled *SX 2000*, was slated for October. This title was a playful nod to the SX 200, a model of Sixties Lambretta scooter – it seemed that Weller had lost none of his infatuation with the cult which had so captivated him in his teens. "It's like a code, in a way," he told TV presenter Jonathan Ross in April. "It gives something to my life. I'm still a Mod. I'll always be a Mod. You can bury me a Mod." In 1992, Paul was even pictured on the front cover of *Scootering* magazine, and discussed the renovation of his recently acquired Lambretta – not that his increasingly hectic schedule would allow him much time to ride it.

Rumours suggested that the Talkin' Loud deal fell through because the Wellers upped their asking price at the last minute. Instead, Paul had to look elsewhere to generate funds. The first move was to sell the lease to Solid Bond Studios, which was valued at just over £100,000. "The reason was economic," explains Dave Liddle, Paul's long-serving guitar technician. "It wasn't that Paul didn't have the money. Nikki worked there, Kenny Wheeler was there, I was there, the old man was there – that was his office. But you've got to keep a studio working all the time and if you're diving in every five minutes doing demos and laying tracks down, you can't let it go to the outside public. Because he doesn't really need a studio all the time, anyway.

It was always a lease rental and the landlords wanted to whack the rent up so high that it wasn't worth keeping it as an office complex."

Liddle hadn't worked with Paul since the twilight days of The Style Council – and just as Mick Talbot had been informed of the group's demise by a letter, so Paul's guitar roadie wasn't given any choice in the matter. "I was made redundant for no apparent reason. The excuse given was that Paul's not going to be working much. But I used to get phoned up – 'Oh, what strings does he use?' 'I'm not working for you anymore,' I'd answer and put the phone down! So I had a break for two years but I got a call in '91 from Paul saying he wanted to see me. They were having a party because Solid Bond was closing and he asked me to come back again."

Dave has observed the tight bond between Paul and his father for two decades: "Paul doesn't do anything he doesn't want to. He's quite a strong-willed person, so he might say, no, I don't want to do that and the old man abides by it. But his dad takes care of business. They organise things together, working as a unit. It always was a unit, always will be." Liddle found the atmosphere was more laid-back on his return. "It's nice and easy now," he admits. "Back in the Seventies, it was busy – but I don't think that's the reason. Since the Paul Weller Movement, it's lightened up and become a nicer place to work. Paul's more relaxed than he's ever been. Going out on tour is funny now, whereas it was a bit of a chore before sometimes. Paul's exact words when I came back were, 'This time we're going to have fun when we go out on tour'. The Style Council was quite a serious band and Paul went through a load of crap in '89 and '90 with the Polydor deal. He wasn't exactly the happiest he's ever been. So he said, 'I guarantee you it's going to be a laugh. We're going to enjoy ourselves! We're not going to do it purely for the dosh.' And it's worked!"

One of Paul's last sessions at Solid Bond yielded a faithful interpretation of 'Don't Let Me Down'. This was donated to a Beatles tribute album, *Revolution No. 9*. The LP was masterminded by the Bradford-based Pax label to raise profits for Oxfam's Cambodian famine relief programme. Meanwhile, Weller signed a deal in Japan (where Paul's profile was far greater than in his home country) with Pony Canyon, who supplied the necessary advance to complete the début LP.

Prompted by his popularity in the Far East, he then assembled a new touring band to play Japan in November 1991, as a prelude to dates in America and a one-off London show. It felt like a Style Council reunion: Helen Turner returned on piano, Zeke Manyika took over percussion and Camille Hinds joined on bass. The new line-up was christened at Brighton's Zap Club, the traditional warm-up gig for ventures abroad, and stayed for the majority of Paul's concerts throughout 1992.

Japan welcomed Weller back with wide open arms and there were none of the empty seats the musician had had to endure in Britain. In return, *Paul Weller* was issued in Japan several months before the album was available elsewhere. To pre-empt the LP's release there, he and Steve White travelled to Tokyo for a low-key promotional show in a small club in March. In front of an invited audience of winners to a magazine competition, Paul performed a relaxed set, previewing much of the new material, accompanied only by his guitar and Steve on bongos or drums. Weller's voice sounded especially strong and, evidently in high spirits, he threw in a couple of unlikely cover versions – a ramshackle rendition of the Lovin' Spoonful's 'Daydream' and a respectable tribute to Marvin Gaye's 'What's Going On'. Most unusual of all was his decision to play The Jam's 'Shopping', which had scarcely been aired live before – if ever. This sense of adventure pervaded the whole event, and it was a feeling which would carry him through his solo career for several years. In the short term, *Paul Weller* entered the Japanese International charts at No. 1 in late April, and stayed there for over a month.

Marvin Gaye's early Seventies classic also provided a fitting finale during one of Weller's first British dates of 1992 in June. During the encore at the Town & Country Club 2, the first of four consecutive shows dotted around London, he welcomed both Mick Talbot and Dee C. Lee onto the stage for an emotional performance of 'What's Going On'. If it felt like a revival of his old band, then The Style Council's concept of a loose aggregate of guest musicians was also present on his début LP. During the sessions, Paul had called on both his wife (who sang backing vocals on four tracks) and friends like Marco Nelson, who also brought along his colleague in the Young Disciples, singer Carleen Anderson, and Robert Howard (occasional bass and backing vocals). On August 6, in fact, Paul guested with Robert at Harlesden's Mean Fiddler Acoustic Room for an encore of two Tim Hardin songs, 'Red Balloon' and 'Reason To Believe', playing guitar on a rendition of T. Rex's 'Life's A Gas'.

After a delay of nearly a year, *Paul Weller* was finally released in Britain in September 1992. Behind the scenes, Weller had secured a UK record deal with Go! Discs, a West London-based record label formed in the early Eighties which had made its name with ostensibly socialist acts – first Billy Bragg and then The Housemartins and spin-off acts The Beautiful South and Beats International. From Weller's point of view, Go! Discs seemed to offer the best compromise of financial incentives and creative freedom: while it was run in a fairly autonomous fashion, by people who came across as music enthusiasts rather than besuited accountants, the organisation could still call upon the might of PolyGram to supply the necessary financial and promotional clout.

"My new LP sounds like British R&B – that's how I describe it," Paul told me at the time. "Not just Sixties – Sixties, Seventies, Eighties, Nineties. It has loads of references to all the music I like, but it also has a contemporary feel as well." The album's opening track, 'Uh Huh Oh Yeh', preceded the LP as a single. The song opened with a phased drum roll, a spacey mix of horns and a funky beat. Above this psychedelic vibe, Weller sang about his childhood in

Woking, the first acknowledgement of his Surrey upbringing since 'Tales From The Riverbank'. The Jam song had been cryptic; 'Uh Huh Oh Yeh', on the other hand, made specific reference to the area around his old home. The first two lines, "I took a trip down Boundary Lane/Try an' find myself again", referred to Boundary Road, which is a couple of streets away from Stanley Road – indeed, the song's subject matter was emphasised by a promotional video shot on location in the back streets of Woking.

Interviewed in Woking by *NME*, Paul spoke about the rediscovery of his home town: "I hadn't been back for about eight years, not since The Style Council started. And I only came back through here because I was going to buy a scooter in Aldershot. It's perfect, innit? Afterwards, I drove back in the car and stopped off here, and went to a few places that I hadn't been to in years. And at the same time, I started playing a few records that I used to listen to then – Stax, R&B, The Small Faces, The Who – and everything started to make some sense again."

It also suggested that, during that period of re-evaluation when his confidence had been shattered after the demise of The Style Council, his thoughts had taken him back to his youth. After Weller had spent most of his life relentlessly moving forward, disregarding his yesterdays – and the people involved in his yesterdays – he was now thinking, and writing, from a more reflective standpoint. One verse encapsulated his new state of mind: "And in my mind I saw the place/As each memory returned to trace/Dear reminders of who I am/The very roots upon which I stand." And there was a direct correlation between the lines, "And all the dreams I had to dream/Were really something, not make believe," and the evocative phrase, "true is the dream mixed with nostalgia", from 'Tales From The Riverbank'.

Aside from its lyrics, 'Uh Huh Oh Yeh' mined the same psychedelic funk-rock seam as 'Into Tomorrow', with stabs of sampled horns from an old Marsha Hunt song, 'Hot Rod Poppa' – it felt like a cross between, say, The Beatles' 'Strawberry Fields Forever' and The Small Faces' 'The Journey'. The single also featured 'Always There To Fool You', which was merely an instrumental version of the title track, a fidgety, sax-led jazz-funk instrumental laced with studio trickery called 'Arrival Time', and best of all, 'Fly On The Wall'. This beautiful, emotion-drenched acoustic ballad remains one of Weller's most impressive songs. "And under my feet, There's nothing to stop my own free fall/Down and down I go/And compared to it all/I'm a fly on the wall": these were typical of Weller's lyrics of the time, the product of a sudden realisation not only of fame's precarious nature but also a personal admission of his insignificance in the grand scheme of things from someone once criticised for his arrogance.

Modesty aside, 'Uh Huh Oh Yeh' put Weller back in the Top 20 for the first time in nearly five years, which led to an appearance on *Top Of The Pops* – though it proved to be his last. "I felt completely removed from all of it," he admitted to *Boston Rock* magazine. "For a start, I felt too old to be on there

234

because it's out-and-out kids' stuff. And there's all these other bands on – these sort of 'rave' bands that were just like a DJ that gets a few dancers in. It was like, 'What are we doing here?' "

Paul Weller was greeted with a surprisingly muted critical response – in fact, the LP was trounced by many reviewers, who considered it bland and directionless. Quite why is difficult to understand, since the album's music was as lavish as its packaging. Many cynics were still wary of Weller's past – after all, this was his first new LP since *Confessions Of A Pop Group*, which was universally treated with a lack of comprehension by the music press. And 1992 was the year when American rock scythed its way through the British independent scene. Grunge arrived on these shores and the critics were too busy foaming at the mouth over Mudhoney and Nirvana to worry about a dodgy old Mod from the home counties who lost the plot some time after 'Town Called Malice'. To the cynics, the album just felt like the latest change in Weller's musical direction to match another new haircut.

Danny Kelly was editor of *NME* at the time. "Radio 5 did a fly-on-the-wall documentary, called *A Week In The Life Of The NME*," he explains. "I wasn't even a Jam fan, I was a Clash fan. But if you listen back to that show, there's a bit about the editorial meeting, with all the young hacks. I came in and said, 'You know what we should do? We should put Paul Weller on the cover.' And there was absolute silence – and disgust because I'm doing this in front of the BBC. 'Paul Weller? Paul Weller? You lost your mind?' I went, 'Paul Weller's got a new record out and I don't care what you people say, he's a very important star.' Now he's on the front cover of the *NME* every three weeks!"

The doubters had overlooked a genuinely strong collection of songs. *Confessions . . .* had succeeded because of its sheer breadth and variety, but *Paul Weller* remains his strongest, most well-rounded collection of songs since *All Mod Cons*. The softly-spoken regret of tunes like 'I Didn't Mean To Hurt You' oozed the kind of bruised emotion that might roughly be defined as soul. Built around a similar backing track to 'Arrival Time', the song's lyrics may well have been linked to Paul's comments in the credits: "Thanks and love to Dee, my (fairly) long-standing and (frequently) long-suffering wife, who's stood by me when I've been way down and hateful for it, for putting up with my many moods . . ." It is fair to conclude that Paul Weller wasn't the easiest person to live with during his soul-searching period of 1989 and 1990.

Hints of The Style Council's gliding soul melodies echoed through the angelic love song, 'Remember How We Started' and the strutting, folky soul groove of 'Amongst Butterflies', which broke into a snatch from 'Arrival Time' as an interlude before one of the album's most haunting songs, 'The Strange Museum'. Co-written with Mick Talbot, this dreamy ballad was memorable not only for the capability of Weller's voice to carry the melody but also because of its vivid, mystical lyrics, all woven into a mellow, jazzy backcloth.

The rest of the album was more upbeat, musically if not lyrically – in fact, it contained some of Weller's most insightful and heartfelt lyrics. Taking a leaf from the feel of Thunderclap Newman's old hit, 'Something In The Air', with a nod towards Curtis Mayfield, 'Bitterness Rising' was delivered like a catharsis: "Or the past will take you/Keep you from the truth/As bitterness rises/From the ashes of your youth". Meanwhile, the music grew from a pleasant R&B groove into an intense funk-rock brew. The same angst ran through much of the album. "They're really my thoughts over the two years leading up to making this LP last year," Paul revealed, "which was kind of a confusing time for me with a lot of personal changes and such." One of the major events was hidden in Paul's romantic credits: "This record is dedicated especially to Nathaniel and Leah – little arrows from our bow, may you soar high and always free." In October 1991, Dee had given birth to the couple's second child. But as his solo career took off, Paul had to make an unhappy compromise between the amount of time he devoted to his family and to his career.

The anthemic 'Bull-Rush' began with the lines, "In a momentary lapse of my condition/That sent me stumbling into a deep despair". But its Small Faces' groove and the melody's fresh, uplifting nature enlivened the mood before breaking out into a psychedelic end refrain borrowed from The Who's 'Magic Bus'. In 'Clues', Weller sang about being "Racked by my own self-doubt/I stumble and fall", but again, the moment of gloomy self-absorption was just one facet. 'Clues' was the album's most complex song instrumentally. The band often veered away from the strident melody to dabble into less structured passages, where Steve White's adventurous drumming bounced off Jacko Peake's swooping flute.

The album finished with 'Kosmos', an experimental collage of funk and psychedelia with heaps of electronic effects from Brendan Lynch as Weller chanted his quest for a sense of identity, "Who am I? What am I? Where am I to go?". The drums were lifted from an old P.P. Arnold tune and the soothing melody was pure Marvin Gaye – and the result was an amalgam of *Sgt. Pepper* and *What's Going On* but from a positively Nineties perspective. Within this climate, a remake of the floating jazz-funk song, 'Round And Round' from the Slam Slam LP, was probably the album's only possible mistake, despite Weller's effort to beef the song up towards the end – but this is a minor quibble. In short, *Paul Weller* was a masterpiece.

It was an indication of the size and loyalty of Weller's audience that the album still reached the Top 10 – since he hadn't yet acquired many new fans. Judging by the crowds at his concerts, it was more a case of Paul reacquainting himself with those who had lost interest during the latter half of the Eighties. The album's cautious success should also be attributed to Go! Discs, who launched an extensive promotional campaign, backed up by widespread radio and TV coverage. Over the next few years, Go! Discs would sustain a slow but steady support of Paul's career in what must rank as one of the most impressive 'comebacks' in British rock history.

In keeping with his growing love of late Sixties singer/songwriters, Weller has recorded numerous radio sessions during his solo career, accompanied only by his acoustic guitar. Especially interesting was a Radio One broadcast in early September 1992, when Paul played a new acoustic ballad, 'Wild Wood'. This had been performed during the summer dates, together with other new songs, 'The Weaver', 'Love Of The Loved' and 'Ends Of The Earth'. Collectively, they lacked the traces of funk which infused his début LP, substituting it for a flavour which critics were wont to call pastoral or rural. A year later, 'Wild Wood' would help catapult him back into the limelight. In fact, producer Brendan Lynch had already revealed during the summer that they were mixing new material and rehearsing new songs for Weller's second solo LP. "I want to get more raw, if anything," Paul stated. "Not rock-y, but just strip it down and make it more live."

The mellow, Marvin Gaye-influenced groove of 'Above The Clouds' was issued as the second single from the album. It was an odd choice: the song's dreamy, soothing vibe lacked the commercial bite of songs like 'Bull-Rush' or even 'Clues' but maybe Paul wanted to counteract the upfront nature of 'Uh Huh Oh Yeh'. Co-produced by Chris Bangs (of Acid Jazz and Galliano fame), the tune had a tranquil, summery atmosphere which might have caught the mood had it been issued earlier in the year. Instead, it felt awkward during the autumnal feel of October and stalled outside the Top 40. Again, the song's lyrics hinted at Weller's state of mind over the previous months: "As my anger shouts/At my own self-doubt/So a sadness creeps/Into my dreams". When Weller's inner emotions were expressed within Jam and Style Council songs, they tended to be externalised as anger against an outside entity. *Confessions Of A Pop Group* contained the first evidence of a more introspective side to his songwriting – and it's this aspect which dominated *Paul Weller*.

The single also boasted a compelling acoustic folk-blues number, 'Everything Has A Price To Pay', and a jazzy update of The Style Council's 'All Year Round', captured on stage that summer in New York City. More revealing was a faithful run through Traffic's 'Feeling Alright'. Featuring extra vocals from Carleen Anderson and Dee C. Lee, this Dave Mason composition had been performed during the summer tour. "I've only bought this in the last year," Paul revealed to *Record Collector*'s Pat Gilbert, referring to Traffic's eponymous second album from which the song was originally taken. "Even though it's twenty four years old, it's had a profound effect on me. Those acoustic sounds. It's given me a different scope as well – made me think differently about music and what I can do with it." Recorded in 1968, *Traffic* had a rootsy, organic feel distinct from the psychedelia of their earlier sound – and its influence could be heard quite clearly in Paul's new material.

Another crucial aspect of Weller's renaissance in the Nineties has been his incessant touring. Prior to the album's release, Paul had embarked on pitstop tours of both Japan (his continued popularity there was reflected by the fact that he comfortably sold out 10,000-capacity stadiums) and North America. The highlight of the US stint occurred at Los Angeles' Greek Theatre, where Weller had the pleasure of welcoming ex-Small Faces organist Ian McLagan on stage.

Towards the end of the year, Paul was barely off the road. An extensive tour to promote the album took in the UK in October – and then much of Europe, for the first time in two years – with a set which included a cover of Aaron Neville's laid-back funk classic, 'Hercules'. And the presence of The Jam's 'Man In The Corner Shop', and Style Council favourites like '(When You) Call Me' and 'Headstart For Happiness', suggested Paul was still happy to dip into his past. To those who had witnessed Paul's earlier solo gigs, it felt like the whole show had been lifted up a rung, both in terms of the venue size and in the strength of Weller's performances – his past edginess melted away as he grew more relaxed on stage. An acoustic performance of The Jam's 'Town Called Malice' was one of several golden oldies aired when the roadshow continued into November with the most extensive US tour of Paul's career. After so many years of openly criticising the country, he now seemed willing to commit himself to playing America – it felt like a show of confidence on Weller's part. The dates culminated in a show in New York's Greenwich Village, where his wife Dee joined him onstage.

While he was over in the States, Paul gave a revealing interview with *Boston Rock* magazine, which covered many aspects of his persona, both past and present. "I don't care what anybody thinks anymore," he stated defiantly, reflecting on his past need to defend himself in the media. "It's my own fault for taking them on in the first place, you know? I should've had enough confidence of character to say, 'Well, fuck you, I ain't got to justify myself to anyone'." Asked if he still believed in the wider potential of pop music, his reply was cautious: "I still believe in it up to a point, yeah, but I guess I'm sorta more realistic about what I can do these days. It can change individuals, I don't know if it can change the world as I once thought it could do."

Having children had made him more pragmatic, too: "You have to be more positive and think of things from their point of view – you want the world to go on, you want things to get better. It's not just for yourself anymore." This view didn't seem to tally with his lack of interest in politics: "I couldn't give a shit about it now, to be quite honest with you," he said. "But also, I think the way the world is now is a different place from ten years ago. We've got to think in global terms." For someone who once cared so passionately about the relevant issues of the day, Weller's complete about-turn was surprising – and could be seen as undermining his earlier stance. However, his lack of enthusiasm was mirrored within the music scene as a whole, which has by and large ignored the social and political realities of Nineties Britain – aside from 'rock'n'roll' issues like drugs – in terms of its lyrical content.

During the early months of 1993, first 'Bull-Rush' and then a fresh song, 'The Weaver', were slated for single release. But nothing had surfaced before Weller played two British dates in March prior to a brief visit to North America. At Leeds' Town & Country Club, Paul was supported by Ocean Colour Scene and at London's equivalent venue in North London two days later, Dr. Robert's new band, Starjuice, were second on the bill. Both acts would also play a crucial role during the sessions for Paul's next LP.

Without the security of Solid Bond Studios to fall back on, Weller had visited several recording facilities before stumbling across the Manor, near a quaint country village named Shipton-On-Cherwell, near Oxford. The studio had been established by Richard Branson in the early Seventies before he launched Virgin Records. One of its major advantages was that it was a self-contained residential studio, which gave musicians the freedom to settle in and, costs permitting, record when they liked. Paul also warmed to the rural ambience of the Oxfordshire countryside. In short, he thought the Manor was the perfect setting for the type of songs he was now writing, and he shacked up there throughout April and May 1993 with an entourage of musicians and producers.

After the prevarication about choosing a new single, Weller eventually opted for one of the songs which had been completed at the Manor. Issued in July, 'Sunflower' began with a effects-laden guitar intro that led to comparisons with The Beatles' 'Lucy In The Sky With Diamonds' and The Faces' 'Flying'. Paul's powerful vocal was built upon an equally punchy guitar riff. Despite some deft touches – Jacko Peake's flute and Paul's Mellotron and Moog blips – the effect was rockier than the feel of his début LP, although the song felt like the logical progression of 'Into Tomorrow' and 'Uh Huh Oh Yeh'. 'Sunflower' was joined on the single by a rampant live medley of 'Bull-Rush' and The Who's late Sixties classic, 'Magic Bus', captured in October 1992 at the Royal Albert Hall. 'Kosmos SXDub 2000', meanwhile, was the first of several overhauls of Paul's songs by producer Brendan Lynch, the best being the more radical 'Kosmos (Lynch Mob Bonus Beats)'. Stripping most of the vocals away, Lynch used the dub techniques of echo and drop-out, adding eerie samples to create a psychedelic collage of sound.

'Sunflower' rewarded Weller with another Top 20 hit – but it represented more than that. It is widely regarded as his best single by his fans, judging by readers' polls in the various fanzines which sprang up following his return. And if there was a watershed when the musician was finally accepted by both the rock critics and a wider audience, then it was Weller's stunning performance of 'Sunflower' on BBC2's *Later With Jools Holland*.

'Wild Wood' was chosen as Weller's next single, an acoustic ballad which attracted adjectives like 'pastoral' and 'rustic' from the music press. This was reinforced not only by its title and the song's gentle melody but also its lyrics. The line, "Find your way out/Of the wild, wild wood", seemed to advocate an escape from stress and "traffics boom" of urban life. The song epitomised his new-found affection for the acoustic approach – just him and his guitar, and an endearingly subtle tune. Whereas the mellower songs on *Paul Weller* echoed early Seventies soul, this was rooted firmly in the singer/songwriter mould. Traces of Neil Young and the late Nick Drake could be heard in 'Wild Wood' but the biggest influence was the late Tim Hardin, who Weller probably discovered via Small Faces' covers of his most famous songs, 'If I Were A Carpenter' and 'Red Balloon'. Paul paid tribute to Hardin by performing another of his best-known songs, 'Black Sheep Boy', which eventually slipped out on a *Volume* magazine compilation.

" 'Wild Wood' is all about these magical memories I have from when I was a kid," he told *NME*. " 'The Place I Love' on *All Mod Cons* is a bit like that, too. 'Monday' on *Sound Affects*, 'Boy About Town' – these are the songs I like now." The simplicity of 'Wild Wood' was matched on the B-side by a sublime, piano-led love song, 'Ends Of The Earth', which completed the picture of a musician who seemed more relaxed in himself. It was as if some of that self-doubt was gradually dissipating, perhaps helped by the tranquil surroundings of the Manor studios, but also by the knowledge that he was finally achieving the sound he'd been striving for since those uncertain dates back in 1990.

That was definitely the impression of *Wild Wood*, the album, which arrived in September 1993. Weller had swapped the sharp, urban edges of The Jam and the cosmopolitan feel of The Style Council for a warm, well-rounded sound. The songs' lyrics were awash with words like "mountains", "country", "season", "lightning", "weaver", "sunflower" and "wood". This might have suggested that Paul had shifted his political sympathies towards the environmentalists, or that he had softened with age, but neither suggestion was strictly true. In his quest to discover a new musical course, Weller had arrived at a style which he felt was authentic, which was deeply rooted in tradition and which shunned the clinical nature of modern-day digital production.

His emphasis was now on playing live and writing durable songs – and other aspects which leant meaning and substance to his work. "Something real is what I'm seeking", sang Weller in 'Has My Fire Really Gone Out?' By now, he had been a pop star for half his life, an artificial environment lacking the boundaries which define most people's lives. True, Paul had a wife and two kids – there is nothing more normal than that – but with *Wild Wood*, Weller finally came to the conclusion that his role in the world was to play music.

Wild Wood was very much an album of different moods, though much of the introspective nature of *Paul Weller* remained. Such was the personal nature of many of its lyrics that it is tempting to find a metaphor lurking beneath the surface: nature's elements of earth, fire, air and water representing aspects of Weller's personality. The accent of the music had also shifted, and the (acid) jazz tinges of his début were virtually absent. The blustering blues rock of '5th Season', which featured Paul's long-time guitar roadie Dave Liddle, began with Weller bellowing angrily, "A storm is raging, inside my head/Why am I so lost and confused/Can't find the reason, for feeling blue". And the self-questioning theme of 'Has My Fire Really Gone Out?' contrasted its goodtime R&B flavour, complete with harmonica – and, as if to wipe away any insecurities, the song ended with a piercing psychedelic rock jam.

The lyrics, too, were defiant, as Steve White later revealed: "He would be saying, 'I've got this new tune, "Has My Fire . . .". It's about all the people who criticise and call me a has-been. This is my way of sticking two fingers up.' Paul has never, ever sat down and said, 'Right, we're gonna do a tune in a Traffic style.' It's an insult to him to believe that he's that contrived about it. He just does what he feels. More and more over that time, his confidence grew as a solo artist."

The vibrant, piano-driven 'Can You Heal Us (Holy Man)' loosely tackled such weighty topics as religion and death. Its mellow funk ending slowed down the riff from Edwin Starr's 'War' into a spiritually-uplifting groove, which was then reprised towards the close of the LP. "I've got little time for organised religion," said Paul of the song's theme. "I think they're a real charade, most of them, and the contradictions are too much for me. But at the same time, I still think that faith is very important. I don't think I have absolute faith yet but I still like the idea that some time I will. I come from a family of atheists, which is good in one way because it's left me clear space to make my own mind up – but I've also inherited their scepticism. With my dad, it's just you're born, you live and then you die."

'Moon On Your Pyjamas' shared a low-key feel with a pretty tune, and a slushy poetic lyric written about Paul's love for his children. 'Country' was a gentle, contemplative song accompanied by acoustic guitar and a stylophone passage from Brendan Lynch which echoed David Bowie's 'Space Oddity'. "I feel the time we've yet to reach," sang Weller, "Is not yet within our belief", reiterating his sense of striving forward to some unfathomable goal in life. This idea was also at the root of 'Foot Of The Mountain' – "Such a long way to climb/How will I ever get up there/Though I know I must try". This captivating acoustic song formed a cornerstone of *Wild Wood* alongside the lengthy 'Shadow Of The Sun', an accomplished exercise in melody and musicianship on which the band indulged in some West Coast-styled instrumental interplay, climaxing in a soaring guitar solo.

It must have been some party down at the Manor – the list of guest appearances ran into double figures, as if passing friends had helped out where they could, a set-up not dissimilar to The Style Council's. "We had a great time and thank you all for it", was the message on the sleeve – and it showed. Weller played a range of instruments – guitar, bass, piano, organ, harmonica, Mellotron, Moog – supported by a core of bassist Marco Nelson and drummer Steve White. And the trio were joined not only by regulars

241

Helen Turner (organ), Jacko Peake (horns and flute) and Max Beesley (Wurlitzer) but also Mick Talbot (organ), Dee C. Lee (backing vocals), Robert Howard (guitar) and Ocean Colour Scene's Steve Cradock (guitar) and Simon Fowler (vocals). To borrow from that old Sly Stone song, *Wild Wood* felt like a family affair – borne out by the photo of Paul, Steve and Marco with their children, sitting in the grounds of the Manor. This tradition of using a pool of musicians was, like *Wild Wood* itself, rooted in the late Sixties/early Seventies, when artists frequently performed on each other's records.

By 1993, Ocean Colour Scene had become embroiled in a dispute with their record label – and their career, as a result, had ground to a halt. "Paul knew it was a bad time for us and we didn't know how long it would last," says Steve Cradock. "So he asked me to play on 'The Weaver'. That was the first time I played with Paul. It was a real education for me. It totally turned around my playing. A lot of real precious moments I've had are just sitting around when Paul's playing the guitar – it's almost spiritual, sometimes." After speculation about its possible release at the start of the year, 'The Weaver' was finally issued in late October as the third single to be lifted from *Wild Wood*. Already a live favourite, this rousing update of British R&B was based around a pounding two-chord riff. The lyric harked back to several moments in Weller's record collection – Humble Pie's "But to follow the weaver of dreams" lyric on their *As Safe As Yesterday Is* album and the "Dreamweaver" of John Lennon's 'God' (on *Plastic Ono Band*), although Paul later cited an old Spooky Tooth song as the initial inspiration.

Another telling influence was heard on *The Weaver EP*, alongside the mellow soul/folk mix that was 'This Is No Time' (a Bill Withers-styled tune co-written with Marco Nelson), and the meandering, laid-back jazz shuffle of 'Another New Day', snatches from which had provided two interludes on *Wild Wood*. Neil Young had written 'Ohio' in 1970 in response to the shooting of demonstrators at Ohio's Kent State University, and recorded the song with America's most successful supergroup of the period, Crosby, Stills, Nash and Young. Weller's live cover reflected his interest in this era, but while his thunderous performance was solid enough, the song's attacking lyrical content only emphasised the lack of a similar drive among Paul's own material.

Weller might have appreciated comparisons with Neil Young; instead, the music press seized upon the idea that he was 'the new Clapton', a suggestion which rankled Paul. The fact that 'Ohio' was recorded at the Royal Albert Hall didn't help, either. The venue was closely associated with Eric Clapton, who played an annual two-week slot at the hall every February. While Neil Young was then experiencing a renaissance prompted by a string of lively and quite different LPs, Clapton seemed to have settled into his brand of dignified, middle-aged blues. Weller patently felt uncomfortable about following this route, but there was no smoke without fire – it should be pointed out that *Wild Wood* wasn't that dissimilar to Clapton's solo recordings of the early Seventies.

Wild Wood was Weller's first LP to be favourably received by the music press since *Our Favourite Shop*. Once again, his face was seen on the front covers of magazines and Radio One broadcast a documentary, *The Paul Weller Story*. Still sceptical of The Style Council, critics compared the album to The Jam in their prime. "He seemed to have crash-landed back in the six months following 'Tales From The Riverbank'," wrote *NME*'s Paul Moody, "folkier, wiser and desperate to re-establish himself as a songwriter." Weller was quite willing to concede that he lost the plot during the late Eighties – perhaps too willing – or, as he put it, "my head was up my arse". Sensitive to criticism, the backlash which had tainted Weller's career during the second half of the Eighties had left its scars.

Within two weeks, *Wild Wood* had sold over 100,000 copies (which was already more than *Paul Weller* had achieved) and all but topped the charts. The album was nominated for the British Phonographic Industry's Brit Awards (as was Weller as 'Best Male Artist') and later made the short-list for the recently-inaugurated Mercury Music Prize. *Wild Wood* was then given a second lease of life in March 1994 (in fact, it returned to the Top 5), when re-promoted with the addition of Paul's new single, 'Hung Up'. Recorded in just three days, this slow, plaintive song crystallised Weller's new-found popularity with his first Top 10 hit for seven years. Spoilt only by a slightly stodgy production, 'Hung Up' attracted comparisons with The Beatles' 'Let It Be' and featured backing vocals from Ocean Colour Scene's Simon Fowler. The naked emotion of Weller's vocal perfectly suited the forlorn, angst-ridden lyrics: "Hidden in the back seat of my head/Some place I can't remember where/I found it just by coincidence/And now I'm all hung up again." The single also featured a yearning acoustic ballad, 'The Loved' (originally titled 'Love Of The Loved', after an early Paul McCartney song), laced with some beautiful flute, which Paul had earlier donated to a flexidisc distributed with the weekly newspaper for the homeless, *The Big Issue*.

★   ★   ★

Between October 1993 and December 1994, Paul Weller was barely off the road, touring around the world. With a new line-up featuring guitarist Steve Cradock, pianist Helen Turner and bassist Yolanda Charles (who had played with Acid Jazz act Raw Stylus and Talkin' Loud's Urban Species as well as the house band on *The Jonathan Ross Show*) – which held steady for over a year – the band played an unpublicised gig at London's Kings College, which was notable for a set which included an exclusive acoustic/harmonica cover of blues artist Taj Mahal's 'Korena'. The show acted as a warm-up before the entourage jetted off to Japan in October, only to return for more UK and mainland European dates, ending 1993 with a couple of isolated concerts in America.

Another tour of Britain was then organised to coincide with 'Hung Up' in

February/March, which also included Paul's first concerts in Ireland for many years — The Jam had never played Northern Ireland because of the possible backlash against their initial use of Union Jack flags as stage props. His growing friendship with Ocean Colour Scene was reflected when he guested with the band at London's Kings Cross Splash Club, playing Erma Franklin's soul classic, 'Piece Of My Heart', which had been revived a year earlier for a Jeans commercial. Ocean Colour Scene's Simon Fowler returned the favour, by taking the microphone while Paul played piano when the song was performed on his British tour.

A circuit around the continent followed in April and then it was off to play a month-long tour the length and breadth of North America in May. A series of German 25,000-seater open-air gigs supporting Herbert Groenmeyer took up most of June. Weller then returned to England to headline two festivals, Glastonbury (which Weller described as "soaring to a fantastic peak") and Phoenix. It was back to Japan again in October and a full itinerary around Britain and Europe kept him busy until the end of 1994, with a set which occasionally featured covers of The Vandellas' 'Heatwave' (an echo of Paul's days with The Jam) as an encore, and a version of Ray Charles' 'What I'd Give', with Paul at the piano and Dave Liddle on bass.

The tour culminated with three sell-out nights at the Royal Albert Hall, which had an aura of the special occasion about them — the auditorium echoed with nervous chatter beforehand and the audience was littered with celebrities. Support slots from Simon Fowler (a solo acoustic set memorable for a crowd-lifting rendition of Oasis' 'Live Forever') and up-and-coming rock band Reef were followed by sets from Weller and assorted guests, including ex-Suede guitarist Bernard Butler on 'Ohio'. The dates also allowed Paul to introduce several new songs — 'Whirlpool's End', 'The Changingman', 'You Do Something To Me' and 'Time Passes'.

On December 3, Weller played a memorial concert at London's Shepherds Bush Empire for Joe Awome, who had worked with Paul since his days as a bouncer at Michael's in the mid-Seventies. Quite apart from acting as a fitting tribute to the late road crew regular, the set that night was memorable for a rousing performance of the Small Faces/P.P. Arnold song, '(If You Think) You're Groovy', with Simon Fowler on vocals.

Weller hadn't committed himself to such an intensive touring schedule since the days of The Jam, but the reasons for his new-found enthusiasm were straightforward enough. His reluctance to embark on those initial tours of 1990 and 1991 stemmed from his lack of confidence, not only in himself and his new material but also in his audience — or lack of one. By 1993, he was on a roll, and comfortable with the songs on *Wild Wood* to the extent that he no longer wished to pay lip service to his past. In Weller's mind, *Wild Wood* was meant to be played live. "I've never known any performer who is so completely and totally happy when he's playing music," says Martin Hopewell, who has been Paul's live agent since the early days of The Jam. "I get the feeling that it doesn't matter if it's just playing the piano. I've never seen anybody as content on stage. From my side, what is annoying is that people view his career in terms of albums, and forget that the mainstay of Paul's career has been his live work, which has been prolific, all over the planet."

A common trend among established rock performers in the early Nineties was to record a concert as part of MTV's *Unplugged* series. After talk of Weller performing such a show towards the end of 1993, the idea fell through. Instead, he celebrated the success of taking *Wild Wood* on the road with a live album issued just over a year later. Borrowing the concept from *Live Rust*, Neil Young's companion volume to his *Rust Never Sleeps* LP, *Live Wood* was a self-explanatory document taped by the Manor Mobile studio during shows in London, Wolverhampton, Amsterdam and Brussels between December '93 and April '94 – although any number of shows might have sufficed.

The overwhelming impression of the LP – or, indeed, of witnessing Paul Weller in concert during this period – was that he wasn't just churning out his new hit album *ad nauseam*. 'Shadow Of The Sun' mutated into a ten-minute rock extravaganza, for example, which tried the patience of those fans reared on his three-minute pop songs, while 'This Is No Time' was extended to make room for some aggressive guitar work. Moments from Paul's record collection were tacked on the end of his songs: 'Remember How We Started' segued into the mid-Seventies fusion of Donald Byrd's late Seventies jazz-funk favourite, '(Falling Like) Dominoes', for example, while 'Bull-Rush' bled into a brief hard rock reading of The Who's 'Magic Bus'; and '(Can You Heal Us) Holy Man' led into Edwin Starr's 'War', harking back once again to his days with The Jam.

As the accompanying *Live Wood* video emphasised, Weller had forged a style of rock that he enjoyed playing on stage – but in a manner which he would have reviled for the best part of the Eighties. Sweating profusely, he interrupted songs with beefy guitar solos, and sang with a gruff, passionate tone which occasionally echoed rock greats like Joe Cocker. The enthusiasm for the *Wild Wood* concept was then taken a stage further with *More Wood (Little Splinters)*, but this compilation of B-sides and other oddities was made available only in Japan.

1994 was a year of consolidation for Weller. Although there was a dearth of new releases, *Wild Wood* was scarcely away from the charts and Paul was just as prominent in the gossip columns of the music press, as he was spotted at numerous press launches, gigs and parties. All this hobnobbing reflected Weller's contentment – at various times in his adult life, Paul had become quite reclusive but that seemed to be in the past. He was also happy to lend a hand when he was called upon to play on friends' records. His guitar playing could be heard on ex-Young Disciples singer Carleen Anderson's cover of the Van Morrison song, 'Who Was That Masked Man', which surfaced on her 'Mama Said' single that year. Weller also played sitar for the first time in his career on a psychedelic dance track, 'Mathar' – a cover of an obscurity by a late Sixties Euro jazz act The Dave Pike Set. Popular in the clubs, the single was credited to Indian Vibes, a pseudonym for Weller, Marco Nelson, Galliano's Crispin Taylor and producer Brendan Lynch and actually charted in France.

Paul also guested on long-time friend Dr. Robert's début solo LP, *Realms Of Gold*, playing guitar on the eventual single, 'Coming Of Grace' and piano on 'Sanctuary' and another song chosen as a single, 'Circular Quay', together with two other tracks. Like Paul's solo recordings, the LP featured a crowd of musicians which dated back to the last days of The Style Council – and both Mick Talbot and Marco Nelson also helped out. When a suitable offer in Britain wasn't forthcoming, Robert had secured a deal with Weller's Japanese label, Pony Canyon, where *Realms Of Gold* was issued in November 1994, together with Dee C. Lee's new album, *Things Will Be Sweeter*. In return, Robert replaced Yolanda Charles on bass during Weller's tour in late 1994, with a set which included 'Circular Quay'.

Live Wood coincided with the release of a new single, 'Out Of The Sinking'. Aired as 'The Sinking' earlier in the year, both in concert and during one of Paul's many acoustic radio sessions, this chunky rock song was firmly rooted in the early Seventies, but interrupted by a power chord crescendo which echoed prime time Steve Marriott. "I wanted to write a great English Mod love song," Paul explained. "How did I feel when I wrote this? Frightened, insecure, crazy but powerful. The middle section is pure Small Faces and proud." The single was backed by another Beatles cover, a faithful run through 'Sexy Sadie', featuring Ocean Colour Scene's bassist Damon Minchella. While this was reflected by various Beatles references on the single's back cover, the cover photo shoot and promo video (with Paul in a fur coat posing outdoors next to guitar amps) borrowed an idea from an old Small Faces clip.

As the year ended, Paul Weller was very definitely the critics' choice. Having won the Ivor Novello award for a 'Lifetime Achievement In Songwriting', a trophy for UK performers which is judged by other songwriters, Weller picked up the music industry's Brit Award for 'Best British Male Artist' for 1994, and was voted 'Best Solo Artist' in both *NME*'s alternative ceremony, the Brats, and the paper's readers' poll. While the impact of Weller's past spread as far as the Edinburgh Fringe Festival, with a play entitled *The Jam Show* based around the characters of Paul, Bruce and Rick, *NME* pledged their final seal of approval of Weller's renaissance by placing an exclusive single on the cover of a September edition of the paper. The lengthy live recording of 'Shadow Of The Sun' from *Live Wood* was joined by Brendan Lynch's remake of 'Sunflower' and 'Wild Wood (Sheared Wood)', a remix by fellow Go! Discs act and the rising stars of Bristol's so-called trip-hop scene, Portishead. That same month, Weller performed

246

live on the BBC's long-running arts programme, *The Late Show*, as one of the nominees for the Mercury Music Prize award for the year's most outstanding album. But perhaps the most telling signal that Weller himself was comfortable with his rejuvenation came with the release in late 1994 of a documentary spanning his whole career. *Highlights And Hang-Ups* didn't pretend to be a dispassionate overview of Weller's musical life: this was an official in-house project narrated by Paolo Hewitt and featuring interviews with Mick Talbot, his wife Dee C. Lee, Billy Bragg, John Weller and Gary Crowley. The project had been in the pipeline for a couple of years; back in 1992, Go! Discs had circulated two promotional half-hour films – one featuring in-concert footage, the other based around a straight interview – which had helped publicise his comeback. Directed by Pedro Romhanyi, who had worked both on *Live Wood* and on several of Paul's videos for his singles, *Highlights And Hang-Ups* was premièred at the National Film Theatre on London's South Bank, on the opening night of *NME*'s series of rock films, *Punk Before And Beyond*, which ran through August.

Paul's choice of archive clips from The Kinks, The Who and The Small Faces showed that his tastes hadn't changed a great deal over the years. This reinforced the overriding impression of the documentary itself – that Weller was still the intense, shy, motivated, headstrong, arrogant individual who had become a pop star on the brink of his nineteenth birthday. "I don't think I've ever played the game," he declared, "going along with what the company wants me to do, or what my audience wants me to do." As the film ended, Paul was asked what he saw, looking back over his life. "Someone who has been able to fulfil a dream in life, which is pretty unique," he admitted. "All those crazy notions I had when I was a kid, about being in a band, let alone making a record – let alone making it, and a lot of people liking what you do. And it all happened." And this was before Paul Weller issued the most successful album of his career.

14

INTO TOMORROW

"Well I talk a lot of shit a lot of the time and people should remember that."

(Paul Weller, NME, 1995)

"Look at Neil Young and Van Morrison – the thing I really admire about them is they've just kept slogging through it. It's taken people years to catch up with them and realise they're really worth something. If it takes that long, well, I can wait."

(Paul Weller, NME, 1993)

Between 1992 and 1994, the music scene had witnessed a tide change in popular opinion. At first, Weller had been roundly dismissed by the critics, but after *Wild Wood*, he was hailed as a warrior returning from the wilderness. Early Nineties indie rock had been shaped by the invasion of American grunge bands, but a backlash against the 'Seattle sound' was already underway by 1993. The arrival of Suede, a camp and very British guitar band who drew heavily on the androgynous glam rock of David Bowie, had catalysed a mood swing within the indie scene. This paved the way for the reincarnation of Blur, survivors from Nineties Manchester-led indie explosion. Their *Modern Life Is Rubbish* album, heavily praised by Paul Weller among others, was followed by 1994's *Parklife*, an LP which defined what was tagged as the 'Britpop' sound – a cheeky amalgam of late Seventies new wave and the mid-Sixties beat of The Kinks, The Small Faces and The Who. Since this might also roughly define the Mod sound as viewed through the eyes of The Jam, Paul Weller was predictably heralded as the 'Modfather' of the scene – a term coined by the music press – just as Neil Young had been lauded as an inspiration for grunge.

As part of their fixation with British culture, Blur flirted with Mod imagery, and singer Damon Albarn was heavily influenced by The Kinks' Ray Davies – whose best songs had acted as microcosms of English life. If it all sounded like The Jam, then it was no coincidence that the music press trumpeted the arrival of another Mod Revival. Unlike the scenario of the late Seventies, there was no real grass roots return to the youth cult, but there was definitely a sea change in people's tastes towards Mod-friendly fashion and Sixties-influenced acts. Mod was no longer a dirty word. Blur had been inspired by The Stone Roses early in their career, but a new band had now arrived as heirs to the Manchester throne. Oasis' first single arrived in April 1994; by September, their début LP was at No. 1 and their lead guitarist and songwriter Noel Gallagher was a pop star. When asked about his influences, Gallagher cited Paul Weller as one of his heroes – and by the end of 1994, the two musicians had struck up a friendship. On December 15, Paul and Noel joined Primal Scream (who shared Oasis' record label, Creation) on stage at the Shepherds Bush Empire for a cover of The Who's 'So Sad About Us'. Weller issued his first single in '77, Primal Scream in '85, Oasis in '94 – but they all seemed to share a love of rock's past achievements which bridged any generation gap.

Weller saw Britpop for what it was – a media invention. While he recognised the renewed vitality within up-and-coming UK guitar bands, which had led to the tag in the first place, Paul was also keen to distance himself from any perceived scene. "I don't think my records are part of the Blur and Oasis thing," Paul declared to *NME* in late '95. "I don't think my success this year has been related to that at all. No-one's gonna buy my record just because Noel said it's good." Nevertheless, Weller sensed the mood swing back towards the kind of British guitar pop that he could relate to. "My favourite record of the year was probably 'Alright' by Supergrass. That was a great teenage pop record. And I really liked the sentiment of that Dodgy tune, 'Staying Out For The Summer' – really up."

Noel Gallagher was also invited to guest on Paul's new album. The sessions had begun the day after his Phoenix Festival appearance in July '94, which yielded the first batch of songs in just two weeks: 'Stanley Road', 'Out Of The Sinking', 'Time Passes . . .', 'Sexy Sadie', 'Whirlpools' End' and 'You Do Something To Me'. Weller then returned to the Manor early in the New Year to record the rest of the LP before the studio was closed for good early that summer. The sessions went well, as Steve White recalled: "That was put together with much more roadwork under our belt. We'd played a lot of the tunes on the tour and we'd gotten the tunes to a higher standard of confidence. So the whole recording time was very short."

For the first three months of 1995, the Weller camp was silent – aside from a mysterious white label 12″ distributed to DJs. 'Lynch Mob Beats' was another of Brendan Lynch's off-the-wall experiments in mixing funk and psychedelia, looping drum beats and a guitar riff from the bare bones of one of Paul's songs – although, in this instance, it wasn't clear what that song was. Later, it was established that 'Lynch Mob Beats' was based loosely on one of the forthcoming LP tracks, 'Whirlpools' End'. Extracts appeared on Weller's next LP (at the end of side one) and the track was eventually chosen as a B-side as 'Steam'. But that promo only gave away one clue as to what was on the horizon: scratched in the run-off groove was a message, 'The Changingman'.

By mid-April, 'The Changingman' had been announced as Weller's next EP, and he performed the song on the Channel 4 music show, *The White Room*. On the same programme, Weller duetted with Noel Gallagher – Paul played piano while the Oasis guitarist nervously strummed along, singing 'Talk Tonight'. For Gallagher, the partnership was the latest of his dreams to come true – Oasis were rewarded that month with their first No. 1 single, 'Some Might Say'. This mutual admiration society worked both ways, though: Weller was seen to be friendly with a group which would be the most popular in Britain before the year was out. And the links between the artists were strengthened when Oasis replaced their drummer with Steve White's younger brother, Alan.

There was no mistaking the autobiographical element of 'The Changingman', which followed a week after the show. The lyrics reiterated his continued attempt to reach some mystical, elusive goal: "What I can't be today, I can be tomorrow". But this restlessness was also matched by the sense of confusion – what Weller called the large expanse of grey in between the black and white world of his youth – with lines like "And the more I see, the more I know/The more I know, the less I understand." Applied to music, that meant his desire to write songs which, in his opinion, might achieve the same greatness as the Sixties rock classics he tried to emulate – music, to his mind, with some palpable meaning. 'The Changingman' came close, although it borrowed its subtle, descending guitar intro from ELO's '10538 Overture' – or that song's inspiration, The Beatles' 'Dear Prudence'.

Paul claimed that the single's title came from hearing his daughter Leah talking about one of her dolls – although it was an uncanny coincidence that Weller's friend Terry Rawlings managed a band of the same name. Regardless of its inspiration, though, 'The Changingman' was a powerful rock record and its faint psychedelic edge managed to invoke the spirit of late Sixties within a modern context. Less impressive was a stodgy cover of Etta James' R&B classic, 'I'd Rather Go Blind', which also featured on the EP. Weller's rendition owed more to Rod Stewart's early Seventies version, and traces of The Faces' barroom atmosphere could also be heard on Paul's acoustic folk-blues tune, 'It's A New Day'.

'The Changingman' was a solid Top 10 hit but its success paled compared with that of Weller's new album. *Stanley Road* entered the charts at No. 1 in May and stayed in the Top 30, by and large, for over a year. Aside from compilations, it was his first LP to be awarded platinum status (for reaching 300,000 sales) and by mid-1996, *Stanley Road* had sold over a million copies and had been nominated for the fourth annual Mercury Music Prize – a remarkable achievement for a record which took barely two months to record. In fact, Go! Discs maintained their promotion drive for over a year. Full-colour ads were placed in over fifteen major publications, over 10,000 posters were plastered across the nation's billboards and the 35,000 postcards distributed via Paul's mailing list were joined by a further 20,000 circulated around London and various record shop advertising displays.

Paul hadn't been so outwardly confident about one of his records since *Our Favourite Shop*. "I would hope that this LP represents a significant change in me and my music," he wrote in Paolo Hewitt's *Days Lose Their Names And Time Slips Away*. "I've reached the bottom at times whilst also soaring to fantastic peaks (Glastonbury '94) and they both seem like scales out of control. I've tried to put some of those feelings into these songs." The album featured a familiar array of musicians, Paul again playing most of the keyboards and guitars and drawing on others where necessary. Dr. Robert, Marco Nelson and Yolanda Charles alternated on bass, and Mick Talbot and Helen Turner had both popped in to play keyboards on a few songs. Now a mainstay of Paul's touring band, Steve Cradock played and sang on several tracks and producer Brendan Lynch and guitar technician Dave Liddle both lent the odd touch here and there – and behind it all was Steve White on drums.

The opening track, 'Porcelain Gods', meandered along in a manner which might well be described as progressive rock, while its brittle melody matched the vulnerability of Paul's lyrics, which questioned the nature of fame. "And how disappointed I am/To find me part of no plan," he sang with a sense of anguish in his voice, "Just a porcelain God, that shatters when it falls." Weller had fallen once but, as the song continued, "I shake it off and start again". And lines like, "Most who see me, see me not for real" and "I hate too what you hate in me" dealt with the complexities of idolatry – from the idol's point of view.

'Porcelain Gods' merged into a raucous, dynamic performance of Dr. John's 'I Walk On Gilded Splinters' – though Paul probably heard the song courtesy either of Marsha Hunt, Steve Marriott (in Humble Pie) or Johnny Jenkins. Noel Gallagher's acoustic guitar contribution was lost in this claustrophobic brew of funky drums, overdriven guitars and Paul's straining-at-the-leash vocals. These songs dominated side one, creating an overriding impression that Weller was rocking out. In fact, the album's ratio between loud, extrovert material and quieter, introspective ballads was roughly the same as previous efforts. One of the oldest songs on the album, the beautiful 'Time Passes . . .', was a mournful tale of lost love perfectly communicated by the heartfelt emotion of Weller's voice.

The final song was linked to a painting on the cover. "On 'Wings Of Speed', I tried to describe the feelings I get from 'The Lady Of Shallot' by John Waterhouse," Weller revealed, "which hangs in a bad spot in the Tate Gallery. I'm not an art buff – I like what I like, etc. – but the lady in the painting looks real." The tune was a graceful attempt at a gospel ballad, although the combination of piano and Carleen Anderson's choral falsetto sounded grandiose. This criticism might also be made of 'You Do Something To Me'. Chosen as the album's second single, this yearning lullaby sounded too earnest, which spoilt what was otherwise an attractive melody. Less ambitious was the sublime 'Broken Stones', a softly-spoken tune which combined an endearing Al Green flavour with a neat lyrical metaphor – people are like "pebbles on a beach, kicked around, all trying to get home". Along similar soulful lines was 'Pink On White Walls', a jolly, swinging R&B affair with music to match its philosophical lyrics.

The title track was the album's central song both physically and conceptually. 'Stanley Road' strutted along, led by Weller's strident piano riff lifted from Van Morrison's 'Moondance'. The lyrics fitted more comfortably into the album as a whole – a nostalgic vision of the street in which Paul spent his childhood. "A hazy mist hung down the street/The length of it's mile/As far as my eye could see/The sky so wide, the houses tall/Or so they seemed to be/So they seemed to me so small": Stanley Road was only a couple of hundred yards but that's long enough when you're still in short trousers, hearing the "rolling stock" on the nearby railway.

Many of the songs had a rougher edge than those on Paul's first two LPs, whose grace and lightness of touch was swapped for a live, very real sound which matched the sweating, earnest, gyrating, intense figure of his live shows. 'Woodcutter's Son', for example, was a gruff rhythm and blues effort – a mid-Nineties take on Bo Diddley via *Exile On Main Street*-era Rolling Stones. When Weller sang, "I'm cutting down the wood for the good of everyone!", it sounded like a response to criticism that he had milked the *Wild Wood* album. And the driving intensity and psychedelic vibe of the lengthy 'Whirlpools' End' hardened up the feel of 'Shadow Of The Sun'. When asked by *NME* in 1993 who he would most like to work with, the first name Paul thought of was Stevie Winwood. Two years later, the ex-Traffic star played keyboards on 'Woodcutter's Son' and piano on 'Pink On White Walls'.

Paul also admired Ronnie Wood, rhythm guitarist with the Rolling Stones, who very nearly played on the album. "We all went for a drink when the Faces reformed to play at the Brit Awards," says Terry Rawlings. "Ian McLagan's there, Ronnie Wood, Bill Wyman, Rod Stewart – they wanted to rehearse at Nomis Studios but couldn't get in and ended up at John Henry's instead. I said, 'Weller's got the big room' so Ronnie says, 'That's why!' Paul wanted Ronnie to play on *Stanley Road* and asked me if I could mention the idea to him. And Ronnie would have done, sure, if he could have got round to it. I said to Ronnie that night, 'Can you ring him up?' Anyway, they carry on drinking. I was staggering along with them, and eventually, Ronnie rang Weller up from a pub in Richmond and said, 'come down, come down!' But Paul was sober, obviously, and everyone else was slaughtered. He said afterwards, 'I couldn't face going down. They were already pissed.' He's terribly shy. He should have pursued the idea, though: that would have been brilliant! Paul Weller is this century's Ronnie Wood!"

After dismissing the idea of posing in an *Abbey Road*-style photo on a zebra crossing, Weller retained The Beatles theme – itself, a nod towards his early teens – by commissioning the work of one of Britain's leading artists, Peter Blake, designer of rock's most famous record cover, *Sgt. Pepper*. Blake created a colourful mosaic of images relevant to Paul's past and present, which harked back both to the sleeve of Sgt. Pepper, and the objets d'art assembled on the cover of *Our Favourite Shop*. Interspersed among the pop-art symbols were allusions to Weller's music heroes (John Lennon, Aretha Franklin, The Small Faces, Stax), fashion (a Mod astride a scooter, The Small Faces), other interests (London, poetry, momentos of trips abroad) and, most important of all, his childhood (old holiday snaps with his parents, George Best, a local Green Line bus and, in the centre, a sign for Stanley Road behind a painting of Paul as a small boy holding a photo of him in 1995).

The theme implied that Weller's life had come full circle. When he was a teenager struggling to break out of Woking, the Surrey backwater was the last place he had wanted to be. The Jam's aggressive edge mirrored Weller's fascination with urban (London) life and he took the first available opportunity to leave home for the capital. Throughout the Eighties, first with The Jam and then The Style Council, Paul was seen to strive onwards and upwards – to varying degrees of success. But there was rarely any hint of harking back to his Woking roots.

Several factors contributed to his change of mood. Firstly, there was nothing like spending time with his children to rekindle memories of his own upbringing. Secondly, Paul's career had followed a cycle back to square one after the demise of The Style Council, and compared with packed houses at Wembley Arena or the Albert Hall, those early solo tours must have reminded him of the years spent playing half-empty dives around Woking. But he would also have been reminded of his past out of circumstance. Prior to recording at the Manor, Paul would often practise at the Black Barn Studio in Ripley, on the outskirts of Woking. And his parents owned a house just outside the town, in addition to their home down in Selsey Bill on the south coast, a legacy from their days holidaying there back in the Seventies. Around the time of writing *Stanley Road*, Paul moved out of the place he had bought with Dee near Holland Park, West London, and into a house next door to his mum and dad. It might have seemed like an odd decision for a man in his mid-thirties – but then his marriage had just fallen apart.

Paul has always kept his private life quite separate from his public persona, but one thing seems clear. Music is the one factor which binds Weller the pop star with Weller the individual and this is where his priorities lay – seemingly at the expense of his relationships with other people. Music appears to be his *raison d'être*, and Weller's state of mind and his songwriting – and therefore, to an extent, his career – have always been interwoven. As a result, he doesn't appear to have been able to divorce his profession from his family life, and the fact that he had married someone who was also involved in music – who was in his band – must have complicated matters further. Whereas Mick Talbot left Galliano that year to spend more time with his family, Paul hadn't really involved himself with Dee's musical pursuits after her Slam Slam LP.

The one emotional bond which has sustained him through thick and thin has been with his parents, who took pride of place in the credits on *Stanley Road*. "I dedicate this record to my Mum and Dad, who've always been there for me and always encouraged me to follow this path," he wrote. "It's also for my wife Dee and our beautiful children." Suddenly, the idea of the boy next door doesn't seem so strange.

Despite the LP's runaway success, it elicited a cautious response from both Weller's fans and music critics. Some of Paul's most loyal admirers were unconvinced by the album's chugging, lumpen production, which occasionally muddied the songs. Whereas a certain zing emanated from *Paul Weller* and *Wild Wood* benefited from a lightness of touch, *Stanley Road* – it was said – suffered in places from a stodgy sound and Paul's thunderous vocal technique. The album duly fared poorly in the journalists' end-of-year summaries.

Despite these reservations, Weller's belief in the album was validated by its overwhelming success – and no-one was more pleased than the artist himself. "It's the best thing for me that I've ever done, the biggest personal achievement," he told *Boys About Town*. "But the fact that so many people liked it quite surprised me. It's quite amazing for me to hear an album which sounds that complete." On his thirty-seventh birthday in late May, he performed four of the songs for *Later With Jools Holland*. By the time the programme was broadcast, Weller was gearing up for another spate of touring that would last until the end of the year. Both Steve Cradock and Damon Minchella were now mainstays in his band, but decked out in Mod clobber and paired to one side of the stage, nodding sagely as Weller twisted and contorted at the other, the scenario did occasionally feel like Paul's fan club was both front-of-stage and on.

Speaking of which, Noel Gallagher joined Weller onstage during a warm-up gig at the 100 Club for 'Walk On Gilded Splinters' and a rendition of Tommy Tucker's old R&B classic, 'High Heeled Sneakers'. Paul returned the favour by playing on Oasis's second album, which met with astonishing success on its release in October. Weller played guitar and sang backing vocals on the album's lengthy finale, 'Champagne Supernova', and contributed to the LP's unnamed instrumental jams which were paired together as 'The Swamp Song' on their 'Wonderwall' single. Noel was often seen socialising not only with Paul but also his long-time cohort Paolo Hewitt, who not only wrote a Cappuccino Kid-style sleeve-note for the Oasis LP but ended up writing a biography about the band.

Two of the songs on Paul's next EP had been floating around for over two years. 'You Do Something To Me' had first been aired on the radio back in

1993, demoed at the Manor on New Year's Day 1994 with a view to being recorded as a possible single and recorded prior to 'Out Of The Sinking'. Paul had written three songs over that Christmas break while staying in Woking – 'Hung Up', 'Time Passes . . .' and a fragile ballad, 'A Year Late'. This last composition appeared on the new EP, together with a cover of an old Stax soul song culled from a recent radio session, William Bell's 'My Whole World Is Falling Down'. Promoted by a video of Weller and friends shot in the countryside around Woking, and his favoured round of festival appearances (such as Phoenix and T In The Park), 'You Do Something To Me' proved to be another sizeable hit.

★ ★ ★

Back in February, Weller had responded angrily to accusations in the tabloid press that he was dating Paul McCartney's twenty-five-year-old daughter Mary. "I'm not an item around town with Mary Mac," he wrote, "I just went to see the Primals with her and some friends." Nevertheless, the connection with the idol of his childhood proved useful after Paul was approached to contribute to a fund-raising album for Brian Eno's War Child charity, which had been founded to help alleviate the suffering of children in war-torn Bosnia. Co-ordinated by Weller's record label, Go! Discs, the *Help* album was recorded in just one day – September 4, 1995 – in different studios around the country by an array of Britain's leading performers, such as Blur, Oasis and Massive Attack. Although the package was anonymous (the different artists weren't credited with the individual contributions), the figurehead of the compilation was undoubtedly a supergroup collective disguised by the moniker of The Smokin' Mojo Filters.

The group's line-up was heralded as the meeting of three generations – Paul Weller, Paul McCartney (guitar, piano, backing vocals), and Noel Gallagher (guitar). Weller explained to *NME* how he roped in the ex-Beatle: "I wrote him a letter about doing the track a while ago and he's just come down and helped us out." The band assembled to record The Beatles' 'Come Together' in the very studio where the song was originally laid down, Abbey Road's famous Studio 2. "We've been jamming it in our soundchecks for ages," Weller added. "It's not meant as some specific comment on the situation." Nevertheless, it felt like a momentous occasion to all involved, a feeling expressed by Paolo Hewitt, who shot home video footage of the event, capturing the whole recording, together with visitors to the studio like supermodel Kate Moss and actor Johnny Depp. "It was unbelievable," Paolo enthused. "You've got this massive studio. McCartney was doing backing vocals downstairs with his headphones on and Paul was up in the control room saying to him, 'Could you do that again please?' This is a man who grew up on McCartney's music. Now he's asking him to re-do vocals – he's producing him!"

Their rendition was solid enough, but the musical worth of the group's performance wasn't the issue. Five days after the session, *Help* made history as the fastest album ever to reach the shops. Sales of some 71,000 copies on its first day of release would have ensured Go! Discs' claim that *Help* was the quickest No. 1 – if chart regulations hadn't excluded various artists LPs.

Early in December, 'Come Together' was issued as the lead song on an EP, alongside other contributions from The Beautiful South, Dodgy and Black Grape. Go! Discs probably left its release too late and the single was lost in the hectic pre-Christmas market, but the sentiment was sound enough. Weller may have lost his past dedication to playing benefit concerts and political rallies, disillusioned with the way in which his wider views interfered with people's appreciation of his music – but he was still willing to contribute to such an unequivocal project. "It's sort of once bitten, twice shy after the whole Red Wedge thing," he admitted. "And to be honest, that's why I'm hanging back a bit this time. We're doing the whole track in one day, which is hard going."

And that wasn't all. On October 28, Paul was one of several musicians who lent his name to a TUC demonstration in Manchester under the banner, Unite Against Racism. And in November 1996, Weller would donate his version of Traffic's 'Feelin' Alright' to the *Childline Charity* record, a PolyGram album designed to both celebrate the tenth anniversary of the organisation and to raise funds. If it all felt like a throwback to the mid-Eighties, then Weller's actions suggested that he still held strong personal convictions – he just chose not to air them as publicly as he had done in the past. A feeling of *déja vu* also surrounded the publication of *Days Lose Their Names And Time Slips Away*, a lavish book of Lawrence Watson photos charting Paul's solo career. Together with a free CD featuring *Stanley Road* demos, the paperback also boasted some previously unpublished examples of Weller's poetry (including the hilarious 'Lambretta Love Poem'), an idea which harked back to his past exploits with Riot Stories.

The last quarter of 1995 was taken up with more touring. Instead of his regular fixture at the Royal Albert Hall, Weller chose to play at the Brixton Academy – rumours suggested he wanted to curb what he viewed as the spreading smear of 'The New Clapton'. The set broke away from Paul's traditional live format by adding an acoustic intermission, where Ocean Colour Scene's Simon Fowler accompanied the band on stage for a run through older songs like The Style Council's 'Down In The Seine' and 'Headstart For Happiness'.

Noel Gallagher guested on 'Come Together' and took over Northern Uproar's support slot for a couple of the shows – and the Oasis guitarist was interviewed together with both Paul and Paolo Hewitt for a Granada TV documentary on The Small Faces as part of Channel 4's *Without Walls* series. *My Generation*, Hewitt's biography of the Sixties legends, had been published earlier in the year. Rumours also emerged that Paul had taped a version of 'I'm Only Dreaming' for a Small Faces tribute album to raise funds for the band's bassist and joint songwriter Ronnie Lane, who was laid up in America suffering from multiple sclerosis. The project was scheduled to appear on Acid Jazz but was delayed for many months. Eventually, Weller played with a Smokin' Mojo Filters-styled scratch band, the Kenney J. Allstars, along-side Small Faces drummer Kenney Jones, Marco Nelson and Mick Talbot. Under the watchful eye of Small Faces producer Glyn Johns, the foursome recorded the Hammond organ-driven instrumental, 'Almost Grown', for Nice Records' *Long Agos And Worlds Apart* LP.

★ ★ ★

In the midst of all his success, a ghost from Weller's past came back to haunt him. In September 1992, *The Sun* newspaper reported that Paul's ex-partners in The Jam were suing both him and his father over a shared bank account for £200,000 royalties, relating to video, merchandising and publishing royalties since the band's split. Buckler and Foxton claimed that a bank account containing a large amount of money was emptied without their knowledge. It was the culmination of a five-year squabble.

"Bruce and I realised around the mid-Eighties that there was a lot of Jam business going on – albums, videos – and nobody was representing our interests," explains Rick Buckler. "PPL money, which is for performing rights, was being paid direct to John Weller, and for eight years, he hadn't sent us our share. When we found out, we quite amicably went back to him and thought he'd be glad to chat to us – it was some old business that needed sorting out, a few grand but nothing to cause any great ruck. The first reaction was that John Weller and Paul immediately went further into their shells. We thought, well, hang on, what's the problem? PPL confirmed that the money went to John. It just seemed very weird. That started the ball rolling.

"Also, me and Bruce had written a third of 'Funeral Pyre', but we weren't getting any money from that either. There were various loose ends that needed sorting out, but we found it difficult, right from the word go. See, all the cheques were made out to The Jam and sent to John Weller. At first, we thought, maybe it was an oversight and he'd just forgotten or hadn't realised. Perhaps we better let him know what the situation is and he'll sort it out. We didn't get that reaction at all. What we got was, no, we're not talking to you, we don't want to know."

One of the few Jam assets which Buckler still possessed was an assortment of the band's early recordings, many of which were taped on reel-to-reel during their rehearsals at Michael's in the mid-Seventies. "I had an album's worth of old material that was done prior to Polydor, which I thought would be a good idea to put out," Rick continues. "I tried various ways and it was blocked every time. Paul said the quality wasn't good enough – but that seems neither here nor there, considering its source. And then John said that the partnership was still in force, therefore them being two partners would stop me from releasing it. You see, all four of us, including John Weller, were even partners in The Jam business. And then John was saying the partnership was not in force, so there was no consistency. But it was part of our business interests and we wanted to get rid of these Jam assets that were still hanging around.

"Bruce approached me and said it would be a good idea if we were represented from The Jam's business point of view. We found there was also money owing to us from PolyGram, because it had been neglected. Nobody knew where the money had gone or who it was sent to. So, at first, it was just a matter of how to find and retrieve it. When you're doing business, you don't want the personal side mixed into it. This was the advantage of having someone representing us."

According to Rick, the pair came up against a brick wall. "We were bemused at first as to why we weren't getting a favourable reaction in trying to set up meetings," adds Buckler. "We had a couple of meetings with John Weller but they weren't very fruitful, which aroused our suspicions – why would they suddenly get cagey? Then they refused to even talk about it. In a way, it was a joke, because PolyGram said they'd paid money over, we know we hadn't received it – and John just clammed up. He wouldn't give an explanation and they kept changing their story."

In March 1993, both the *Daily Mirror* and the weekly music press claimed that The Jam were to reform, with headlines like "Jamming again". It was suggested that there would be four 'secret' reunion gigs in America, but the source of these rumours were thought to be a ruse on the part of Foxton and Buckler's management to embarrass Weller. Needless to say, Paul wasn't interested in the proposition – in an age where many of his contemporaries, such as The Buzzcocks and more recently The Sex Pistols, have opted for nostalgia, Weller is one of the few musicians who has continued to move forward. Asked in 1991 if he was a traitor to the punk spirit, his reply was typically brusque: "Bollocks – go and ask all the reformers. It's a joke."

"We threatened court action but then they dug their heels in," Rick continues. "I think they were making it financially difficult for us to pursue this claim so that we'd drop it. But because they'd played that card, they played it all the way to the end. It not only made it expensive for us, it was for them as well – which was silly because the initial sums we were after didn't even get near the legal costs. The only thing we heard from Paul was favourable. After setting a date in the high court, he didn't want to appear but eventually gave a statement. In there, he said something along the lines of, 'if we owe the boys money, we'll pay them'. We suspected all along that Paul didn't really know the facts and figures. In an interview, Paul said quite confidently that it had been kicked out of court – when it hadn't. We thought he was being fed misinformation."

The animosity between the two camps was exacerbated by the publication in January 1994 of *The Jam – Our Story*. Buried within this light-hearted account of the band's progress from Woking to Wembley was an underlying animosity between 'the other two' and the Wellers. The book's last sentence said it all: "There were actually three people in The Jam," commented Bruce. "And two weren't Paul Weller." Bad blood also seemed to surround a story that Paul would donate around £20,000 to save the Horsell Common Muslim Cemetery in the woods on the edge of Woking, "where I played as a child" – Weller had chosen the site as one of his favourite aspects of Woking in a questionnaire in *NME* and it featured in one of his promo videos. A few months later, Buckler was featured in the *Woking News And Mail* saying that, since Paul's contribution had never arrived, he would sell some of his personal Jam memorabilia to help with the proceeds.

"At that moment when the band split up, we trusted John," Rick concludes. "We'd been with him right from the beginning and it was inconceivable that there would be any scurrilous activity. So, quite naïvely, we thought we'd done OK out of The Jam – we weren't ripped off. This is why, when we got back in touch with John, we didn't think it would be a problem and we'd sort this thing out. And then that would be that and we'd all get on with our own lives again – but it didn't turn out to be!"

Certainly, there appears to be no love lost between the Wellers and The Jam's ex-rhythm section. In an interview in 1995, Weller was asked if he felt he was on the same wavelength as the other two: "Not at all. I didn't talk much about music with them, didn't go out and buy records together. I didn't really like them that much, anyway." This bad feeling reached its zenith with a widely-publicised and protracted court case between Paul and John Weller and Foxton and Buckler, which was eventually settled on February 28, 1996. The Jam's rhythm section had been seeking more than £100,000 in royalties, merchandising rights and group assets. The petty details of the case were trivial and irrelevant. Those on both sides of the fence swamped any attempts to sift through the quagmire of litigation with sour memories and pure hearsay, throwing up as many contradictions about the case as facts. But the salient point about the whole unfortunate affair was that both sides admitted, at least privately, that the dispute should never have reached the courts.

★ ★ ★

A far more worrying bombshell arrived in late 1995, when Paul's father fell ill and spent some time in hospital, recovering from a triple heart bypass operation. The whole Weller roadshow ground to a rapid halt, as dates were cancelled and other arrangements frozen until John was well again. A long-standing dispute with Paul's younger sister Nikki aside (they didn't speak for four years or so after they tried to oust Paul's minder Kenny Wheeler), the bond within Paul's family had grown tighter throughout his solo career and the impact of his dad's continued guidance can't be underestimated.

One of those who has witnessed the relationship since the early days of

The Jam is Paul's booking agent, Martin Hopewell. "They've become so ingrained in my entire life for as long as I can remember," he says. "John is a genuinely extraordinary character. If this business didn't have him, it would be so much the poorer and less colourful for it. He's completely and totally one hundred per cent devoted to Paul's career – and always has been."

John Weller has earned the respect of the music industry for his no-frills approach. "He's focused on getting the very best for Paul at all times," Martin explains, "and if anybody – me included – appears to be slipping up on that, my God you're in trouble. He's a serious ringmaster for the whole circus that surrounds Paul but he's also, for all of that, one of the nicest people. Anybody who can be at the steering wheel of a career like Paul's, and see him do it three times internationally, has got to be doing something very much right. That's never been done by anybody before and John never claims to be a trained manager. He hasn't changed at all, not one jot, not even to look at. He still has the same bloody jacket, the same bag – the same John.

"Paul's a lovely blend between his dad and his mum – Ann's equally important, a great influence. You can be in worse trouble with her, quietly in the background, than you can be with John. But she's a lovely lady. She speaks her mind, which is where a lot of Paul's bluntness comes from. And John is not exactly known for his feats of diplomacy either. Straight-talking people. No mincing around. Paul, when he first started out, was a kinda gauche, quiet sort of chap. What happened is that he matured into this person who has every right to behave like a complete arsehole popstar – if anyone ever did have – and yet has managed to remain a real human being, not at all stuck-up, with his feet firmly planted on the ground."

The most enduring relationship in Paul's life, then, has been the bond between himself and his mother and father, and he has felt comfortable within the extended family framework around him which is dominated by men of his dad's age. This generation gap has also existed within his band, where he has been happy to play with musicians who were scarcely old enough to remember The Jam. But few of his musician friends are his contemporaries – the one exception being Dr. Robert, who has followed a parallel musical path to Weller since the mid-Eighties.

After all the activity which surrounded *Stanley Road*, Paul Weller kept a low profile during the early months of 1996. His current standing as one of Britain's leading performers was recognised both by the Brits (he retained the award for 'Best Male Solo Artist') and *NME*'s corresponding Brat Award. For the second year running, Paul didn't collect his award at the Brits' ceremony, opting instead for a curt, pre-recorded acceptance speech. Excuses were made for his shyness – and his father graciously accepted the prize – but Weller spoke harshly of the event in a letter to *Boys About Town*. Dismissing tabloid jibes, he wrote, " 'millionaire pop-star' is just the Establishment's way of trying to belittle people or put them in their place (the class war's still real). The Brits is a silly fucking circus – the Establishment's Entertainment wing."

Twenty years in the music business evidently hadn't softened Paul's view of the industry.

To tie in with the Brits award, BBC2's *Later With Jools Holland* gave over a whole episode to Paul, together with his usual array of musicians, plus veteran reggae trombonist Rico Rodriguez (who'd played on The Jam's *Setting Sons* album) and Mercury-nominated trumpeter Guy Walker. Broadcast twice across a late February weekend, this was the first time that the long-running music show had been devoted to one artist. During the performance, Weller looked tired – and although he breathed new life into the oldest songs of the programme, The Jam's 'Tales From The Riverbank' (with altered lyrics) and The Style Council's 'Down In The Seine', the strain of five years' constant recording and touring was beginning to show.

Go! Discs responded to Weller's trophies with their own tribute – a limited reissue available for one week only of 'Out Of The Sinking' (the album version with vocal overdubs from Carleen Anderson). Together with a couple of songs taken from radio sessions, the single sported a cover of Bob Dylan's classic, 'I Shall Be Released', which was taken from the forthcoming British film, *Hollow Reed*. The fact that the movie starred Ian Hart, the actor who had twice played John Lennon, hadn't gone unnoticed by Paul.

The success of both *Stanley Road* and Oasis' *(What's The Story) Morning Glory* laid the foundations for the return of a more traditional rock sound based around solid playing, strong tunes and an air of craftsmanship. Weller called it "an older sound, what I'd call a real sound, not poxy drum machines!" In Oasis' case, there was barely a whiff of the punk energy which had infused both their début LP and the whole Britpop phenomenon. The first benefactors of this mood swing within the music scene were Ocean Colour Scene, who relaunched their career to great effect in February 1996 with 'The Riverboat Song', a driving riff rock song on which Steve Cradock's guitar duelled with Weller's organ playing. Both the single and the ensuing *Moseley Shoals* album were produced by Brendan Lynch, and echoed the early Seventies rock of Free or Thin Lizzy, but with a Mod-ish mid-Nineties twist. Paul also played on *Moseley Shoals* – guitar on 'The Circle' (later chosen as a single) and piano and backing vocals on 'One For The Road'. When Ocean Colour Scene performed on *Later With Jools Holland* in late May, Paul sat in on keyboards. He also popped up as a guest when the band played at the HMV megastore in London's Oxford Street to launch *Moseley Shoals* in April. Paul shared much in common with the band – both musically and socially – but the extent of his patronage was surprising. He definitely seemed to enjoy taking part in the band's remarkable success, but in a peripheral role away from the limelight. It may have just been a show of mutual support, returning the favour for the band's crucial role within both his touring band and his records. Neil Young has Crazy Horse; Paul Weller has Ocean Colour Scene.

To some critics, Paul's association with OCS, Noel Gallagher and a host of other like-minded musicians felt too cosy. As *Moseley Shoals'* tenancy in the Top 10 spread across the summer of 1996, selling over a million copies, the music press ran articles with headlines like 'Dadrock' and 'Noelrock'. There *was* no scene, of course; just a clutch of artists who shared a common sense of musical heritage, but it culminated in a spoof feature in *Select* about a supposed supergroup:

"Seemingly, Paul has an album out in May under the title of the Yer Blues Band, which features him working with Noel Gallagher, Steve White, Ocean Colour Scene, Bobby Gillespie, Denise Johnson (Primal Scream), Liam Tyson (Cast), Martin Blunt (The Charlatans), Andy Bell (Ride), Richard Ashcroft (The Verve) and seemingly even Paul McCartney. The album's title is *The Smokestack Sessions* and will be out on Creation." This skit on the Smokin' Mojo Filters had many people fooled; Creation were inundated with phone calls, after the piece reported that just twelve cassettes of the album were in existence. It seemed that Paul's very public affirmation of his wish to play 'Maximum R&B' (a reference to that old Who slogan) didn't necessarily meet with the approval of some journalists . . .

★ ★ ★

On June 9, 1996, Paul Weller played the most spectacular concert of his career. Bearing in mind his declaration that "I wouldn't do places like Wembley again, I hated it when we did it as The Style Council," the only choice was to organise an outdoor show. So, in front of some 35,000 cheering fans in North London's Finsbury Park – his largest-ever UK audience aside from appearances at festivals – he played with an enthusiasm and vitality which belied the fact that he had just passed his thirty-eighth birthday. "It's nice doing the festivals," says Dave Liddle. "I mean, if you offered Paul a million quid to play Wembley Arena, he'd probably say no. But stick him in Finsbury Park in front of people in the open air and he hasn't got the weight on his back. He likes headlining, don't get me wrong, but I think also he likes supporting because he can walk on stage, he isn't the main act and he has a good time."

The event was tagged a 'Lazy Sunday Afternoon With Paul Weller', another allusion to Paul's obsession with The Small Faces, with a line-up of assorted friends and like-minded acts, from The Bluetones and Reef to Dr. Robert. Although Paul seemed daunted by such an enormous crowd – his between-song banter was brief, even by his standards – the event was a definite success. P.P. Arnold and Simon Fowler joined the band towards the end for a version of '(If You Think) You're Groovy' and the show climaxed when Primal Scream's Bobby Gillespie came on to perform the Scream's 'Movin' On Up'. No lesser publication than *The Guardian's* Saturday supplement, *The Guide*, celebrated the occasion by giving away a free CD with the headline, "Splendour In The Grass".

Over the past few years, Paul had told his record label on several occasions that he wanted to take time off. After the runaway success of *Wild Wood*, he took a breather – only to then decide that he wanted to "record some new songs I've just written", which led to 'Out Of The Sinking' and the first sessions for *Stanley Road*. Once that album and subsequent tours were out of the way, Weller decided to keep relatively quiet during 1996. For the most part, he stuck to his pledge – a new album wasn't scheduled until 1997 – but Paul kept cropping up, either with friends like Ocean Colour Scene or in his own right.

In July, for example, he reunited with one of his oldest friends, Steve Brookes, at a Woking pub where Dave Liddle's band Blues Express were playing, Paul joining the ensemble on stage for a version of 'High Heeled Sneakers'. "It's just nice to go to the pub again and see a rocking live blues band," commented Weller. Back in 1995, Paolo Hewitt had put Paul back in touch with The Jam's co-founder after filming *Highlights And Hang-Ups*, Weller endorsing Steve's poignant, self-published account of his days with The Jam, *Keeping The Flame*. Two days later, Noel Gallagher introduced a surprise support slot from Paul at one of soul singer Gabrielle's shows at Soho's legendary jazz club Ronnie Scott's. Weller performed three acoustic songs – 'Waiting On An Angel' (by US singer/songwriter Ben Harper), Ocean Colour Scene's 'The Circle' and a new song, 'Up In Suze's Room', which echoed the jazz/R&B crossover of *Café Bleu*-era Style Council.

The following month, Paul issued his only new release of the year, the strutting 'Peacock Suit' – previewed at both the Finsbury Park event and during a special *Top Of The Pops* performance. The production was rougher and more aggressive than most of *Stanley Road* and Weller growled and barked as if straining on a leash, a throwback to the 'angry' days of The Jam. An intense, masculine R&B workout, 'Peacock Suit' was played hard and fast; only the groovy funk-rock refrain at the end softened the blow. The song's stripped-bare approach was perfectly captured by the promotional video, Weller and Cradock duelling on Rickenbackers (including Paul's distinctive pop-art guitar, another nod to his past) in a spartan, brick-walled basement.

To tie in with its release, Weller headlined another festival – Virgin's V96 event at Chelmsford's Hylands Park. It was the end of an era for Paul: Steve Cradock and Damon Minchella had decided they should concentrate on Ocean Colour Scene and this was to be their last performance in Weller's backing band. Neil Young lost his Crazy Horse, Bob Dylan his Band – and the group dressed up in suits to mark what Paul called their Candlestick Park, a reference to the Beatles' farewell concert. He then knuckled down to the business of writing songs for the follow-up to *Stanley Road*. As a result, the rest of '96 was quiet, aside from an appearance on the New Years Eve Hootenanny edition of *Later With Jools Holland*. Instead of performing with his own band, Paul was accompanied by Jools' Rhythm And Blues Orchestra for two soul covers (Billy Preston's 1973 single, 'Will It Go Round In

Circles' and William Bell's 'I Forgot To Be Your Love'), alongside 'Come Together'.

Weller surfaced again in February 1997, sporting long sideburns and looking distinctly uncomfortable as he posed on the cover of women's magazine *Elle* with supermodel Kate Moss. Weller had been swayed when he was told that the photographer was none other than Sixties icon David Bailey; inside, under the headline 'Supermods From Surrey', Paolo Hewitt chatted to the pair about their shared working class suburban backgrounds. Weller seemed tickled: "I loved it when I was in New York and saw this big picture of Kate in Times Square. I thought, she's from Croydon and she's on a billboard in Times Square. You can harp on about humble beginnings but I think it's fucking wicked!" Paul also seemed more comfortable with his own fame but as critical as ever of the media's hypocritical gaze: "It would be great if we could celebrate a bit of success in this country. But anyone who wins . . . it's don't go too far, don't get above your station, know your place. It's the tail-end-of-the-Empire class thing. It's not so much among the people, it's the media and the establishment."

That same month, Weller aired five new songs during a warm-up set for Ocean Colour Scene at the Royal Albert Hall. Paul also joined the band onstage for an encore of Ronnie Lane's 'The Poacher'. Meanwhile, reports seeped out that Weller, Noel Gallagher and Pete Townshend were recording the song for an MCA fund-raising EP for Lane, hosted by Ocean Colour Scene at their Moseley Shoals studios. But nothing was issued prior to Lane's death in June 1997. And in May, Paul and Noel Gallagher guested on stage at the Charlatans' Brixton Academy concert for the National Missing Persons' Helpline.

★ ★ ★

Weller's past accomplishments have been recycled on a regular basis ever since the success of his solo career – every few months sees the arrival of another Jam or Style Council compilation. But perhaps the last word on The Jam's achievements arrived in the shape of *Direction, Reaction, Creation*, a lavish boxed set containing their complete recordings and issued in May 1997 to commemorate the twentieth anniversary of their first release, 'In The City'. This five-CD collection sold well enough to reach the Top 10, an unknown feat for expensive box sets and testament both to the enduring affection with which The Jam are regarded by thirty-something Jam fans – who still constitute Weller's core audience.

Many punters were lured by the fifth disc, which mopped up some unreleased works-in-progress, allowing greater insight into Paul's writing process at the time – not least, his technique of rescuing the odd lyric or refrain from abandoned songs for later compositions. Take 'Worlds Apart': snatches from this upbeat tune (accompanied by piano instead of guitars) were resurrected for both 'In The Crowd' and 'Strange Town', while the middle eight from 'Beat Surrender' surfaced instead on a prototype for 'Solid Bond In Your Heart'. Meanwhile, The Jam's enormous influence was reflected by a tribute album, *Fire 'N' Skill*, assembled by Simon Halfon, featuring artists as diverse as The Prodigy, The Beastie Boys, Dodgy, Texas, Reef, Gene and Everything But The Girl, together with more predictable names – Ocean Colour Scene, Noel Gallagher, Primal Scream.

To Weller himself, The Jam era must seem like an eternity ago. "There are people out there the same as me – thirty-five years old with two kids who met their wife at a Jam gig in '79," he reflected. "We've all grown up together and we've been through a lot. As long as it doesn't get too nostalgic or too sentimental, I'm happy."

★ ★ ★

While the music press busied itself with gushing Jam testimonials, the Weller camp were finally resolving an ongoing dispute about Paul's record contract – after Go! Discs ceased operations in a sea of acrimony following a prolonged tug-of-war with PolyGram in what must surely rank as one of the most bloody disputes within the music industry of the Nineties. Apparently, the problem revolved around PolyGram's original contract with label boss Andy MacDonald: they had invested a 49% share in Go! Discs (with MacDonald retaining the remaining 51%), but only on the proviso that, at a later date, either PolyGram or MacDonald would buy out the other party. That later date was 1996 and after it became clear that Go! Discs' parent company weren't willing to cooperate, MacDonald sold his share on August 20, 1996, for a sum rumoured to be approaching twenty million pounds. MacDonald promptly resigned, commenting in the press that he was effectively forced out. In the resultant turmoil, Go! Discs dissolved, staff were made redundant and their Hammersmith HQ was eventually taken over by Polydor.

From the Wellers' point of view, they felt reluctant to co-operate with PolyGram. After all, the corporation's flagship label was Polydor, who had unceremoniously dumped Paul back in 1989. Sure, Go! Discs was a part of that same empire – but MacDonald had run what felt like an autonomous outfit, with a strong belief in giving his musicians artistic control, and Paul felt comfortable with the relaxed atmosphere created by Go! Discs' personnel at the Go! Discs' office.

Now, the situation had changed, and while other Go! Discs outfits like Gabrielle, The Beautiful South and Portishead were shuffled among PolyGram's other labels, the Weller camp kept extremely quiet. Rumours circulated that Paul might follow MacDonald to his new record company, Independiente (which had hitched up with Sony), or maybe he might sign to Oasis' label Creation or even Richard Branson's V2. This hearsay was unfounded, though: Paul's contract tied him to PolyGram for two further studio albums. Basically, Paul wanted to continue working with his old marketing and publicity team and the stalemate of those winter months allowed him to renegotiate a new contract in which this was possible.

In late spring 1997, PolyGram announced that Paul Weller had moved to Island Records. The label was a logical home: twenty years ago, Paul had liked the idea of Polydor because of its Who connotations; Island also had an impressive track record, with late Sixties acts like Traffic, Spooky Tooth and Nick Drake. But the rest of the deal was more unusual, as a *Music Week* report revealed:

"Island and Independiente are to create a joint marketing team to work with Paul Weller, following their unique deal unveiled last week," it revealed. "Independiente managing director Mike Heneghan says the team will be drawn from personnel at both Island and Independiente. Island MD Marc Marot believes it is a first for the industry. 'It's a cool deal. It's quite common for companies to co-operate internationally, but I've not heard of one like this. Independiente will be involved in all the things labels do for artists. It will be able to watch over and protect its investment, and we get the best quality advice because Andy MacDonald and his team have had a very close and profitable relationship with Paul in the past.' " The bulletin also suggested that a *Greatest Hits* was slated for late 1998, to be followed by the final album of Weller's deal. Paul would then transfer to Independiente on a long-term contract.

All of which meant that the publicity campaign for Weller's new album was delayed until the last possible moment. Ignoring Island's pleas, Paul decided to stick with his Go! Discs press officer, Pippa Hall, who had recently helped set up a new PR company, Monkey Business; another ex-Go! Discs employee joined Paul at his Solid Bond offices. And this was the set-up behind the launch of *Heavy Soul* in late June.

The launch pad for a string of outdoor appearances to promote the album over the summer (T In The Park and a pair of concerts in Sheffield and Crystal Palace under the banner, *A Day At The Races*) was Weller's headline slot at the 15,000-strong Cardiff Bay Big Noise Festival on May 11. After supporting sets from the likes of Space and Gene (and, way down the bill, Delta, who are managed by Paul's sister), Weller introduced a new backing band – Matt Deighton (ex-front man with Acid Jazz act Mother Earth) on rhythm guitar and Yolanda Charles, who returned on bass after Weller had an alleged falling-out with Marco Nelson. Collectively, the pair lent a funkier edge to the proceedings than, say, the Ocean Colour Scene guitarists. Broadcast live on the radio and on Welsh TV, the show previewed three songs from Paul's forthcoming LP.

The two-part title track, 'Heavy Soul', sounded like an anguished battle cry, all angst-ridden R&B and claustrophobic guitar riffs. Its bullish blues picked up where 'Porcelain Gods' left off, while the lyrics could easily be applied to his conflict with PolyGram: "I'm touched by the thought that I can't be bought . . . 'cos I'm a heavy soul". More buoyantly melodic was

'Friday Street' (as in 'Friday On My Mind' and 'Dead End Street'), a pleasantly flowing song with a title that suggested a less literal extension of the 'Stanley Road' idea. 'Mermaids' shared this refreshingly tuneful edge, with its loose rhythm, jangly guitar and an anthemic "sha la-la la-la" chorus (as in 'Sha-la-la-la-lee'). Dedicated to "anyone from the Home Counties", 'Mermaids' harked back to The Style Council in their heyday.

Each Paul Weller solo album has been progressively less smooth. *Paul Weller* retained some of The Style Council's polish; *Wild Wood* dropped the acid jazz tinges for a more earthy feel; and *Stanley Road* was characterised by its solid live production. Recorded early in '97 at Van Morrison's Woolhall Studios in Bath, *Heavy Soul* appeared to be a logical development of Weller's obsession with a back-to-basics approach – but maybe he'd gone too far. Its jagged edges were off-putting, rather as if we'd been given a rough-and-ready prototype instead of the finished album. The lyrics were often difficult to decipher and instruments were sometimes buried beneath the album's murky production. In attempting to convey the bruised emotion of British blueswailers like, say, Marriott or Joe Cocker, Paul's voice sometimes sounded wayward and off-key. The songs tended to be built upon a solid platform of guitar riffs rather than overtly tuneful melodies and the rhythm section all too often felt lacklustre. The whole effect verged on being too earnest, too serious, too . . . well, heavy.

However, *Heavy Soul* is a more carefully crafted affair than first impressions suggested. 'Brushed' is an intense rollercoaster of blues funk, Weller's aggressive hollering offset by some searing guitar stabs and electronic mischief from oscillator operator Brendan Lynch. Ploughing a parallel Stonesy vein, 'Golden Sands' is Paul's brashest take on late Sixties Stax R&B, evoking the hazy Southern States heat with a stomping soul rhythm and some gliding, Dr. John-styled electric piano from Jools Holland.

If these heavier soul workouts dominated the ears, then the album's most accomplished tunes were those of a less upfront nature. 'Up In Suze's Room' is a beautiful song (though we're none the wiser as to the identity of the lady in question). The acoustic 'Driving Nowhere' has a mournful quality and that introspective Sunday feeling which matches lyrics like, "I'm still drifting, I've got no faith". 'I Should Have Been There To Inspire You' is a lengthy piano ballad with a country-ish flavour, a mature, smoky barroom lament in the vein of 'Wings Of Speed'. Then there's 'Science' with its crisp, snappy drumbeat, the perfect backdrop for the song's light, floating atmosphere as Paul returns to his lyrical quest for a sense of identity – "I can be who I am/I have no pretence". Which leaves the most endearing moment on *Heavy Soul*: 'As You Lean Into The Light' is an atmospheric tune (file under 'Country'), dreamy and softly spoken one moment, hoarse and defiant at others.

The whole *Heavy Soul* package was strongly rooted in a Sixties/Seventies rock crossover – from the artwork depicting the album title in post-*Rubber*

Soul psychedelic writing to the late Sixties pink Island label design. Gone were the rose-tinted reminiscences of his Woking childhood that adorned *Wild Wood* and *Stanley Road*: "Like all nostalgia, it wears thin after a while," he admitted in 1996. "So I've stayed in Woking quite a lot this year-and-a-half. It was nice at first but I've got a bit bored now – the nostalgic part has run its course. But I suppose there always comes a point when people go back and plug in again to their roots. It's been twenty years since I left Woking – at that time, I couldn't wait to get away!"

Bearing in mind Paul's other working title for the album, *Raving R&B*, it seemed clear in which direction Weller was heading. Coupled with traces of Free, Humble Pie and The Faces within the music, this invariably led some critics to pan Weller for adopting what they deemed a retrogressive stance. In fairness, Paul's relentless worship of his idols may have led to the odd derivative refrain or obvious reference to the past, but he has achieved way too much in the last twenty years to take any accusations of plagiarism that seriously.

★　★　★

Heavy Soul was released in late June 1997 and entered the chart at No. 2 behind Radiohead's fortnight-old *OK Computer*. Though it's unlikely he'd have unseated Oxford's finest at their commercial zenith, Weller's chances weren't helped by what can only be described as a record-company cock-up. The initial release with five postcards, labelled as a 'collectors edition', was banned from chart inclusion because the rules specified a maximum of four!

Ironically, had they been stapled together, the cards would have counted as a non-bannable booklet – but, as it was, label reps were sent scurrying countrywide to remove the offending extra item and post them to chart compilers CIN as proof of compliance. Singles 'Friday Street' and 'Mermaids' would peak in the lower reaches of the UK Top 30, 'Brushed' rising higher to No. 14.

Though *Mojo* magazine's review was typical in claiming the album favoured conviction over content and was "light on strong tunes", Weller would later deny that he had made *Heavy Soul* deliberately uncommercial in an attempt to get out of his contract. "When Go! Discs got taken over by PolyGram," he said, "I thought 'Fuck this – I'm gonna make the record anyway.' Same as I did with my first solo album, when I didn't have a deal either. I wouldn't make a record for contractual reasons."

A six-month world tour in support of the release included two weeks in North America, the highlight a sell-out date at New York's Roseland Ballroom, but trouble loomed in early November on the occasion of the 40th date in Paris. The gendarmerie were called to the Warwick Hotel off the Champs Elysées, where Weller and chums trashed a room after the hotel's manager had refused to open the bar around midnight. According to a police spokesman, "He spent about eight hours in a cell and was released without charge the next morning, having come to a financial settlement with the hotel."

Ironically, a *NME* feature of July '97 had reported Weller swearing off the demon drink "after waking up in a ditch one morning", but he would later dismiss the incident in a *Guardian* interview as "pissing about that got out of hand. We'd been on the Eurostar and there was free drink that we'd been knocking back. It wasn't even my room, just my name that was in the papers." Four and a half grand later (and lighter), he was home to play the Kilburn National dancehall in London by the week before Christmas. And for fans short of gift ideas, a visit to the merchandise stand would reveal a range of tour souvenirs that included a Paul Weller Ben Sherman shirt (£35), beanie hat (£15) or, for the financially challenged, a mug for their cappuccino (just £5).

A quiet start to 1998 was broken with the announcement of a 13-date UK and Eire tour, kicking off in Blackburn in late June. It closed in a one-day open-air festival, the British Summer Time concert in London's Hackney, played in the hand-picked company of Ian Dury, sometime Weller backing vocalist Carleen Anderson and Finlay Quaye.

The year would see Polydor release the final, dancefloor-orientated Style Council album, *Modernism: A New Decade* eight years after they'd originally rejected it. "It puts a big smile on my face," confessed a vindicated Weller, who simultaneously admitted he hadn't listened to it for a couple of years. "It still sounds all right to me, (though) it'd have been too early for a lot of people. Garage was still very much an underground thing at the at time."

Not only did the album appear, it lent its name to a box set containing over six hours of Style Council music – effectively the whole of their front-line studio output. The set, released in September, consisted of 90 tracks spread over five CDs, of which the 'missing' album was the last eight tracks on CD5. Compiler Dennis Munday chose not to include anything from the live *Home And Abroad*, the 'odds and sods' collection *Here's Some That Got Away* or many of the 12″ mixes, but the result went a long way to provoking re-evaluation of Weller's most critically reviled project.

In addition to the music, the box included an extensive booklet with forewords by Pat Gilbert and Paul Weller, an interview with Weller by Paolo Hewitt, compiler's notes by Munday, The Style Council Diary compiled by John Reed, a three-part set of biographical sleeve notes by Gilbert, Reed and Hewitt, a complete discography and numerous rare photos from the Polydor archives.

The impression that 1998 was to be a 'year off', at least by Weller's workaholic standards, was confirmed by the announcement of a long-awaited hits collection. *Modern Classics*, with its double-edged title, arrived in November and would push its way into the crowded pre-Christmas chart at No. 7. Though it wouldn't make further progress against similar collections from U2, Phil Collins, Mariah Carey, M People and George Michael, UK sales soon earned it platinum status, over 300,000 copies passing across the counter within a month of release.

The 16 tracks posed few surprises, though the now difficult to find single 'Hung Up' was included alongside more predictable choices. As with all such exercises, a new track was included in the package, and this, 'Brand New Start', distinguished itself as a No. 16 single. 'Wild Wood', which had made it to 14 at the first time of asking in 1993, would follow up with a No. 22 singles placing early in 1999.

Reviews for the album were typically polarised, *New Musical Express*'s David Stubbs grudgingly awarding it a four out of ten mark: Stubbs was later the recipient of a phone call suggesting they should meet to "sort it out". That said, a four-page interview gave Weller the chance to retaliate more publicly. "You all sit behind your word processors having it large," he grumbled, "but I never see anyone coming up to me face to face. I was written off for fucking years, then all of a sudden it's all right to like me again. Now the backlash may be starting again."

Not in all quarters. A month before release, Paul had been granted the accolade of Best Songwriter at *Q* magazine's ninth annual awards. While R.E.M. stole the spotlight with a Lifetime Achievement Award, the Bard of Woking was particularly chuffed to receive his accolade from none other than Motown legend Edwin Starr. "He's the man, you know what I mean?" said the soul disciple, sporting a suit almost as natty (but not as star-spangled) as Edwin himself. "Not much to say as usual, but thank you very much for this – and a nice video selection, as well."

The reference was to a montage of clips including the Style Council's 'Long Hot Summer' which had elicited a round of tittering from the assembled, inebriated multitudes. Weller was the ninth recipient of the award and found himself in the exalted company of such former role models as Van Morrison (1995) and Paul McCartney (1997).

Christmas was celebrated in the company of Ocean Colour Scene, playing London's Brixton Academy in a benefit for a charity for the homeless. (May the following year would see them sharing a stage again, this time at the Forum in North London in a benefit for the victims of conflict in Kosovo that also featured Noel Gallagher and Supergrass.) And he used a special programme – *Paul Weller Uncut*, premiered in early December by cable channel VH1 – as a platform to announce he "wouldn't be playing Jam songs again." Needless to say, his ever-changing moods would render this a red herring.

But he clearly got a greater kick out of new material, and more was on the way. Released in July 2000, *Heliocentric* – his fifth solo studio album, and fifteenth in all – took its name from the studio in which part of it was recorded. 'Centred round the sun' is the dictionary definition, in case you wondered. Confusingly, a new song, titled 'Helioscentric' (note the added 's') would be released as a bonus track on first single, 'He's The Keeper'.

Heliocentric the album found Weller seemingly at ease with his past, while looking to the future. As Robert Wyatt once said, Weller is adept at making "new furniture seasoned from old wood". Ocean Colour Scene's Damon Minchella and Steve Cradock were among the supporting musical cast. The Internet website music365.com gave the album the best possible review, their Gary Crossing judging it "quite possibly the man's finest solo effort to date" and according it a maximum five stars.

Proceedings kicked off on a suitably upbeat note with the aforementioned 'He's The Keeper', an emotive ode to revered Small Faces/Faces bassman Ronnie Lane who'd died in 1997. "He's the one knight on a knackered stallion," ran the lyric, "his rusty armour so undervalued."

This was one of the few tracks kept from original sessions for an album he decided was going to turn out "too much like Heavy Soul Pt II and I wanted to stay away from that". What he was aiming for this time was "pastoral and folky, (with) a warm, mellow feel to it". As with his first solo release, comparisons would be made to Traffic, the archetypal Sixties British band whose 'organic' feel Paul admired. "The actual recording of the tracks," he explained, "was real quick. We only spent 4–5 days at a time and got as much done as possible in those short spaces of time. All the tracks are live performances."

It wasn't long before the vulnerability kicked in with 'Frightened', its swirling string arrangement coming courtesy of Nick Drake cohort Robert Kirby. Said Paul: "Robert was brilliant and really understood that I was after something really special. We spent a long time over getting the arrangements right." The rocking 'There Is No Drinking After You're Dead' was soon to become a live staple, as would album closer 'Love-Less', ("I gotta need to be loved, yes I want to be loved like anyone else") and the mid-paced 'Back In The Fire'. Both the latter echoed the Style Council sound.

The lyrics of 'Dust And Rocks' and 'With Time & Temperance' seemed to deal with the down-side of relationships, while 'Picking Up Sticks' unusually teamed organ with hurdy-gurdy. The album's second single would be 'Sweet Pea, My Sweet Pea', a pleasing slice of summer pop released in August. It was dedicated to daughter Leah, and managed to steer just the right side of McCartney-esque sentimentality.

On the other side of the coin, 'A Whale's Tale' seemed inspired by the music business in general, and quite possibly the PolyGram/Go! Discs situation in particular, with its barbed lyric: "You don't even know me but you own me the same . . . and if all fails you can pull on the line, it's a whale's tale I leave behind."

Heliocentric was released in mid-April into a chart still dominated by albums that had made it big the previous Christmas: Moby's *Play*, Tom Jones' *Reload*, pop efforts from Sporty Spice and Westlife plus Travis' *The Man Who*, now one year old and seven times platinum. Happily, *Heliocentric* proved a much-needed breath of fresh air by entering at No. 2. It would clock up seven weeks in the Top 75 and go gold (100,000 sales) before being displaced by the incoming likes of Eminem and Toploader.

A major UK tour to push the product – his first in two years – sold out within hours of its announcement and saw Paul playing to in excess of 100,000 people, and was followed by the customary round of appearances at the summer's UK festivals. A special gig at the Royal Albert Hall in May was played with a full orchestra, and would emerge in November as a video/DVD release.

The year of 2000 had found Weller content in his newly rediscovered family life: Child number four had arrived, courtesy of his current girlfriend Sami Stock, and as he confessed to Q magazine, "My son's nearly 12, so to go through (fatherhood) again is exciting." It was therefore especially upsetting that the month of October should have brought drama in the shape of an unlikely – and, as it quickly proved, unsubstantiated – rape allegation that was trumpeted out of all proportion by the red-top tabloid press.

Weller had been arrested, interviewed and released on police bail after a 36-year-old woman accused him of sexually assaulting her in Farnham, some 12 miles from Woking, four years earlier. Happily, after one fraught week, Surrey police confirmed the matter would not be the subject of further police investigation. "I'm relieved at this outcome and sincerely hope it is the end of the ordeal," said Weller with feeling after charges were dropped. "From the start I have emphatically denied the allegation. Rape is despicable, and to be accused of the crime has been one of the most depressing moments of my life."

Yet his good name had been dragged through the mud, however briefly, and he took the opportunity to make that point. "I doubt very much that the news of my innocence will make the same headlines as the story of my arrest. The current legal system, in which only the alleged victim in a rape case is guaranteed anonymity, seems grossly unfair.

"My name has been tarnished, even though there is no substance in the allegation. While I understand the need for anonymity, it should be extended to both parties in such cases, especially prior or any criminal charges being brought."

Having weathered that unexpected and unwelcome storm, next on the agenda was an appearance with Paul's Mod heroes The Who. Seemingly unwilling or unable to retire, the surviving trio of Pete Townshend, Roger Daltrey and John Entwistle, with Zak Starkey on drums and John Bundrick on keyboards, played a charity show at the Royal Albert Hall on November 27 with special guests including Paul, Noel Gallagher, Bryan Adams, Eddie Vedder (Pearl Jam), Kelly Jones (Stereophonics) and violinist Nigel Kennedy. The whole was filmed for video/DVD release, something the publicity-shy Weller found not a little disconcerting.

"It was bad enough rehearsing with Pete (Townshend) but, with the TV crew and cameras and more people milling about than Oxford Street, it was

crazy." Though they rehearsed 'Sunrise' from *The Who Sell Out*, the song
selected for the final show was the more upbeat 'So Sad About Us' from
1966's *A Quick One*, while Paul returned to the stage with fellow guests for
Tommy's climactic 'See Me, Feel Me'. Having recorded 'Instant Karma' for a
Channel 4 TV special to mark the 60th anniversary of John Lennon's birth,
he would also wax a cover of the single B-side 'Circles' for a Who tribute
album, *Substitute*, to released the following year.

Last in a retrospectively related sequence of events was the publication of
The Soul Stylists: (Forty Years of Modernism), a book written by cohort Paolo
Hewitt for which Weller was credited with 'Concept & Introduction'.
"From Mod to Casual, from Skinhead to Northern Souler, the soul stylists
are an amazing family joined together by a tradition of secrecy, exclusivity
and absolute indifference towards the outside world."

The project for 2001 was an acoustic tour, which would be recorded for a
live album. Weller's reference point for a classic concert LP was *Donny
Hathaway Live*, while the process of choosing a set list was, he explained, not
so much creating a retrospective show or a greatest hits. "I'm trying to find
something in each song that shows the lineage between all my work . . .
something I've never really done up until now."

Unfortunately, having returned home from his first live dates in Belgium
and Holland, Weller fell downstairs and broke the thumb of his left-hand.
This caused the postponement of Irish shows due to take place later in
February. Shows in Germany and Italy were also rescheduled.

There was an unforced intimacy about the performances that was appealing, and extended to varying the running order to include guest spots. The
Dublin show on 19 March, for instance, saw local singer Yvonne Tipping
take the stage with Weller to encore with John Martyn's folky classic 'May
You Never'.

Meanwhile, 'The Loved' (B-side of 1994's 'Hung Up') saw him miss out
the verse 'That's someone's son sleeping in the gutter . . .' When asked why
he didn't perform it, he replied simply "Because I don't like it."

A tribute gig was held at London's Astoria in April to mark the tenth
anniversary of Steve Marriott's death. Surviving members of Small Faces and
Humble Pie mingled with contemporary superstars, and it was no surprise to
see Weller prominent in proceedings. Teaming up with Noel Gallagher and
Gem Archer from Oasis, he performed half a dozen Small Faces classics:
'Become Like You', 'I'm Only Dreaming', 'Here Comes The Nice', 'Get
Yourself Together', 'All Or Nothing' and 'Tin Soldier'. Proceedings were
filmed for the obligatory DVD to come.

Three days later, Paul played an acoustic date in the BBC Radio Theatre
in London for broadcast by Radio 2, the audience of just a few hundred
comprising on-air competition winners. The March–May period also saw
him try his hand at radio presenting with a series on the same channel.
Paul Weller's *Vinyl Classics* was an easy-paced ramble through the record

collection he had put together over the past 20 years.

"I'm going to be playing some of my favourite soul, jazz, R&B records," ran the press release, "the sort of thing I jump around my living room to. I think it's really fascinating the love affair that British working-class people have had with black Afro-American music, and I'm one of them. I'm a fan as well and a follower." The first programme paid tribute to Curtis Mayfield, who'd died in late 1999, allowing him to reminisce about his meetings with the late soul superstar.

Six British city hall dates, billed as the Paul Weller Acoustic Tour 2001, were followed by the first festival of the season, Scotland's T in the Park. US dates in July included a trio of gigs at the House of Blues in LA, followed by one apiece in New York and Boston. Festivals followed in August at Dranouter, Belgium and the Witnness Festival, Dublin. Japan was also briefly visited for dates in Tokyo and Osaka.

As far as new acts went, Weller was plugging The Coral and Symian who, he felt, sounded "a bit different, and not your usual run of the mill, post-Oasis guitar bands". But the passing of legendary bluesman John Lee Hooker, a Mod icon in the Sixties, led an admiring Paul to remark that "he was still cool right up until the end." Hooker, he said, was "one of the originators, I don't honestly feel I'm that important in musical history. That's not being humble, that's just fact."

Former record label Polydor clearly held him in somewhat higher regard. In May they released two box sets of Jam singles, 18 discs in total divided between 1977–79 and 1980–82 and augmented where possible by visual CD-ROM content. An approving Weller thought they "looked nice, given that Polydor have all the rights to my back catalogue and are free to do what they will. They did a very tasteful job."

Weller's acoustic touring continued through the autumn of 2001, the final leg starting in Utrecht, Holland, on October 31 and passing through Germany before finishing with two dates at the Royal Albert Hall before Christmas. By that time, *Days Of Speed* had not only been released but promoted by an acoustic session for Virgin Radio and a special edition (devoted entirely to him) of BBC TV's *Later With Jools Holland*, the latter screened on October 5.

The album hit the Top 3 in late October beneath another new entry from Starsailor, a new band Weller clearly rated ("I thought they were great, I really love 'Fever' and the guy's voice is pretty soulful") and renascent teen queen Kylie Minogue. A slow decline down the Top 40 was reversed just before Christmas when the now platinum-rated album picked up to No. 27. Well-connected fans had already picked up on a promotional set which spread the album's 18 tracks over three discs.

The credit for sifting through every song from every gig went to Pete Mason at Independiente, who earned an executive producer credit for his persistence. Ten different shows were pillaged, the mostly fruitful being

Dornbirn in Austria which yielded four. Three songs dated from Jam days – 'English Rose' (introduced as "here's an old tune"), 'That's Entertainment' and the closing 'Town Called Malice', while 'Down In The Seine' and 'Headstart For Happiness' were the Style Council representatives.

The performances were simple, sparse but effective – just one man and his acoustic guitar – and served as a palate-cleanser before he kicked off the second decade of his solo recording career. The likely musical direction of his next studio would be "more raw (than *Heliocentric*) but not 'bigger' in any other way, perhaps more concise in the arrangements, hopefully a bit more soul and funk. I hope my next record is released in the US, but we don't have a record label as yet."

The year 2002 started for Paul Weller in the familiar surroundings of the Royal Albert Hall, where he played a charity gig on February 9. Paul performed a regular set and was joined on stage by Noel Gallagher and Kelly Jones. Van Morrison and Steve Winwood had been scheduled to appear with Paul as special guests, but 'other commitments' intervened. The ex-Led Zeppelin pairing of Page and Plant also appeared separately on the night.

A studio date was arranged early in the year with acoustic bluesman Terry Callier. John Martyn and Death In Vegas had been other collaborators in 2001, though the fruits of these unions had yet to be revealed at the time of writing.

Paul's own LP had originally been scheduled for March/April release, but was set to be beaten to the shops by the Jam *BBC Sessions*. (A collection of solo rarities and B-sides was also in the pipeline.) The *BBC Sessions* would be following in the footsteps of role models The Who and Small Faces, and though the *Peel Session* from May 1977 had already been issued, there remained two more in later '77 and '79 plus one for Kid Jensen in 1978 – the same year they'd been taped for an *In Concert* broadcast.

★ ★ ★

Paul Weller is unique. He has been a pop star for all of his adult life. He has been a spokesman for a generation, a political firebrand and a fashion guru. He has been a campaigner for causes, a working-class hero and the Mod-father. He is a cat who has already had three musical lives. But above all, he has proved beyond all reasonable doubt his ability to write a good three-minute pop tune with enough edge, verve and sheer quality to rank among the best of them. His lifelong passion for music has driven him to dizzying peaks that have stood him apart from his peers – and troughs which less hardy souls would never have survived. We will probably never solve that other billion dollar question – what actually drives Weller towards his unreachable goal? That's because he himself doesn't know the answer. Driven by an unshakable, headstrong conviction and undeniable talent, he truly is a man of ever-changing moods.

As Stevie Winwood once sang, who knows what tomorrow may bring? But the last word has to go to Paul Weller, who had this to say to *NME* in 1993: "I really believe more and more that I'm just good at what I do. Playing guitar, singing songs and that's about it. People who look for more than that are going to be disappointed. All I wanted to do from the age of twelve was be in a group. When I was fourteen, I eventually got round to learning the guitar and I started going out playing gigs in pubs and clubs, playing Chuck Berry or whatever else had three chords. Twenty years on, that's what I'm still doing. That's the end of my story, really."

Discography

- All the releases by The Jam and The Style Council are on Polydor unless otherwise stated.
- All the releases by Paul Weller are on Go! Discs unless otherwise stated.
- All the singles originally came in pictures sleeves and are 7″ editions unless otherwise stated.
- All the vinyl LPs except In The City and the first two on Respond came with their own unique inner sleeves.
- Cassette editions exist for all the albums but are only included here if they feature exclusive material.
- This discography only includes those various artists compilations which feature exclusive material.

THE JAM

PRE-POLYDOR RECORDINGS

8/73   **Blueberry Rock/Takin' My Love**   acetate
Notes: Recorded at Eden Studios, Kingston

11/73   **Some Kinda Lovin'/Making My Way Back Home**   acetate
Notes: Recorded at Fanfare Studios, North London

Other songs which exist on tape:
1973/74   cassette
[1]Taking My Love/Eight Days A Week/Some Kinda Loving/Little Girl Crying/World Without Love/Oh Carol/Remember/Jailhouse Rock/I Saw Her Standing There/Love Has Died/Feels So Good/That Way/Little Queenie/Baby I Don't Care/Twist And Shout/Love, Love, Loving/Crazy Old World/Like I Love You/You And The Summer/Say Goodbye/[2]She Don't Need Me/When I'm Near You/Love's Surprise/Love Has Died/She's Coming Home/Loving By Letters
Notes: One of the many revelations of Steve Brookes' mid-1996 biography of his time with The Jam, *Keeping The Flame*, was this old C120 cassette of early rehearsals, entitled *The Jam – Live*. For detailed annotations of the songs' origins, refer to Steve's book. The first side was recorded at the Woking Working Men's Club one Sunday afternoon, probably late '73 or early '74, while the second side, featuring all-original material, was probably taped a couple of months later.

1974   Loving By Letters/More And More
Notes: Recorded at Bob Potter's studio, Mytchett, Surrey

3/75   Walking The Dog/I Will Be There/Hundred Ways/Forever And Always
Notes: Recorded at TW Studios, Fulham

10/75   Again/Takin' My Love
Notes: Recorded at Bob Potter's studio, Mytchett, Surrey

5/76   Left, Right And Centre/Non-Stop Dancing
Notes: Recorded at Bob Potter's studio, Mytchett, Surrey

Pre-Polydor recordings of the following songs are also known to exist: Uptight, Dancing In The Street, Cheque Book, Soul Dance, When I Needed You, Please Don't Treat Me Bad, Back In My Arms Again, So Sad About Us, I Got By In Time, In The City, Sounds From The Street and Time For Truth

SINGLES
(Chart position in brackets)

4/77	**In The City/Takin' My Love**	2058 866	(40)
7/77	**All Around The World/Carnaby Street**	2058 903	(13)
10/77	**The Modern World/Sweet Soul Music/** **Back In My Arms Again/Bricks And Mortar** (Part) (last three tracks recorded live at 100 Club 11.9.77)	2058 945	(36)
2/78	**News Of The World/Aunties And Uncles** (Impulsive Youths)/**Innocent Man**	2058 995	(27)
8/78	**David Watts/'A' Bomb In Wardour Street** (double-A-side)	2059 054	(25)
10/78	**Down In The Tube Station At Midnight/** **So Sad About Us/The Night**	POSP 8	(15)
3/79	**Strange Town/The Butterfly Collector**	POSP 34	(15)
8/79	**When You're Young/Smithers-Jones**	POSP 69	(17)
10/79	**The Eton Rifles/See-Saw**	POSP 83	(3)
3/80	**Going Underground/** **The Dreams Of Children** (double-A-side)	POSP 113	(1)
	Going Underground/ **The Dreams Of Children//** **Away From The Numbers/The Modern World/** **Down In The Tube Station At Midnight** (double pack)	POSPJ 113/ 2816 024	

Notes: Second disc recorded live at Rainbow Theatre, 3.12.79, not 3.11.79 as stated on label

8/80	**Start!/Liza Radley**	2059 266	(1)

2/81	**That's Entertainment/ Down In The Tube Station At Midnight** (Live Version) (West German import)	Metronome 0030.364	(21)

5/81	**Funeral Pyre/Disguises**	POSP 257	(4)

10/81	**Absolute Beginners/ Tales From The Riverbank** (with lyric insert)	POSP 350	(4)

2/82	**Town Called Malice/Precious** (double-A-side)	POSP 400	(1)
	Town Called Malice	POSPX 400	

(Live at Hammersmith Palais 14.12.81)/**Precious** (Extended Version)
(12″, double-A-side, striped die-cut sleeve)

6/82	**Just Who Is The 5 O'Clock Hero?/ The Great Depression** (West German import)	2059 504	(8)
	Just Who Is The 5 O'Clock Hero?/War/ The Great Depression (12″, West German import)	2141 558	

9/82	**The Bitterest Pill (I Ever Had To Swallow)/ Pity Poor Alfie–Fever**	POSP 505	(2)

Notes: B–side tracks segued

11/82	**Beat Surrender/Shopping**	POSP 540	(1)
	Beat Surrender/Shopping//Move On Up/ Stoned Out Of My Mind/War	POSPJ 540	

(double pack, gatefold sleeve, War is different version from 2141 558)

	Beat Surrender/Shopping/Move On Up/ Stoned Out Of My Mind/War (12″)	POSPX 540	

ALBUMS

5/77	**In The City**	2383 447	(20)

[1]Art School/I've Changed My Address/Slow Down/I Got By In Time/Away From The Numbers/Batman Theme/[2]In The City/Sounds From The Street/Non-Stop Dancing/Time For Truth/Takin' My Love/Bricks And Mortar

11/77	**This Is The Modern World**	2383 475	(22)

[1]The Modern World / London Traffic / Standards / Life From A Window / The Combine / Don't Tell Them You're Sane / [2]In The Street Today / London Girl/ I Need You (For Someone)/Here Comes The Weekend/Tonight At Noon/In The Midnight Hour

11/78   **All Mod Cons**   POLD 5008   (6)
[1]All Mod Cons/To Be Someone (Didn't We Have A Nice Time)/Mr. Clean/David Watts/English Rose/In The Crowd/[2]Billy Hunt/It's Too Bad/Fly/The Place I Love/'A' Bomb In Wardour Street/Down In The Tube Station At Midnight
Notes: English Rose is omitted from track listing on back cover; David Watts and 'A' Bomb In Wardour Street are different versions from those on single; Down In The Tube Station At Midnight is longer than single version

11/79   **Setting Sons**   POLD 5028   (4)
[1]Girl On The Phone/Thick As Thieves/Private Hell/Little Boy Soldiers/Wasteland/[2]Burning Sky/Smithers–Jones/Saturday's Kids/The Eton Rifles/ Heatwave
Notes: Track listing on back cover initially on printed sticker; The Eton Rifles is different to single version

11/80   **Sound Affects**   POLD 5035   (2)
[1]Pretty Green/Monday/But I'm Different Now/Set The House Ablaze/Start!/That's Entertainment/[2]Dream Time/Man In The Corner Shop/Music For The Last Couple/Boy About Town/Scrape Away
Notes: Start was a remix of the single version

3/82   **The Gift**   POLD 5055   (1)
[1]Happy Together/Ghosts/Precious/Just Who Is The Five O'Clock Hero?/"Trans-Global Express"/[2]Running On The Spot/Circus/The Planner's Dream Goes Wrong/Carnation/Town Called Malice/The Gift
Notes: Initially in pink–and–white striped 'gift' paper bag

12/82   **Dig The New Breed** (live)   POLD 5075   (2)
[1]In The City / All Mod Cons / To Be Someone / It's Too Bad / Start! / Big Bird / Set The House Ablaze/ [2]Ghosts/Standards/In The Crowd/Going Underground/The Dreams Of Children/That's Entertainment/Private Hell

5/01   **45rpm: The Singles 1977–79**   Polydor 587 610-2
        (9CD)
In The City (& video)/Takin' My Love/All Around The World/Carnaby Street/Modern World/Sweet Soul Music (Live)/Back In My Arms Again (Live)/Bricks & Mortar (Live)/News Of The World (& video)/Aunties And Uncles/Innocent Man/David Watts/"A" Bomb In Wardour Street/Down In The Tube Station At Midnight/So Sad About Us/The Night/Strange Town (& video)/The Butterfly Collector/When You're Young (& video)/Smithers-Jones/Eton Rifles/See Saw

5/01   **45rpm: The Singles 1980–82**   Polydor 587 978-2
        (9CD)
Going Underground (& video)/The Dreams Of Children/(Live) Away From The Numbers/The Modern World/Down In The Tube Station At Midnight/Start!/Liza Radley/That's Entertainment (& video)/Down In The Tube Station At Midnight/Funeral Pyre (& video)/Disguises/Absolute Beginners (& video)/Tales From The Riverbank/A Town Called Malice (& video)/Precious/Just Who Is The 5

O'Clock Hero (& video)/War/The Great Depression/The Bitterest Pill (I Ever Had To Swallow) (& video)/Pity Poor Alfie/Fever/Beat Surrender/Shopping/Move On Up/Stoned Out Of My Mind/War

OTHER SINGLES

12/80   **Boy About Town/Pop Art Poem**   Lyntone LYN 9048
       (flexidisc with *Flexipop* magazine; hard vinyl test pressings also mailed out)
Notes: Boy About Town was a different version from that on Sound Affects

1981   **When You're Young**   Lyntone (no cat. no.)
       (fan club flexidisc)

2/82   **Tales From The Riverbank** (re-recorded)   Lyntone (no cat. no.)
       (fan club flexidisc)

12/82   **Move On Up** (live)   PAOLO 100
       (flexidisc with *Melody Maker* music paper)

RETROSPECTIVE SINGLES

In both April 1980 and January 1983, Polydor reissued The Jam's singles back catalogue, many of which re-charted. During the second of these campaigns, That's Entertainment [POSP 482] and Just Who Is The 5 O'Clock Hero? [2229 254] received a UK release.

3/90   **Town Called Malice/Absolute Beginners**   Old Gold OG 9894

            Beat Surrender/   OG 9895
            The Bitterest Pill (I Ever Had To Swallow)

            The Eton Rifles/   OG 9896
            Down In The Tube Station At Midnight

            Going Underground/Start!   OG 9897
Notes: Two-on-one couplings of their greatest hits as part of oldies series

7/90   **The Peel Session**   Strange Fruit
       (12″ EP; recorded 26.4.77; also on CD, reissued   SFPS 080/SFPSCD 080
       1996)
       In The City/Art School/I've Changed My Address/The Modern World

6/91   **That's Entertainment/**   PO 155   (57)
            Down In The Tube Station At Midnight (live)

            That's Entertainment/   PZ/PZCD 155
            Down In The Tube Station At Midnight (live)/
            Town Called Malice (live) (12″/CD)
Notes: These live B-sides are the same recordings as those which appeared on original singles

| 4/92 | **Dreams Of Children/** | PO 199 |
| | **Away From The Numbers** | |

Dreams Of Children/ PZ 199
Away From The Numbers/The Modern World (12″)
Last two tracks recorded live at Rainbow Theatre, 3.12.79, not 3.11.79 as stated

Dreams Of Children/ PZCD 199
Away From The Numbers/The Modern World (CD)

COMPILATION ALBUMS

10/83   **Snap!** (double LP)   SNAP 1   (2)
[1]In The City/Away From The Numbers/All Around The World/The Modern World/News Of The World/Billy Hunt/English Rose/Mr. Clean/[2]DavidWatts/'A' Bomb In Wardour Street/Down In The Tube Station At Midnight/Strange Town/ The Butterfly Collector/When You're Young/Smithers-Jones/Thick As Thieves/ [3]The Eton Rifles/Going Underground/The Dreams Of Children/That's Entertainment (Demo)/Start!/Man In The Corner Shop/Funeral Pyre (Remix)/[4]Absolute Beginners/Tales From The Riverbank/Town Called Malice/Precious/The Bitterest Pill (I Ever Had To Swallow)/Beat Surrender
The LP initially came with **Live!** EP recorded at Wembley Arena 2 & 3.12.82 [SNAPL 45]: Move On Up/Get Yourself Together/The Great Depression/But I'm Different Now
Notes: CD entitled Compact Snap! issued 9/84 [821 712-2]

7/91   **Greatest Hits** (LP/CD)   849 554-1/2   (2)
In The City/All Around The World/The Modern World/News Of The World/ David Watts/Down In The Tube Station At Midnight/Strange Town/When You're Young/The Eton Rifles/Going Underground/Start!/That's Entertainment/Funeral Pyre / Absolute Beginners / Town Called Malice / Precious / Just Who Is The Five O'Clock Hero?/The Bitterest Pill (I Ever Had To Swallow)/Beat Surrender

1991   **Live At The Roxy**   Receiver
       (LP, unreleased, test pressings only)
Notes: Recorded at the London punk venue in 1977, this album was shelved before release

4/92   **Extras** (double LP/CD)   513 177-1/2   (15)
[1]The Dreams Of Children/Tales From The Riverbank/Liza Radley*/Move On Up/Shopping/Smithers-Jones/[2]Pop Art Poem/Boy About Town/A Solid Bond In Your Heart*/No One In The World*/And Your Bird Can Sing*/Burning Sky*/Thick As Thieves*/[3]Disguises/Get Yourself Together*/The Butterfly Collector/The Great Depression/Stoned Out Of My Mind/Pity Poor Alfie-Fever/ [4]But I'm Different Now*/I Got You (I Feel Good)*/Hey Mister*/Saturday's Kids*/ We've Only Started*/So Sad About Us/The Eton Rifles*

Notes: Tracks marked (*) are previously unissued studio demos; Get Yourself Together features newly recorded vocal; Smithers-Jones is B-side version; Boy About Town is remix of flexidisc version

10/92 **Wasteland** (CD) Pickwick PWKS 4129P
News Of The World/Burning Sky/Saturday [sic] Kids/Art School/In The Street Today/Non-Stop Dancing/Wasteland/In The City/Strange Town/Standards/'A' Bomb In Wardour Street/In The Crowd/London Girl/David Watts/I Got By In Time/All Around The World
Notes: A pointless and arbitrarily compiled budget compilation

5/93 **Beat Surrender** (CD) Spectrum 550 006-2
Beat Surrender/Town Called Malice/Pretty Green/That's Entertainment/The Gift/ Carnaby Street/Batman Theme/In The City/All Mod Cons/The Modern World/ When You're Young/Funeral Pyre/Private Hell/In The Midnight Hour
Notes: A pointless and arbitrarily compiled budget compilation – again

10/93 **Live Jam** (double LP/CD) 519 667-1/2 (28)
The Modern World / Billy Hunt / Thick As Thieves / Burning Sky / Mr. Clean / Smithers-Jones/The Eton Rifles/Away From The Numbers/Down In The Tube Station At Midnight/Strange Town/When You're Young/'A' Bomb In Wardour Street / Pretty Green / Boy About Town / Man In The Corner Shop / David Watts / Funeral Pyre / Move On Up / Carnation / The Butterfly Collector / Precious / Town Called Malice / Heatwave
Notes: Town Called Malice is taken from the original 12″; Away From The Numbers, The Modern World and Down In The Tube Station At Midnight were originally featured on the double pack of Going Underground

7/96 **The Jam Collection** (double LP/CD) 531 493-1/2 (58)
Away From The Numbers / I Got By In Time / I Need You (For Someone) / To Be Someone (Didn't We Have A Nice Time) / Mr. Clean / English Rose / In The Crowd/It's Too Bad/The Butterfly Collector/Thick As Thieves/Private Hell/ Wasteland/Burning Sky/Saturday's Kids/Liza Radley/Pretty Green/Monday/Man In The Corner Shop/Boy About Town/Tales From The Riverbank/Ghosts/Just Who Is The 5 O'Clock Hero?/The Great Depression/Shopping

5/97 **Direction, Reaction, Creation** (5-CD box set) 537 143-2 (8)
Notes: Comes with 88-page colour booklet. 1st 4 CDs contain entire Jam output, avoiding the odd alternative version and demos from Extras. 5th CD contains previously unissued material, plus flexidisc version of Tales From The Riverbank. Tracks marked (*) feature Paul Weller only:
In the City/Time For Truth/Sounds From The Street/So Sad About Us/ Worlds Apart/Billy Hunt (Alternate Version)/It's Too Bad/To Be Someone/David Watts/Best Of Both Worlds/That's Entertainment/Rain*/Dream Time*/Dead End Street*/Stand By Me*/Every Little Bit Hurts*/Tales From The Riverbank (Alternate Version)/Walking In Heaven's Sunshine/Precious*/Pity Poor Alfie (Swing Version)/

The Bitterest Pill (I Ever Had To Swallow) (First Version)/A Solid Bond In Your Heart★

REISSUE ALBUMS

9/80	**In The City/This Is The Modern World** (double LP/double cassette)	2683 074/ 3574 088
2/83	**All Mod Cons/Setting Sons** (two-on-one cassette)	3574 098
6/83	**Sound Affects/The Gift** (double cassette)	TWOMC 1
8/83	**In The City** (LP, mid-price reissue)	SPELP 27 (100)
4/84	**This Is The Modern World** (LP, mid-price reissue)	SPELP 66
6/87	**Dig The New Breed** (LP, mid-price reissue)	SPELP 107

REISSUE CDs

6/90	**In The City**	817 124-2
6/90	**This Is The Modern World**	823 281-2
1989	**All Mod Cons**	823 282-2
1987	**Setting Sons**	831 314-2
5/88	**Sound Affects**	823 284-2
6/90	**The Gift**	823 285-2
6/90	**Dig The New Breed**	810 041-2
6/90	**Compact Snap!**	815 537-2

Notes: During the above reissue campaign in June 1990, the vinyl LPs were also reissued with corresponding numbers

1/91	**In The City/This Is The Modern World**	847 730-4
7/97	**Snap!** (remastered CD)	821 712-2
7/97	**In The City** (remastered CD)	537 417-2
7/97	**This Is The Modern World** (remastered CD)	537 418-2
7/97	**All Mod Cons** (remastered CD)	537 419-2
7/97	**Setting Sons** (remastered CD)	537 420-2
7/97	**Sound Affects** (remastered CD)	537 421-2
7/97	**The Gift** (remastered CD)	537 422-2

9/97   **Greatest Hits** (remastered CD)   537 423-2

Notes: Each of The Jam's studio albums were reissued on CD in 1997 in remastered form with new sleeve-notes, together with the two retrospectives.

IMPORTANT VARIOUS ARTISTS COMPILATIONS

11/81   **When You're Young** (live)   NME 001
on *Dancin' Master* cassette, mail-order via *NME* music paper

11/92   **Pretty Green** (Demo 10.6.80)   Select/Polydor
on *Maximum Bliss* cassette free with *Select* magazine   (no cat. no.)

GUEST APPEARANCES

PETER GABRIEL
5/80   Peter Gabriel (LP)   Charisma   (1)
Paul Weller played guitar on **And Through The Wire**   CDS 4019

THE PURPLE HEARTS
1980   **Concrete Mixer** (Paul Weller plays piano)   Well Suspect SUSS 1
On Various Artists LP, *The Beat Generation And The*   [issued 12/84]
Angry Young Men; reissued on Re-Elect The President
NIXON 3, 4/87; reissued on CD, Captain Mod
MODSKA CD 3, 11/96

THE NIPS
10/81   **Happy Song/Nobody To Love** (7")   Test Pressing TP 5
Produced by Paul Weller, who may have contributed guitar to the B-side

OTHER IMPORTANT SINGLE

THE JOLT
2/79   Maybe Tonight/I'm In Tears/**See Saw**/   Polydor 2229 215
        Stop, Look (EP; also as 2-track promo)
Features See Saw, written for the band by Paul Weller

TRIBUTE LPs

8/96   **The Jam Tribute – The Modern World**   Flavour TFCK 87520
        (Japanese CD)
Notes: Compiled by UK label Detour

9/97   **Fire 'N' Skill** (CD)   Polygram

Notes: Compiled by Simon Halfon, this Jam covers CD is scheduled to feature Beastie Boys, Dodgy, Everything But The Girl, Noel Gallagher, Gene, Ocean Colour Scene, Primal Scream, Prodigy, Reef, Silversun, 60Ft Dolls and Texas

SPOKEN-WORD INTERVIEW RECORD

1980s   **Interview with Paul Weller & Bruce Foxton**   PJAM1
(picture disc)

VIDEOS

6/82   **Trans Global Unity Express**   Spectrum 791 526-2
Town Called Malice/Carnation/Precious/Ghosts/Move On Up/Private Hell/Pretty
Green/"Trans-Global Express"/The Gift
Notes: In concert at Birmingham Bingley Hall 21.3.82; reissued on Channel 5
CFV 00082, 8/86

11/83   **Video Snap!**   Spectrum 040 190-2
In The City / Art School / News Of The World / Strange Town / The Butterfly
Collector/When You're Young/Going Underground/Dreams Of Children/ Start!/
Funeral Pyre/Town Called Malice/Precious/The Bitterest Pill (I Ever Had To
Swallow)/Absolute Beginners/That's Entertainment
Notes: Companion release to the Snap! album; features promo videos plus live clip of
The Butterfly Collector; reissued on Channel 5 CFV 00292, 9/86

7/91   **Greatest Hits**   PolyGram 083 436-3
(same tracks as Video Snap!)
Notes: Companion release to the Greatest Hits album; Greatest Hits and Trans
Global Unity Express later combined onto one video [PolyGram 630 062-3, 1/94];
later reissued on 4 Front 638 958-3, 6/96

IMPORTANT VARIOUS ARTISTS VIDEOS

2/83   **Kids Like You And Me**   3M MMM 5001
In The City/Mr. Clean/'A' Bomb In Wardour Street (all tracks live, 1978)
Notes: Concert film of the Reading Rock Festival

12/83   **Top Of The Pops**   BBC V 3023
Beat Surrender (studio performance on *Top Of The Pops*, 1982)

10/84   **The Rock Revolution**   Peppermint 6123
In The City/Tonight At Noon (both tracks live)
Notes: Later abridged as Rock Rebels (Video Gems R1047, 7/86), featuring just In
The City

10/86   **Punk In London**   Hendring WRIT 001
Carnaby Street/In The City (both tracks live in 100 Club, 1977)
Notes: German-made documentary about British punk scene; reissued as Punk In
London '77 (Studio K7 006, 9/91)

10/86   **British Rock – Ready For The 80's**   Hendring WRIT 003
All Around The World/The Eton Rifles/David Watts (all tracks live)

Notes: German-made documentary about British music scene at the start of the Eighties; reissued as Punk And Its After Shocks (Studio K7 010, 1/92)

| 11/89 | **Top Of The Pops – 25 Years Vol. 2** | Telstar TVE 1009 |

The Eton Rifles (studio performance on *Top Of The Pops*, 1979)

THE STYLE COUNCIL

SINGLES

| 3/83 | **Speak Like A Child/Party Chambers** | TSC 1 | (4) |

| 5/83 | **Money-Go-Round** (Parts 1+2) (with picture insert) | TSC 2 | (11) |

Money-Go-Round/
Headstart For Happiness/Mick's Up (12″) — TSCX 2

| 8/83 | **À Paris** EP | TSC 3 | (3) |

Long Hot Summer/Party Chambers/
The Paris Match/Le Départ

À Paris EP (12″) — TSCX 3
Long Hot Summer (Extended Version)/
Party Chambers/The Paris Match/Le Départ

| 11/83 | **A Solid Bond In Your Heart/** | TSC 4 | (11) |

It Just Came To Pieces In My Hands/
A Solid Bond In Your Heart (Instrumental)

A Solid Bond In Your Heart/ — TSCG 4
It Just Came To Pieces In My Hands/
A Solid Bond In Your Heart (Instrumental)
(alternative gatefold sleeve)

| 2/84 | **My Ever Changing Moods/Mick's Company** | TSC 5 | (5) |

My Ever Changing Moods (Long Version)/ — TSCX 5
Spring, Summer, Autumn/
Mick's Company (12″)

| 5/84 | **Groovin': You're The Best Thing/** | TSC 6 | (5) |

The Big Boss Groove (double-A-side)

Groovin': You're The Best Thing — TSCX 6
(Long Version)/**You're The Dub Thing/**
The Big Boss Groove (12″)

Notes: You're The Best Thing was remix of version on Café Bleu LP

10/84	**Shout To The Top/Ghosts Of Dachau**	TSC 7	(7)
	Shout To The Top/Shout To The Top (Instrumental)/**The Piccadilly Trail/ Ghosts Of Dachau** (12″)	TSCX 7	
5/85	**Walls Come Tumbling Down!/ The Whole Point II/Blood Sports**	TSC 8	(6)
	Walls Come Tumbling Down!/ Spin' Drifting/The Whole Point II/Blood Sports (12″, initially with poster; last two tracks as Council Folk Club Presents . . .)	TSCX 8	
6/85	**Come To Milton Keynes/ (When You) Call Me**	TSC 9	(23)
	Come To Milton Keynes/ (When You) Call Me (alternative gatefold sleeve)	TSCG 9	
	Come To Milton Keynes/ Our Favourite Shop (Club Mix)/ **(When You) Call Me/The Lodgers** (Club Mix) (12″)	TSCX 9	
9/85	**The Lodgers** (re-recorded)/ **You're The Best Thing★/The Big Boss Groove★**	TSC 10	(13)
	The Lodgers (re-recorded)/ **You're The Best Thing★/The Big Boss Groove★// You're The Best Thing/The Lodgers** (shrinkwrapped double pack)	TSC DP 10	
	The Lodgers (re-recorded) (Extended Mix)/ **The Big Boss Groove★/Move On Up★/ Money-Go-Round–Soul Deep–Strength Of Your Nature** Medley★/ **You're The Best Thing★** (12″)	TSCX 10	

Notes: All formats have photo insert; tracks marked (★) recorded live in Liverpool & Manchester, 1985

3/86	**Have You Ever Had It Blue/ Mr. Cool's Dream**	CINE 1	(14)
	Have You Ever Had It Blue (Uncut Version)/ **With Everything To Lose** (Recorded Live In London Dec. '85) (cassette, free with initial copies of CINE 1 in printed PVC sleeve)	CINEC 1	
	Have You Ever Had It Blue (Uncut Version)/ **Have You Ever Had It Blue** (Cut Version)/ **Mr. Cool's Dream** (12″)	CINEX 1	
1/87	**It Didn't Matter/All Year Round**	TSC 12	(9)
	It Didn't Matter/It Didn't Matter (Instrumental)/**All Year Round** (12″)	TSCX 12	

3/87	**Waiting** (Vocal)/**Francoise** (Vocal)	TSC 13	(52)
	Waiting (Vocal)/**Francoise** (Vocal)/ **Francoise** (Theme From "JerUSAlem")/ **Waiting** (Instrumental) (12″)	TSCX 13	
10/87	**Wanted/The Cost/The Cost Of Loving**	TSC 14	(20)
	Wanted/The Cost/The Cost Of Loving (12″, with picture inner sleeve)	TSCX 14	

Also on CD [TSCCD 14] and cassette [TSCMC 14] with same tracks
Notes: The Cost is an instrumental version of the slower re-recording of The Cost Of Loving

5/88	**Life At A Top Peoples Health Farm/ Sweet Loving Ways**	TSC 15	(28)
	Spank! (Live At A Top Peoples Health Club)/ **Life At A Top Peoples Health Farm** (7″ Version)/**Life At A Top Peoples Health Farm** (Um & Argh Mix)/**Sweet Loving Ways** (12″/CD)	TSCX 15/ TSCCD 15	

Notes: 7″ and 12″ have picture inner sleeves

7/88	**1-2-3-4 – A Summer Quartet** EP **How She Threw It All Away/Love The First Time/ Long Hot Summer/I Do Like To Be B-Side The A-Side** (last track credited as The Mixed Companions)	TSC 16	(41)
	1-2-3-4 – A Summer Quartet EP **How She Threw It All Away/ Love The First Time/Long Hot Summer** (Tom Mix)/ **I Do Like To Be B-Side The A-Side** (12″/CD)	TSCX 16/ TSCCD 16	

Notes: 7″ and 12″ have picture inner sleeves; I Do Like To Be B-Side The A-Side is re-recording of Mick's Company

2/89	**Promised Land** (Juan Atkins Mix)/ **Can You Still Love Me?**	TSC 17	(27)
	Promised Land (Juan Atkins Mix)/ **Can You Still Love Me?** (box set with poster)	TSCB 17	
	Promised Land (Longer Version)/ **Promised Land** (Pianopella Version)/ **Can You Still Love Me?** (Dub)/ **Can You Still Love Me?** (Vocal) (12″/CD)	TSCX 17/ TSCCD 17	

Promised Land	TSCXS 17	
(Joe Smooth's Alternate Club Mix)/		
Can You Still Love Me? (Club Vocal)/		
Can You Still Love Me?		
(12 O'Clock Dub) (12″ remix)		

5/89	**Long Hot Summer** 89 Mix/	LHS 1	(48)
	Everybody's On The Run		

Long Hot Summer 89 Mix (Extended Version)/ LHSX 1/
Everybody's On The Run (Version One)/ LHSCD 1
Everybody's On The Run (Version Two)
(12″/CD)

Notes: B-side mixed by Freddie Bastone and featuring Brian J. Powell on vocals

7/89 **Sure Is Sure/Love Of The World** TSCX 18
(unissued but 12″ acetates exist)

Notes: Boy Who Cried Wolf was issued as a single instead of Come To Milton Keynes in many countries other than the UK (including North America and Australia)

THE COUNCIL COLLECTIVE SINGLE

12/84	**Soul Deep** pt 1/**Soul Deep** pt 2	MINE 1	(24)

Soul Deep/A Miner's Point MINE X1
(12″; B-side is interview)

Soul Deep (Club Mix)/**Soul Deep** MINEX 1
(12″; plain black sleeve)

RETROSPECTIVE 7″ EPs

12/87 **Café Bleu** (also on CD [TSCCD 101]) TSCEP 1
Headstart For Happiness/Here's One That Got Away/Bleu Café/Strength Of Your Nature

12/87 **The Birds And The B's** (also CD [TSCCD 102]) TSCEP 2
Piccadilly Trail/It Just Came To Pieces In My Hands/Spin' Drifting/Spring, Summer, Autumn

12/87 **Mick Talbot Is Agent '88** TSCEP 3 (100)
(also CD [TSCCD 103])
Mick's Up/Party Chambers/Mick's Blessings/Mick's Company

ALBUMS

9/83   **Introducing The Style Council**   815 277-1
(Mini-LP, Dutch import)
[1]Long Hot Summer/Headstart For Happiness/Speak Like A Child/[2]Long Hot Summer (Club Mix)/The Paris Match/Mick's Up/Money-Go-Round
Notes: The cassette edition [815 531-4] added two extra tracks, Party Chambers and Le Depart; although not credited, Long Hot Summer is Extended Version

3/84   **Café Bleu**   TSCLP 1   (2)
(with A5 booklet)
[1]Mick's Blessings / The Whole Point Of No Return / Me Ship Came In! / Blue Café/The Paris Match*/My Ever Changing Moods*/Dropping Bombs On The Whitehouse/[2]A Gospel/Strength Of Your Nature/You're The Best Thing/Here's One That Got Away/Headstart For Happiness*/Council Meetin'
Notes: The Whole Point Of No Return is omitted from track listing on back cover; tracks marked (*) are re-recordings of earlier releases; LP was titled My Ever Changing Moods in U.S.A. with different track listing

6/85   **Our Favourite Shop**   TSCLP 2   (1)
(gatefold sleeve with photo insert)
[1]Homebreakers / All Gone Away / Come To Milton Keynes / Internationalists / A Stones Throw Away/The Stand Up Comic's Instructions/Boy Who Cried Wolf/[2]A Man Of Great Promise/Down In The Seine/The Lodgers (or She Was Only A Shopkeeper's Daughter)/Luck/With Everything To Lose/Our Favourite Shop/Walls Come Tumbling Down!
Notes: Cassette edition adds Gary Crowley Meets The Council, a track-by-track interview with the band; CD edition [825 700-2] adds different version of Shout To The Top; LP was titled Internationalists in U.S.A. with different track listing

5/86   **Home & Abroad** (live)   TSCLP 3   (8)
(with 'Live! The Style Council' 'obi' wraparound band)
[1]My Ever Changing Moods/The Lodgers/Headstart For Happiness/(When You) Call Me / The Whole Point Of No Return / [2]With Everything To Lose / Homebreakers/Shout To The Top/Walls Come Tumbling Down!/Internationalists
Notes: The CD edition [829 143-2] adds two extra tracks, The Big Boss Groove and Our Favourite Shop

2/87   **The Cost Of Loving**   TSCLP 4   (2)
(double pack of 2 × 45rpm 12"s)
[1]It Didn't Matter/Right To Go/[2]Heavens Above/Fairy Tales/[3]Angel/Walking The Night/[4]Waiting/The Cost Of Loving/A Woman's Song
Notes: A Woman's Song is omitted from track listing on inside of gatefold sleeve and inner sleeves

6/88　**Confessions Of A Pop Group**　　　　TSCLP 5　　(15)
(with foldout lyric insert)
[1]The Piano Paintings: It's A Very Deep Sea/The Story Of Someones Shoe/Changing Of The Guard/The Little Boy In A Castle/The Gardener Of Eden (A Three Piece Suite)/[2]Confessions Of A Pop-Group: Life At A Top Peoples Health Farm/Why I Went Missing/How She Threw It All Away/Iwasadoledadstoyboy/Confessions 1, 2 & 3/Confessions Of A Pop Group

8/89　**Modernism: A New Decade**　　　　TSCLP 6
(unissued but acetates exist)
(alias **A Decade Of Modernism** or **1990: A New Decade In Modernism**)
[1]That Spiritual Thing/Everybody's On The Run/Love Of The World/Sure Is Sure/
[2]A New Decade/Can You Still Love Me?/The World Must Come Together/Hope (Feelings Gonna Getcha')
Note: Hope (Feelings Gonna Getcha') exists on separate acetate or white label promo

8/98　**Modernism: A New Decade**　　　　557 789-2
　　　　Box Set
Disc 1
Speak Like A Child/Party Chambers (Vocal Version)/Money-Go-Round (Bert Bevans Alternate Remix)/Headstart For Happiness (Money Go Round B-side Version)/Mick's Up/Long Hot Summer/The Paris Match (Weller's vocal Version)/Le Départ/A Solid Bond In Your Heart/It Just Came To Pieces In My Hands/My Ever Changing Moods (12" Version)/Micks Company/Spring Summer Autumn/Mick's Blessings/The Whole Point Of No Return/Me Ship Came In!/Blue Café/The Paris Match (Tracey Thorn Version)/My Ever Changing Moods (Long Slow Version)/Dropping Bombs On The Whitehouse/A Gospel

Disc 2
Strength Of Your Nature/You're The Best Thing/Here's One That Got Away/Headstart For Happiness (Cafe Bleu Version)/Council Meetin'/The Big Boss Groove/Shout to the Top/Ghosts of Dachau/The Piccadilly Trail/Soul Deep (Bert Bevans Remix)/Walls Come Tumbling Down!/The Whole Point II/Bloodsports/Spin' Drifting/Homebreakers/All Gone Away/Come To Milton Keynes/Internationalists/A Stone's Throw Away/The Stand Up Comic's Instructions/Boy Who Cried Wolf

Disc 3
A Man Of Great Promise/Down In The Seine/The Lodgers (Or She Was Only A Shopkeeper's Daughter)/Luck/With Everything To Lose/Our Favourite Shop/(When You)Call Me/Have You Ever Had It Blue (Uncut Version)/Mr. Cool's Dream/It Didn't Matter/All Year Round/Right To Go/Heavens Above/Fairy Tales/Angel/Walking The Night/Waiting/The Cost Of Loving/A Woman's Song/Françoise

Disc 4

Wanted/The Cost Of Loving (12" Version) (Slow Version)/Life At A Top peoples health farm (Um & Argh Mix)/Sweet Loving Ways/It's A Very Deep Sea/The Story Of Someone's Shoe/Changing Of The Guard/The Little Boy In A Castle A Dove Flew Down From The Elephant/The Gardener Of Eden (A Three Piece Suite) In the Beginning – The Gardener Of Eden –Mourning The Passing Of Time/Why I Went Missing/How She Threw It All Away/Iwasadoledadstoyboy/Confessions 1,2 & 3/Confessions Of A Pop Group/In Love for The First Time/I Do Like To Be B-side The A-side/The Mixed Companions

Disc 5

Promised Land (Longer Version)/Can You Still Love Me?/Long Hot Summer '89/Everybody's On The Run/Modernism: A New Decade 49.33 Reviewed/A New Decade/Can You Still Love Me?/The World Must Come Together/Hope (Feelings Gonna Getcha')/That Spiritual Thing/Everybody's On The Run/Love Of The World/Sure Is Sure

OTHER SINGLES

12/84	**It Just Came To Pieces In My Hands**	Lyntone
	(Coventry)/**Speak Like A Child** (London)	LYN 15344/45
	(Live fan club flexidisc)	

9/85	**My Ever Changing Moods**	GIV 2
	(Live in Liverpool 6.85)	
	(on *NME* Drastic Plastic EP given away with the *NME* music paper)	

9/85	**Walls Come Tumbling Down!**	HOT 001
	(Live at Manchester Apollo 14.6.85)	
	(on The Hit Red Hot EP given away with issue 1 of *The Hit* magazine)	

1985	**Long Hot Summer/(When You) Call Me/**	883 478-1
	Internationalists	
	(Australian 12"; also on 2-track 7")	
	Notes: Live on 18.8.85 at Sports & Entertainment Centre, Melbourne, Australia)	

1/90	**Speak Like A Child/Long Hot Summer**	Old Gold OG 9924

1/90	**You're The Best Thing/**	Old Gold OG 9929
	My Ever Changing Moods	

IMPORTANT PROMOTIONAL RELEASES

4/83	**Money-Go-Round/Money-Go-Round**	TSCX 2
	(Dance Mix) (12", white label)	
	Notes: B-side unavailable commercially in the UK	

| 4/85 | **Walls Come Tumbling Down!/** | TSC DJ 8 |
| | **The Whole Point II/Blood Sports** (7″) | |

Notes: Censored A-side, "You don't have to take this *rap*"

| 8/85 | **The Lodgers** (Extended Mix)/ | TSCCM 10 |
| | **The Lodgers** (Club Mix) (12″, white label) | |

A-side differs from Extended Mix released commercially in the UK

| 2/87 | **Angel/Heavens Above** (12″) | COST 2 |

Notes: This was planned as a single but scrapped after this promo

| 5/88 | **Interview With The Style Council** (LP) | TSCIN 1 |

Notes: In addition, several unique edits were created for the American market

KING TRUMAN SINGLE

| 2/89 | **Like A Gun** (various mixes) (12″) | Acid Jazz JAZID 9 |

Notes: Essentially a Style Council release, which was quickly withdrawn

COMPILATION ALBUMS

| 3/89 | **Singular Adventures Of The Style Council** | TSCTV 1 | (3) |

[1]You're The Best Thing/Have You Ever Had It Blue/Money-Go-Round/My Ever Changing Moods/Long Hot Summer/The Lodgers/Walls Come Tumbling Down!/ [2]Shout To The Top/Wanted/It Didn't Matter/Speak Like A Child/A Solid Bond In Your Heart/Life At A Top Peoples Health Farm/Promised Land
Notes: The CD edition has Alternate Mixes of You're The Best Thing and The Lodgers, 12″ versions of Money-Go-Round, Have You Ever Had It Blue, My Ever Changing Moods and Long Hot Summer 89 and two extra tracks, How She Threw It All Away and Waiting

| 10/91 | **Headstart For Happiness –** | Pickwick |
| | **The Style Council Collection** (CD) | PWKS 4090P |

Long Hot Summer/Why I Went Missing/Angel/Waiting/Move On Up (Live)/ Spring, Summer, Autumn/Blue Café/Come To Milton Keynes/Wanted/Heavens Above/Everybody's On The Run (Version One)/Spin' Drifting/It Just Came To Pieces In My Hands/Mr. Cool's Dream/Headstart For Happiness

| 6/93 | **Here's Some That Got Away** (CD) | 519 372-2 | (39) |

Love Pains★/Party Chambers/The Whole Point II/Ghosts Of Dachau/Sweet Loving Ways/A Casual Affair★/A Woman's Song/Mick's Up/Waiting On A Connection★/ Night After Night★ / The Piccadilly Trail / (When You) Call Me / My Very Good Friend★ / April's Fool★ / In Love For The First Time / Big Boss Groove / Mick's Company / Blood Sports / Who Will Buy / I Ain't Goin' Under★ / I Am Leaving★ / A Stones Throw Away
Notes: Tracks marked (★) were previously unissued; Who Will Buy was previously issued in Japan as B-side to It Didn't Matter

3/96   **The Style Council Collection** (CD)   529 483-2

Speak Like A Child/Headstart For Happiness/Long Hot Summer/The Paris Match/ It Just Came To Pieces In My Hands/My Ever Changing Moods/The Whole Point Of No Return/Ghosts Of Dachau/You're The Best Thing/The Big Boss Groove/ Man Of Great Promise/Homebreakers/Down In The Seine/A Stones Throw Away/With Everything To Lose/Boy Who Cried Wolf/The Cost Of Loving/ Changing Of The Guard/Why I Went Missing/It's A Very Deep Sea

t.b.a.   **The Style Council In Concert**   t.b.a.

Meetin' (Over) Up Yonder★/Up For Grabs★/Long Hot Summer/One Nation Under A Groove★/Le Départ/Spring, Summer, Autumn/Hangin' On To A Memory★/It Just Came To Pieces In My Hands/Here's One That Got Away/My Ever Changing Moods/Man Of Great Promise/Boy Who Cried Wolf/A Stones Throw Away/Speak Like A Child/Mick's Up/You're The Best Thing/Move On Up/Down In The Seine/It's A Very Deep Sea/Heavens Above

Notes: This follow-up release to 1986's Home & Abroad featured four exclusive songs, marked (★) but has still to be released

IMPORTANT VARIOUS ARTISTS LPs

4/86   **Have You Ever Had It Blue**   Virgin V 2386
            (slightly different mix)
            on soundtrack, *Absolute Beginners* (also issued as double LP)

8/85   **Come To Milton Keynes** (Instrumental)   Natalie LIE 2
            on *Sons Of Jobs For The Boys*

GUEST APPEARANCES, ETC.

BANANARAMA

3/83   **Dr. Love**   London   (7)
            on their LP, *Deep Sea Skiving*   RAMA 1
Notes: Song given to them by Paul Weller

ANIMAL NIGHTLIFE

1984   **Mr Solitaire**/Lazy Afternoon (also on 12″)   Island   (25)
            Paul Weller sings backing vocals on A-side   IS 193

BAND AID

12/84   **Do They Know It's Christmas?**/   Mercury   (1)
        Feed The World   FEED 1
            (also on 12″ [FEED 112] & shaped picture disc [FEED P1])
Notes: Multi-artist charity single featuring Paul Weller; reissued 12/85 (No. 3)

DIZZI HEIGHTS
4/85   **The Gospel!/Instrumental** (7"/12")   Parlophone
                                                        (12) DIZZ 1
Notes: Re-recording of Paul Weller's Café Bleu song with Steve White on drums

DEE C. LEE
10/85   **See The Day/The Paris Match**   CBS A 6570   (3)

        See The Day/The Paris Match/Luck   CBS TX 6570
        (Live Version)/**Don't Do It Baby** (Club Mix) (12")
Notes: The Paris Match is by 'the Council Quartet', i.e. The Style Council; Luck is a
Style Council song

CHAIRMEN OF THE BOARD Featuring GENERAL JOHNSON
9/86   **Lover Boy/Lover Boy** (Instrumental Mix)   EMI 5585   (56)

        Lover Boy (Extended Mix)/   12EMI 5585
        Lover Boy (Instrumental Mix) (12")

        Lover Boy (Extended Mix)/   12EMID 5585
        Lover Boy (Instrumental Mix)//**Give Me Just A Little More Time/
        (You've Got Me) Dangling On A String**
        (12", double pack, gatefold sleeve)
Notes: Lover Boy remixed at Solid Bond Studios by Paul Weller with keyboard solo
by Mick Talbot

THE JAZZ DEFECTORS
8/87   **The Jazz Defectors**   Factory FACT 205
Notes: LP produced by Paul Weller and Mick Talbot

LISA M
9/89   **Going Back To My Roots** (Dynamite Mix)/   Zomba JIVE(T) 221
        (Back To The Beats Mix)/Make It Right (12"; also on 7")
Notes: Going Back To My Roots Produced by Paul Weller and Mick Talbot

SLAM SLAM (Dee C. Lee)
9/90   **Something Ain't Right** (D Beat Slammin' Mix)/ MCA MCAX 1444
        Something Ain't Right (Jammin' Urban Mix)/
        Free Your Feelings (12")
A-side written by Paul Weller, who was also involved in the production

5/91   **Free Your Feelings** (LP/CD)   MCA(D) 10147
[1]Move (Dance All Night)/Something Ain't Right*/Free Your Feelings/What
Dreams Are Made Of*/Giving It Up*/[2]You'll Find Love*/Depth Charge/Round
& Round*/Tender Love*/Nothing Like It*
Notes: Tracks marked (*) are written or co-written by Paul Weller; Move (Dance All
Night) (7/89) and Free Your Feelings (5/91) were also released as singles but these
aren't Paul Weller songs

OTHER IMPORTANT LPs

VARIOUS ARTISTS
1990   **A Certain Kind Of Freedom** (LP)   Urban 841 923-1
Co-ordinated and featuring Steve White, plus Mick Talbot

TALBOT WHITE
1994   **United States Of Mind** (LP/CD)   Boogie Back
                                                    BBRLP 003
Collaboration between the two ex-members of The Style Council; also features
Jacko Peake and Camelle Hinds, who have worked with Paul Weller

SPOKEN-WORD INTERVIEW RECORDS

4/87   **Interview Picture Disc** (12″)   Baktabak
Interview from 1985 Australian tour   BAK 2032

4/88   **Interview 1988**   STYLE 7
(7″, on blue vinyl [500 only] or picture disc [2000 only])

VIDEOS

11/83   **What We Did On Our Holidays**   PolyGram
          The Video Singles Part 1   040 189-2
Speak Like A Child/Money-Go-Round/Long Hot Summer/A Solid Bond In Your
Heart
Notes: Promo videos for first four singles, plus Le Départ played over credits; reissued
on Channel 5 CFV 00282, 3/86

9/84   **Far East & Far Out –**   PolyGram 040 369-2
          Council Meeting In Japan
Intro – Me Ship Came In!/The Big Boss Groove/Here's One That Got Away/
You're The Best Thing/It Just Came To Pieces In My Hands/Mick's Up/Dropping
Bombs On The Whitehouse/Long Hot Summer/My Ever Changing Moods/Le
Départ/The Whole Point Of No Return/Money-Go-Round/Headstart For
Happiness/Speak Like A Child/Reprise – Le Départ
Notes: In concert in Japan, 5.5.84; also on CD Video (Laservision 040 369-1);
reissued on Channel 5 SPC 00302, 7/86; and on Spectrum SPC 00032, 10/89; US
and Japanese CD Videos add 5 extra tracks

12/85   **What We Did The Following Year**   PolyGram 041 322-2
          The Video Singles Part 2
You're The Best Thing/Shout To The Top/The Lodgers/My Ever Changing Moods/
Boy Who Cried Wolf/Walls Come Tumbling Down!/Come To Milton Keynes
Notes: More promotional videos; reissued on Channel 5 CFV 05082, 10/86

5/86   **Showbiz! – The Style Council Live!**   PolyGram 041 371-2
The Big Boss Groove/(When You) Call Me/Shout To The Top/Homebreakers/
With Everything To Lose/Our Favourite Shop/Headstart For Happiness/Long Hot

Summer / Walls Come Tumbling Down! / A Stones Throw Away / Soul Deep –
Medley (Soul Deep–Strength Of Your Nature)/Internationalists
Notes: In concert at Wembley Arena, 1985; companion release to Home & Abroad
live album; also on CD Video (080 038-1, 10/88); reissued on Channel 5 CFV
06182, 3/87

2/87   **Jerusalem**   Palace PVC 3014M
Angel/It Didn't Matter/Heavens Above/Fairy Tales
Notes: Half-hour movie starring the band, which was also shown at the cinema and
during concerts

10/88   **Confessions Of A Pop Group**   Channel 5 CFV 07512
It's A Very Deep Sea/Why I Went Missing/Life At A Top Peoples Health Farm/
Changing Of The Guard/How She Threw It All Away/Confessions Of A Pop Group
Notes: Companion release to Confessions Of A Pop Group album; also on 8" CD
Video (PolyGram 080 384-9)

3/89   **The Video Adventures Of The Style Council**   Channel 5 CFV 07842
        (Greatest Hits Vol. 1)
You're The Best Thing/Have You Ever Had It Blue/Money-Go-Round/My Ever
Changing Moods/Long Hot Summer/The Lodgers/Walls Come Tumbling Down/
Shout To The Top!/Wanted/It Didn't Matter/Speak Like A Child/A Solid Bond In
Your Heart/Life At A Top Peoples Health Farm/Promised Land
Notes: Companion release to The Singular Adventures Of The Style Council album;
reissued on 4 Front 083 512-3, 7/91

CD VIDEO SINGLES

These 5" discs all feature several audio tracks, ending with one audio-visual track

11/88   **À Paris**   PolyGram 080 206-2
Long Hot Summer (Extended Version) / Party Chambers / The Paris Match /
Le Départ/Long Hot Summer

11/88   **Have You Ever Had It Blue**   PolyGram 080 336-2
Have You Ever Had It Blue (Uncut Version)/Mr. Cool's Dream/With Everything
To Lose/Have You Ever Had It Blue

11/88   **How She Threw It All Away**   PolyGram 080 400-2
How She Threw It All Away/Love The First Time/Long Hot Summer (Tom
Mix)/How She Threw It All Away

4/89   **Life At A Top Peoples Health Farm**   PolyGram 080 560-2
Life At A Top Peoples Health Farm (Extended Remix)/Spank!/Sweet Loving
Ways/Life At A Top Peoples Health Farm

IMPORTANT VARIOUS ARTISTS VIDEOS

9/84   **Video Bongo**   NME/Maxell V 002
Notes: mail–order only via NME music paper

1/85   **Video Aid**   Virgin 102
Both the above exclusively feature the promo video for The Big Boss Groove

VIDAID
12/84   **Band Aid – 'Do They Know It's Christmas'**   PolyGram 041 121 2
Includes documentary on the making of the record

10/86   **Absolute Beginners – The Musical**   Virgin VVP 160
Have You Ever Had It Blue
Notes: Video release of movie with Eddie O'Connell lip-synching to Style Council song; reissued on VVL VVD 160, 7/93

4/88   **Red Wedge – Days Like These**   Virgin VVD 237
Don't Look Any Further/Move On Up/Madness
Notes: This 1986 Newcastle City Hall concert by the Red Wedge collective includes The Style Council joining the likes of Madness, Billy Bragg and Lloyd Cole; Paul Weller shares lead vocals with Junior on Don't Look Any Further, and also contributes vocals on Move On Up and Madness; he also provides comments during interview clips between songs

6/88   **Freedom Beat**   Hendring HEN 2 087
Move On Up (live, 1986)
Notes: Anti-apartheid concert held on Clapham Common

12/88   **Curtis Mayfield Live At Ronnie Scott's,**   Hendring HEN 2 151
London
Notes: Interspersed within live footage, Paul Weller interviews Curtis Mayfield

PAUL WELLER

All the releases by Paul Weller are on Go! Discs unless otherwise stated. Cassette editions exist for all Paul Weller's singles, which share the same tracks as the 7" editions.

THE PAUL WELLER MOVEMENT SINGLE

5/91   **Into Tomorrow/Here's A New Thing**   Freedom High   (36)
                                            FHP 1

         Into Tomorrow/Here's A New Thing/   Freedom High
         That Spiritual Feeling/Into Tomorrow   FHPT 1/FHPCD 1
         (8-Track Demo) (12"/CD)
Notes: Freedom High was Paul Weller's own label; That Spiritual Feeling was recorded by The Style Council

PAUL WELLER SINGLES

8/92	**Uh Huh Oh Yeh/Fly On The Wall**	GOD 86	(18)

Uh Huh Oh Yeh/Fly On The Wall/ GOD X 86/
Arrival Time/Always There To Fool You GOD CD 86
(12″/CD Digipak)

10/92	**Above The Clouds/**	GOD 91	(47)

Everything Has A Price To Pay

Above The Clouds/ GOD X 91/
Everything Has A Price To Pay/ GOD CD 91
All Year Round (Live at New York City The Ritz 25.7.92)/
Feeling Alright (12″/CD)

7/93	**Sunflower/Bull-Rush–Magic Bus**	GOD 102	(16)

(Live at Royal Albert Hall 10.92)

Sunflower/Kosmos SXDub 2000/ GOD X 102/
Bull-Rush–Magic Bus GOD CD 102
(Live at Royal Albert Hall 10.92)/
That Spiritual Feeling (New Mix) (12″/CD)

Notes: That Spiritual Feeling features The J.B.'s; Kosmos SXDub 2000 is remix of Kosmos

8/93	**Wild Wood/Ends Of The Earth**	GOD 104/	(14)

(7″/10″ with poster/CD Digipak with 5 prints) GOD T 104/
GOD CD 104

10/93	**The Weaver** EP:	GOD 107/	(18)

The Weaver/This Is No Time/ GOD T 107/
Another New Day/Ohio GOD CD 107
(Live at Royal Albert Hall 10.92) (EP/numbered 10″/CD)

3/94	**Hung Up/Foot Of The Mountain**	GOD 111/	(11)

(Live at Royal Albert Hall 23.11.93)/ GOD X 111/
The Loved/Kosmos (Lynch Mob Bonus Beats) GOD CD 111
(EP/12″/CD)

10/94	**Out Of The Sinking/Sexy Sadie**	GOD 121	(20)

Out Of The Sinking/Sexy Sadie/Sunflower GOD X 121/
(Lynch Mob Dub) (12″/CD) GOD CD 121

4/95	**The Changingman/I'd Rather Go Blind/**	GOD 127/	(7)

It's A New Day, Baby/ GOD CD 127
I Didn't Mean To Hurt You (Live at Royal Albert Hall) (EP/CD)

300

7/95	**You Do Something To Me/**	GOD 130/	(9)
	My Whole World Is Falling Down★/	GOD CD 130	
	A Year Late/Woodcutter's Son★ (EP/CD)		

Tracks marked (★) were recorded live on Radio One's *The Evening Session* 5.95

9/95	**Broken Stones/Steam**	GOD 132/	(20)
	(7″/CD)	GOD CD 132	

Notes: Steam was originally circulated as a promo 12″, Lynch Mob Beats

2/96	**Out Of The Sinking** (LP Version)/	GOD 143/	(16)
	I Shall Be Released/Broken Stones/	GOD CD 143	
	Porcelain Gods (numbered EP with postcard/CD)		

Last two tracks recorded on Dutch radio K.R.O. Radio 3, 1.10.95
Notes: This reissue with different B-sides and a different sleeve was available for one week only

8/96	**Peacock Suit/Eye Of The Storm**	GOD 149/	(5)
	(7″/Digipak CD)	GOD CD 149	

7/97	**Brushed/Ain't No Love In The Heart Of**	Island IS/	(14)
	The City/Shoot The Dove/As You Lean	CID 666	
	Into The Light (Acoustic Version)		
	(7″/CD)		

9/97	**Friday Street/Sunflower/Brushed/**	Island	(21)
	Mermaids (live)	CID676/IS676	
	(7″/CD)		

11/97	**Mermaids/So You Want To Be A Dancer/**	Island	(30)
	Everything Has A Price To Pay ('97 version)	CID683/IS683	
	(7″/CD)		

11/98	**Brand New Start/Right Underneath It/**	Island	(16)
	The Riverbank	IS/CID711	
	(7″/CD)		

1/99	**Wild Wood/Ends Of The Earth**	Island	(22)
	(CD billed as Paul Weller vs Portishead)	CID734/IS734/	
		12IS734	

4/00	**He's The Keeper/Helioscentric/**	Island	(–)
	Bang-Bang	CID760/IS760/	
		562 655-1/2	
		Island	
		CID760/562 655-2	

| 8/00 | **Sweet Pea, My Sweet Pea/** | Island | (44) |

8/00   **Sweet Pea, My Sweet Pea/**   Island   (44)
      Back In the Fire (BBC Radio Version)**/**   CID764/IS764/
      There's No Drinking After You're Dead   562 869-1/2
      (Noonday Underground Remix)

GUEST APPEARANCE ON WHO TRIBUTE ALBUM
6/01   **Circles**   Edel 0126242ERE
      on Substitute: The Songs Of The Who

THE SMOKIN' MOJO FILTERS SINGLE

12/95   **Come Together/**(tracks by other artists)   GOD 136/   (19)
      (EP/CD)   GOD CD 136
Notes: Beatles cover version featuring Paul Weller and his band, plus Noel Gallagher and Paul McCartney; taken from *Help* album

ALBUMS

9/92   **Paul Weller** (LP/CD)   828 343-1/2   (8)
(LP has gatefold sleeve with stapled–in lyric booklet)
[1]Uh Huh Oh Yeh/I Didn't Mean To Hurt You/Bull-Rush/Round And Round/ Remember How We Started/Above The Clouds/[2]Clues/Into Tomorrow/Amongst Butterflies/The Strange Museum/Bitterness Rising/Kosmos

9/93   **Wild Wood** (LP/CD)   828 435-1/2   (2)
(LP has gatefold sleeve & 'obi' wraparound band; initially with poster)
[1]Sunflower/Can You Heal Us (Holy Man)/Wild Wood/Instrumental (pt 1)/All The Pictures On The Wall/Has My Fire Really Gone Out?/Country/[2]5th Season/The Weaver/Instrumental (pt 2)/Foot Of The Mountain/Shadow Of The Sun/Holy Man (Reprise)/Moon On Your Pyjamas

4/94   **Wild Wood** (LP/CD)   828 513-1/2   (2)
(LP has gatefold sleeve & 'obi' wraparound band; initially with poster)
Reissue with extra track Hung Up (end of side 1 after Country)

9/94   **Live Wood** (double LP/CD)   828 561-1/2   (13)
[1]Bull-Rush–Magic Bus / This Is No Time / All The Pictures On The Wall / Remember How We Started – Dominoes/Above The Clouds/[2]Wild Wood/ Shadow Of The Sun / [3](Can You Heal Us) Holy Man – War / 5th Season / Into Tomorrow/[4]Foot Of The Mountain/Sunflower/Has My Fire Really Gone Out?

5/95 **Stanley Road** (LP/CD)   828 619-1/2   (1)
(LP has gatefold sleeve with *Excerpts* booklet)
[1]The Changingman/Porcelain Gods/I Walk On Gilded Splinters/You Do Something To Me/Woodcutter's Son/Time Passes/[2]Stanley Road/Broken Stones/Out Of The Sinking/Pink On White Walls/Whirlpools' End/Wings Of Speed
Notes: Out Of The Sinking features Carleen Anderson's additional backing vocals missing from earlier single version

5/95 **Stanley Road**   850 070-7/828 620-2
Limited edition box set of 6 x 7″ singles in 7″ box or CD in 12″ box

6/97 **Heavy Soul** (LP/CD/   Island ILPS/   (2)
Foldout CD in card cover with 5 postcards)   CID/CIDX
                                                     8058
[1]Heavy Soul/Peacock Suit/Up In Suze's Room/Brushed/Driving Nowhere/I Should Have Been There To Inspire You/[2]Heavy Soul Pt. 2/Friday Street/Science/Golden Sands/As You Lean Into The Light/Mermaids
Notes: The Japanese edition adds Eye Of The Storm

11/98 **Modern Classics** (LP/CD)   Island   (7)
                                                     ILPS/CIDD
                                                     8058/524 609-1/2
Out Of The Sinking/Peacock Suit/Sunflower/The Weaver/Wild Wood/Above The Clouds/Uh-Huh Oh-Yeh/Brushed/The Changingman/Friday Street/You Do Something To Me/Brand New Start/Hung Up/Mermaids/Broken Stones/Into Tomorrow

4/00 **Heliocentric** (LP/CD)   Island   (2)
                                                     ILPS/CIDD
                                                     8093/542 394-1/2
He's The Keeper/Frightened/Sweet Pea, My Sweet Pea/A Whale's Tale/Back In The Fire/Dust And Rocks/There's No Drinking, After You're Dead/With Time & Temperance/Picking Up Sticks/Love-Less

10/01 **Days Of Speed** (LP/CD)   Independiente   (3)
                                                     ISOM26LP/CD
Brand New Start/The Loved/Out Of The Sinking/Clues/English Rose/Above The Clouds/You Do Something To Me/Amongst Butterflies/Science/Back In The Fire/Down In The Seine/That's Entertainment/Loveless/There's No Drinking After You're Dead/Everything Has A Price To Pay/Wild Wood/Headstart For Happiness/Town Called Malice

SELECTED MAGAZINE & BOOK FREEBIES

1993   **The Loved**   (WELLER+F1)
(blank clear flexidisc given away with *The Big Issue* magazine)
Notes: Different version to B-side of Hung Up

9/94   **Shadow Of The Sun**   PNME 1
          (Live at Wolverhampton Civic Hall 9.3.94)/
          Sunflower (Lynch Mob Dub Edit)/**Wild Wood**
          (Sheared Wood – Remixed by Portishead with A. Utley)
Given away with *NME* music paper, double-A-side

1/95   **This Is No Time**   NME BRAT 95
          (Live at Royal Albert Hall 11.94)
On various artists cassette *NME Brat Pack '95* given away with 28.1.95 issue of *NME*

9/95   **Stanley Road/Porcelain Gods/Time Passes/**   DAYS 1
          Broken Stones/You Do Something To Me
(CD, Demo versions of songs from Stanley Road)
Available by mail-order to purchasers of book, *Days Lose Their Names And Time Slips Away*

1/96   **Stanley Road** (Demo)   NME BRATS 96
On various artists cassette *NME Brat Pack '95* given away with 27.1.96 issue of *NME*

1/96   **Talk Tonight**   Q/Channel 4
                                        (no cat. no.)
By Noel Gallagher with Paul Weller on piano on various artists cassette *The White Room Album* given away with 2.96 edition of Q magazine (issue 113)

6/96   **Into Tomorrow/Wild Wood/**   PWGCD 1
          Out Of The Sinking (CD)
Given away with *The Guide*, part of *The Guardian* newspaper's Saturday edition

IMPORTANT JAPANESE CDs

4/92   **Paul Weller**   Pony Canyon
                                        PCCY 00337
With a unique version of Here's A New Thing instead of Strange Museum

6/94   **More Wood (Little Splinters)**   Pony Canyon
                                        PCCY 00509
Japanese-only compilation of B-sides and other non-album tracks

IMPORTANT PROMOTIONAL RECORDS

1993   **Bull-Rush** (edit)/**Amongst Butterflies**   CDP 874
        (Acoustic)/**Bitterness Rising** (Acoustic) (U.S. CD)
The 'Acoustic' versions weren't issued in the UK

1994   **Kosmos** (Bonus Beats 6.11)/   PRO 1117 DJ
        (Lynch Mob Bonus Beats 7.04) (U.S. 12″)
Features an exclusive edit of the remix

1/95   **Lynch Mob Beats**   LYNCH 1
        (12″, stamped 1-sided white label promo)
Radical remix of Whirlpools' End; later released as Steam

6/95   **A Conversation With Paul Weller**   PRCD 7007-2
        (Interview CD)
This digipak promo CD was given away free with initial U.S. copies of *Stanley Road*

IMPORTANT VARIOUS ARTISTS LPs

1991   **Don't Let Me Down**   Pop God
(cover of The Beatles song)   PGLP 09/PGCD 09
on Beatles covers LP/CD, *Revolution No. 9*, for Oxfam's Cambodia appeal

1993   **Above The Clouds** (Acoustic)   Radio
on *2 Meter Sessies Volume 4*   474 719-2
(Dutch CD, featuring exclusive radio sessions)

3/94   **Black Sheep Boy**   Volume
(cover of Tim Hardin song)   99VCD9/99VLP9
on *Volume Nine* CD or double LP, with 192-page 'book' magazine, issue 9

9/95   **Come Together**   Go! Discs   (1)
(cover of The Beatles song as The Smokin' Mojo Filters)   828 682-1/2
on *Help* double LP/CD, a fund-raising project for War Child campaign

9/96   **Almost Grown**   Nice NYCE 1(CD)
On Small Faces tribute LP/CD *Long Agos and Worlds Apart*
Notes: Credited to Kenney J. All Stars, this cover version features Paul Weller, the
Small Faces' drummer Kenney Jones, and producer Glyn Johns

GUEST APPEARANCES

MOTHER EARTH
3/93   **Mr Freedom** EP   (12″/CD)   Acid Jazz
Paul Weller sings backing vocals on the title track   JACID 62T/CD
Notes: Weller also plays harp on an unissued cover of the Small Faces' The Universal;
Mr Freedom was taken from Mother Earth's The People Tree album (Acid Jazz
JAZID 083, 2/94, No. 45)

CARLEEN ANDERSON
5/94   Mama Said/You've Got To Earn It/   Circa YRCDG 114
        Who Was That Masked Man?/If You Knew (Demo) (CD)
Paul Weller plays guitar on the B-side, a cover of the Van Morrison song

INDIAN VIBES
9/94   **Mathar** (12″/CD)   Virgin France
                                                        DINST/DINSD 136
Indian Timebomb Breaks/Dawson's Dub Hands On/Radio Mix/Discovery Of
India Mix/Ballistics In Traffic Mix/Lynch Mob Beats
Weller plays electric sitar, acoustic and electric guitar on this cover of a track by
German jazz guitarist Volker Kriegel, which was originally released by the Dave Pike
Set on MPS Records in 1969; also features Marco Nelson and Galliano's Crispin
Taylor; produced by Brendan Lynch; also available as 7-track French mini-LP

DR. ROBERT
11/94   Realms of Gold (Japanese CD)   Pony Canyon
                                                        PCCY 00646
Notes: Paul Weller plays guitar on **Comfort Of The Clan**, backing vocals on **The
Coming Of Grace**, piano on **Circular Quay** and guitar, bass and percussion on
Have No Roots

1/96   **Realms Of Gold** (LP/CD)   Permanent
Notes: Belated and amended UK issue   PERM LP/CD 40
The Coming of Grace and Circular Quay were also issued as singles

OASIS
10/95   (What's The Story) Morning Glory?   Creation   (1)
         (double LP/CD)   CRE LP/CD 189
Paul Weller plays lead guitar and adds backing vocals to **Champagne Supernova**,
and plays guitar on the two unnamed instrumental jams

11/95   Wonderwall/Round Are Way/   Creation   (2)
         The Swamp Song/The Masterplan (CD)   CRESCD 215
Weller plays guitar and harmonica on The Swamp Song
(12″ omits The Masterplan but includes The Swamp Song)

OCEAN COLOUR SCENE
2/96   **The Riverboat Song**/So Sad (7″/CD)   MCA   (15)
Paul Weller plays organ; produced by Brendan Lynch   MCS/MCSTD 40021

4/96   Moseley Shoals (double LP/CD)   MCA   (2)
                                                          MCA/MCD 60008
Paul Weller plays guitar on **The Circle**; organ on **The Riverboat Song**; piano and backing vocals on **One For The Road**

9/96   **The Circle**/Mrs. Jones/Cool Cool Water/   MCA   (6)
          Top of the World   MCSTD 40077
Paul Weller plays guitar on The Circle

3/97   B-Sides, Seasides And Freerides (CD)   MCA   (3)
Gatefold digipak in outer card cover with booklet   MCD 60034
Paul Weller plays organ on **Chicken Bones And Stones**, which also appeared on the single The Day We Caught The Train

TALBOT-WHITE
9/97   Riding The Rapids (CD)   New Note
                                        NNCD 1002
Paul Weller plays guitar on 'Max's Mad Mix' of **Off The Beaten Track**
Notes: Also available on a 4-track CD single and 12″ white label promo

VARIOUS ARTISTS
8/97   **Long Live Tibet** (CD)   EMI CDEM 3768
Includes Lining Your Pockets by Ocean Colour Scene featuring Paul Weller on piano and backing vocals

ROBERT WYATT
9/97   **Shleep** (CD)   Hannibal HNCD 1418
Paul Weller plays guitar and sings harmony vocals on Free Will And Testament; and plays guitar on Blues In Bob Minor

VIDEOS

7/91   **The Paul Weller Movement Live**   Video Collection
                                                    VC 4103
Tin Soldier/Headstart For Happiness/Round And Round/Kosmos/That's Entertainment / Piccadilly Trail / Into Tomorrow / Ummh! / Long Hot Summer/ Homebreakers / Carnation / Bitterness Rising / Here's A New Thing / Precious / Tales From The Riverbank/My Ever Changing Moods
Notes: In concert at London's Brixton Academy 20.4.91; reissued on Music Club MC 2093, 10/92; reissued again on Video Collection MC 2093, 5/97

9/94   **Live Wood**   PolyGram 632 360-3
Bull-Rush–Magic Bus/Hung Up/Wild Wood/Has My Fire Really Gone Out?/
Remember How We Started/Above The Clouds/Sunflower/Can You Heal Us
(Holy Man)/5th Season/Into Tomorrow/Foot Of The Mountain/Shadow Of The
Sun
Notes: In concert at Wolverhampton Civic Hall 9.3.94; companion release to the
Live Wood album

11/94   **Highlights And Hang-Up's**   PolyGram 633 678-3
Notes: Initially mail-order only; in the shops from 2/95; documentary spanning the
whole of Paul Weller's career, with unique live clips; 1st 500 had free promo CD,
Sexy Sadie (PN PCD 2)

Notes: Live Wood and Highlights And Hang-Up's later combined on PolyGram 043
580-3, 9/96

9/00   **Paul Weller Live At The Royal Albert Hall**   Warner Music Vision
                                                         8573 85205-2 (DVD)/
                                                         3 (VHS)
Peacock Suit/Friday Street/He's The Keeper/Back In The Fire/Dust & Rocks/Out
Of The Sinking/Heavy Soul/Time & Temperance/Frightened/You Do Some-
thing To Me/Changing Man/Porcelain Gods/There Is No Drinking After You're
Dead/As You Lean Into The Light/Broken Stones/Picking Up Sticks/Love-
Less/Woodcutter's Son

GUEST APPEARANCE ON VIDEO
9/01   **The Who Live At The Royal Albert Hall**   Aviva International
                                                         IX0834MYUKD (DVD)
                                                         IX0831MYUKV (VHS)
Weller performs with The Who on 'So Sad About Us' and 'See Me, Feel Me'

JAMMING! LABEL

SINGLES

RUDI
9/81   When I Was Dead/Bewerewolf/   CREATE 1
        The Pressure's On (with lyric insert)
Notes: co-produced by Paul Weller but he was uncredited

ZEITGEIST
12/81   Ball Of Confusion (Pt 1)/   CREATE 2
        Ball Of Confusion (Pt 2)/Don't Hold On

RUDI
2/82   Crimson/14 Steps   CREATE 3

ZEITGEIST
6/82   Stop/Time Won't Tell (also on 12″)   (12) CREATE 4

APOCALYPSE
9/82   Teddy/Release!   CREATE 5
Notes: A-side produced by Paul Weller

11/82   Teddy/Release/Home Of The Brave   12 CREATE 5
            (12″ reissue)
Notes: Re-recorded version of A-side not produced by Paul Weller

ZEITGEIST
10/82   Over Again/Ripped (also on 12″)   (12) CREATE 6

RESPOND LABEL Mark I

SINGLES

Respond was initially distributed and run through Polydor:

DOLLY MIXTURE
11/81   Been-Teen/Honky Honda/Ernie Ball   RESP 1

THE QUESTIONS
2/82   Work And Play/Work And Play Part II   RESP 2
Notes: Produced by Paul Weller

THE RIMSHOTS
2/82   Sweet Talk/What's The Matter Baby?   RESP 3

DOLLY MIXTURE
3/82   Everything And More/   RESP 4
            You And Me On The Sea Shore

URBAN SHAKEDOWN
7/82   The Big Bad Wolf/Rap The Wolf   RESP 5

THE QUESTIONS
10/82   Work And Play/Saved By The Bell   RESP 7
            Work And Play (Extended Version)/   RESPX 7
            Saved By The Bell (Extended Version) (12″)
Notes: Re-recorded version produced by Paul Weller

THE QUESTIONS
1/83   Someone's Got To Lose/   RESP 8
            The Groove Line (unissued)

1/83   Someone's Got To Lose/(Instrumental)/   RESPX 8
            The Groove Line (12″, unissued)

RESPOND LABEL Mark II

SINGLES

Respond was then distributed and run through A&M:

TRACIE
3/83   The House That Jack Built/Dr. Love   KOB 1   (9)

The House That Jack Built/Tracie Talks/   KOBX 1
The House That Jack Built (Instrumental Version)/Dr. Love (12″)
Notes: Tracie is backed by the Soul Squad, led by Paul Weller, who also produced the single, co-designed the sleeve, wrote Dr. Love and interviewed Tracie on Tracie Talks; A-side is written by The Questions

THE QUESTIONS
4/83   Price You Pay/The Groove Line   KOB 702   (56)

Price You Pay/The Groove Line/   KOBX 702
Price You Pay (Instrumental) (12″)

THE MAIN T POSSEE
5/83   Fickle Public Speakin'/Version   KOB 703

Fickle Public Speakin'/Extended Version (12″)   KOBX 703
Notes: An alias for Vaughn Toulouse; Paul Weller wrote the backing music and co-produced the single – and played on it, together with Mick Talbot

TRACIE
7/83   Give It Some Emotion/The Boy Hairdresser   KOB 704   (24)

Give It Some Emotion/Tracie Raps/   KOBX 704
Give It Some Version (12″)
Notes: Tracie is backed by the Soul Squad, led by Paul Weller, who also produced the single, co-wrote The Boy Hairdresser and interviewed Tracie on Tracie Raps; Give It Some Emotion is written by A Craze

THE QUESTIONS
9/83   Tear Soup/The Vital Spark   KOB 705   (66)
Tear Soup (Extended Version)/The Vital Spark   KOBX 705
(Extended Version) (12″)

A CRAZE
10/83   Wearing Your Jumper/She Is So   KOB 706
Wearing Your Jumper/She Is So/   KOBX 706
Dub, But Not Mute (12″)
Notes: A-side produced by Paul Weller; Mick Talbot plays Wurlitzer

THE QUESTIONS

2/84	Tuesday Sunshine/The House That Jack Built	KOB 707	(46)
	Tuesday Sunshine (Jock Mix)/	KOBX 707	
	Tuesday Sunshine (Sass Mix)/The House That Jack Built/		
	No One (Long Version) (12″)		

TRACIE

3/84	Soul's On Fire/You Must Be Kidding	KOB 708	(73)
	Soul's On Fire (Long Version)/	KOBX 708	
	You Must Be Kidding (12″)		

Notes: Co-produced by Paul Weller, who also co-wrote Soul's On Fire and played guitar under pseudonym of Jake Fluckery; You Must Be Kidding is written by A Craze

THE QUESTIONS

5/84	Building On A Strong Foundation/	KOB 709
	Dreams Come True	
	Building On A Strong Foundation	KOBX 709
	(Long Version)/Dreams Come True/Acapella Foundation (12″)	

TRACIE

5/84	(I Love You) When You Sleep/	KOB710	(59)
	Same Feelings Without The Emotions		
	(I Love You) When You Sleep/	KOBX 710	
	Same Feelings Without The Emotions/Moving Together (Club Mix) (12″)		

Notes: Co-produced by Paul Weller; A-side written by Elvis Costello

M.E.F.F.

9/84	Never Stop (A Message)/Nzuri Beat/	KOBX 711
	Non-Stop Electro (12″)	

Notes: The only single from Steve White's band; A-side is produced by Paul Weller; later reissued on Re-Elect The President label

THE QUESTIONS

9/84	Belief (Don't Give It Up)/	KOB 712
	A Month Of Sundays (double-A-side)	
9/84	Belief (Don't Give It Up) (Extended Mix)/	KOBX 712
	A Month Of Sundays (12″)	

ALBUMS

VARIOUS ARTISTS

10/83   Love The Reason   RRL 501

[1]Work'n'Play by The Questions/She Is So by A Craze/Give It Some Emotion by Tracie/Peace, Love And Harmony by N.D. Moffatt/Mama Never Told Me by Tracie & The Questions/Building On A Strong Foundation by The Questions/[2]Fickle Public Speakin' (Remix) by The Main 'T'-KO/Keeping The Boys Amused by A Craze/History Of The World by The Big Sound Authority/The House That Jack Built by Tracie/Give It Up Girl by The Questions

Notes: Paul Weller played, co-produced, co-designed the sleeve and wrote the sleeve notes

TRACIE

5/84   Far From The Hurting Kind   RRL 502   (64)

[1]Thank You/Moving Together/Spring, Summer, Autumn★/What Did I Hear You Say/Far From The Hurting Kind★/[2](I Love You) When You Sleep/Soul's On Fire★/Nothing Happens Here But You★/I Can't Hold On 'Til Summer/Dr. Love★. Tracks marked (★) were written or co-written by Paul Weller.

Initially with free poster.

Notes: Tracie is backed by Kevin Miller (bass), Helen Turner (keyboards) and Steve Sidelnyk (drums), who all played with Weller, who co-produced and guested as Jake Fluckery (guitar); What Did I Hear You Say, Moving Together and I Can't Hold On 'Til Summer were written by The Questions

THE QUESTIONS

10/84   Belief   RRL 503

[1]Belief/All The Time In The World/The Bottom Line/Month Of Sundays/Someone's Got To Lose / Body And Soul / [2]Tuesday Sunshine / December / The Learning Tree/Drop That Burden/Everything I See

Notes: Steve White plays drums on Someone's Got To Lose

Much of the Respond output has been reissued on CD in Japan

RESPOND LABEL Mark III

Respond returned to Polydor for its final releases:

TRACIE YOUNG

7/85   I Can't Leave You Alone/19 – The Wickham Mix SBS 1   (60)
       (7″ Version)

       I Can't Leave You Alone (Pick 'n' Mix)/   SBSX 1
       19 – The Wickham Mix/I Can't Leave You Alone (12″)

Notes: Paul Weller received a co-songwriting credit on the B-side

VAUGHN TOULOUSE

8/85	Cruisin' The Serpentine/	SBS 2/SBSX 2
	You See The Trouble With Me (also on 12″)	

TRACIE YOUNG

10/85	Invitation/The Country Code	SBS 3
	Invitation (RSVP Mix)/The Country Code/	SBSX 3
	Invitation (12″)	

Tracie then stayed at Polydor for the following singles:

TRACIE YOUNG

7/86	We Should Be Together/Find It In Your Nature	POSP 805
7/86	We Should Be Together (The Jezamix)/	POSPX 805
	We Should Be Together/	
	Find It In Your Nature (12″)	

Notes: A-side features Steve White on drums

TRACIE YOUNG

10/86	(When You) Call Me/Italian Girl	POSP 823/
	(also on 12″)	POSPX 823

Notes: A-side is a cover of the Style Council song; Steve White played drums

Bibliography

Much as I would like to claim that every anecdote and each scrap of information presented in *My Ever Changing Moods* has never before been reported, this is not the case, and I gratefully acknowledge the many writers and publishers of the various sources I have accessed during the course of my research.

While this is the first biography to deal with the whole of Paul Weller's career, several other books have focused on the individual components:

THE JAM
Paul Honeyford, *The Modern World By Numbers* (Eel Pie, 1980)
Miles, *The Jam By Miles* (Omnibus Press, 1981)
Paolo Hewitt, *A Beat Concerto* (Omnibus Press, 1983; reprinted & expanded 1996, Boxtree)
Mike Nicholls, *About The Young Idea – The Story Of The Jam 1972-1982* (Proteus, 1984)
Alex Ogg, Bruce Foxton & Rick Buckler, *Our Story* (Castle, 1993)
Steve Brookes, *Keeping The Flame* (Sterling, 1996)
Steve Keegan, *The Jam Live* (unpublished)

There were also several magazine-styled Jam biographies. Chief among them were:

Chris Charlesworth, *Living On Borrowed Time* (Arlington Press, 1982)
Richard Lowe, *Modern Rock Icons: The Jam* (Virgin, 1997)

THE STYLE COUNCIL
Andrea Olcese, *Internationalists – Introducing The Style Council* (Riot Stories, 1985)
Iain Munn, *Mr. Cool's Dream* (Whole Point, 1996) (39 Boase Avenue, St. Andrews, Fife KY16 8BX)

PAUL WELLER
Paolo Hewitt, *Days Lose Their Names And Time Slips Away* (Boxtree, 1995)

In addition, the following books were useful:
Colin MacInnes, *Absolute Beginners* (Allison & Busby, 1959)
Adrian Henri, Roger McGough, Brian Patten, *The Mersey Sound* (Penguin, 1967)
Richard Barnes, *Mods!* (Eel Pie, 1979)

Various, *Cool Cats* (Eel Pie, 1981)
B. George & Martha DeFoe, *International Discography Of The New Wave*
    (Omnibus, 1982)
Robin Denselow, *When The Music's Over – The Story Of Political Pop*
    (Faber & Faber, 1989)
Jon Savage, *England's Dreaming* (Faber & Faber, 1991)
Mark Paytress, *Twentieth Century Boy* (Sidgwick & Jackson, 1992)
Mark Davison & Ian Currie, *Surrey In The Sixties* (Frosted Earth, 1994)
D.J. Taylor, *That's Entertainment* (essay in *Love Is The Drug*, Penguin, 1994)
George Gimarc, *Punk Diary (1970–79)* (Vintage, 1994)
Peter Ackroyd, *Blake* (Sinclair-Stevenson, 1995)
Kevin Pearce, *Something Beginning With O* (Heavenly, 1990s)
Michael Heatley, *Paul Weller In His Own Words* (Omnibus Press, 1997)
Steve Malins, *Paul Weller: The Unofficial Biography* (Virgin, 1997)

Other Weller-related publications also proved essential, such as *The Style Population* (the Style Council's fan club magazine) and the various songbooks and tour programmes.

On occasion, I also delved through the archives of the popular music press, including:
The Face, Jamming!, Melody Maker, New Musical Express, Record Collector, Record Mirror, Smash Hits, Sounds, Mojo, Q, Vox, Select, Volume.

More thorough in their coverage of Paul Weller's career have been the slew of fanzines which have accompanied his return as a solo artist in recent years:
Neil Allen, *Start!*
    Publication devoted entirely to The Jam.
    (2 Woolpack Close, Rowley Regis, Warley, West Midlands B65 8HY)

Julie Kershaw, *Ooh Aah, Paul Weller*
    A humorous, light-hearted side to Paul Weller's career.
    (4 Ennerdale Road, Formby, Liverpool L37 2EA)

David Lodge & Paula Cuccurullo, *Boys About Town*
    This most popular of Weller fanzines now boasts over thirty issues.
    (P.O. Box 12318, Edinburgh EH11 1YD)

Mark Ridlington, *Groovin'*
    Still in its infancy, this claims to be "for the complete Paul Weller fan".
    (4 North Croft, St. Johns, Worcester WR2 4HH)

Scott Moskowitz, *Soul Museum*
    An American effort which mimics the style of *Boys About Town*.
    (P.S.C. Box 7669, CAFRB, NM 88103-7669, USA)

Fabrice Bonanno, *The Woking Wonder*
French language fanzine, the first non-English publication devoted to Weller
(3 Ave De Savoie, 78140 Vélizy, France)

9/02 (45381)